SOCIAL WORK MACRO PRACTICE

SOCIAL WORK MACRO PRACTICE

SECOND EDITION

F. Ellen Netting
Virginia Commonwealth University

Peter M. Kettner
Arizona State University

Steven L. McMurtry
University of Wisconsin-Milwaukee

 LONGMAN

An imprint of Addison Wesley Longman, Inc.

New York • Reading, Massachusetts • Menlo Park, California • Harlow, England
Don Mills, Ontario • Sydney • Mexico City • Madrid • Amsterdam

Acquisitions Editor: Janice E. Wiggins
Editor-in-chief: Priscilla McGeehon
Marketing Manager: Wendy Albert
Supplements Editor: Tom Kulesa
Project Coordination and Text Design: York Production Services
Cover Designer: Kay Petronio
Art Coordination: York Production Services
Full Service Production Manager: Valerie Zaborski
Manufacturing Manager: Hilda Koparanian
Electronic Page Makeup: York Production Services
Printer and Binder: Maple-Vail Book Manufacturing Group
Cover Printer: Coral Graphic Services, Inc.

Library of Congress Cataloging-in-Publication Data
Netting, F. Ellen.
    Social work macro practice / F. Ellen Netting, Peter M. Kettner,
  Steven L. McMurtry. — 2nd ed.
        p.   cm.
    Includes index.
    ISBN 0-8013-1611-1
    1. Social service.   2. Social service—United States.
    3. Macrosociology.   I. Kettner, Peter M., 1936–   . II. McMurtry,
  Steven Lloyd.   III. Title.
    HV41.N348   1997
    361.3′2—dc21   97-13944
                                                                   CIP

Copyright © 1998 by Addison Wesley Longman, Inc.

ISBN 0-8013-1611-1
 234567890—MA—009998

To my father, Millege H. Daniel, who taught me
to value the printed word
F. E. N.

To G-Y, Caitlin, and Alex
S. L. M.

CONTENTS

CHAPTER 6:   Understanding a Community Human Service System   159

PART III THE ORGANIZATION AS THE ARENA OF CHANGE   189

CHAPTER 7:   Understanding Organizations   191

PREFACE TO THE SECOND EDITION

Macro practice has come to mean many different things to different people, so we feel it is important to share our perspective at the outset. In reviewing and using our first edition, a number of faculty members across the country have shared with us their concerns that the book does not cover areas such as policy, administration, or planning. At the same time we were intrigued to learn that our textbook was being used in courses on human behavior and policy practice, as well as in community analysis and organization analysis courses at both graduate and undergraduate levels.

It is likely that a wide variety of curriculum designs and different ways of dividing up curriculum content accounts for the varying perspectives on how this book can be used. While we are pleased that so many faculty have found so many uses for the book and its content, we would also like to take this opportunity to clarify our perspective about the purpose of the book.

We are aware that the history of social work as a profession has been marked by shifts in the dominant focus from intervention with individuals to intervention with and within larger systems. Early perspectives on the latter tended to focus primarily on policy-level involvements (especially legislative processes) and community organizing (using Rothman's classic models of locality development, social planning, and social action). As the need for social work administration content was recognized and incorporated into the curriculum of many schools of social work, this topic was also embraced as an area of concentration for those who preferred to work with and within larger systems.

However, as we taught our required foundation-level courses on community and organizational change, and as we worked with students and professionals in the field, we became aware of the changing dynamics of practice and expectations for practitioners. Both students and practitioners were working with populations such as the homeless, members of teen street gangs, victims of domestic violence, the chronically unemployed, and other disenfranchised groups. While it will always be true that social workers will need casework and clinical skills to help people in need on a one-to-one basis, it was becoming increasingly evident to us that they were also expected to intervene at the community level. Typical activities included promoting the development of shelters, developing neighborhood alternatives to gang membership and juvenile incarceration, or addressing chronic unemployment as a community problem.

This is not new. Such activities closely mirror the work of settlement-house workers in the early days of the profession. Yet many social work students have traditionally seen themselves as preparing strictly for interventions at the individual or family level. It is unexpected and disconcerting when they find themselves being asked to initiate actions and design interventions that will affect large numbers of people and attack problems at the community or organizational levels. A major goal of this book, then, is to recapture a broader definition of social work practice that recognizes the need for workers to be able to bridge these distinctions if they are to provide effective services.

When social work practice with macro systems is seen as the realm solely of administrators, community organizers, program planners, and others, a vital linkage to millions of people who struggle daily with environmental constraints has been severed. Social workers who see clients every day, we believe, are the ones who are most aware of the need for macro-level change. Macro practice, understood within this context, defines the uniqueness of social work practice. Many disciplines claim expertise in working with individuals, groups, and families, but social work has long stood alone in its focus on the organizational, community, policy, and political contexts within which its clients function. The concept of the person-in-environment is not simply a slogan that makes social workers *aware* of environmental influences. It means that we recognize that sometimes it is the *environment* and not the *person* that needs to be changed.

Macro-level change may, but does not necessarily always, involve large-scale, costly reforms at the federal and state levels or the election of candidates more sympathetic to the poor, neglected, and underserved in our society. Sometimes useful macro-level change can involve organizing a local neighborhood to deal with deterioration and blight, sometimes it may mean initiating a self-help group and stepping back so that members will assume leadership roles. The focus of this book is on enabling social work practitioners to undertake whatever types of macro-level interventions are needed in an informed, analytical way and with a sense of confidence that they can do a competent job and achieve positive results.

ORGANIZATION

The book is organized into four main parts. **Part I** begins with a brief history of social work as a profession and highlights examples of macro practice in the interest of acquainting students with the rich traditions of macro-level change that all social workers inherit when they enter the profession. We also address ethical dilemmas that social workers may face when using micro-level strategies. In this first section we also introduce the concept of analyzing macro systems, and we guide the student through the early phases of the process. A new contribution to the second edition is that we have subdivided this analysis into three distinct but overlapping topics: analysis of the problem, analysis of the population, and analysis of the arena (the organization and/or community where the change will take place). Guidelines for problem and population analysis are incorporated into the first section, and students are referred to available literature and other resources to complete these analyses.

Parts II and III focus on community content and organizational content, the component that we have referred to as analysis of arena. These sections of the book are more comprehensive because the content is provided in the text itself and is designed to walk a student through a community and/or organizational analysis in preparation for proposing change that is relevant to the arena within which it will take place.

Finally, in Part IV we have designed a practice model for planned intervention that we believe is applicable to both communities and organizations, and that we sincerely hope addresses the realities of practice. We attempt to give recognition to the fact that when a caseworker or administrator becomes involved in a change effort, clinical or administrative responsibilities do not stop. By sharing organizing responsibilities with others and by clearly defining and analyzing the problem, population, and arena for intervention, we believe the busy practitioner can bring about organizational and community change necessary to improve the quality of life for the intended beneficiaries of the change.

A familiar dilemma we faced in preparing the book concerned organizing the material for the purpose of teaching in contrast to organizing it in ways that reflect the realities of daily practice. One comment we received on the first edition of the book was that it went too far in cautioning the reader to consider all alternatives and perspectives before proceeding with planned change. While we recognize that social movements and societal change would not occur if passion and risk-taking did not incite people to action, we believe we must always be mindful that we are attempting to reach an audience of new professionals who are just entering the field of social work. We would be remiss if we did not suggest that they critically consider the implications of their actions, for we believe that professionals have to be responsible for what they do. It is difficult to embrace this responsibility without recognizing the potential implications of one's actions. As in one-on-one practice, new professionals engaging in macro-level interventions need to act methodically early in their careers, in contrast to the practiced professional who can more swiftly accomplish the analytical work and move to action. We hope that the contents of this book are helpful in developing that professional, analytical mind set, and that social workers at all levels throughout organizations and communities are able to move skillfully from interventions with clients to interventions at the organization and community levels, depending on need.

NEW EDITION FEATURES

The second edition of *Social Work Macro Practice* has been thoroughly updated and revised to make it an even stronger and more user-friendly text:

- We have added a new chapter on community theory.
- We have revised material on planned change and included this material in Chapter 3 so that students will first learn the concepts that guide the planned change model before they focus on arenas (the communities and organizations where the change will take place). The revision of planned change includes a new focus on the intersection of population, problem, and arena.
- We have revised and updated content on assessing communities (Chapter 5); human service systems (Chapter 6); and human service organizations and theory (Chapter 7).
- We have integrated more examples and content on diversity throughout the text. Of note is the careful attention paid to including material on persons with disabilities.
- We have brought the content on values and ethics into the first chapter and have included a summary of the newly revised NASW Code of Ethics.
- We have updated references and materials throughout the book and have added suggested readings to all chapters in order to provide direction to other resources for students and faculty.
- Also new to the second edition is an *Instructor's Manual* that is organized in chapters that correspond to those in the text. In each chapter of the manual, we have included: notes to instructors, learning objectives, key concepts, discussion questions, exam questions, exercises and assignments, sample syllabi, and sample student papers.

In our first edition, students and faculty alike seemed to find that the frameworks we provided were "user-friendly" and easy to follow. We have kept those frameworks throughout the book and have tried to strengthen them. However, we caution the reader to recognize that in our attempt to make these tools easy to use we may falsely imply that step-by-step completion of all tasks will inevitably lead to success. Obviously, the world is far too complex for "cookbook" approaches that are followed in lockstep. Our intent is to provide tools and frameworks that have records of success and offer a reasonable likelihood for future successes if used appropriately. We readily recognize that ours is not the only approach, nor is it necessarily the best approach in all circumstances. We remain interested in any approach that provides students and practitioners with viable alternatives.

As with the first edition, we have designed this book to mesh well with a variety of contemporary policy textbooks, and we have made every attempt to remind the reader that planned change approaches, such as the one presented herein, occur within a political environment that is constantly changing. We hope readers will always use our planned change approach with an eye to the political environment as well as to the iterative nature of how change processes occur.

F. Ellen Netting
Peter M. Kettner
Steven L. McMurtry

ACKNOWLEDGMENTS

As we finish this second edition, much has changed since our 1993 publication. We are now scattered in three different geographical locations: Virginia Commonwealth University in Richmond, Arizona State University in Tempe, and the University of Wisconsin at Milwaukee. We are indebted to colleagues at all three universities who have given us constructive feedback.

At Virginia Commonwealth University, much appreciation is due to Leavelle Cox, David Fauri, Mary K. Rodwell, Robert Schneider, and Joseph Walsh, who shared their own and their students' insights with us after using our book in the classroom. We are especially grateful to King Davis for granting us permission to use his definition of social justice, Elizabeth "Lib" Hutchison for sharing her work on community theory with us, to Stephen F. Gilson for his assistance in integrating content on persons with disabilities into our book.

We are also indebted to colleagues who provided feedback as they used our textbook at other universities. Deep gratitude goes to Diane Kaplan-Vinokur at the University of Michigan who sent us extensive feedback, along with copies of course materials into which she integrated our book. We appreciate as well the guidance provided by other reviewers who provided careful and thoughtful assessments of earlier drafts: Neal S. Bellows, Syracuse University; William Boline, Governors State University; Dwight J. Hymans, Ball State University; Terry Tirrito, University of South Carolina; and Marion Wagner, Indiana University.

To our editor, Janice E. Wiggins, we express our appreciation for her oversight, interest, and assistance as we revised our text. To our former editor, David Estrin, we are grateful for the support he provided in making our first edition a success.

Most of all we thank the students and practitioners who, often in the face of seemingly insurmountable barriers, continue to practice social work the way it was intended. They intervene at whatever level is needed. They persist with what may appear to be intractable problems and work with clients who have lost hope until hope can be rediscovered and pursued. Their spirit and dedication continually inspire us in our efforts to provide whatever guidance we can for the next generation of social workers.

PART **1**

Values and Historical Perspectives

The first part of this book is intended to provide the definitions, background information, and context for the subsequent parts.

Chapter 1 attempts to accomplish the following: offer a definition of macro practice, present case vignettes to illustrate the fit between macro and micro social work practice, explain the rationale for preparing all social workers to undertake macro-practice activities, introduce the values and ethics of the profession, and focus on professional identity.

Chapter 2 attempts to accomplish the following: trace the historical development of traditional macro-practice roles and identify ways in which contemporary trends have affected these roles.

Chapter 3 attempts to accomplish the following: provide an overview of how one prepares for macro-level interventions so that change can occur in organizations and communities and explain how to complete an analysis of problem and of population.

CHAPTER 1

An Introduction to Macro Practice in Social Work

Overview

MACRO PRACTICE IN CONTEXT

This book is intended for all social workers, regardless of whether they specialize in micro or macro tracks within schools of social work. We define macro practice as professionally guided intervention designed to bring about planned change in organizations and communities.

Micro practice includes "professional activities that are designed to help solve the problems faced primarily by individuals, families, and small groups. [It typically] focuses on direct intervention on a case-by-case basis or in a clinical setting (Barker, 1995, p. 234).

This book is designed to be an introduction to the macro practice roles social workers play. Although some practitioners will concentrate their efforts primarily in one arena rather than another, in some situations all social workers will engage in macro-level interventions as the appropriate response to a need or a problem. Given this perspective, our book reflects a generalist orientation in which we believe that all social workers must have both micro- and macro-level skills. Although there is some disagreement over how to define generalist social work practice, "there appears to be definitional agreement on the centrality of the multi-method and multi-approaches, based on an eclectic choice of theory base and the necessity for incorporating the dual vision of the profession on private issues and social justice concerns" (Landon 1995, p. 1103). It is our contention that this dual vision is essential to good social work practice.

This book is not designed to prepare practitioners for specialist roles such as full-time agency administration, program planning, community organization, or policy analysis. Social workers who assume full-time macro roles will need a more advanced understanding than this book will provide. This is not a book on specialization. The roles discussed in this and the following chapters are ones that competent social work practitioners will play during their professional careers.

In preparation for writing this book, we talked with a number of our former students who are now practicing social workers, some of whom work directly with clients and some of whom are planners, managers, or administrators. We asked them what they would say to students about the differences between their expectations of social work practice when they were students and their actual experiences over the past few years. Here are some of the things they said: "As a student, I have this very vivid memory of being idealistic. I liked social work's emphasis on serving clients as the primary focus of attention, and I thought that would carry over to my professional practice. Instead, I find that my professional life is dominated by two things: fellow employees and money. In making decisions we find that we have to deal much more with staff egos than with client needs. And the 'bottom line' mentality that pushes budget issues into every discussion and decision has been a real disappointment."

A second student had this to say: "What makes this profession worthwhile for me is that there is a core of very committed people who really live up to the ideals of the profession. They're very talented people who could make a lot more money elsewhere, but they believe in what they're doing, and it is always a pleasure to work with them. Our biggest frustration has been that there are so many people (like state legislators, for example) who wield so much power over this profession, but who have no understanding of what social problems and human needs are all about. Even though professionals may have spent the better part of their careers trying to understand how to deal with people in need, their opinions and perspectives are often not accepted or respected."

A social worker recently employed by a community-based agency on an Indian reservation shared his experience. "Culture is so important to the work we do. I constantly have to ask indigenous people for advice so that I do not make assumptions about the people with whom I work. The concept of community and what it means to this tribe, even the value of the land as a part of their tradition, is so crucial. It is much more complex than I had assumed when I was in school."

Another former student reinforced the importance of community. "The thing that has surprised me is how much I need to know about the community—people's values, where funding comes from, how to assess community needs. Even though I do direct practice, I am constantly pulled onto task forces and committees that have to deal with the broader community issues."

Another former student was disappointed about the impact of limited resources on practice and employee morale: "It really wears you down after awhile when everything is decided in terms of money. Furniture in our waiting room is falling apart, the place needs to be painted, there are so many things we should do to improve our efficiency and effectiveness, but we can't because we can't afford them. Just once I'd like to have the resources to really do things right, the way they can in big corporations."

However, lest we begin to believe that the commercial sector does not have its own limitations, the clinical director of a private for-profit adoption agency had these words to say: "Unlike a lot of social workers, I work in a for-profit agency, and business considerations always have to be factored into our decisions. We have a fairly small operation, and I think the agency director is responsive to my concerns about how clients are treated, but I've still had to get used to the tension that can arise between making a profit and serving clients."

A child protective services worker had this to say: "It's really hard to describe. Within a few days last year in my caseload there was a death of a child, another of my kids was abandoned in our waiting room, and there were threats of violence against our staff from people who think we just indiscriminately take children away from their parents. I often think of going into other lines of work, but there are lots of intangible rewards in social work, and other professions have their headaches, too."

The director of a social services unit in a hospital talked about another client group, the elderly: "I have been here long enough to see the advent of diagnosis-related groups. This is the Medicare system's way of making sure older patients are discharged efficiently, and if they are not the hospital has to pick up the tab." She went on to explain how health care social workers are struggling to understand their roles which are reimbursed and defined by funding sources. Understanding the way in which health care organizations are changing, diversifying, and turning outward to the community has become critical for social workers who are encountering other professionals in roles similar to their own. As social work departments are decentralized into cost centers, social workers must understand why these administrative decisions are being made and find ways to influence future decision making. Many of these social workers entered health care systems with the idea of providing

counseling. What they are doing is advocacy, solution-focused and crisis intervention, case management, and discharge planning. These roles require an in-
depth understanding of macro issues.

On a final note, a direct practice student who recently graduated made this
statement: "This may sound negative, but it is not meant to be. My education
in social work taught me how little I know. I feel as if I have just scratched the
surface. Learning is a long ongoing process. I work in a head injury center and
what I learned from having had exposure to macro practice roles is that you
have to know the organization in which you work, particularly the philosophy
behind what happens there. This is more important than I ever imagined."

These quotations tell their own stories. The issues facing social workers in
their daily practice are not limited to client problems. Many problems must be
addressed at the agency or community level if social workers are to be effective in serving their clients. Many of these problems require changing the
nature of services, programs, or policies. Most require an understanding of
funding issues. We thank our former students for helping us raise these issues.

WHAT IS MACRO PRACTICE?

As stated earlier, *macro practice* is professionally guided intervention designed
to bring about planned change in organizations and communities. Macro
practice, as all social work practice, draws from theoretical foundations while
simultaneously contributing to the development of new theory. Macro practice is based on any of a number of practice models, and operates within the
boundaries of professional values and ethics. Macro-level activities engage the
practitioner in organizational, community, and policy areas. In today's world,
macro practice is rarely the domain of one profession. Rather, it involves the
skills of many disciplines and professionals in interaction.

Macro activities go beyond individual interventions but are often based
on needs, problems, issues, and concerns identified in the course of working
one-on-one with clients. There are different ways to conceptualize the arenas
in which macro social work practice occurs. Rothman, Erlich, and Tropman
(1995) identify three arenas of intervention: communities, organizations, and
small groups. We have selected communities and organizations as the arenas
on which we will focus the majority of this book, folding small group work in
as a critical part of most interventions in both communities and organizations.
Small groups are defined as "a tangible collection of people who can discuss
matters personally and work together in close association." (Rothman et al.
1995, p. 13). It is our contention that small groups are often the nucleus
around which change strategies are developed in both communities and organizations and are therefore more logically conceptualized as part of the strategy or medium for change more often than the focus of change.

Other writers focus on the policy context (Fisher 1995; Flynn 1992; Jansson 1994) in which macro intervention occurs. Organizational and communi-

ty arenas are deeply embedded in political systems. Fundamental to macro change is an understanding of overriding ideologies and values that influence local, state, and national politics.

Levels of Involvement in Social Work Practice

Social work practice is broadly defined and allows for intervention at the micro (individual, group, or domestic unit) level, and at the macro (organization and community) level. Social workers who undertake macro-level interventions will often be engaged in what is called "policy practice" (Jansson 1994), since policy change is so integral to what happens in organizations and communities. Given this division of labor, some professional roles require that the social worker be involved full time in macro practice. These professional roles are often referred to by such titles as planner, policy analyst, program coordinator, community organizer, manager, or administrator.

The micro service worker or clinical social worker also bears responsibility for initiating change in organizations and communities. The micro service worker is often the first to recognize patterns indicating the need for change. If one or two clients present a particular problem, the logical response is to deal with them as individuals. However, as more and more persons present with the same situation, it rapidly becomes evident that something is awry in the systems with which these clients are interacting. It then becomes incumbent upon the social worker to help identify the system(s) in need of change and the type of change needed. The nature of the system(s) in need of change may lead to community-wide intervention or intervention in a single organization.

Take, for example, the discovery by the staff of a Senior Center that there are a number of elderly persons in the community who, because of self-neglect, are socially isolated and possibly malnourished. A caseworker could follow up on each person, one at a time, in an attempt to provide outreach and needed services. This would probably result in a hit-or-miss approach and could take a very long time to get to everyone in need. Another option would be to deal with the problem from a macro perspective—to invest time in organizing the resources of the agency and the community to identify elderly people who may need the kind of service the Senior Center has to offer and to ensure that services are provided through a combination of staff and volunteer efforts.

This may seem like a complex undertaking for someone who came into social work expecting to work with people one at a time. While it's true that macro-level interventions can be complex, we will attempt to provide a somewhat systematic approach that hopefully will make such undertakings more manageable. Remember, too, that these efforts are typically accomplished with the help of others—not alone.

A Systematic Approach to Macro Social Work Practice

Figure 1.1 illustrates an approach that can be used by social workers to identify, study, and analyze the need for change and eventually to propose

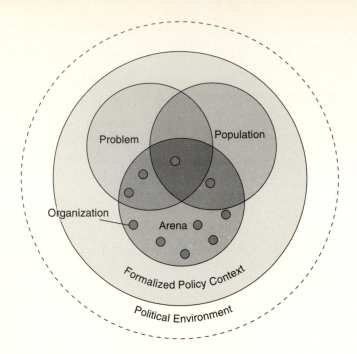

FIGURE 1.1   Macro Practice Conceptual Framework

solutions. A problem may be brought to a social worker's attention by a client. A group of residents within a neighborhood may present issues and concerns that need to be addressed. Issues in the workplace, such as the quality of service to clients, may surface and require organized intervention. Community problems may be so glaring that the need for change comes from many different directions. Regardless of how social workers identify change opportunities, they function in a political environment that cannot be ignored.

In Figure 1.1 there are three overlapping circles. These are intended to illustrate the focal points of the social worker's efforts in undertaking a macro-level change episode. We will refer to these focal points as (1) problem, (2) population, and (3) arena.

Good social work practice requires understanding persons within their environments. A social worker cannot expect to help a client who is addicted to alcohol, for example, if the social worker does not understand both the phenomenon of alcoholism and the background of the person addicted. In carrying out episodes of macro practice, the social worker must understand not only the problem (alcoholism) and the population (elderly, retired males, for example), but also the arena (community or organization) within which the problem is happening. Understanding communities and organizations adds a dimension of complexity to macro practice, but this understanding is a critical precursor to successful macro-level intervention.

In the course of developing an understanding of problem, population, and arena, the social worker will inevitably focus on the areas of overlap depicted in Figure 1.1. Continuing with the example of alcoholism among elderly, retired males, it would be important to review the literature on the phenomenon of alcoholism and on the population of elderly, retired males. But as the change agent builds a body of knowledge about problem and population, it becomes especially important to focus on the overlap between the two areas: alcoholism and its unique impact on elderly, retired males.

Likewise it is important to understand how the phenomenon of alcoholism affects the local community (the overlap between problem and arena), and to what extent the needs of the population of elderly, retired males are understood and addressed in the local community (overlap between population and arena). Ultimately, in an episode of macro practice, the objective is to work toward an understanding of the area in which all three circles overlap (alcoholism and its impact on elderly, retired males in XYZ town).

As the social worker and other change agents study the situation, they will gain at least some level of understanding of (1) basic concepts and issues surrounding alcoholism, (2) elderly, retired males, (3) the local community and/or relevant organizations, (4) alcoholism as it affects elderly, retired males, (5) alcoholism and how it is addressed in the local community, (6) how the needs of elderly, retired males are addressed in the local community, and finally (7) the problem and needs of elderly, retired males in the local community who are addicted to alcohol.

Social and community problems and needs must also be addressed in the context of formalized policies that may have an impact on the problem, the population, or the community or organization. In addition, dealing with social and community problems and needs effectively requires an awareness of the political environment within which the change episode will be undertaken. For these reasons, we have placed the three circles (problem, population, and arena) within a larger circle with a solid line, depicting the formalized policy context. Finally, the dotted outer circle is intended to depict the political environment. The importance of and the need for understanding the policy and political contexts cannot be overemphasized.

The Interrelationship of Micro and Macro Social Work Practice

Given the complexity of macro interventions, practitioners may begin to feel overwhelmed. Is it not enough to do good direct practice or clinical work? Is it not enough to listen to a client and offer options? The answer is that professional practice focusing only on an individual's intrapsychic concerns does not fit the definition of social work. Being a social worker requires seeing the client as part of multiple, overlapping systems that comprise the person's social and physical environment. The profession of social work is committed to seeking social justice in concert with vulnerable and underserved populations, and macro practice skills are necessary in confronting these inequalities. If the social worker is not willing to engage in some macro-practice types of activities relating to these environments, then he or she is not doing social work.

Similarly, social workers who carry out episodes of macro practice must understand what is involved in the provision of direct services to clients at the individual, domestic unit, or group levels. Without this understanding, macro practice may be carried out in the absence of an adequate grounding in understanding client problems and needs. The interconnectedness of micro and macro roles is the heart of social work practice. In short, it is equally important for social workers to understand the nature of individual and group interventions as it is to understand the nature of organizational, community, and policy change.

Because we believe that all social workers are professional change agents, we use the terms *social worker, professional,* and *change agent* interchangeably throughout this book. Social workers are always change agents because they are constantly identifying changes that need to occur to make systems more responsive or sensitive to target population needs. Change is so much a part of social work practice that one cannot separate the two. We are aware that other professionals may also see themselves as change agents. It is important for the contemporary macro practitioner to collaborate and partner with other professionals in the community so that the knowledge of diverse fields can be used in planning effective change. *Professional* is a term that implies identification with a set of values that places the best interests of the client first and relies on knowledge, judgment, and skill to act on those values. Later in this chapter we discuss the meaning of professional values that unite social workers across roles, arenas, and areas of emphasis.

THREE CASE EXAMPLES

Some of the aspects of macro social work practice that need to be understood by the student and the beginning practitioner can perhaps best be illustrated by case examples. We selected the following examples because they contain similar themes but focus on three different target population groups: children, elderly and disabled persons, and women. As these cases and the workers' thoughts are presented, we encourage the reader to think about how macro-level change might be approached by beginning with a study of the *problem,* the *population,* and the *arena* within which change might take place.

CASE EXAMPLE 1:   Child Protective Services

Child protective services (CPS) workers are responsible for dealing with the abuse and neglect of children. When reports of alleged abuse or neglect come to the unit, the CPS worker is responsible for investigating the report and making decisions about the disposition of the case. It is a very demanding and emotionally draining area of specialization within the field of social work. One CPS worker several years ago took the time to record the details of a particular case, and also shared with us a list of dilemmas and contradictions he had recorded over the years, in the interest of helping new workers be better prepared for what they will face as they enter practice.

Friday, 10:40 a.m.   Supervisor called to inform me about a report of neglect. She felt it should be checked out today, because it sounded too serious to be left over the weekend. According to the neighbor's report, parents have deserted and abandoned three minor children.

11:10 a.m.   Got in my car and headed for the address on the intake form. I know the neighborhood well. It is the poorest in the city and not a safe neighborhood at night. A high percentage of families receive some kind of assistance. Homes are run down, streets are littered, any sense of pride has long been abandoned.

11:40 a.m.   The house at the address given is among the most run-down in a seriously deteriorating neighborhood. The house had no front steps, just a cinder block placed in front of the door. Window casings were rotting out for lack of paint. There was no doorbell. I knocked. There was rustling inside, but no answer. I waited and knocked again. I walked around and peered through a window and saw a small child, about three years old I guessed, curled up in a chair. An older girl, about age eight or nine, peeked out from behind a doorway.

I remembered that the oldest child was named Cindy, so I called out to her. After a bit of conversation I persuaded her to let me in. I quickly recognized that this would not be an ordinary case. A foul smell hit me so hard it made my eyes water. I used my handkerchief to filter the air. The worst odors were coming from the bathroom and kitchen. The water had evidently been shut off—toilets were not working and garbage was piled up. The kitchen was littered with fast food containers, possibly retrieved from the dumpsters of nearby fast food outlets.

There were three very frightened children—Cindy 9, Scott 6, and Melissa 3. None would talk.

12:35 p.m.   I made arrangements to transport them to the shelter and went back to the office to do the paperwork.

2:15 p.m.   A previous neglect report revealed the following:

Father: Stan, age 27, unemployed, in and out of jail for petty theft, public intoxication, and several other minor offenses. Frequently slept in public parks or homeless shelters. Rarely showed up at home any more. Several police reports of violence against wife and children. Admits paternity for only the oldest child.

Mother: Sarah, age 25. AFDC recipient, high-school dropout, never employed. Tests performed in connection with one attempt at job training revealed borderline retardation. While child care skills have always been minimal, there is no previous history of abandonment of children. Whereabouts at this time are unknown.

3:35 p.m.   Filed the appropriate forms with agency and the police. Dictated case for the record. Children placed at Vista Shelter until a more permanent placement can be arranged.

Over the years as this CPS worker had dealt with similar cases, he had kept a running list of the kinds of dilemmas, frustrations, and contradictions he and his colleagues regularly faced. These are excerpts from his list:

1. Abused and neglected children are the saddest victims of all. They brought nothing on themselves, yet their chances of success are extremely limited. Success, to a large extent, correlates with a child's ability to perform in school. A child's performance will be hindered by moving from shelter to foster home to home, changing schools, missing many days, lacking consistent parental support and help, having poor clothing, diet, and self-esteem, and other barriers. We can predict failure, but we can't seem to do anything to change it. Could a macro-level preventive effort be launched that focuses on success for these children?

2. A disproportionately high percentage of lower socioeconomic status teens get pregnant and drop out of high school, go on welfare, parent poorly, and recycle many of their problems to the next generation. How can we interrupt this pattern? Current programs seem to focus primarily on survival in terms of shelter, food, clothing, and medical care, but do not change the behavior patterns. Can we organize an intensive effort to help young women make informed decisions during this highly vulnerable time in their lives?

3. Lots of people in this wealthy country are worse off than lots of animals in this country. There ought to be minimum standards for food, clothing, housing, and medical care below which no one should be allowed to fall. Governments at all levels claim lack of resources, and legislators seem bent on blaming the victims, when it is clearly a matter of priorities. Could we focus attention on this issue by organizing a panel of experts to establish these types of standards for our community and give them maximum publicity?

4. The corporate sector has reaped enormous benefits from our economic system. Gross national product continues to grow and many corporations are moving from a national to an international market. As a sort of a "return" or "payback" for their success, the corporate sector donates a few dollars to charitable organizations. Rarely do they get involved directly in the habilitation or rehabilitation of human beings, even though they control the means to self-sufficiency and success. If

all employable people were somehow tied to a job with benefits, the need for income assistance and human services would be greatly reduced. Perhaps a few community-minded business owners would be willing to experiment with "adopting" families by providing employment, training, and scholarships.

5. Bureaucracy has a tendency to become an end in itself. Its manuals become a way of life for many of its employees. People in severe emotional pain bring their needs to our agency and we look up an answer in the manual and quote it to them. Sometimes all they want is to make contact with a human being, and they are unable to do so in our agency. Can we change this agency to make it more responsive to those it serves even though it is a large bureaucratic organization?

CASE EXAMPLE 2: Case Management with Elderly and Disabled Persons

Case managers work in a variety of public and private settings. They are responsible for screening potential clients, assessing client needs, developing case plans, mobilizing resources to meet identified needs, and monitoring and evaluating services provided. The case manager in this example works for a nonprofit agency in an inner-city neighborhood, where many of her clients have lived all their lives. She is assigned to the home and community-based long-term care unit, and carries a caseload of about 100 elderly and disabled clients. As part of the program evaluation, she was asked to keep a diary of what happened during a typical day. The following are excerpts from her diary.

Wednesday, 7:30 a.m.   Arrived early to catch up on paperwork. Organized documents from eight cases, including two new care plans and five medical reports.

8:00–8:10 a.m.   Mrs. Garcia, a 79-year-old woman, called. She was distraught over a letter received from the Social Security office, thinking it meant her benefits would be cut off. Explained that it was a form letter, indicating a routine change, not affecting the amount of her check. Knowing that she is often forgetful and has a hearing problem, made a note to make home visit tomorrow to be certain she understands what was said.

8:10–8:30 a.m.   Met with Jim from In-Home Support Services. Mr. Thomas, a 93-year-old man, had fallen last night and was in Mercy Hospital. Homemaker had found him when she arrived at 7:00 this morning. He is not expected to live. Homemaker is very upset. Called his daughter and will plan to meet her at hospital later this morning.

8:30–9:30 a.m.   Staff meeting regarding 10 clients discharged from City Hospital with inadequate discharge plans. Discussed how to work better with discharge planners from hospital since this situation continues to be a problem. As I left meeting, another case manager told me that my client, Mrs. Hannibal, had refused to let the home health nurse into her apartment.

9:30–9:45 a.m.   Called Mrs. Hannibal, no answer. Called the lifeline program to meet me at her apartment.

9:45–10:00 a.m.   Drove to Mrs. Hannibal's apartment. No one answered my knock, so got manager to let me in. Mrs. Hannibal had been drinking and was acting paranoid. Threw bottle at me and screamed "no one is going to get me out of here. I'll never go to a home. I'll die first." Worked with lifeline staff to get Mrs. Hannibal calmed down. She is a 67-year-old widow. She goes in and out of the hospital every two months. Has a severe drinking problem.

10:00–11:00 a.m.   Arrived at Mercy Hospital. Met Mr. Thomas's daughter. She was in tears, saying it was all her fault, that if he had been living with her this would have never happened. Talked with her regarding her father's desire to live alone, that this had been his choice. Contacted hospital social worker to work with daughter.

11:15–12:00 a.m.   Back to office. Wrote up visits to Mrs. Hannibal and Mr. Thomas. Called two new referrals and set up appointments to do assessments tomorrow. Received call from Mrs. Roman, age 83. She is lonely and wondered when I would be seeing her. Her husband died last week and she is crying. Has no family. Assured her I would come see her on Friday.

12:00–12:30 p.m.   Ate lunch with Adult Protective Services (APS) worker. Discussed abusive relationship of Mr. and Mrs. Tan, a couple in their 60s living in public housing. Agreed to work closely with APS regarding this situation.

12:45–2:00 p.m.   Conducted in-home assessment for new client, Ms. Johnson. She was released from the hospital yesterday and is receiving home-delivered meals and in-home nursing. Small house is a mess, roaches everywhere. Needs chore and housekeeping services, but there's a long waiting list. Called and cajoled volunteers at senior center to help her temporarily. Ms. Johnson was too weak to complete full assessment, will come back tomorrow.

2:30–3:30 p.m.   Attended public hearing preceding the planning process for the area agency on aging. Presented written and verbal documentation of problems in working with my caseload. Discussed the need for more flexibility in providing services to disabled clients under age 60. Gave examples of three clients on caseload who are in their 40s and have severe mobility problems.

3:45–4:15 p.m.   Stopped by Sunnyside Nursing Home to see Mrs. Martinez. Has been my client for five years and was just admitted to Sunnyside. Doesn't know me and seems confused. Checked with facility social worker regarding what medications she is on and agreed to call physician regarding potential drug interactions. Made note to check with local long-term care ombudsman about any complaints against this facility. Also made mental note to check on Mrs. M's disabled daughter who is still in the home and will need supportive services previously provided by her mother.

4:45–5:15 p.m. Returned to office, found out Mr. Thomas had died. Called his daughter. Called physician about Mrs. Martinez's medications. He was angry and told me it's none of my business. Received call from home health aide referring client to us. Had to tell her that client did not qualify for our services, but referred her to a for-profit agency in town. Returned a call about assistive technology that might help several clients with disabilities.

5:00–5:30 p.m. Tried to clean up desk. Decided to stop by and check on Mrs. Garcia on my way home.

Just as the CPS worker had kept a running list of the kinds of dilemmas he faced through the years, the case manager had kept a list of her dilemmas as well. In preparation for the public hearing of the area agency on aging, she had updated the list in hopes something could be done to address her ongoing frustrations, particularly about persons with disabilities who were not yet 60 years old. Excerpts from her list follow:

1. So many of the older people I see have had problems all their lives. You can almost tell what's going to happen in their old age by what happens to them as they go through life. Drug and alcohol problems only seem to get worse. If someone had intervened when they began having these problems it would have been much easier, because the behavior patterns are set by the time I encounter them. I know people can change at any age, but the older they get the harder it is to do so. Is there some way we could organize a prevention effort to prepare middle-aged people for their senior years?

2. Although some of our resources can be used to serve any older person in need, most of our funding is tied to income eligibility. Slots for people who aren't destitute are quickly filled and there is a long waiting list. So clients above the income eligibility level are referred to for-profit agencies or to other nonprofits that have sliding fee scales. The irony is that the ones who have set a little money aside are usually the same ones who get left out in the cold. These clients can't afford to pay the full cost of services but fall just above our eligibility guidelines. It seems that in our society if you aren't really poor or really rich, you had better hope your health holds out or you'll have nowhere to turn. Couldn't we organize this group to help each other and advocate for their own needs?

3. I'm concerned about our younger clients who have disabilities. So many of the places that claim to have their best interests at heart are not complying with the Americans with Disabilities Act. Water fountains aren't accessible, elevators are out of order, and ramps are poorly lit at night. I'm constantly reminding people who should know better that these policies are important. The problems caused by noncompliance are very demoralizing to our clients.

4. I'm learning some revealing things about case management. Case managers attempt to coordinate what is really a nonsystem of services. If we had a real system we wouldn't need to pay people like me and we could put those resources toward client services. Even our professional organizations have bought into it. The National Association of Social Workers and the National Council on Aging have developed guidelines and standards for case management. There is even a journal on case management. We are investing a lot in institutionalizing case management when it often just covers up the real problem—that we don't have a service-delivery system in place. Until we get agencies in this community to collaborate in establishing a coordinated and accessible system of services, case management efforts will be of limited use.

5. How does one maintain a client-centered perspective in a cost-obsessive environment? Working closely with health care organizations has shown me the contrasts between the ideal and the reality of managed care. Ideally, managed care is supposed to view clients as whole people, recognizing that their psychosocial as well as their medical needs must be addressed. In reality, many people view managed care simply as a mechanism for containing costs. As a case manager in a managed care environment, it's really hard to explain to higher-ups that case management can be intensive and long-term and that it requires balancing advocacy and gatekeeping roles. How can I show administrators the effect that cost decisions have on clients' lives? What kind of documentation can I keep so that decision makers will benefit from what I know about my clients?

6. Old people are not a homogeneous group. There are vulnerable subpopulations that get lost when one talks about "the aged." Most clients in my caseload are women who live alone and are often members of oppressed groups. Because many have been oppressed all their lives, they are practically "invisible" now. How do we familiarize policy makers with the unique needs of these clients?

CASE EXAMPLE 3: Displaced Homemaker Services

Many communities have designed programs and services to address the special needs of women. One such program targets displaced homemakers, persons who have experienced sudden and often traumatic change in their lives through separation, divorce or widowhood. Having devoted their time to homemaking, they often encounter emotional and financial distress when their relationships change.

A social worker was hired by a coalition of community groups interested in women's issues. Her task was to assess the status of displaced homemakers within the community and to make recommendations to the coalition. Excerpts from her field notes follow.

Tuesday, 8:00–9:00 a.m.   Met with representatives from two state agencies to locate data on women in the workforce. Very productive meeting which resulted in identification of three studies on workforce characteristics. In addition, was referred to two groups that had conducted needs assessments on women's concerns in adjacent communities.

9:30–11:00 a.m.   Drove to the community center to observe a support group for women experiencing divorce. Group was led by a member of the coalition. Twelve persons attended. Topics discussed were: no work experience outside the home and the accompanying economic fears, problems as single parents with sole responsibility for taking care of children, emotional distress and grief over marital breakup, and lack of marketable skills and/or education needed to locate employment.

This meeting made me aware of how uncertain and vulnerable these women feel. Several of the women had been married for over 20 years. Many emotions were expressed during the meeting. Some women said they were angry, others indicated they felt depressed.

11:30–1:00 p.m.   Left support group to meet with five representatives from the AFDC program. We discussed the results of a recent survey of AFDC recipients. Although many of the women interviewed had been separated and divorced after only five years, 20% were teen mothers who had never married. We discussed the concept of displaced homemakers and whether the AFDC respondents could be described in this way. Certainly many of their needs for marketable skills, education, and money paralleled the needs of the morning's support group. However, the workers felt that they could not be described as displaced homemakers because they had seldom had the opportunity to be in a homemaking role for extended periods of time. This precipitated a long discussion regarding how we should define the target group.

1:30–3:00 p.m.   Drove to the senior citizens center to meet with the widow's support group. They had requested a speaker from the coalition. After my brief presentation, the group discussed their concerns. Five of the 20 persons present had worked outside the home all their lives and another eight had worked outside the home part-time. The remaining seven described themselves as displaced homemakers who had been widowed in their fifties and had experienced severe financial problems when their spouses had died. They encouraged the coalition to focus on preparing women to understand finances and to obtain skills that would make them more marketable.

3:15–4:30 p.m.   Tried to collect my thoughts. Returned several phone calls and began reading the state reports obtained this morning. The reports focused on the menial jobs filled primarily by women, often without adequate benefits.

4:30–6:30 p.m.   Drove across town to a dinner meeting with representatives from the gay and lesbian rights alliance. They indicated that the design of our programs would need to include lesbian women who were often raising children on their own or with partners. While some were struggling with financial issues, their primary concerns were around dealing with public attitudes that were often hostile toward their raising their own children.

The dilemmas experienced by this social worker are somewhat different from the previous two case examples. This professional was hired to assess a community situation described to her by members of a coalition. Her direct practice background gave her considerable insight in understanding women's issues, yet her first days on the job required a great deal of reflection. She outlined a number of questions and concerns.

1. Defining a target group or population sounds simple enough, but it isn't always clear. As I met with various community groups I realized that many population groups—young mothers, middle-aged widows, women of divorce at all ages, and lesbian women—were in need of varying degrees of support. The coalition needs to remain open to various groups, but must recognize that with limited resources there are often trade-offs of depth for breadth. Having a sincere commitment to serving all in need does not help to resolve the dilemma. How can we make an informed decision about who is most in need of what we have to offer and how can resources be invested to get the best possible return?

2. Not only is it difficult to define the problem, but there will be continued danger as we analyze the problem. Too often we view women's issues in a "we-they" context that would really alienate men and some women. Can we frame the problems and issues we confront so that we don't impose dichotomous thinking on the process—as if everyone who doesn't think like us is against us?

3. There are themes that seem to emerge across all the groups. Women keep talking about how devalued they feel and support groups focus on finding one's voice. Why does it take a crisis before we socialize women to find their voices and to value who they are? Should we consider, as

one element of this coalition effort, a prevention and early intervention component?

4. Coalition building is essential to community ownership of a problem. The coalition that wants to assess the status of women is composed of community-based women's groups. Where are the men? Many of the powerful leaders and groups in the community are not part of this coalition. What other groups should be involved? How can we build a base that ensures broad support from the community?

5. In the women I've observed I have seen tremendous strength. Yet we always focus on the weaknesses of their economic and social dependency. Is it possible that helping professionals may see deficits before they see strengths? How can we develop the strengths of women in this community and build leadership in spite of the fact that the community tends to discourage leadership roles for women?

SURVIVING THE DILEMMAS

We have presented these rather lengthy scenarios and the accompanying concerns expressed by social workers in an attempt to characterize the kinds of issues and problems social workers face almost every day. The nature of a capitalist economy is that some people are able to compete and to succeed while others are not. For the most part, social workers deal with those who are not able to care for at least a part of their own needs. It should be clear by this time that casework alone cannot address large-scale community problems. Social workers must also master the skills involved in organizing people who may want change and have good intentions but need coordination and direction. Faced with these contrasts, Sherman and Wenocur (1983) say that a practitioner has a number of options. We agree that options are available and we categorize them as follows:

1. *Burn out and leave.* Frustrated and burned out practitioners may decide to leave the organization in which they work or to leave social work altogether. Unable or unwilling to continue to deal with the ambiguities inherent in their professional practice, leaving becomes their option of choice.

2. *Burn out and stay.* Some practitioners may burn out but remain on the job. Social workers can get caught in believing that they are working at impossible jobs. They stay in the system and feel powerless, accepting that they, too, are victims of the things they cannot control. They may do the basics of what has to be done with clients and ignore the larger issues, which means that they accept organizational norms and relinquish the advocacy role. This is a tempting option because taking on the larger issues can add many hours of work to an already busy week for what often seems like an impossible task. The profession, then, ceases to be a calling and becomes "just a job."

3. *Develop tunnel vision.* Even social workers who are not burned out, may develop a sort of tunnel vision. These practitioners may remain very committed to clients but choose to ignore conflict by focusing on an area of expertise or assuming a set of responsibilities that establishes an independent base of power within the organization. Although this is similar to option 2, the difference is that the social worker remains committed to clients from a casework perspective. They acknowledge the problems and concerns that arise, but typically stay out of the central life of the organization and community. They avoid controversy.

4. *Channel energies elsewhere.* Some social workers become activists, joining as many organizations and efforts as time and energy will allow. Rejecting the norms of what is viewed as a flawed organization, these persons try to effect systemic change through whatever means possible. Adopting an independent stance from the organization in which he or she works, the social worker quickly becomes a maverick or "house radical." Often these persons become labeled as uncooperative and immature, losing credibility as they fight for change.

5. *Initiate change.* Together with concerned colleagues, clients, and citizens, practitioners can apply professional knowledge and skill toward an orderly, systematic change effort designed to resolve at least a part of a problem and, hopefully, work toward its reduction and eventual elimination. This is the approach taken by social workers who are committed to clients, community, career, and profession. Together with colleagues, workers form committees and task forces with the intent of changing organizational and community problems. Initiating feasible change means that the social worker must be selective, recognizing that not every problem can be addressed and that choices must be made regarding which problems on which to focus. Working toward change calls for sound judgment and discretion.

Much of the work done by social workers who work toward feasible change is what we refer to as macro practice, and is carried out with widely varying degrees of skill. The purpose of this book is to present a theoretical base and a practice model designed to assist the professional social worker in bringing about change in organizations and communities. We not only encourage its readers to become change agents within the organizations and communities in which they will work, but we believe that the value base of social work demands it.

THE FOUNDATION OF MACRO PRACTICE

Understanding the professional mission of social work is essential to recognizing why macro practice is important. In a provocative argument, Specht and Courtney (1994) challenge social work's contemporary interest in the popular psychotherapies that have diverted social work from its original mission and vision of the perfectibility of society. There is a yet unfulfilled mission for social work: to deal with the enormous social problems under which our society staggers, the social isolation of the aged, the anomie experienced by youth, the neglect and abuse of children, homelessness, drug addiction, and the problem of those who suffer from AIDS.

Our mission should be to build a meaning, a purpose, and a sense of obligation for the community. It is only by creating a community that we establish a basis for commitment, obligation, and social support. We must build communities that are excited about their child care systems, that find it exhilarating to care for the mentally ill and the frail aged, and that make demands upon people to behave, to contribute, and to care for one another. (p. 27)

Similarly, the person-is-political perspective underscores the belief that individuals cannot be viewed separately from the larger society. The actions, and even the inactions, of individuals influence those around them and may have broad implications for others within an organization or community. Bricker-Jenkins and Hooyman (1986) explain that:

just as no "private realities" exist apart from political processes, there are no private solutions. Given that we are interconnected and the sum of our individual actions create the social order, we are thereby responsible to each other for our actions. Accordingly, failure to act is to act; likewise, failure to work to transform social and political realities is to support the status quo. (p. 14)

For those social workers who do feel a sense of commitment to bring about positive change not only for individual clients but for whole neighborhoods, organizations, and communities, the question becomes: How is it possible to meet all the expectations of a job and still be involved in dealing with larger issues? In Chapters 3 to 11 of this book we will attempt to develop a framework that makes it both possible and manageable to carry out episodes of change.

Before we embark on the change model, it is necessary first to develop a foundation for macro practice. That foundation, we believe, is made up of values, ethics, an understanding of the role and expectations of a professional, an understanding of some of the basic principles on which macro practice is based, and an understanding of the historical roots of macro practice. In this section we will focus on values, ethical dilemmas, professional identity, and basic principles of macro practice. Chapter 2 will be devoted to a review of the history of macro practice in social work.

Values

Values are fundamental to social work practice. Barker (1995) defines values as "the customs, standards of contact and principles considered desirable by a culture, a group of people, or an individual" (p. 399). He goes on to explain that in 1982, social workers, as a professional group, stated some of the overriding values for their practice. These values were published in the *NASW Standards for the Classification of Social Work Practice*. They were:

- "Commitment to the primary importance of the individual in society,
- Respect for the confidentiality of relationships with clients,
- Commitment to social change to meet socially recognized needs,
- Willingness to keep personal feelings and needs separate from professional relationships,
- Willingness to transmit knowledge and skills to others,
- Respect and appreciation for individual and group differences,
- Commitment to develop clients' ability to help themselves,
- Willingness to persist in efforts on behalf of clients despite frustration,
- Commitment to social justice and the economic, physical, and mental well-being of all in society, and
- Commitment to a high standard of personal and professional conduct." (Barker 1987, p. 171)

These values do not cover the entire NASW Code of Ethics, but they do provide a general orientation to the positions taken by the profession on the larger issues relating to responsible and conscientious professional behavior. In all social work practice, there is clearly an expectation that the social worker will, when the situation calls for it, become involved beyond the simple needs of a "case" or client and initiate change at the organizational or community level.

Because codes of ethics serve as guidelines for professional practice, it is imperative that students know the content and the limitations of written codes. Figure 1.2 provides a summary of the major principles contained in the NASW Code of Ethics.

The NASW Code of Ethics is intended to introduce a perspective that drives practitioners' thinking, that establishes criteria for selecting goals, and that influences how information is interpreted and understood. Regardless of which role the social worker plays, whether it is community organizer, political lobbyist, or direct practitioner, these professional actions are not value-free.

Ethical Dilemmas

Although values tell us what is important, ethics are the operationalization of values or the behavior that occurs in carrying out those values. The Code of Ethics, therefore, reflects the values of social work, but its intent is to provide direction for what actually happens in social work practice.

In many situations, social work practice presents ethical dilemmas. A dilemma implies that one is faced with a situation that necessitates a choice between equally important values. For example, a social worker who values a child's right to a safe and secure environment, must also value the parents' rights to have a say in their child's future. The retirement community administrator who values the freedom of a disruptive resident must also value the

FIGURE 1.2   NASW Code of Ethics
Summary of Major Principles & Standards

Summary of Ethical Principles

Value: Service
Ethical Principle: Social workers' primary goal is to help people in need and to address social problems.

Value: Social Justice
Ethical Principle: Social workers challenge social injustice.

Value: Dignity and Worth of the Person
Ethical Principle: Social workers respect the inherent dignity and worth of the person.

Value: Importance of Human Relationships
Ethical Principle: Social workers recognize the central importance of human relationships

Value: Integrity
Ethical Principle: Social workers behave in a trustworthy manner.

Value: Competence
Ethical Principle: Social workers practice within their areas of competence and develop and enhance their professional expertise.

Summary of Ethical Standards

1. **The Social Worker's Ethical Responsibilities to Clients**
    1.01. *Commitment to Clients.* Social workers' primary responsibility is to promote the well-being of clients.
    1.02 *Self-Determination.* Social workers respect and promote the rights of clients to self-determination and assist clients in ther efforts to identify and clarify their goals.
    1.03 *Informed Consent.* Social workers should provide services to clients only in the context of a professional relationship based, when appropriate, on valid informed consent.
    1.04 *Competence.* Social workers should provide services and represent themselves as competent only within the boundaries of their education, training, license, certification, consultation received, supervised experience, or other relevant professional experience.
    1.05 *Cultural Competence and Social Diversity.* Social workers should understand culture and its function in human behavior and society, recognizing the strengths that exist in all cultures.
    1.06 *Conflicts of Interest.* Social workers should be alert to and avoid conflicts of interest that interfere with the exercise of professional discretion and impartial judgment.
    1.07 *Privacy and Confidentiality.* Social workers should respect clients' right to privacy.
    1.08 *Access to Records.* Social workers should provide clients with reasonable access to records concerning the clients.
    1.09 *Sexual Relationships.* Social workers should under no circumstances engage in sexual activities or sexual contact with current clients, whether such contact is consensual or forced.
    1.10 *Physical Contact.* Social workers should not engage in physical contact with clients when there is a possibility of psychological harm to the client as a result of the contact (such as cradling or caressing clients).
    1.11 *Sexual Harassment.* Social workers should not sexually harass clients.
    1.12 *Derogatory Language.* Social workers should not use derogatory language in their written or verbal communications to or about clients.
    1.13 *Payment for Services.* When setting fees, social workers should ensure that the fees are fair, reasonable, and commensurate with the services performed.
    1.14 *Clients Who Lack Decision-Making Capacity.* When social workers act on behalf of clients who lack the capacity to make informed decisions, social workers should take reasonable steps to safeguard the interests and rights of those clients.
    1.15 *Interruption of Services.* Social workers should make reasonable efforts to ensure continuity of services in the event that services are interrupted by factors such as unavailability, relocation, illness, disability, or death.

1.16. *Termination of Services.* Social workers should terminate services to clients and professional relationships with them when such services and relationships are no longer required or no longer serve the clients' needs or interests.

2. **Social Workers' Ethical Responsibilities to Colleagues**
   2.01 *Respect.* Social Workers should treat colleagues with respect and should represent accurately and fairly the qualifications, views, and obligations of colleagues.
   2.02 *Confidentiality.* Social workers should respect confidential information shared by colleagues in the course of their professional relationships and transactions.
   2.03 *Interdisciplinary Collaboration.* Social workers who are members of an interdisciplinary team should participate in and contribute to decisions that affect the well-being of clients by drawing on the perspectives, values, and experiences of the social work profession.
   2.04. *Disputes Involving Colleagues.* Social workers should not take advantage of a dispute between a colleague and an employer to obtain a position or otherwise advance the social workers' own interests.
   2.05 *Consultation.* Social workers should seek the advice and counsel of colleagues whenever such consultation is in the best interests of clients.
   2.06 *Referral for Services.* Social workers should refer clients to other professionals when the other professionals' specialized knowledge or expertise is needed to serve clients fully or when social workers believe that they are not being effective or making reasonable progress with clients and that additional service is required.
   2.07 *Sexual Relationships.* Social workers who function as supervisors or educators should not engage in sexual activities or contact with supervisees, students, trainees, or other colleagues over whom they exercise professional authority.
   2.08 *Sexual Harassment.* Social workers should not sexually harass supervisees, students, trainees, or colleagues.
   2.09 *Impairment of Colleagues.* Social workers who have direct knowledge of a social work colleague's impairment that is due to personal problems, psychosocial distress, substance abuse, or mental health difficulties and that interferes with practice effectiveness should consult with that colleague when feasible and assist the colleague in taking remedial action.
   2.10 *Incompetence of Colleagues.* Social workers who have direct knowledge of a social work colleague's incompetence should consult with that colleague when feasible and assist the colleague in taking remedial action.
   2.11 *Unethical Conduct of Colleagues.* Social workers should take adequate measures to discourage, prevent, expose, and correct the unethical conduct of colleagues.

3. **Social Worker's Ethical Responsibilities in Practice Settings.**
   3.01 *Supervision and Consultation.* Social workers who provide supervision or consultation should have the necessary knowledge and skill to supervise or consult appropriately and should do so only within their areas of knowledge and competence.
   3.02 *Education and Training.* Social workers who function as educators, field instructors for students, or trainers should provide instruction only within their areas of knowledge and competence and should provide instruction based on the most current knowledge available in the profession.
   3.03 *Performance Evaluation.* Social workers who have responsibility for evaluating the performance of others should fulfill such responsibility in a fair and considerate manner and on the basis of clearly stated criteria.

3.04   *Client Records.* Social workers should take reasonable steps to ensure that documentation in records is accurate and reflects the services provided.

3.05   *Billing.* Social workers should establish and maintain billing practices that accurately reflect the nature and extent of services provided and that identify who provided the service in the practice setting.

3.06   *Client Transfer.* When an individual who is receiving services from another agency or colleague contacts a social worker for services, the social worker should carefully consider the client's needs before agreeing to provide services.

3.07   *Administration.* Social work administrators should advocate within and outside their agencies for adequate resources to meet clients' needs.

3.08   *Continuing Education and Staff Development.* Social work administrators and supervisors should take reasonable steps to provide or arrange for continuing education and staff development for all staff for whom they are responsible.

3.09   *Commitments to Employers.* Social workers generally should adhere to commitments made to employers and employing organizations.

3.10   *Labor-Management Disputes.* Social workers may engage in organized action, including the formation of and participation in labor unions, to improve services to clients and working conditions.

4. **Social Workers' Ethical Responsibilities as Professionals.**

4.01   *Competence.* Social workers should accept responsibility or employment only on the basis of existing competence or the intention to acquire the necessary competence.

4.02   *Discrimination.* Social workers should not practice, condone, facilitate, or collaborate with any form of discrimination on the basis of race, ethnicity, national origin, color sex, sexual orientation, age, marital status, political belief, religion, or mental or physical disability.

4.03   *Private Conduct.* Social workers should not permit their private conduct to interfere with their ability to fulfill their professional responsibilities.

4.04   *Dishonesty, Fraud and Deception.* Social workers should not participate in, condone, or be associated with dishonesty, fraud, or deception.

4.05   *Impairment.* Social workers should not allow their own personal problems, psychosocial distress, legal problems, substance abuse, or mental health difficulties to interfere with their professional judgment and performance or to jeopardize the best interests of people for whom they have a profesional responsibility.

4.06   *Misrepresentation.* Social workers should make clear distinctions between statements made and actions engaged in as a private individual and as a representative of the social work profession, a professional social work organization, or the social worker's employing agency.

4.07   *Solicitations.* Social workers should not engage in uninvited solicitation of potential clients who, because of their circumstances, are vulnerable to undue influence, manipulation, or coercion.

4.08   *Acknowledging Credit.* Social workers should take responsibility and credit, including authorship credit, only for work they have actually performed and to which they have contributed.

5. **Social Workers' Ethical Responsibilities to the Social Work Profession**

5.01   *Integrity of the Profession.* Social workers should work toward the maintenance and promotion of high standards of practice.

5.02   *Evaluation and Research.* Social workers should monitor and evaluate policies, the implementation of programs, and practice interventions.

FIGURE 1.2 NASW Code of Ethics   *continued*
Summary of Major Principles & Standards

6. *Social Workers' Ethical Responsibilities to the Broader Society*
   6.01   *Social Welfare.* Social workers should promote the general welfare of society, from local to global levels, and the development of people, their communities, and their environments.
   6.02   *Public Participation.* Social workers should facilitate informed participation by the public in shaping social policies and institutions.
   6.03   *Public Emergencies.* Social workers should provide appropriate professional services in public emergencies to the greatest extent possible.
   6.04   *Social and Political Action.* Social workers should engage in social and political action that seeks to ensure that all people have equal access to the resources, employment, services, and opportunities they require to meet their basic human needs and to develop fully.

Reprinted with permission from The National Association of Social Workers, Inc., Copyright 1996.

---

importance of being responsive to the larger resident community. Inherent in both situations are dilemmas. A choice between equally important values may have to be made when there is no easy or obviously right and wrong solution.

Reamer (1995) explains that social workers' views of values and ethics have matured and that no one could have predicted the types of dilemmas contemporary society poses. For example, practitioners will deal with clients who are child molesters, wife beaters, people who sell drugs to children, skinheads who commit hate crimes and a host of other persons who act on values alien to social work. Fortunately, the field of professional and applied ethics in social work emerged during the 1970s, and today there is growing literature and energetic dialogue addressing the complex value issues that arise in social work practice (Reamer 1995).

Jansson (1994) emphasizes ethical principles that are critical in analyzing policy practice decision making. He lists the principles of autonomy, beneficence, social justice, fairness, freedom, preservation of life, honesty, confidentiality, equality, due process, and societal or collective rights (p. 50). Depending on the ethicist or philosopher one reads, different principles may take precedence. Realizing that many principles have relevance to macro social work practice, we select three principles to illustrate ethical dilemmas that social workers face:

- Autonomy
- Beneficence
- Social Justice

Autonomy.   Autonomy is based on self-determination and freedom. It implies that each person should have the right to make his or her own life

choices. Concepts such as empowerment are built on the principle of autonomy, implying that power or control over one's life means seizing the opportunity to make one's own decisions. As an example, the pro-choice proponents
in the abortion controversy advocate for autonomy, a woman's right to
choose. This stance conflicts with a number of religious codes that argue the
immorality of abortion and state that the right of the unborn child must be
considered as well. Although autonomy may be perceived as individualistic
and therefore more relevant to direct practice situations, one has only to be involved in the heated debate over abortion to realize the ethical dilemma involved in situations in which the autonomy of both parties cannot be equally
respected.

Beneficence.   Beneficence is based on doing good for others, as well as not
doing harm. This principle is probably a primary motivator for those professionals who work in health and human service settings. It is their hope that
they will find ways to assist others in making life more meaningful.

Beneficence requires that the professional view clients holistically. Jansson
uses examples of a physician who treats a woman's presenting medical problem but does not consider her inability to afford a healthy diet, and a lawyer
who assists with a divorce but does not consider the financial implications for
the divorcee. Beneficence requires that the physician would refer the woman
to a food bank, a social worker, or to the food stamp office and that the
lawyer would refer the client to a financial counselor. Jansson says that all
professionals are morally obligated:

> to make their professional recommendations with a sensitivity toward their
> clients' economic, social, and policy realities, and to engage in brokerage, liaison,
> and advocacy work for specific clients to improve their economic and policy reali-
> ties. (1994, p. 36)

Beneficence, then, means that all professionals must consider multiple client
needs. Social workers, however, define themselves as being particularly sensitive to seeing persons in their environments. If social workers fail to see the
broader needs of their clients, then they have neglected the principle of
beneficence.

Social Justice.   Social justice is a complex ethical principle. Ideally, social
justice is achieved when there is a fair distribution of society's resources and
benefits so that every individual receives a deserved portion. Social work is in
the business of distributing and redistributing resources, whether they are as
tangible as money and jobs or as intangible as status and stigma. Undergird-
ing the distribution of resources in our society are value considerations that influence the enactment of laws, the enforcement of regulations, and the frameworks used in making policy decisions.

Reid and Billups (1986) tell us that the Code of Ethics instructs social
workers to "promote social justice" and to ensure that "persons have access
to resources" (p. 7). King Davis (1995) has developed a definition:

Social justice is a dynamic goal or condition of democratic societies and includes equitable access to societal institutions, resources, opportunities, rights, goods, services, responsibilities for all groups and individuals without arbitrary limitations based on observed or interpretations of differences in age, color, culture, physical or mental disability, education, gender, income, language, national origin, race, religion or sexual orientation.

Given the incredible range of social justice issues encompassed in this definition, it is clear that macro practitioners are constantly facing justice-related dilemmas. Jansson (1994) points out that social justice is based on equality. Given the many entrenched interests one encounters in local communities, it is likely that social workers will focus their efforts on particularly oppressed target population groups and will always be discovering new inequalities.

Concerns about justice are exacerbated when clients cannot pay for services. As long as clients can pay, professional decision making may not conflict with the larger society because resources do not have to be redistributed. Conceivably, as long as clients can pay for professional services, professions can operate within the market economy. Private practice and fee-for-service agencies conform to this model. Quality care is exchanged for economic resources, often in the form of third-party payments. The key to this model is that the client has access to the resources or has insurance coverage.

This model breaks down, however, when clients cannot pay. Most social work clients are in the situations they are in because their incomes are inadequate to meet their needs and other resources are not available. An AIDS patient may find himself unable to pay for his care at the same time his needs increase because he is fired from his job when news about his disease becomes known. An older woman could avoid institutional care by hiring an in-home caregiver, but despite having considerable lifetime savings, medical expenses from her husband's terminal illness now leave her with too few funds to meet her own needs. A youth who has grown up in poverty knows exactly what it means when the model breaks down. For him, a broken model has been a way of life, and he has no expectation of nor any reason to strive for a better standard of living.

The reality we face is that our society's health and human service systems are driven by considerations of whether resources are available to pay for (or to subsidize) the services clients need. If resources are not available, the AIDS patient and the older woman may be forced to expend all their own resources before ending up in public institutions, and the minority youth may continue in a cycle of insufficient education, housing, health care, and job opportunities. In this resource-driven system, social workers may have difficulty maintaining a vision of the compassionate community in which mutual support is provided to all those in need. These dilemmas face social workers because the profession is enmeshed in issues of redistribution.

Balancing autonomy, beneficence, and justice demands an analytical approach to decision making and intervention. Inevitably, the macro practitioner will face ethical dilemmas that go beyond the bounds of the Code of Ethics. This requires that he or she have a strong professional identity.

Professional Identity

Lengthy lists of characteristics have been proposed to describe a "profession." Gustafson (1982) identifies three principal characteristics common to all professions: (1) people-oriented purpose, (2) an extensive knowledge base, and (3) mechanisms of control.

First, professions "exist to meet the needs of others" within the larger community (Gustafson 1982, p. 508). Professions are therefore client-oriented and conform to a set of values that encapsulate the community good that is to be served. Activities designed only to serve the political or economic needs of powerful community members, even though they may be carried out by skilled individuals, do not qualify as professional endeavors.

Second, professions require mastery of a large body of theoretical, research-based, and technical knowledge. Professional judgment derives from the ability to apply knowledge skillfully in a workable manner. Gustafson argues that professional practitioners prefer guidelines rather than rules because guidelines offer direction rather than rigid formulation. They allow professionals to exercise discretion and to use their judgment. However, professionals also carry enormous responsibility because what they decide and how they act will affect both their clients and the multiple constituencies previously discussed. Every choice is a value judgment.

Gustafson's third characteristic of professions is that they place many social controls on professional activities. In social work, these controls include the accreditation activities carried out by the Council on Social Work Education (CSWE) to ensure the quality and consistency of degree programs in social work; the sanctioning capacity of the National Association of Social Workers (NASW); the NASW Code of Ethics, which provides basic value guidelines through which professional judgment is applied; and the credentialing and licensing requirements in various states. In short, there are many mechanisms for overseeing what occurs under the guise of professional practice.

Professional identify, according to Gustafson (1982), is built on the sense of calling that draws individual social workers to professional practice. "A profession without a calling lacks moral and humane roots, loses human sensitivity, and restricts the vision of the purposes of human good that are served" (p. 501). Quality of motivation and an in-depth vision of the needs to be served are the distinguishing characteristics that make a profession a calling (Gustafson 1982).

Certainly, each practitioner will have a vision of what the social work profession can be. The vision may be as broad as a higher quality of life for all and a better society, and may never be achieved as fully as one would like. Gustafson (1982) and Sullivan (1995) suggest that one major barrier to a shared vision is professional specialization. As the social work profession has developed (and as human service organizations have become larger and more bureaucratized), multiple specialties have emerged. For example, it is not uncommon to have social workers describe themselves as psychiatric social workers, geriatric specialists, child welfare workers, etc. These specialties denote the target populations with whom these practitioners work. Just as common are terms such as medical social worker or behavioral health specialist, indicating a setting in which these professionals are employed. Terms such as planner, community organizer, case manager, and group worker describe actual functions performed by social workers. Specialization can contribute to tunnel vision, in which one begins to focus on specific areas of expertise to the exclusion of broader concerns.

Bureaucratization can be a barrier to professional vision. As professional organizations have developed and grown, as settings in which social workers function have become multipurpose and have diversified their programs, and as communities have established numerous mechanisms that structure interaction amomg units within those communities, it is easy to lose one's professional sense of the broader vision. Sometimes there are so many impediments to instituting change in an organization or community that the change agent becomes frustrated.

Fabricant (1985) discusses the "industrialization" of social work practice, particularly in large public welfare agencies. In his discussion, he argues that social work is losing is aspects of "craft." A craft implies that the person responsible for beginning the professional task sticks with it until the end. For example, if a social worker provides intake for the client, that same social worker assesses the client, contracts with the client regarding a care plan, and continues to work with the client until the goals of that plan are achieved. This provides both the worker and the client with a sense of continuity, with ownership of the entire process, and with a shared understanding of what the outcome is to be.

As our health and human service delivery systems have become more and more complex, as new actors enter the arenas, and as professionals specialize, it becomes rare for the practitioner to see an intervention from beginning to end. As tasks become more standardized and routinized, social workers may feel bound by rules rather than directed by flexible guidelines that facilitate discretion and judgment. These changes can jeopardize the maintenance of a professional vision that transcends individual organizations and communities.

Although there are barriers to achieving an in-depth vision, we believe that professional vision is built on a commitment to serve diverse people within a society that does not always perform this function well and at times actually denies support to oppressed populations. The challenge is to work toward the development of comprehensive, effectiveness-based health and human service systems within local communities. This often requires the practitioner to understand situations without accepting "what is," to analyze dilemmas with the full realization that an ethical response is a choice among values, to envision competent and compassionate alternatives to what currently exists, and to skillfully use a macro practice model to change "what is" to "what could be."

In many ways it is this commitment to the understanding and changing of larger systems that defines social work. Sullivan (1995) argues that the very nature of professionalism implies a responsibility to the larger society. "The professions are important because they stand for, and in part actualize, the spirit of vocation. Professionalism promises to link the performance of specific tasks with the larger civic spirit" (p. 10). He goes on to say that professional "integrity is never a given, but always a quest that must be renewed and reshaped over time" (p. 220). Professional integrity means that those persons who call themselves professionals will remember that the center of their practice is always the client. Social work is only one of many helping professions, but its unique contribution is to serve as a constant reminder that people are multidimensional and that they must be viewed in the context of their environments.

Some Basic Principles of Macro Practice

Having examined issues of values, ethics, and professional identity, we end this chapter with a set of principles designed to guide the social worker involved in macro-level change episodes through the many decisions and choices that must be made. Each of these assumptions will be evident in future chapters, so we will only briefly describe them here.

Informed Approach.   First, the macro practitioner approaches the need for change with an understanding and expectation that decisions will be based on as complete a set of data and information as time and resources allow. Informed decision making is pursued in a systematic and scholarly manner, using the best available theoretical, research-based, and practice-based knowledge.

Consumer Input and Participation.   Although it may be more time consuming and take more energy to include clients in change processes, the social worker must always look for client input. Finding new and meaningful ways to facilitate consumer as well as citizen participation in organizational and community arenas is an ongoing challenge for the dedicated professional.

Critical Thinking.   Fitting problems to solutions is based on thorough analysis. Defining the problem to be changed requires integrating what clients have to say with scholarly research and practice results. This analytical process is dynamic and interactive, often causing the change agent to reframe the original problem statement. This process is iterative, meaning that new information constantly requires rethinking. But once the problem statement is agreed upon, social workers must ascertain that their interventions make sense in relation to the problem at hand. Interventions often require a creative imagination that goes beyond traditional approaches.

Goal Directedness.   Goals are broadly defined aims toward which practitioners guide their efforts. They are usually long-term and sometimes idealistic. However, goals provide a vision shared by clients and colleagues—a hope of what can be—and they assist the practitioner in maintaining a focus.

Outcome Orientation.   Outcomes are defined as quality-of-life changes in clients' lives based on the interventions jointly planned by practitioners and clients. Much of the history of social work practice has been focused on process—what the social worker does. Interventions of the future will be driven by outcomes—what change is expected to be achieved by and for the target population as a result of this change effort. Balancing the importance of process and the push for accountability through outcome measurement is part of contemporary practice.

Social workers have the opportunity to make change occur. Based on a set of values, macro social work practice progresses in an informed manner, incorporating clients into the dynamic process, designing interventions to meet well-analyzed problems. Broad goals and specific outcomes provide the focused direction.

SUMMARY

In this chapter we have tried to provide the basic foundations on which students can build an understanding of social work macro practice. We defined macro practice as professionally guided intervention designed to bring about planned change in organizations and communities, and we began a discussion of the circumstances leading to the need for planned change. A conceptual framework was provided.

We used comments from former students who are now practicing social workers to illustrate how the circumstances that are often most important or troubling to social workers are not only the concerns of their clients but also issues such as the management of their organization or the resources available within their communities. These points were reinforced through three case vignettes showing how policies, program structures, resource deficits, and other macro-related criteria have much to do with social workers' ability to be effective in their jobs.

One way that social workers sometimes respond to these realities is to give up fighting against them. This is done through burning out and leaving the profession, burning out and staying in the profession, developing tunnel vision, and redirecting one's energies beyond the employing agency. However, social workers who are skilled in macro practice have another option—to use their understanding of macro systems to bring about needed changes in these systems. These skills are not and should not be limited to those who are working in traditional macro-practice roles such as administration or planning. Instead, they are critical for all social workers to know, including those engaged mostly in micro practice.

The value base of social work is summarized most succinctly in the NASW Code of Ethics, which embodies the profession's orientation to practice. Intervening at any level presents ethical dilemmas that must be faced by the practitioner. In many cases no right or wrong answer is present, and the appropriate course of action is not at all clear. In such cases, the practitioner's job can be facilitated by analyzing the situation in terms of three or more basic, though sometimes conflicting, ethical principles. *Autonomy* refers to the value we ascribe to an individual's right of self-determination. *Beneficence* refers to the value of helping others. *Social justice* is ensuring equal access to resources and equitable treatment. Macro practitioners may find that their job is one of balancing these values. In micro practice, for example, one must often temper the desire to help (and our notions of how best to solve a client's problem) with a recognition of the client's need for personal autonomy. From a macro practice perspective, social justice considerations may demand that we focus not only on individual helping but on attempts to alter macro systems that fail to distribute resources in a fair manner.

Working through these dilemmas aids in the development of a professional identity that incorporates both micro and macro practice aspects. Just as the profession must be built on social workers who are committed to making a difference in the lives of individual clients, these same workers must also be committed to making a difference in the systems within which clients live and upon which they depend.

Parts II, III, and IV of this textbook will provide a macro practice model to guide social workers in undertaking change processes. But first, Chapters 2 and 3 will complete this part of the book by providing a more detailed history and preparation for change perspectives for macro practice in social work.

REFERENCES

Barker, R. L. (1995) *The social work dictionary.* Washington, DC: National Association of Social Workers.

Barker, R. L. (1987) *The social work dictionary.* Silver Spring, MD: National Association of Social Workers.

Bricker-Jenkins, M., and N. R. Hooyman. (1986) *Not for women only.* Silver Spring, MD: National Association of Social Workers.

Davis, K. (1995) *Definition of social justice.* Unpublished paper.

Fabricant, M. (1985) The industrialization of social work practice. *Social Work,* 30(5), 389–95.

Fisher, R. (1995) Political social work. *Journal of Social Work Education,* 31(2), 194–203.

Flynn, J. P. (1992) *Social agency policy: Analysis and presentation for community practice.* Chicago: Nelson-Hall.

Gustafson, J. M. (1982) Professions as "callings." *Social Service Review,* 56(4), 501–15.

Jansson, B. S. (1994) *Social policy: From theory to policy practice* (2nd ed.). Pacific Grove, CA: Brooks/Cole.

Landon, P. S. (1995) Generalist and Advanced Generalist Practice. In *The Encyclopedia of Social Work* (19*th* ed., 2:1101–1108). Washington, DC: National Association of Social Workers.

Reamer, F. G. (1995) *Social work values and ethics.* New York: Columbia University Press.

Reid, P. N., and J. O. Billups. (1986) Distributional ethics and social work education. *Journal of Social Work Education,* 22(1): 6–17.

Rothman, J., J. L. Erlich, and J. E. Tropman. (1995) *Strategies of community intervention* (5th ed.) Itasca, IL: F. E. Peacock.

Sherman, W. R., and S. Wenocur. (1983) Empowering public welfare workers through mutual support. *Social Work, 28*(5), 375–9.

Specht, H., and M. E. Courtney. (1994) *Unfaithful angels.* New York: The Free Press.

Sullivan, W. M. (1995) *Work and integrity: The crisis and promise of professionalism in America.* New York: Harper/Collins.

SUGGESTED READINGS

Austin, M. J., and J. I. Lowe. (1994) *Controversial issues in communities and organizations.* Boston: Allyn & Bacon.

Bargal, D., and H. Schmid (guest eds.) (1992) Organizational change and development in human service organizations. *Administration in Social Work,* 16 (3/4), entire issue.

Fabricant, M. B., and S. Burghardt. (1992) *The welfare state crisis and the transformation of social service work.* Armonk, NY: M.E. Sharpe.

Inglehart, A. P., and R. M. Becerra. (1995) *Social services and the ethnic community.* Boston: Allyn & Bacon.

Lakey, B., G. Lakey, R. Napier, and J. Robinson. (1995) *Grassroots and nonprofit leadership.* Philadelphia: New Society Publishers.

Mayers, R. S., F. Souflee, and D. J. Schoech. (1994) *Dilemmas in human service management: Illustrative case studies.* New York: Springer.

McInnis-Dittrich, K. (1994) *Integrating social welfare policy and social work practice.* Pacific Grove, CA: Brooks/Cole.

Perlmutter, F. D., ed. (1994) *Women and social change.* Washington, DC: National Association of Social Workers Press.

Tropman, J. E., J. L. Erlich, and J. Rothman. (1995) *Tactics and techniques of community intervention* (3rd ed.). Itasca, IL: F. E. Peacock.

CHAPTER 2

The Historical Roots of Macro Practice

TRENDS UNDERLYING THE EMERGENCE OF SOCIAL WORK ROLES

Preceding the birth of social work as a profession, a number of societal trends had appeared that eventually brought about recognition of the need for macro-level responses to social problems. Among these, Garvin and Cox (1995) call attention to: (1) social conditions, (2) ideological conflicts, and (3) oppressed populations. These are helpful divisions that we will also follow in our discussion.

Social Conditions

The first U.S. census in 1790 revealed a national population of less than 4 million. By 1900 this number had grown to almost 92 million, and recent figures placed the population at over 260 million in 1994. The period of fastest growth was in the 1800s, when the nation's population increased by more than one third every 10 years throughout the first half of the century and, despite the death and destruction of the Civil War, continued to grow by more than 25 percent per decade during the century's second half. The rate of growth moderated after 1900, with increases diminishing to about 11 percent per decade since 1960. Still, in raw numbers, the nation continues to add roughly 25 million persons to its population every 10 years.

Immigration.   Immigration has always been a critical element in population growth in the United States. One of the first massive waves of immigrants came in the 1840s. To the East Coast came Irish and German immigrants fleeing famine and political upheaval, respectively. To the West Coast came the Chinese to obtain employment during the California gold rush. Successive waves followed from Southern and Eastern Europe as well as Asia, reaching a peak during 1900–1910 when immigrants totaled over six million and accounted for almost 40 percent of the nation's population growth. Though arrivals slowed after 1920, the proportion of population growth accounted for by immigration has risen recently, and since 1980 immigration has accounted for between 27 and 31 percent of population growth each year (U.S. Bureau of the Census 1995a). At present, about five percent of people in the United States were born outside its boundaries. Mexico is the most common birth country among these individuals, yet it still accounts for only 20 percent of the total (U.S. Bureau of the Census 1995b).

Industrialization.   Accompanying the country's population growth was a rapid shift toward industrialization of its economy. Axinn and Levin (1992) use the production of cotton in the South as a way of illustrating the effects of this shift. Total cotton production was only 6000 bales the year before the invention of the cotton gin in 1793, after which it grew to 73,000 bales by 1800 and almost four million bales near the start of the Civil War in 1860. This type of dramatic change transformed working life throughout the country. In 1820, for example, nearly 3 of every 4 workers were employed in agriculture, a ratio that dropped to less than 2 in 5 by 1900, and is currently about 1 in 35. Similarly, the contribution of the agricultural sector to overall national income fell from 20 percent in the 1880s to just 2 percent in 1995 (U.S. Bureau of the Census 1995b).

The economic opportunity generated by increasing industrialization was a key enabling factor for the rapid growth of the nation's population. This is because the wealth generated by an expanding industrial economy meant that many more people could be supported than in previous agricultural economies. Trattner (1995) calls particular attention to the vast growth in national wealth that occurred following the Civil War. In just the 40 years between 1860 and 1900, for example, the value of all manufactured products in the country grew sixfold and total investment in industry grew by a factor of 12.

Urbanization.   The combination of population growth and industrialization brought about increased urbanization. As recently as 1910, over half the population still lived in rural areas; by 1980, almost three fourths lived in urban areas. Warren (1978) notes that no U.S. city had a population of 50,000 as of the 1790 census, whereas almost 400 such cities existed by 1970. In 1995 this number had grown still higher, to a total of 615 cities (U.S. Bureau of the Census 1995b). Initially, much of this growth occurred in the urban core of large industrial cities, compared to the more recent increases taking place in suburbs and medium-sized cities. Still, no American city had reached a population of one million until the 1880s, while today more than half (55%) of all U.S. residents live in the 51 metropolitan areas having populations of a million or more (U.S. Bureau of the Census 1995a).

Change in Institutional Structures.   Accompanying these trends were fundamental changes in the institutional structure of society, especially with regard to the system of organizations that meet people's needs. In the early 1800s, these organizations tended to be informal, few in number, and small in scope (e.g., families, churches, and schools). Engaged primarily in agriculture and living in rural areas, people were largely self-sufficient and depended on these organizations for a relatively narrow range of needs. With the advent of industrialization, however, new technologies were linked with advances in methods of organizing, and a new social structure began to emerge. The hallmark of this structure is a complex system of highly specialized organizations designed to meet very specific needs. These range from accounting firms to computer manufacturers to adoption agencies, and they exemplify the enormous diversity and complexity of modern society. The specialization of these organizations allows them to do a few tasks very efficiently and in great quantity. However, this specialization also makes them very dependent on other organizations for resources such as power, raw material, and trained personnel, even if they may not always recognize this dependence.

People in today's society benefit enormously from the vast production of these organizations, but like the organizations they, too, are more specialized in their roles. Instead of learning the range of tasks necessary for basic self-sufficiency, individuals in society now concentrate on learning specific skills that will allow them to carry out certain functions, usually within an organization. This specialization allows both individuals and organizations to do particular tasks more effectively, and society as a whole is more productive. However, a corollary effect of specialization is that almost no individuals or organizations are wholly self-sufficient, and the interdependence among members of society is greater than ever before. Moreover, when for various reasons individuals cannot meet their needs through the roles they are able to fill, they are much more dependent than in the past on assistance from societal institutions. This is a prime reason for the development of social work as a profession.

Changes in broad social conditions that contributed to the development of social work thus included population growth, industrialization, urbanization, and changes in the institutional structure of society that led to increased specialization and interdependence. The institutional changes were particularly relevant to social work because they most directly influenced the development of services to people in need.

Ideological Conflicts

Not surprisingly, changes in broad social conditions coincided with considerable ideological change. Garvin and Cox (1995) identify several viewpoints that arose during the late 1800s in response to these conditions. These include Social Darwinism, radical ideology, and liberalism. In the late 1800s, Herbert

Spencer, an English writer, applied Charles Darwin's biological theories to society. Social Darwinism particularly focused on the concept of "survival of the fittest," reasoning that persons with wealth and power in society achieved this status because they were more fit than those without such resources. It was also hypothesized that, though in the biological world genetic mutations could survive and overcome inferior traits, in societies some groups are inherently inferior. Not surprisingly, this philosophy was embraced by many of the wealthy. It was used to argue that little should be done for the poor and dispossessed on the grounds that such help would simply perpetuate social inferiority.

Social Darwinism also provided ideological support for the philosophy of manifest destiny, which helped to fuel westward expansion during the latter half of the 1800s. Coined by a politician in 1845, this term described the belief that God had willed the land to the Anglo-Saxon race to build a Utopian world. Such a world would fuse capitalism, protestantism, and democracy, and in it Anglo-Saxon peoples were not to dilute their superiority by marrying members of other races (Jansson 1988).

Partly as a reaction to the racism and classism inherent in these views, but also in response to the growing influence of Karl Marx and other socialist writers, a radical ideology developed. This view is closely associated with the rise of the labor movement, which drew its strength from the terrible conditions afflicting most industrial laborers at the time. One goal of the proponents of this view was the transfer of industrial control from capitalists to trade unions. However, the growing plight of the poor also led to broader organizing efforts designed to mobilize and empower all those in the low socioeconomic class (Garvin & Cox 1995).

Liberalism arose partly as a secular expression of the Judeo-Christian values of egalitarianism and social responsibility, which were seen as a means of tempering the excesses of a laissez-faire economic system. In this view, human rights supersede property rights, and society is seen as having a responsibility for promoting the collective good. One of the expressions of liberalism was scientific charity, which advocated "a method of investigation and planned helping, case by case, that would build on and strengthen the informal or natural 'fountains of charity' and not displace or weaken them" (Leiby 1987, p. 764). This view was to contribute powerfully to the rise of some of the earliest non-religiously based human service agencies—the Charity Organization Societies—in the late 1800s.

Oppressed Populations

New social conditions such as the changing face of the U.S. population and shifts in ideology intensified prejudicial attitudes and discriminatory behavior toward certain groups. As is often the case, these beliefs and actions were commonly directed toward groups already suffering the harshest effects of rapid social change. The following review thus concentrates on trends affecting populations whose members would later become focuses of attention for professional social workers.

Native Americans.   Among Indian people in the 1800s and early 1900s oppression was literally governmental policy, enacted via war, forcible relocation, deliberate spread of disease, contravention of treaties, and confinement to reservations. The Removal Act of 1830 gave the federal government the right to relocate any native groups living east of the Mississippi River. For many tribes this move meant virtual genocide. Relocation of the Cherokee nation in 1838, for example, produced massive losses from disease and exposure, becoming known as the Trail of Tears. Beginning in the 1890s, generations of Native American youth, whose families had previously been forced onto reservations, were required to attend off-reservation boarding schools where they were forbidden the use of their own language and made to "think, act, look and be, in every way possible, like members of white society" (Beane 1989, p. 38). Though the goal of this policy was to speed assimilation into white culture, the main effect was to severely damage Native American family life.

Latinos.   More than 100,000 indigenous Spanish-speaking people in the Southwest became part of the United States following the Mexican-American War in 1848. The war had begun primarily as a result of U.S. military incursions into Mexico, and the Treaty of Guadalupe Hidalgo that ended it included specific protections regarding property rights and civil liberties for those who became part of the United States. Nonetheless, many of these people were forced from their lands. Language was also a common tool of oppression, with Latinos being denied participation in voting and public education because they were not proficient in English. Following the beginning of the Mexican Revolution in 1910, large waves of Mexican immigrants began to face similar barriers. During the Depression years of the 1930s, unemployment pressures led to huge deportations of supposedly illegal residents, as many as half of whom were in fact U.S. citizens (Gibson 1987).

African Americans.   African Americans were treated poorly despite their emancipation from slavery in the Civil War. The Freedmen's Bureau, set up in 1865 to assist the transition of freed slaves, was a rare example of federal involvement in the provision of social welfare services. Though it lasted only six years, it did assist many former slaves in finding employment or gaining access to education and health care. More typical of black people's experiences, however, was the founding, also in 1865, of the Ku Klux Klan. Its reign of terror in the South lasted almost 100 years, effectively denying many African Americans the freedoms they had supposedly gained. In the courts, rulings supporting Jim Crow legislation had similar effects. The U.S. Supreme Court's landmark *Plessy v. Ferguson* decision of 1896 upheld the segregationist doctrine of "separate but equal" facilities, in this case with regard to public transportation. Trattner (1995) notes that even in the Progressive Era and the New Deal years, social welfare gains had a much greater impact on poverty among white than among black persons.

Asian Americans.   On the West Coast, Chinese immigrants had been exploited as cheap labor. When economic conditions changed, hostility resulted in violence. In 1882, Congress enacted the Chinese Exclusion Act, which became permanent in 1902 (Garvin & Cox 1995). This act outlawed all Chinese immigration until its repeal in 1943. Japanese immigration increased between 1890 and 1907, resulting in changes to California state laws that restricted the ability of the Japanese to own or even lease property. Later, in one of the most egregious examples of governmental discrimination by race, hundreds of thousands of Japanese were forcibly relocated to internment camps during the Second World War.

Women.   Though the roots of feminism emerged during the 1800s, most women remained relegated to traditional subordinate roles. Women's suffrage was identified as a central goal at an early national Women's Rights Convention in 1848. However, despite ceaseless efforts by pioneers of women's rights such as Elizabeth Cady Stanton and Susan B. Anthony, full voting rights for women were not achieved until the ratification of the 19th amendment to the U.S. constitution in 1919. Meanwhile, viewed as keepers of the hearth and nurturers of the family, women were placed on a pedestal of romantic idealization that also served as a prison to constrain their thoughts and actions (Jansson 1988).

Persons with Disabilities.   Laws urging charitable and considerate treatment of persons with disabilities date to the Code of Hammurabi and ancient Judeo-Christian writings, yet in practice many societies have dealt harshly with their disabled members. Even in the relatively enlightened Greek and Roman cultures, accepted practices included infanticide, enslavement, concubinage, and euthanasia (Trattner 1995). More recent societies have renounced these practices, but their treatment of persons with disabilities has still been affected by longstanding tendencies to view a disability as somehow the fault of the disabled or as punishment for unspecified sins. Terms such as "crippled" or "simple minded," which have only recently faded from common usage, are instructive because (1) they describe disabilities through pejorative terms and (2) they define disability as some form of deficit vis-à-vis others in the population, though research has shown that persons with disabilities do not perceive themselves in terms of deficiencies (Wright 1988).

In the United States after the Civil War, battlefield injuries were one of the few categories of disabilities receiving public attention. In 1866 Mississippi spent one fifth of its state funds on artificial limbs for wounded veterans (Ward 1990), yet at the same time no public system existed in the state to serve the needs of persons with mental retardation. Even for veterans, available assistance was usually very limited and did little to foster independence or integration with the rest of society. Not until the Veterans Rehabilitation Act of 1918 and the Civilian Vocational Rehabilitation Act of 1920 were federal programs established to promote greater participation and self-sufficiency. These were followed by income assistance programs created by the Social Security Act of 1935 (Percy 1989).

Gay Men and Lesbian Women.   Members of the gay and lesbian community, because of longstanding and widespread persecution, were traditionally the most hidden of oppressed groups. For many years homosexuality was viewed primarily through the lens of religious taboos and was thus considered sinful behavior. However, English law, unlike that of many other European countries, made homosexuality a crime as well, and as recently as 1816, English sailors were executed for the crime of "buggery" (Marotta 1981). English legal codes on homosexuality were adopted in the United States, and, though not always enforced, they were often used selectively as a means of harassment. More recently, drawing in part on theories advanced by Sigmund Freud, gays and lesbians were considered mentally ill, and could be forcibly subjected to hospitalization or other measures designed to cure their "perversions" (Szasz 1965).

The Development of Social Work

The oppression of ethnic minorities, women, and sexual minorities predated the development of the social work profession. The profession, thus, was born into an environment in which social change was needed. The effects of oppression, ideological shifts, and broad social changes created social pressures that could not be indefinitely ignored. The first organized efforts to respond to these pressures also formed the basis for development of social work. Among these efforts were the Charity Organization Societies (COS) and the settlement house movement.

Local COS agencies, which began forming in the 1870s, were usually umbrella organizations that coordinated the activities of a wide variety of charities created to deal with the problems of immigrants and rural transplants who were flooding into industrialized northern cities in search of jobs. Social Darwinism provided the philosophical roots of the movement, thus the "scientific charity" provided by COS agencies tended to be moralistic in tone and oriented mostly toward persons deemed able to become members of the industrial workforce (Axinn & Levin 1992). Workers in the COS agencies were often volunteers, especially middle- and upper-class women, who served as "friendly visitors" to poor individuals and families. The volunteers tended to share idealistic goals of providing the poor with an opportunity to better themselves, but they had a high stake in weeding fraudulent claimants from the ranks of those seen as both truly needy and open to reform (Chambers 1985).

While the COS movement represented one response to human need, settlement houses adopted a different approach. Conditions in the crowded slums and tenement houses of industrial cities in the late 1800s were as dire as any in the nation's history, and the goal of the settlement houses was to attack these problems on a systemic level. This meant an approach to practice that emphasized societal as well as individual and group reform. Many of the settlement houses served as religious missions and, like the COS members, did their share of proselytizing and moralizing. Nonetheless, they were also more willing to meet their mostly immigrant constituents on their own grounds and to believe that chasms of class, religion, nationality, and culture could be spanned. In addition, their societal vision tended to be pluralistic—whereas COS workers feared organized efforts such as the labor movement, settlement leaders tended to support these endeavors. They also played prominent roles in the birth of organizations such as the National Association for the Advancement of Colored People, the Women's Trade Union League, and the American Civil Liberties Union.

Women played a major role in building the foundations of social work in both the COS and settlement house movements. Benevolent work was viewed as compatible with women's nurturing roles in society, and, ironically, even the social change roles played by women were justifiable as "'civic housekeeping' [that] was but an extension of women's concern for family welfare into the public sphere" (Chambers 1986, p. 13). Also, Trattner (1995) notes that since elected office was effectively denied to most women, an alternative chosen by many was to pursue their interest in social and political issues through involvement in the settlement houses and other efforts.

Early Social Work Education

Service responsibility gradually began to shift from volunteers to paid employees. COS workers emphasized the need for a systematic approach to their work, while settlement house workers demanded training on how to effect social change. Both traditions "developed and promoted neighborhood-based research" (Brieland 1990, p. 135). This need for education and research contributed to the organization of schools of social work. The New York School of Philanthropy began in 1898 as a summer training program of the New York Charity Organization Society, and the Boston School of Social Work was jointly founded by Simmons and Harvard colleges in 1904, also in response to prompting from local COS agencies (Trattner 1995). Meanwhile, persons involved with the settlement house movement helped establish the Chicago School of Civics and Philanthropy in 1907 (Jansson 1988).

Accompanying these efforts, a debate ensued over whether the fledgling profession should focus on macro or micro social work models. Macro models, concerned with fundamental social policy issues, demanded an academic curriculum based on social theory and an orientation toward analysis and reform. A parallel movement, represented by Jane Addams, emphasized training for political activism. It promoted not only economic reforms but also a pacifist agenda (e.g., advocating peace negotiations instead of military involvement in World War I). In contrast, micro models focused on case-by-case assistance and required that caseworkers learn how to conduct field work.

An important turning point in this debate was the 1915 meeting of the National Conference of Charities and Corrections, described as the "most significant event in the development of the intellectual rationalization for social work as an organized profession" (Austin 1983, p. 359). Abraham Flexner, the most prominent national figure in medical education, was asked to address the issue of whether social work was truly a profession. He argued that social work still lacked certain characteristics of a profession and could more appropriately be called a semi-profession, a view that Austin (1983) says was typically applied to careers in which women predominated. Flexner's six characteristics of a true profession were: (1) professionals operate intellectually with large individual responsibility; (2) they derive their raw material from science and learning; (3) this material is applied practically; (4) an educationally communicable technique exists; (5) there is a tendency toward self-organization or association; and (6) professions become increasingly altruistic in motivation (Austin 1983).

In a more or less unquestioning response to Flexner's remarks, social workers hurried to adopt these characteristics. In 1917, Mary Richmond published *Social Diagnosis,* which brought one-on-one casework practice to the fore and cast it firmly in a traditional, professional mold. As Reisch and Wenocur (1986) argue, the book "redefined investigation as diagnosis and thereby linked social work to the occupational symbols of the medical and legal professions" (p. 77). The focus on diagnosis was further strengthened by the influence of Freudian psychotherapy, which became the dominant theoretical basis for casework practice throughout almost the next half-century.

COMMUNITY ORGANIZATION AND SOCIAL REFORM

Though inconspicuous and not specifically professionally focused, the development of macro-practice models continued. By 1920, the first social work textbook on community organization had appeared, and at least 5 more books on the subject were written within the next 10 years. Organizational theorists such as Mary Follett and social work educators such as Eduard Lindeman called attention to the possible role to be played by small primary groups working to strengthen local areas within larger communities (Garvin & Cox 1995). However, differences had already begun to arise concerning the appropriate focus of macro-level interventions. On one side were those who advocated for grass-roots efforts in effecting community change, and on the other were those who argued for greater involvement in policy development and agency-based provision of services.

In addition, a radical social work movement emerged in the mid-1920s that reached a peak in the New Deal Era and was embraced as a part of professional identity in the early 1940s. Unionization efforts in the late 1920s and early 1930s resulted in social workers such as Bertha Capen Reynolds collaborating with other professions to reduce management abuses and ameliorate the effects of workforce reductions and pay cuts. Social workers also marched side by side with residents of urban slums demanding improved housing conditions. These social workers were mostly young, held low-level positions such as case managers and community action organizers, and did not strongly identify with "professional" social workers (Wagner 1989).

Effects of the Great Depression

The Great Depression, which began with the stock market crash of 1929, became a watershed event in the history of macro practice. In the four-year period from 1929 to 1933, the gross national product of the United States fell by almost half, and unemployment reached 25 percent. The resulting impoverishment of vast segments of the population raised doubts about traditional notions that poor people were responsible for their own plight and could solve it through personal reform. As Axinn and Levin (1992) note:

> The depression brought forcibly to consciousness the point that one could be poor and unemployed as a result of the malfunctioning of society. The temporary relief programs developed to meet the exigencies of the depression acknowledged the existence of this kind of poverty and of a "new poor." The later permanent programs of the Social Security Act recognized the possibility of inherent societal malfunctioning. (p. 171)

This was the point that settlement leaders and social reformers had long argued, and it was to play an influential role in the development of Franklin D. Roosevelt's New Deal programs. A number of social workers and agency administrators who had supported New Deal–like reforms during Roosevelt's term as governor of New York later assumed key positions in his presidential administration. Harry Hopkins, head of the Federal Emergency Relief Administration (FERA), and Frances Perkins, Secretary of Labor, were the most visible of this community (Jansson 1988).

Social Work and Social Change

In an atmosphere of sweeping change, radical social workers cooperated with mainstream social work leaders during the late 1930s. The radical journal, *Social Work Today,* began to pay attention to social work practice, muting somewhat its traditional view that casework constituted a "Band-Aid" approach to client problems. Radical elements within the profession remained identifiable as the left wing in social work, but they were less dramatically differentiated from the liberal social work professional leadership. These shifts were facilitated by the achievement of mutual goals such as the Social Security Act in 1935 and passage of the National Labor Relations Act, which ensured labor's right to organize, strike, and bargain collectively. The latter act marked the beginning of a period of great successes on the part of the labor movement in organizing much of the industrial workforce in the country.

After the mid-1930s, large governmental agencies began to dominate the provision of human services, and the battle of social work roles shifted to this arena. Reisch and Wenocur (1986) note that advocates of the casework model were well placed in many of these organizations and developed job specifications that largely excluded community organizers. However, members of the Rank and File Movement of radical social workers also became involved in the public services arena, and they brought with them their emphasis on large-scale social reform (Wagner 1989).

These developments in the 1930s and 1940s set the stage for many later social movements. Though the 1950s were not a time of great tumult, key events occurred during the decade that were to open the door for considerable social change in the 1960s. One landmark example was the 1954 Supreme Court decision that struck down "separate but equal" policies in public education. Ensuing efforts to overturn school segregation became the foundation of the Civil Rights Movement. Beginning with the Montgomery, Alabama, bus boycott the following year, Martin Luther King, Jr., and the Southern Christian Leadership Conference carried out a campaign of nonviolent resistance through sit-ins and demonstrations. Other groups such as the Congress on Racial Equality (CORE) and the Student Nonviolent Coordinating Committee sponsored "freedom rides" and trained young whites and blacks from elsewhere in the country to assist with organizing efforts in the South. Both the Voting Rights Act of 1964 and the Civil Rights Act of 1965 were passed largely as a result of these efforts.

In response to the struggles of blacks in the South and elsewhere, other social change movements began to address the interests of other traditionally oppressed groups. Cesar Chavez's United Farm Workers began organizing the predominantly Chicano field workers in the Southwest, and the La Raza movement sought to gain political power for Hispanics through voter registration drives and other efforts that had worked well in the South. The American Indian Movement (AIM) called attention to governmental policies that had often worsened rather than ameliorated problems in Native American communities. Writings such as Betty Friedan's *The Feminine Mystique* (1963) became a catalyst for the Women's Movement, which sought to extend into the social and economic realms the type of equality women had gained in voting rights through the suffrage movement. Episodes of "gay-bashing" by citizens and police officers in New York led to a disturbance called the Stonewall Riot. This in turn helped lead to the Gay Liberation movement, the first large-scale effort to overcome prejudice and discrimination against homosexuals. Finally, the counterculture movement, student unrest (through groups such as Students for a Democratic Society), and protests against the Vietnam War combined to make the late 1960s the most turbulent period of the century in terms of mass social movements. Participation in these events provided on-the-job training for many community activists who later became professional social work practitioners.

Also in the 1960s, expanded governmental social programs, though sometimes ill-conceived, provided new opportunities for community-level interventions. One stimulus for these changes was renewed awareness of the plight of poor people, brought on in part by books such as Michael Harrington's *The Other America* (1962). John Kennedy's election in 1960 on a platform of social activism also played a part, resulting in programs such as Mobilization for Youth, inner-city delinquency prevention efforts, and the Peace Corps. On an international basis, these efforts helped refine models of community development (Trattner 1995).

In 1964, Lyndon Johnson's call for a war on poverty led to the passage of a vast array of social welfare programs. These programs left a mixed legacy of results but provided an opportunity for testing macro-practice models. One of the most important examples was the Community Action Program (CAP), part of the Economic Opportunity Act of 1964, which was a keystone of antipoverty legislation. The goal of CAP programs was to achieve better coordination of services among community providers and to facilitate citizen participation in decision making through "maximum feasible participation of the residents of the areas and the members of the groups being served" (U.S. Congress 1964, p. 9). Accordingly, CAP agencies were created in neighborhoods and communities throughout the country, recruiting residents to serve as board members or as paid employees alongside professionally trained staff members.

In their evaluation and critique of CAP initiatives, Peterson and Greenstone (1977) argue that the design and implementation of the programs largely undermined the first objective of improving coordination of services. However, they also contend that CAP agencies achieved considerable success in their second objective of facilitating citizen participation, particularly in African-American communities. In their view, "the contribution of [CAP agencies] to the organizational resources of local black communities was substantial. CAP's distinctive mission began the formation of new political linkages between black Americans and the political order" (pp. 272–4). Other programs were less successful and in some cases resulted in harsh criticisms of social workers and their efforts. Within the field itself, however, accomplishments such as those of the CAP agencies helped to reestablish the importance of macro-practice roles.

Reflecting this trend, the Council on Social Work Education (CSWE) in 1962 recognized community organization as a method of social work practice comparable to group work and casework. In 1963, the Office of Juvenile Delinquency and Youth Development of the U.S. Department of Health, Education, and Welfare funded CSWE to develop a curriculum for training community organizers. Between 1965 and 1969, the number of schools of social work providing training in community organization rose by 37 percent, eventually including virtually every school in the country (Garvin & Cox 1995). Community organization thus emerged as a legitimate part of social work practice.

MACRO PRACTICE IN ORGANIZATIONS

The Organizational Context of Social Work

Communities are macro systems in which all social workers interact and for which practice models have evolved. However, communities themselves are comprised in large measure of networks of organizations, and it is these organizations that usually hold the direct responsibility for carrying out basic community functions. As such, organizations are a second type of macro system with which social workers must be familiar. One important consideration regarding human service organizations is historical patterns of shifting emphasis between centralization and decentralization of agencies and services.

England's Elizabethan Poor Law of 1601, the first written law establishing a governmental system of services for the poor, adopted a decentralized approach to providing services. Under this law, assistance to the poor was a local function (as was taxation to pay for the assistance), and responsibility for service provision rested with an individual "overseer of the poor." This model was retained more or less intact in the American colonies, and until the 1800s relief efforts for the needy remained primarily local and small in scale.

The reformist movement of the early nineteenth century began a slow transition to larger-scale services in the form of state-run asylums for dependent children, the mentally ill, and others. Later, as population, urban concentration, and service needs increased, so did the diversity of both public and private programs. Eventually, it became apparent that some sort of coordinating mechanism was needed for these various efforts. As Trattner (1995) notes:

> The situation in Massachusetts was typical. In 1859, the commonwealth had three state mental institutions, a reform school for boys, an industrial school for girls, a hospital, and three almshouses for the state or nonresident poor. In addition, four private charitable institutions—schools for the blind, the deaf and dumb, the feeble-minded, and an eye and ear infirmary—received state aid. Each of these was managed by its own board of trustees. So uncoordinated a system not only increased the cost of operation, but it did not provide for a channel of communication between institutions; a reform in one, then, might not be implemented in the others. The situation obviously called for some method of state supervision (p. 81).

The result was the creation of what became known as the State Boards of Charities, first in Massachusetts in 1863, then in another fifteen states by the mid-1890s. These boards represented the first real involvement of state governments in centralized coordination of welfare services, and they helped to establish standards for the administration of human service organizations.

For roughly the next 65 years, much of the development of human service organizations took place in the private sector. The formation of the COS agencies and settlement houses was a partial recognition of the advantages of establishing standard service practices within the framework of a strong organizational base. Efforts toward developing more comprehensive public agency involvement in social welfare services occurred during the Progressive movement in the early 1900s. One example was the creation of the first state public welfare department in Illinois in 1917. Still, the focus remained very much on decentralized service provision. There was relatively little growth among human service organizations in the public sector.

It was not until the Great Depression that public organizations for the provision of human services were established on a large scale. The New Deal programs created an infrastructure of organizations at the federal level that became both the foundation of the welfare state and the first large, governmental human service bureaucracies. In addition, a key function of these agencies was to distribute relief funds to various states, and this in turn helped to spur the creation of state-level public welfare organizations. Some programs, such as the Federal Emergency Relief Administration (FERA) and the Work Projects Administration (WPA) were established to respond directly to Depression-era problems and thus were relatively short-lived. Others, such as the Social Security Administration, formed the institutional basis of ongoing federal social welfare programs, and they continue to play major roles. With the creation in 1956 of the Department of Health, Education, and Welfare (now the Department of Health and Human Services), most of these agencies were combined into a single, cabinet-level organization through which governmental social welfare programs were centralized.

Since its early development, most professional social work practice has been carried out from within some type of organizational base. However, these organizations varied over time, and the skills needed for effective practice within them also changed. For example, in the early years of social work education, attention toward models of practice in social work organizations focused primarily on preparing a limited number of macro practitioners to assume roles as administrators of small agencies, usually in the private sector. The goal was to provide skills such as fund raising, working with voluntary boards, and supervising direct-service workers.

With the growth of large public bureaucracies and nationwide networks of affiliated agencies in the private sector, the size and complexity of human service organizations changed. The role of macro practitioners within these organizations was also forced to change. For example, trends such as the increased size of human service organizations, their increased complexity and diversity of services, and changes in standard budgetary policies forced administrators to seek new skills. Lewis (1978) calls particular attention to the growth of concern for fiscal accountability that first became a dominant issue in the late 1960s. He argues that these concerns forced social work administrators to shift from "problem solvers" to "managers." Implicit in this shift was a change in administrative orientation, moving away from external considerations of how best to deal with specific social problems and toward internal considerations such as budgetary compliance and operational efficiency. Considerable concern still exists that if social work administrators do not acquire these skills, leadership of human service agencies will pass to persons from other disciplines who do possess such training.

Concern has also arisen that administrative decisions in human service agencies have become overwhelmed by managerial concerns and no longer reflect the consideration of client needs. In response, a number of writers (Patti 1987; Rapp & Poertner 1992) and others have called for the development of a *client-driven* model of administrative practice in which the achievement of desirable outcomes for clients becomes the primary criterion for decision making. The intent of this model is to view administrative practice in social work as a unique blend of managerial skills combined with broader knowledge of social problems and the means of addressing these problems.

Finally, just as views of the role of human service administrators have changed, so too have notions about the organizations in which they work. Since most social workers now operate within the context of some type of organization, their understanding of that organization may have much to do with the ability to do their job well. A classic work by Robert Pruger (1973) addressed the question of how social workers can function effectively within organizations. He makes the point that social workers have two major roles—the *helper* role defines their activities as a social worker who assists clients with various problems, while the *organizational* role defines the responsibilities they have for completing forms, making reports, attending meetings, and other organizational tasks. These roles may compete, and the clash between them may lead to a worker's inability to meet either satisfactorily. For example, a worker may have so many forms to fill out that he or she has little time for listening to detailed client problems. Pruger argues that a third role is possible in which the worker develops skills in mediating the conflicts between the other two roles. In particular, the worker learns either to meet organizational demands without sacrificing professionalism or to attempt to alter the demands to make them more consistent with the expectations of professional practice. This relates closely to the fifth option of initiating change that is part of the discussion in Chapter 1 about how social workers maintain themselves in difficult circumstances.

CONTEMPORARY TRENDS

At the beginning of this chapter, we discussed major historical trends affecting the development of the social work profession. Using the model of Garvin and Cox (1995) these are: (1) social conditions, (2) ideological conflicts, and (3) oppressed populations. In this section, we examine these same areas in terms of their influence on contemporary developments in the field.

Social Conditions

The combined effect of population growth, urbanization, industrialization, and changes in institutional structures have created communities that are very different today from those in the early years of the profession. Though these changes have fostered improvements in areas such as health, income, transportation, and others, not all aspects of the transformation have been positive. Warren (1978) calls attention to these concerns, noting that

> discerning Americans have come to the uneasy realization that all is not right with their community living, that undesirable situations appear with growing frequency

or intensity and that these are not the adventitious difficulty of one community or another so much as the parts of a general pattern of community living. (p. 14)

Warren calls this the *community problem,* and as an element of contemporary society, it is an important concern for macro practitioners.

One aspect of this problem has to do with the consequences of *urbanization.* Though they offer many benefits, large, complex cities also breed large, complex problems, and the very size and complexity of a community can interfere with solving these problems. One casualty resulting from metropolitan growth, for example, is a sense of solidarity within the community. Small-town shared views of the common good are possible in large measure because in small towns each person can be personally acquainted with a substantial proportion of the town's other residents. This is impossible in large cities, and in fact the average city dweller meets most other residents only as blurred faces passing by in other vehicles or on busy sidewalks. Identification with the community thus tends to devolve into a narrow parochialism based on units such as a single apartment building, an area of gang turf, an ethnic enclave, or a neighborhood defined by a particular employer or institution such as a factory, church, or college. The greater the number of these communities-within-communities, the more difficult it is to identify and serve the interests of the whole.

Closely tied to these consequences of urbanization is the *loss of geographic relevance* of many communities. In small-town America, communities were largely defined in terms of residents' physical proximity, as well as commonalities such as topography, soil conditions, water supply, and other correlates of geographic closeness. People lived in the same place they worked, often remained there throughout their lives, and shared with their neighbors both fortune and misfortune (droughts, floods, good and bad harvests, and so forth). In contrast, many cities are now so immense that residents in one area may share little with those in another in terms of their economic base, political environment, lifestyle, or even climate and terrain. Because geographic, legislative, and social boundaries often intermingle and evolve, it may be difficult even to define the boundaries of a given community.

As residents' identification with local connections has ebbed, the importance of *extracommunity affiliations* has greatly expanded. These affiliations define the relationships between community organizations and related institutions outside the community. For example, an automobile plant may be essential to the economy of a particular community. Its most important ties, however, may not be to the community but to the home office of its corporation in another city far away. A decision to close the plant might come entirely from the home office, yet it is the community that would bear the most severe consequences of this decision. Loss of control over such decisions renders the community extremely vulnerable, yet an excessive concern for external affiliations may also blind community members to critical local needs.

In addition to community issues, contemporary developments in the organizational structure of human services are also important to consider. One parallel between communities and organizations is that both have continued to grow and become more complex. In the organizational realm, this has giv-en rise to the *bureaucratization* of service systems. The term *bureaucracy* has taken on a number of mostly negative connotations that, as we shall discuss in Chapter 7, may or may not always be accurate. Here we refer to bureaucrati-zation as the growth in size and structural complexity of human service orga-nizations. This has been especially true in public agencies, which have general-ly continued to expand since the New Deal.

Bureaucratic organization is a means of structuring tasks and relation-ships among organizational members in order to maximize operational effi-ciency. Specialization of task is one aspect of bureaucratization, and as we discussed earlier, these sorts of changes coincided with the vast increase in productive capacity associated with modern industrial organizations. The problem with bureaucracies is that they often become as machinelike as the tools they employ, and the result can be a rigid and dehumanizing style of operation. This style usually grows more pronounced as the organization gets larger, and vast governmental human service agencies have become some of the most notorious examples of the negative aspects of bureaucratic structure.

Partly in response to this problem, *privatization* became a significant trend during the past two decades. Although the term can be used in many ways, we define privatization as "the deciding, financing, or providing of human services by the private sector to clients for whom the public sector is responsible" (Netting, McMurtry, Kettner, & Jones-McClintic 1990). This trend may be more accurately termed "reprivatization" because of its focus on returning to the private sector for responding to human need.

Beginning in the 1960s, recognition of the limitations of government bureaucracies prompted growth in *purchase of service contracting*. Public agencies paid for services, but these were provided to their clients by private organizations. Between 1973 and 1984, for example, nonprofit purchase of service contracts grew from $262 million to $664 million (Kettner & Martin 1987). Decision-making and financing functions remained governmental responsibilities, whereas the function of providing services shifted to the pri-vate sector. This arrangement was probably well accepted in many communi-ties, since going to a local nonprofit agency to receive services is often less stig-matizing for clients. However, other trends accompanying the move toward privatization complicated the community service delivery system.

For example, during the early 1980s, conservative views toward human services, combined with an economic slowdown, led to decreased public fund-ing and decentralization of decision making. This meant that many nonprofit agencies, which had previously grown larger on public dollars, were suddenly faced with stiff competition for very limited resources. For example, facing a shortage of patients, hospitals began diversifying into service areas other than primary health care (i.e., substance abuse centers, home health, etc.). For-prof-it organizations began moving into human service provision, seeking clients who could pay for their own services.

The effect of this trend on community human service systems has been felt most strongly in the provision of services to low-income clients. Formerly, many of these clients were served by nonprofit agencies either through contracts with public agencies or through offsetting revenues earned from clients who were able to pay. Now, government funds are more scarce and paying clients are often siphoned off by hospitals and for-profit providers. Many nonprofit agencies no longer have resources to pay for services to poor clients, and there is increasing competition between nonprofits for the funds that are available (McMurtry, Netting, & Kettner 1991).

Yet another trend is the advent of *computerization*. Society is moving toward a model in which information and services rather than manufactured goods are the most important commodities. As this takes place, the character of the workplace will also change. For example, more and more workers are now staying home for part or all of the work week, carrying out their tasks over the phone via voice links or via computer modems that allow them to connect to national and international networks. Over time, these changes have the potential of dramatically altering the nature of community life. At the very least, such changes are likely to modify traditional commuting patterns, as more workers "go to the office" at home. Farther in the future they may even reverse urbanization trends, contributing to smaller and more decentralized communities.

Social workers' roles will inevitably be affected by these changes. For example, reports indicate that the most-affluent and least-affluent segments of society have each grown in recent years while the middle class has shrunk (Hacker 1996). Apparently, those with the necessary education and skills to participate in the information revolution have prospered while many other members of society have faced increasing difficulty maintaining their standard of living. In particular, the diminished number and importance of manufacturing and other blue-collar jobs has closed off traditional routes to middle-class prosperity for many of society's members. This will further complicate the task of social workers attempting to assist society's poorest members, because few will have the highly specialized technical skills necessary to qualify them for better-paying jobs.

The way social workers do their jobs will also change. Some writers have noted that "social workers write reports and progress notes, pull and read numerous files, take case histories and develop diagnoses, tap into local area resource networks, keep in touch with professional developments, and provide facts and figures to contribute to agency accountability process" (Parker et al. 1987, cited in Ginsberg 1988, p. 71). Computers are well suited for assisting in these functions, and they are becoming increasingly common tools for many social workers. For example, many agencies are now providing social work staff with powerful laptop computers that they can carry with them when making home visits to clients. Workers can complete case notes, fill out forms, administer assessment tools, and perform other tasks directly on the computer while in the field. With proper equipment they can also use

phone lines to dial in to agency records or bibliographic sources. Upon returning to the office, they can then upload information into larger data bases useful in monitoring and evaluating agency services overall.

However, some writers argue that these changes pose dangers for the profession. Fabricant (1985) asserts that the computer revolution is but another
manifestation of the ongoing process of "de-skilling" social workers. One
example he offers is workers who determine eligibility for benefits such as
AFDC and food stamps. These positions are commonly filled not by professional social workers but by poorly paid and sometimes poorly trained clerical
staff whose job is simply to input data into computers. It is the computers that
then determine most clients' eligibility, absent any professional judgment. Fabricant therefore argues that if social workers cannot learn to adapt to and control new technologies (as well as other social trends we have discussed) they
risk being controlled by them.

Finally, broad aspects of macro practice may be affected by the *welfare
reform* movement and its as-yet uncertain effects on the structure of human
service organizations. A central issue is the argument of welfare critics such
as House Speaker Newt Gingrich, who contends that not just the policies
guiding welfare but its structures are to blame for problems in the system.
He argues that effective reform requires the elimination of "the bureaucracies that are exploiting [welfare children] instead of helping" (Gingrich
1995). Even critics of the dramatic welfare reform measures passed in 1996
focus on the organization of welfare services as the source of problems. One
of the most pointed attacks was by *Newsweek* columnist Joe Klein who
wrote:

> The current welfare system is an abomination. It is inflexible, bureaucratic, heart-
> less. . . . It is a system based on an assumption that has proved mistaken: that so-
> cial work is a profession. It isn't. It is a *calling*. The work of caring for the poor is
> best done by inspired individuals and institutions, not career government workers.
> . . . We have tried to bureacratize charity and have failed miserably. (1996, p. 45)

As this quote suggests, the development of large organizations to respond
to the equally large scale of human services has had the effect of associating
the entire profession of social work with large-scale governmental organizations. Though this is an inaccurate perception it is widely held, and now
both large organizational structure and the profession as a whole are being
cast as failures because social problems such as poverty have not disappeared.

Edwards, Cooke, and Reid (1996) argue that this perception will contribute to trends such as the privatization movement discussed above, and it
may also alter the organizational character of human service agencies:

> This situation will likely accelerate management changes that are already appar-
> ent in response to the shift of social policy. Downsizing or "right-sizing" is occur-
> ring in many social services organizations, a process driven by both budget con-
> straints and the necessity for organizations to compete on service-product cost.

The result is smaller and flatter organizations in which fewer people supervise more workers (p. 473).

These authors argue that the "devolution revolution" will intensify trends such as the decentralization of services from the federal to state levels. Also, managers of human service organizations will become less concerned with the implementation of social policies and more oriented toward responding to market forces impinging on the organization. This may lead to human service organizations that are led predominantly by administrators trained as professional business executives rather than as professional social workers.

Ideological Conflicts

As with the discussion of broad social conditions, Warren's (1978) notion of "the community problem" also provides a starting point for addressing contemporary ideological trends. One issue concerns community members' increasing difficulty in achieving a *sense of community*—the psychological feeling of belonging that is critical to both individuals and communities. This feeling should arise from individuals' awareness of the roles they play as useful contributors to the well-being of the community. In historic times, such roles were easier to perceive, as when a person was perhaps the only grocer, teacher, baker, blacksmith, or midwife in the community. In complex modern communities, however, few people have unique roles, and their activities are often so specialized that their contribution to the community good is seldom apparent either to them or to other community members.

The loss of a sense of community in turn induces feelings of *alienation* from both the community and the larger society. Alienation is often described as a sense of rootlessness, whereby individuals perceive themselves as isolated from social groups with which they might naturally identify. Persons experiencing alienation feel estranged or set apart from social and cultural connections, and they tend to be both less productive and less able to cope with the strains of daily living. Sometimes a vicious cycle can occur in which the complexity and impersonality of community living breeds alienation, and its sufferers in turn feel even less able to manage such complexity. Feelings of separation that are also part of the experience of alienation fall especially hard on traditionally disadvantaged populations who are already worse off than other community members. Also, one consequence of alienation appears to be a rise of self-serving and antisocial behaviors in which concern for community good (in the absence of a clear perception of the community and one's role therein) is subordinated to individual interests. It is this phenomenon that has been labeled by some social commentators and political figures as a breakdown in "civility" in social relationships.

Current writers also agonize over the mounting tension between individualism and the collective or common good. This issue has gained attention over the past 30 years, and it has greatly influenced the way individuals, communities, and societal responses to social welfare are perceived. One corollary issue involves disagreements over where decisions should be made to best serve individuals and community needs. As noted earlier, this is being played out in current policy debates as to whether state and local versus national authorities should control public programs. In general, political conservatives argue that local governments are best situated to discern local needs and tailor appropriate responses. Those with more liberal views argue for broad-scale programs that reduce inequities existing between communities and establish general standards for services or benefits.

Oppressed Populations

Terminology.   A valuable contemporary lesson that has emerged in dealing with oppressed populations is the importance of language. Social workers need to understand that terms used to define and distinguish special populations have also been applied adversely to reinforce stereotypes or further isolate the members of these groups.

Abramovitz (1991) provides a glossary of terms to increase awareness about "hidden messages conveyed in everyday speech" (p. 380). For example, she discusses the "feminization of poverty" as a phrase that calls attention to the economic concerns of women but may also imply that poverty is a new issue for women. She argues instead for the term "povertization of women," which better reflects the long history of women's economic disadvantage. Similarly, the sociological term *underclass,* which has been suggested as a replacement for *multiproblem, disadvantaged,* and *hard to reach* poor people, may stigmatize the persons so described (pp. 380–1).

Since the 1950s, there have been movements toward more accurate or less historically laden language when referring to special populations. For example, among ethnic and racial groups, blacks adopted the term *black* as a preferred descriptor in the 1960s and 1970s, supplanting the old, segregation-linked terms of *Negro* and *colored.* Many now argue in favor of the term *African American.* Similarly, *Native American* has been promoted as more accurate than the term *Indian,* but many native people continue to refer to themselves as American Indians. The term *Hispanic* is used as a generic expression to represent persons of Latin ancestry, including Puerto Ricans, Cuban Americans, Mexican Americans (who also call themselves "Chicanos"), and others. However, the term *Latino* is also gaining acceptance. The term *white,* despite its common usage, is a poorly defined term, but it remains more broadly applicable than *Anglo* or *Caucasian.*

A recent study on these issues was conducted as a supplement to the May 1995 Current Population Survey, a monthly telephone survey conducted on a sample of roughly 60,000 households for the Bureau of Labor Statistics (1995). The study was designed to determine the preferences of individuals in various ethnic and racial groups regarding the term they prefer to be used to describe their group. The terms favored by a majority of each group are to be used henceforth in censuses and other government surveys. Results showed that, among blacks, the preferred self-descriptive term is "black," which was favored by 44 percent of black respondents, followed by "African American" (28%) and "Afro-American" (12%). Among persons of Hispanic origin, the overwhelming choice was "Hispanic" (58%), followed by "of Spanish origin" (12%) and "Latino" (11%). Indian respondents showed a moderate preference for the term "American Indian" (50%) over "Native American" (37%). Finally, among whites "white" was greatly preferred (62%) over "Caucasian" (17%). No information on preferred terms was collected for other ethnic or racial groups.

The term *persons with disabilities* is considered appropriate to refer broadly to individuals having different physical or mental capacities from the norm. Recently, the term *differently abled* has been advocated as a way to avoid categorizing members of this group in terms of their perceived limitations, but this phrase has not yet gained wide usage. With respect to sexuality, *gay* and *lesbian* have been preferred terms for at least the past two decades. Members of both groups were previously referred to as being distinguished by their *sexual preference,* but the term *sexual orientation* is now considered more appropriate because it reflects research indicating that sexuality is more a matter of biology than choice. With respect to gender, some feminist writers have argued for use of the terms *womyn* or *wimin* on the basis that they are less derivative of "men." As yet these terms do not appear to have been adopted into wide usage.

We recognize the extreme importance of language, and it is our intent in this book to reflect that importance in our use of terms. Given the changing times in which we live, when some terms seem to be nearing the end of their useful lives and others seem to be emerging, we use most of these terms interchangeably. In some instances, where the use of a more traditional term seems more appropriate, we use such terms as black, white, Hispanic, and Indian. In other cases, where newly emerging terms seem appropriate, we will use African American, Native American, and Latino. Our intention is to be sensitive to the convictions and wishes of as many people within these population groups as possible, and to offend as few as possible. We hope the reader is not confused by this mixed use of terms, but instead recognizes it as evidence of the dynamic, changing nature of modern language.

Relative to earlier periods in our nation's history, the recent past has been marked by significant gains by ethnic and racial groups, women, and gays and lesbians in their struggle to achieve equal standing in society. However, though progress has undoubtedly been made, the struggle has by no means been won. For example, success in reducing societal acceptance of prejudicial attitudes and overt acts of discrimination is tempered by the fact that these attitudes and behaviors have in some cases become simply more covert and thus more difficult to confront. Also, hard-won political victories have not always been matched by comparable economic gains, and for some groups conditions have in fact grown much worse.

Native Americans.   Native Americans clearly benefitted in important ways from the social upheavals of the 1960s, with groups such as the American Indian Movement (AIM) helping to focus attention on the troubled relationship between tribal organizations and the federal government. As a result, tribal governments were able to diminish the paternalistic influence of agencies such as the Bureau of Indian Affairs and gain greater autonomy over their own operations. For example, the Indian Child Welfare Act of 1978 gave jurisdiction of child welfare cases to tribal rather than state courts, thus placing tighter controls on practices such as the adoption of Native American children by non–Native American families. Other examples of helpful federal legislation include the 1978 Religious Freedom Act, which benefitted members of the Native American Church, and the 1988 Gaming Regulatory Act, which confirmed that tribes may create gambling establishments on reservation land if the state in which it is located also allows betting of some form.

Nonetheless, Native Americans have a more distinct cultural heritage than many other ethnic groups, and the struggle to simultaneously preserve this heritage and integrate with the rest of society has taken its toll. Poverty on some rural reservations is as pervasive and severe as anywhere in the country, and little progress has been made in improving economic conditions in these areas. Another major concern is health care. The Indian Health Service, which was created to meet treaty-based federal guarantees for health care provision to Indian people, has a record of inconsistent and sometimes dramatically inferior care. It currently faces both budgetary cutbacks and controversy over the extent of its responsibility for providing services to urban as well as reservation-based populations. One reason for the high level of concern about health care is the high rate of diseases such as diabetes and heart ailments, to which members of some tribal groups may be genetically predisposed. Also, alcoholism rates, especially among adult males living on reservations, remain high. One report estimated the annual age-adjusted alcoholism mortality rate among Native Americans to be four times higher than that for the general population (U.S. Department of Health and Human Services 1990), and it remains an indication of the difficulty faced by Indian people in adjusting to life in two different worlds.

Latinos.   The Latino population is one of the fastest growing ethnic groups in the country, having increased in number by 53 percent between 1980 and 1990, due in roughly equal parts to immigration and births to residents (Curiel 1995). As a whole, Hispanics tend to be younger than the rest of the population and mostly urban. Not quite two thirds are of Mexican descent, 14 percent are from Central and South American countries, 13 percent are Puerto Rican in origin, and 5 percent are from Cuba (U.S. Bureau of the Census 1995a). Population concentrations are in southwestern and midwestern states for Mexican Americans, New York for Puerto Ricans, and Florida for Cuban Americans (Curiel 1995). As is typical of groups with a high concentration of recent immigrants who are still struggling to gain equal economic footing, socioeconomic status across Hispanic groups is lower than that of non-Hispanics, though Chavez (1991) reports that earnings of Mexican-American men had reached about 93 percent of whites at that time.

Of perhaps greater concern are problems of high school dropout rates and persistent language barriers. These related concerns have been the source of considerable controversy. For example, in recent years voters in some southwest states passed "English-only" initiatives designed to restrict official use of Spanish in areas such as public education and voting. The expressed goal of this movement is to force Spanish speakers to learn English and thus integrate more fully into society. Critics charge that it has had the opposite effect, especially among children who have greater difficulty in school because they must learn in an unfamiliar language.

African Americans. For blacks victories in the Civil Rights Movement of the 1950s and 1960s meant the rejection of segregationist practices that had prevailed since the Civil War. These gains helped spur electoral successes, particularly on the local level. For example, in 1991, four of the six largest cities in the nation—New York, Los Angeles, Philadelphia, and Detroit—were led by African-American mayors. Some economic progress has also been made in areas such as the expansion of the black middle class, which was fueled in part by growth in the numbers of African Americans working in professional and managerial jobs.

Unfortunately, from a social work perspective the more telling figures concern African Americans who did not share in these economic gains, especially the inner-city poor. Consider, for example, the following statistics published by the Children's Defense Fund (1990) concerning the plight of young African-American children. Relative to white children, they are:

78 percent more likely to die at birth;

twice as likely to be a low-birth-weight child;

three times more likely to be born into a poor family;

four times more likely to be born to an unmarried mother;

four times more likely to experience nutritional deficiencies.

Black children are also 30 to 50 percent more likely than white children to die of injuries due to fires or household accidents (Leashore 1995), and death by firearms claims 11 times more young black males than white males aged 15 to 19 years (Children's Defense Fund 1994).

Events such as the Million Man March by African-American men in Washington in 1995 illustrate the variety of efforts being made to acknowledge and address these problems. It also points out the increasing emphasis within the black community on addressing problems through strengthening basic institutions such as families and neighborhoods. Efforts to highlight the unique African-American heritage through holiday celebrations such as Kwanzaa are also a part of this movement.

Asian Americans.   Considerable public attention has recently been directed toward the educational achievements of Asian American youngsters, who, for example, have led all other ethnic groups in standardized test scores and rates of college completion (U.S. Department of Education 1988). Unfortunately, this success has sometimes masked problems facing other Asian Americans, particularly Southeast Asian immigrants whose numbers have increased rapidly in the past 20 years. Many of these people are refugees from regional wars who arrived penniless and without other family members. Once here, they had to cope with "(1) the great disparity between their culture and American society, (2) the lack of an already established ethnic community to help them adjust, and (3) the poor economic conditions in this country at the time of their arrival" (Kitano 1987, p. 168). As a result, they are now struggling to overcome lingering problems of poverty, poor housing, and racial discrimination.

Women.   Women's advancement in recent years has been marked by both progress and disappointment. One of the most important gains was the development of women's groups such as the National Organization for Women (NOW), which was organized in the mid-1960s. NOW and other organizations formed the core of the Women's Movement, which has had considerable success in calling attention to institutional sexism present in employment, government policy, and language. These efforts helped produce tangible gains, such as the narrowing of the difference in earnings between men and women. As of 1992, women on average earned 80 percent as much as men, up from 64 percent in 1985 (Gottlieb 1995; U.S. Bureau of the Census 1987). A significant defeat was the failure of the Equal Rights Amendment, intended to be an important protection against gender-based discrimination. Unfortunately, the amendment drew vociferous opposition by other women's groups who felt that it would undermine traditional roles. In 1982, it failed due to lack of ratification by a sufficient number of states. Its downfall serves to illustrate that sexual stereotyping exists on the part of both men and women, and its elimination will require continued efforts on a society-wide basis.

Persons with Disabilities.   The Rehabilitation Act of 1973 and the subsequent Rehabilitation Act Amendments of 1974 were for persons with disabilities what the Civil Rights Act had been for other groups. They prohibited discrimination against anyone who currently had or had in the past "a physical or mental impairment which substantially limits one or more of such person's major life activities" (Rehabilitation Act of 1973). The act also was the first to require that public facilities be made accessible to disabled persons, and it laid the groundwork for the expansion of these requirements to all commercial properties through the Americans with Disabilities Act of 1990. Another example of related legislation was the 1975 Education for All Handicapped Children Act, which required children with developmental disabilities to be given access to mainstream public education rather than the traditionally segregated "special education" system. The unifying feature of these and other

initiatives was that they had the goal of achieving the fullest possible participation in society by persons with disabilities. They also endeavored to do
away with programs, practices, and attitudes that emphasized differences
rather than commonalities between disabled persons and the rest of society.

Gay Men and Lesbian Women.   A combination of factors has helped to
ease the isolation of and institutional discrimination toward gay men and lesbian women. One factor has been research results providing evidence that homosexuality is a basic and possibly genetically inherited trait in many people.
These results have reduced some of the fear and misunderstanding of gays and
lesbians on the part of heterosexuals, though progress has been slower in promoting the general social consensus that sexual orientation, whether innate or
developed, should make no difference in how a person is treated. An important advancement has been the increase in political activism on the part of
both gays and lesbians. Lesbian women, for example, were an integral part of
the Women's Movement and have both contributed to and benefitted from its
achievements. Marotta (1981) notes that many gay males were inspired by the
work of black civil rights leaders in the 1950s and 1960s, and this helped lead
to the formation of organizations such as the Gay Liberation Front. These organizations have been pointedly visible in their advocacy and lobbying efforts
and have helped many men accept and acknowledge their sexual orientation.
In addition, gay and lesbian activism has led to the repeal of antihomosexual
laws and the passage of ordinances against discrimination based on sexual
orientation.

   On the other hand, lobbying efforts by gay and lesbian groups have
generally been more successful at the local level than at the state and
national levels. For example, members of the armed forces remain under the
threat of immediate dismissal for identifying themselves as homosexuals.
Moreover, gays and lesbians are still targets for individual acts of discrimination and violence, and in most states they remain subject to arrest and
prosecution for consensual sexual behavior. Finally, the AIDS epidemic has
struck a severe blow to the gay male community, and irrational fear of the
disease has compounded the problem of discrimination experienced by all
homosexuals.

Lingering Problems.   Overall, though public acts of discrimination were increasingly condemned during and after the 1960s, prejudicial attitudes toward
sexual and ethnic differences and toward women remain. In addition, many
overtly discriminatory laws were altered, but blatant discrimination often
gave way to more subtle forms. For example, with respect to attitudes toward
racial and ethnic differences, Austin (1988) cites a 1986 study by Shuman,
Steeh, and Bobo indicating that "while racial equality is supported in principle, negative attitudes toward governmental economic initiatives explicitly intended to redress the consequences of past racial discrimination are, in fact,
widespread throughout the United States" (p. 58). Perhaps the best evidence

of this is the continuing and often divisive debate over affirmative action policies governing hiring, admissions, and other actions.

Health and human service programs often reflect the status quo because
they address the symptoms of oppression rather than the causes. Professionals
frequently assume they know the causes of oppression, and hence the needs of
consumers, rather than asking the people they serve. During recent decades,
however, efforts such as the social movements and citizen participation activities described above have taken initial steps to address the needs of special
populations in a more comprehensive and consumer-involved manner. Still,
the task for practitioners remains that of finding interventions that are sensitive to the needs of these populations (Kettner, Daley, & Nichols 1985).

THE IMPORTANCE OF CHANGE

The development of social work macro practice has been accompanied by a
number of changes over the years. In fact, change is one of the few constants
in modern life. Nevertheless, change is not always seen as desirable or favorable, and resistance to change occurs as individuals, groups, and organizations
attempt to hold on to the familiar. Brager and Holloway (1978) define three
types of change that affect health and human service providers: people-
focused change, technological change, and structural change.

People-focused change centers on alterations in values, knowledge, and
skills. Because it involves the values that underlie our attitudes and perceptions, people-focused change is often very difficult. Yet, in dealing with trends
such as oppression, social workers are commonly faced with the need to
change people's values, knowledge, and skills.

Technological change refers to alterations in the process of service delivery, those activities and procedures that guide policy and program implementation. Since the days when COS staffers and settlement house workers
demanded training to become more systematic in how they approached individuals, groups, and communities, professional technologies have evolved and
changed. The current explosion in computers and information technology is
another example of this change, and such advances have the capacity to make
meaningful improvements in the provision of human services. At the same
time, however, these changes tax practitioners' ability to stay current in their
methods, adapt to new service approaches, and apply new technologies in a
humane way so that clients are not depersonalized in the process.

Structural change deals with how units within a system relate to one
another. Reprivatization of services represents this type of change, in that it
has the potential to fundamentally alter the process of meeting the needs of
disadvantaged persons in society. However, its success requires that services
not be driven solely by the criterion of expending the minimum resources possible. Instead, change must be managed in such a way that effectiveness is
maximized at the lowest cost possible.

As can be seen in our description of these three types of change, each raises important professional questions. Should macro practitioners react to trends, attempting to respond as spontaneous changes occur within the environment? Should they seize opportunities to plan community changes to address human need by selecting and utilizing the available tools? Can new structures be created or existing structures be altered to improve a community's ability to both meet individual needs and reinforce its own cohesiveness? We believe that a planned change model can be successfully applied by social workers to address problems in macro systems. Chapter 3 will introduce the basic elements of such a model by discussing how to identify macro-level problems and target populations.

SUMMARY

The need for social workers to be able to understand and practice in macro systems is based on both the history of the social work profession and the society in which it evolved. The effects of immigration, industrialization, and rapid population growth led to concentrations of people in large urban areas, where, for the first time, modern institutional structures (e.g., highly specialized organizations) began to arise. So, too, did modern problems of urban poverty, alienation, loss of a sense of community, and others. The types of service that developed to address these problems were affected by new ideologies. Social Darwinism led to assistance that was often paternalistic and judgmental, but this was tempered by liberalism and even radical ideologies that led to much more proactive helping efforts.

The traditions of the COS agencies, with their emphasis on case-level practice, and the settlement houses, with their more community-oriented efforts, led to a dualistic professional model that continues today. Within this model, social workers must be able to perceive their clients not only as individuals with personal problems; they must also understand clients as members of larger community systems, and they must be prepared to intervene at the community level as well.

Moreover, social workers themselves typically work within formal organizations, and the actions of these organizations also have much to do with how well social workers can do their jobs. Over time, these organizations have tended to become more complex and more bureaucratized, meaning that they may be more efficient, but they may also be more rigid and less focused on client interests. Other organizational trends such as reprivatization and computerization similarly present both risks and opportunities for social workers practicing within them. Understanding these trends and acquiring skills in bringing about planned change within organizations are one approach for reducing the risks and maximizing the opportunities.

A critical point in this chapter was that a meaningful understanding of the development of modern macro systems and of the social work profession requires an awareness of the history of oppressed groups within society. Macro-level systems can either overcome or exacerbate institutionalized oppression, depending on how they are structured. For example, protections supposedly guaranteed to African Americans and Hispanics through the Emancipation Proclamation and the Treaty of Guadalupe Hidalgo were undermined by other economic and social policies that effectively continued the oppression. Complex urban, industrial communities produced vast wealth during the past century, but this was not always shared by ethnic groups segregated (formally or informally) in ghettos or on reservations. Highly bureaucratized organizations became very efficient at processing individual clients in standardized ways, but they did not reliably advance in their ability to meet specific individual needs or to avoid practices that institutionally discriminate against particular groups.

Traditional debates about whether social workers should pursue casework, group work, or community organization seem less important in light of these realities. Macro systems pervade all types of social work practice, and the ability to recognize and redirect their influence is critical to all social workers, regardless of their primary role.

REFERENCES

Abramovitz, M. (1991) Putting an end to doublespeak about race, gender, and poverty: An annotated glossary for social workers. *Social Work, 36*(5): 380–4.

Austin, D. M. (1983) The Flexner myth and the history of social work. *Social Service Review, 57*(3): 357–77.

Austin, D. M. (1988) *The political economy of human service program.* Greenwich, CT: JAI Press.

Axinn, J., and Levin, H. (1992) *Social welfare: A history of the American response to need* (3rd ed.). New York: Longman.

Beane, S. (1989) Indian child welfare social policy history. In E. Gonzalez-Santin, ed., *Defining entry-level competencies for public child welfare workers serving Indian communities.* Tempe, AZ: School of Social Work, Arizona State University.

Brager, G., and Holloway, S. (1978) *Changing human service organizations: Politics and practice.* New York: Free Press.

Brieland, D. (1990) The Hull-House tradition and the contemporary social worker: Was Jane Addams really a social worker? *Social Work, 35*(2): 134–38.

Bureau of Labor Statistics. (1995) A Current Population Survey supplement for testing methods of collecting racial and ethnic information: May 1995. Washington, DC: U.S. Department of Labor.

Chambers, C. A. (1985) The historical role of the voluntary sector. In G. A. Tobin, ed., *Social planning and human service delivery in the voluntary sector* (pp. 3–28). Westport, CT: Greenwood Press.

Chambers, C. A. (1986) Women in the creation of the profession of social work. *Social Service Review, 60*(1): 3–33.

Chavez, L. (1991) *Out of the barrio: Toward a new politics of Hispanic assimilation.* New York: Basic Books.

Children's Defense Fund. (1990) *S.O.S. America: A Children's Defense Fund budget.* Washington, DC: Author.

Children's Defense Fund. (1994) *The state of America's children yearbook, 1994.* Washington, DC: Author.

Curiel, H. (1995) Hispanics: Mexican Americans. Encyclopedia of social work (19th ed., 2: 1233–44). Washington, DC: National Association of Social Workers.

Edwards, R. L., P. W. Cooke, and P. N. Reid. (1996) Social work management in an era of diminishing federal responsibility. *Social Work, 41*(5): 468–80.

Fabricant, M. (1985) The industrialization of social work practice. *Social Work, 30*(5): 389–95.

Friedan, B. (1963) *The feminine mystique.* New York: Norton.

Garvin, C. D., and F. M. Cox (1995) A history of community organizing since the Civil War with special reference to oppressed communities. In J. Rothman et al., eds., *Strategies of community intervention* (5th ed.; pp. 26–63). Itasca, IL: F. E. Peacock.

Gibson, G. (1987) Mexican Americans. *Encyclopedia of social work* (18th ed., 2: 135–48). Silver Spring, MD: National Association of Social Workers.

Gingrich, N. (1995) *To renew America.* New York: Harper Collins.

Ginsberg, L. H. (1988) Data processing and social work management. In P. R. Keys and L. H. Ginsberg, eds., *New management in human services.* Silver Spring, MD: National Association of Social Workers.

Gottlieb, N. (1995) Women overview. *Encyclopedia of social work* (19th ed., 3: 2518–28). Washington, DC: National Association of Social Workers.

Hacker, A. (1996) Meet the median family. *Time, 147*(5): 41–3.

Harrington, M. (1962) *The other America: Poverty in the United States.* New York: Macmillan.

Jansson, B. S. (1988) *The reluctant welfare state.* Belmont, CA: Wadsworth.

Kettner, P. M., J. M. Daley, and A. W. Nichols (1985) *Initiating change in organizations and communities.* Monterey, CA: Brooks/Cole.

Kettner, P. M., and L. L. Martin (1987) *Purchase of service contracting.* Newbury Park, CA: Sage.

Kitano, H. H. L. (1987) Asian Americans. *Encyclopedia of social work* (18th ed., 1: 156–71). Silver Spring, MD: National Association of Social Workers.

Klein, J. (August 12, 1996) Monumental callousness. *Newsweek,* 45.

Leashore, B. R. (1995) African Americans overview. *Encyclopedia of social work* (19th ed., 1: 101–15). Washington, DC: National Association of Social Workers.

Leiby, J. (1987) History of social welfare. *Encyclopedia of social work* (18th ed., 1: 755–77). Silver Spring, MD: National Association of Social Workers.

Lewis, H. (1978) Management in the nonprofit social service organization. In S. Slavin, ed., *Social administration: The management of the social services.* New York: Council on Social Work Education.

Marotta, T. (1981) *The politics of homosexuality.* Boston: Houghton Mifflin.

McMurtry, S. L., F. E. Netting, and P. M. Kettner. (1991) How nonprofits adapt to a stringent environment. *Nonprofit Management and Leadership, 1*(3): 235–52.

Netting, F. E., S. L. McMurtry, P. M. Kettner, and S. Jones-McClintic. (1990) Privatization and its impact on nonprofit service providers. *Nonprofit and Voluntary Sector Quarterly, 18*(1): 33–46.

Patti, R. J. (1987) Managing for service effectiveness in social welfare: Toward a performance model. *Administration in Social Work, 11*(3/4): 7–21.

Percy, S. L. (1989) *Disability, civil rights, and public policy.* Tuscaloosa, AL: University of Alabama Press.

Peterson, P. E., and J. D. Greenstone. (1977) The mobilization of low-income communities through community action. In R. H. Haveman, ed., *A decade of federal antipoverty programs: Achievements, failures, and lessons.* New York: Academic Press.

Pruger, R. (1973) The good bureaucrat. *Social Work, 81*(4): 26–32.

Rapp, C. A., and J. Poertner (1992) *Social administration: A client-centered approach.* New York: Longman.

Rehabilitation Act of 1973, P.L. 93-112, 87 Stat. 335 (1973).

Reisch, M., and S. Wenocur. (1986) The future of community organization in social work: Social activism and the politics of profession building. *Social Service Review, 60*(1): 70–93.

Richmond, M. (1917) *Social diagnosis.* NY: Russell Sage Foundation.

Szasz, T. S. (1965) Legal and moral aspects of homosexuality. In J. Marmor, ed., *Sexual inversion: The multiple roots of homosexuality.* New York: Basic Books.

Trattner, W. I. (1995) *From poor law to welfare state: A history of social welfare in America* (5th ed.). New York: Free Press.

U.S. Bureau of the Census. (1987) Statistical abstract of the United States. Washington, DC: U.S. Government Printing Office.

U.S. Bureau of the Census. (1995a) Statistical Abstract of the United States (115th ed.). Washington DC: U.S. Department of Commerce.

U.S. Bureau of the Census. (1995b) Population Profile of the United States. Washington DC: U.S. Department of Commerce.

U.S. Congress. (1964) Act to Mobilize the Human and Financial Resources of the Nation to Combat Poverty in the United States, 188–452, 88th Congress, 2nd Session.

U.S. Department of Education. (1988) Digest of educational statistics, 1988. Washington, DC: National Center for Educational Statistics.

U.S. Department of Health and Human Services. (1990) Seventh Special Report to the U.S. Congress on Alcoholism and Health from the Secretary of the Department of Health and Human Services. Rockville, MD: National Institute on Alcohol Abuse and Alcoholism.

Wagner, D. (1989) Radical movements in the social services: A theoretical framework. *Social Service Review, 63*(2): 264–84.

Ward, G. C. (1990) *The Civil War: An illustrated history.* New York: Alfred A. Knopf.

Warren, R. L. (1978) *The community in America* (3rd ed.). Chicago: Rand McNally.

Wright, B. A. (1988) Attitudes and the fundamental negative bias: Conditions and corrections. In H. E. Yuker, ed., *Attitudes toward persons with disabilities.* New York: Springer.

SUGGESTED READINGS

Abramovitz, M. (1988) *Regulating the lives of women: Social welfare policy from colonial times to the present.* Boston: South End Press.

Adam, B. D. (1995) *The rise of a gay and lesbian movement.* New York: Twayne Publishers.

Calloway, C. G. (1995) *The American revolution in Indian country: Crisis and diversity in Native American communities.* New York: Cambridge University Press.

Day, P. J. (1989) *A new history of social welfare.* Englewood Cliffs, NJ: Prentice-Hall.

Erlich, J. L., and F. G. Rivera (1992) *Community organizing in a diverse society.* Boston: Allyn & Bacon.

Hochman, A. (1994) *Everyday acts and small subversions: Women reinventing family, community, and home.* Portland, OR: Eighth Mountain Press.

Horton, J. O. (1993) *Free people of color: Inside the African American community.* Washington, DC: Smithsonian Institution Press.

Inglehart, A. P., and R. M. Becerra (1995) *Social services and the ethnic community.* Boston: Allyn & Bacon.

Lundblad, K. S. (1995) Jane Addams and social reform: A role model for the 1990s. *Social Work, 40*(5), 661–9.

Okihiro, G. Y. (1994) *Margins and mainstreams: Asians in American history and culture.* Seattle: University of Washington Press.

Shorris, E. (1992) *Latinos: A biography of the people.* New York: Norton.

Simon, B. L. (1994) *The empowerment tradition in American social work: A history.* New York: Columbia University Press.

Specht, H., and M. E. Courtney (1994) *Unfaithful angels: How social work has abandoned its mission.* New York: The Free Press.

Treanor, R. B. (1993) *We overcame: The story of civil rights for disabled people.* Falls Church, VA: Regal Direct.

CHAPTER 3

Understanding the Problem and the Target Population

Overview

Summary
References
Suggested Readings
Appendix

Social work is a profession oriented toward action and change. People who practice social work commit themselves to serve as a resource for those who have problems, who have limited or no control over the changes that need to be made in order to resolve their problems, and who request or are willing to accept help.

The majority of social workers deal with change directly with clients, usually working with individuals one-on-one or with families or small groups. Some practitioners focus on community-wide problems. Others work in the areas of planning, management, and administration of organizations. Regardless of the professional social worker's practice orientation, it is crucial that practitioners of all types understand that, while some problems can be resolved at an individual or family level, others will require intervention that takes in a broader scope, including the need to effect changes in organizations and communities.

Managing macro-level change requires a good deal of professional knowledge and skill. Poor management and flawed decision making in the change process can result in serious setbacks, sometimes making things worse for those already in need. On the other hand, many very positive changes in organizations and communities have been orchestrated by social workers and others who have carefully planned, designed, and carried out the change process.

It is not unusual for direct practitioners to have clients ask for help with problems that appear to be individual or interpersonal but, upon further probing turn out to be macro-level problems. A family that loses its primary source of income, is evicted, and finds that there is a three-month waiting list to get into a homeless shelter represents a symptom of a community problem. Clearly, their immediate shelter problem must be resolved, but just as obviously the community-wide lack of emergency housing must be addressed.

A mother may describe the pressures put on her son to join a gang and become involved in the drug trade. While the immediate need for this family can perhaps be met by building a support system for the boy designed to keep him in school, in a part-time job, and in constructive activities, this casework approach would not solve the problem for the many other families who must live daily with the same threats.

Identifying and dealing with organizational and community conditions, problems, and needs presents a complex set of challenges to a social worker. Over the years, the image of the change agent has developed around some of the early social change pioneers—people like Dorothea Dix or Florence Kelley. Others view change agents as superorganizers like the late Saul Alinsky, or as high-profile advocates like Ralph Nader who have had great success in bringing about social change through nationwide organization and exceptional political skill. In reality, most social workers have neither the resources, the media exposure, the charisma, the experience, the following, nor the power that these leaders have had available to them. Yet, in spite of seemingly overwhelming challenges, social workers have been effective in bringing about changes in organizations and communities.

Effectiveness does not necessarily come from the power of personality or the ability to mobilize thousands to a cause. It comes from careful, thoughtful, and creative planning undertaken by a group committed to change, and the tenacity to see it through to completion. The change effort may be guided, led, or coordinated by a professional social worker, but those involved will represent a broad range of interest groups.

THE SOCIAL WORKER'S ENTRY INTO AN EPISODE OF MACRO-LEVEL CHANGE

As noted in Chapter 1, social workers find themselves drawn into episodes of macro practice through a number of different avenues, which we have referred to as (1) problem, (2) population, and (3) arena. The following examples will illustrate these different points of entry into an episode of change.

A clinical practitioner with a Family Service Agency may discover that she has five or six clients who are single parents and unable to find affordable child care. Working with this group's *problem* (children that need to be cared for while the parent is at work) as her point of entry into the episode of change, the social worker and others develop a plan for child care for the children of these clients and perhaps for many others in the same situation.

In another case a social worker may find that the housing agency he works for has not been responsive to requests for assistance from people with AIDS. In this instance the worker's point of entry into the episode of change may be through the *population* of people with AIDS, helping them to organize themselves to take their concerns to the city council or funding source.

Or perhaps a school social worker attends a meeting to orient parents to school programs and to meet school personnel. She finds the primary concern of parents is that their children are alone from the time school gets out until the parents get home from work. In this instance, the worker's point of entry into the episode of change may be the community or neighborhoods within the school's boundaries, perhaps beginning with a door-to-door or mailed survey of community residents to assess need. This represents an entry through the community *arena*.

The point is that in the practice of social work one finds many avenues or points of entry that lead to the use of macro-practice skills. In this chapter we will focus on understanding *problem* and *population*, two of the three domains through which social workers become involved in community and

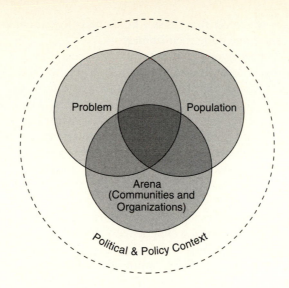

FIGURE 3.1   Understanding Problem, Population and Arena

organizational change. In addition we will specify the major tasks to be undertaken within each domain.

Problem, population, and arena can be thought of first as separate circles, each of which must be thoroughly explored in its own right. Second they can be thought of as intersecting circles in which the most critical knowledge and information is at the points of overlap. Figure 3.1 illustrates how each of these domains have unique as well as overlapping elements.

In this chapter we will focus on understanding the problem and the population(s) affected. In the following chapters we will explore ways of understanding the arenas in which macro practice is carried out: communities and organizations.

GUIDELINES FOR PLANNING CHANGE

Initiating an episode of organizational or community change involves some disciplined study and fact gathering as well as skillful organizing and intervention. Within the core group of those who decide that further exploration of a problem is warranted, early decisions must be made about collaboration and sharing of responsibility.

Skills are needed in the areas of library research, data collection, interviewing representatives of affected populations and informed analysis based on findings. Remember that it is likely that the case to be made in favor of change will be taken to a decision-making body and possibly to a funding source. People who accept responsibility for making decisions and allocating funds have a right to expect that those who come before them are knowledge-able, informed, and have done their homework.

Doing one's "homework" in this instance means taking a disciplined, methodical approach to understanding the problem, the population and the arena. Referring back to Figure 3.1 as a guide to our study of these three domains, we first approach them as separate circles. This means that we might, for example, look only at the "problem" domain, attempting to under-stand everything we can within the limited time frame available about the problem under consideration. In this early phase of the process we would not limit our focus to the impact of the problem on the local community.

If the focus of study is on teen violence, it is important to know as much as possible about the phenomenon itself. What do experts say is the etiology (cause-and-effect relationship) of violence? What does the research say about the importance of early nurturing experiences? About the need for an identity? About social skills? About employment skills? The time will come when we will apply these findings to the local community. First we must understand the phenomenon itself—to explore the entire circle as it applies to the problem.

Often in the course of this study, information will be found on the over-lapping areas of problem and population. In the course of attempting to understand teens, for example, we may come across studies on teen violence. In most cases (but not all) these studies or summaries of existing knowledge about problem and population will be even more valuable than studies of problem alone or population alone. Each new finding should be treasured as an addition to a body of knowledge that brings the change agent closer to understanding the problem. In this manner, the change agent and others involved in the change effort gradually move toward understanding the prob-lem and population as they currently exist in the local community.

Ultimately, the information and knowledge that will be of the highest value to local decision makers will be that which is found where the three circles in Figure 3.1 intersect; that is, where knowledge of problem, population, and arena overlap to aid in understanding how these domains interact with each other to create the current situation and explain how it is unique to this local community.

We are not proposing here an exhaustive study that goes on for months or years. There is rarely time or resources for such a study, and responding in a timely manner is often critical to success. However, plunging into a proposed solution without doing the necessary homework is equally risky. Our intent in this and the following chapters is to lay out a format for systematic study of each of the three circles in Figure 3.1 that can be accomplished within a rea-sonable amount of time (a few weeks to a few months, depending on the peo-ple and the skills involved) and with a small core team of four or five people committed to bringing about needed change.

Focus A: Understanding the Problem

Community leaders and activists are often so anxious to make change happen that they begin at the point of proposing solutions. Too much violence? Let's hire more police! Too many teen pregnancies? Let's take away welfare! While these overly simplistic "solutions" will inevitably emerge in any episode of change, it is the responsibility of the social worker in a professionally guided change effort to make certain that alternative perspectives are adequately explored before proposing a solution.

There are a couple of reasons for exploring multiple perspectives on the problem. First, leaping to propose quick solutions in a macro-practice context is exactly parallel to telling clients in micro-practice situations exactly how to solve their problems. This sort of instant advice-giving behavior is, of course, one of the first things that social workers studying good direct-practice techniques learn *not* to do. Second, quick and easy solutions usually are based on the assumption that the problem in question has one primary cause. In fact, as we will discuss in greater detail later in this chapter, virtually no social problem has only one cause. Many different factors come into play in the development of a social condition, and changing that condition almost always necessitates addressing more than one of these factors.

Take, for example, a community in which highway deaths due to alcohol are up 37 percent in the past two years. How might the causes in this case be defined? One group will be convinced that the cause is lack of strict enforcement of existing laws prohibiting driving under the influence of drugs or alcohol. Another group will describe causes as easy availability of alcohol to teenagers. Another will see alcohol abuse as a symptom of increasing stress. Still another will see it as a symptom of family breakdown. These represent just a few of the perspectives that might be introduced in an attempt to understand some of the reasons behind driving under the influence of alcohol or drugs, even when there is agreement that the increase in drug- and alcohol-related highway deaths is the problem.

This early analytical work is a very important part of the change process. We propose that change agents proceed with a set of tasks designed to gather as much useful information about the problem as is available. These tasks are designed to produce as thorough an understanding as possible of the problem and population in as short a time as possible.

Task 1: Identify the Community or Organizational Condition.   Questions to be asked for this task include:

- What is the difference between a condition and a problem?
- What does this community or organization consider to be its priority problems?
- In approaching an episode of change, how should the condition statement be framed?

A condition is a phenomenon that is present in a community or organization that may be troublesome to a number of people, but that has not been formally identified, labeled, or publicly acknowledged as a problem. Every organization and community is full of both conditions and problems. Social consequences of urban living such as traffic, air pollution, crime, drug abuse, broken families, and suicide can all be considered social or community conditions. Similarly, in rural communities isolation, inaccessible health care, or a declining economic base can all be considered social conditions.

The same concept applies to organizations, where troublesome phenomena are also present, but have not necessarily been formally identified or labeled as a problem. For example, staff in a long–term care facility for the elderly may be concerned about what they consider to be overmedication of some of the residents. Similarly, program managers may recognize a troublesome trend to extend services to those who can pay while offering only a waiting list to those who cannot.

To be defined as a problem, a condition must in some way be formally recognized and incorporated into a community's or an organization's agenda for action. This may mean that elected officials propose formal programs or policy solutions. It may mean that a task force within an organization is officially sanctioned to address the condition. Or it may mean that a group who experiences or sees the effects of the condition takes steps to bring about broader recognition of the presence of the condition and its problematic nature. Regardless of the form it takes, formal recognition is important for legitimization.

The distinction between a condition and a problem is significant to a social worker planning a macro-level intervention. If a condition has not been formally recognized in some way, the first task must be to obtain that formal recognition. For example, for many years homelessness was dealt with as a personal employment problem, child maltreatment as a family matter, and AIDS as a personal health problem. Most communities simply viewed these as existing conditions, not as social or community problems. When these conditions began to affect greater segments of society and reached the point at which they could no longer be ignored, national, state, and local community leaders began to perceive them as problems. Once formally recognized and acknowledged as problems (usually as a result of persistent media attention), these conditions become candidates for organized interventive efforts. The creation of task forces for the homeless in cities across the country, child abuse and neglect reporting laws, and federal funding for AIDS research are results of recognizing conditions and defining them as problems.

A first task in problem identification, then, is to develop a condition statement. A condition statement must include (1) a target population, (2) a geographical boundary, and (3) the difficulty facing the population. Statements should be descriptive, as objective as possible, and based on findings to date.

Statements will be adapted depending on whether the condition exists within a community or in an organization. For example, a condition statement might be, "Suicide among teenagers in Preston County is increasing." Generally speaking, the more precise the statement, the greater the likelihood of a successful intervention. The above statement, for example, could vary from extremely general to very specific, as depicted in Figure 3.2.

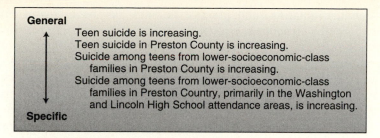

General

Teen suicide is increasing.
Teen suicide in Preston County is increasing.
Suicide among teens from lower-socioeconomic-class
    families in Preston County is increasing.
Suicide among teens from lower-socioeconomic-class
    families in Preston Country, primarily in the Washington
    and Lincoln High School attendance areas, is increasing.

Specific

FIGURE 3.2   Sample Condition Statements

A similar process within an organization would begin with a general statement. For example, an organizational condition might involve an increasing dropout rate among single-parent families in a family counseling program. Data and information would need to be compiled to help pinpoint the condition as precisely as possible.

Condition statements are made more precise through a process of research and documentation of the nature, size, and scope of the problem. As one proceeds with the subsequent tasks in problem analysis, the condition statement will be refined many times as new facts and findings emerge. The statement, however, should not be changed without the knowledge and support of those involved in the change effort.

Task 2: Review the Literature on the Condition, Problem or Opportunity. With regard to this task, relevant questions include:

- What literature is considered key to understanding the condition, problem, or opportunity?

- What frameworks are useful in understanding the condition, problem, or opportunity?

The challenge to the change agent in Task 2 is to become as much of an expert on the condition, problem, or opportunity as possible in the time available. Few experiences are more embarrassing than to be making a public presentation to a decision-making or funding body and to be exposed as less knowledgeable than the audience.

In recent years, literature reporting empirical testing of theoretical and practice-related questions has increased dramatically in the social sciences. A number of journals are now devoted almost exclusively to reporting research in social work and related fields (e.g., *Social Work Research, Journal of Social Service Research, Research on Social Work Practice*). Others examine practice issues (e.g., *Practice Digest, Social Work with Groups, Journal of Marriage and the Family, Journal of Gerontological Social Work*). A computerized search of the literature should quickly produce a listing of relevant literature, and a scan of the titles will guide the change agent toward those articles that appear to be most useful in understanding the condition, problem, or opportunity.

Research, evaluation, and practice findings can be useful in problem analysis. Formally structured, rigorously designed research projects hold the greatest promise for generalizability, assuming that populations, problems, and conditions are comparable. Evaluations of existing social service programs can be informative, but they often lack the methodological rigor of organized research. Reports of practice findings tend to be the least formal in terms of their data collection, analysis, and reporting of findings, yet they can be helpful and informative as long as the user is cautious in interpreting findings and deriving applications.

One feature that can be useful in attempting to understand a phenomenon is the way in which the author has conceptualized the condition, problem, or opportunity. In compiling an article for publication it is incumbent on the author to present some framework or format for analysis that sheds light on the topic under study. In a study of elder abuse, for example, does the author break the topic down by levels of severity? By classification of the perpetrators? By victims? What concepts (and what technical terms) are presented that help us to better understand the phenomenon of elder abuse? Achieving this beginning level of understanding of the condition, problem, or opportunity under study prepares the change agent for the next task—of collecting supporting data.

Task 3: Collect Supporting Data.   Among the questions to be asked for this task are:

- What data are most useful in describing the condition, problem, or opportunity?
- Where can useful data and information be found?
- How should data be displayed in order to make the case for change clearly and concisely?

There was a time when a community could become sensitized to a condition and recognize it as a problem based on a few incidents. Churches started orphanages and counties started poor houses with little or no data beyond personal knowledge of a few people in need and the expectation that there would be more.

In the complex communities of today, however, with so many social and community problems competing for limited resources, data must be compiled to document the size and scope of a problem or need. Collecting data on a community social condition or problem can be a challenge. Ideally, in dealing with teen pregnancy, for example, one would hope to find powerful statistics that clearly demonstrate something like the following:

- There are 3279 pregnant teens in Clifton County.
- Lack of early intervention can be expected to result in 1200 premature births, including a high risk of stillbirth or mental retardation.
- Lack of help with child care and parenting can be expected to result in an abuse and neglect rate of 22 percent, or 721 abused and neglected children.

- The retarded, abused, and neglected children born this year alone can be expected to cost the state $4.5 million per year for at least the next 20 years for various forms of care and treatment.

- An early intervention program for 3279 pregnant teens will cost $1.5 million and can be expected to reduce the incidence of premature delivery to about 300, resulting in an improved quality of life for over 400 children and an annual savings to the state of over $2 million.

These kinds of figures make it clear that it is a case of paying something now for prevention or paying many times more than that amount later for care, maintenance, or perhaps rehabilitation. However, though these kinds of statistics are much desired and preferred, they are rarely accessible. Instead, individuals initiating change must rely on what is available: census data, community needs assessments, levels of demand for service as reported by agencies, rates of service, data generated by hospitals, schools, and police departments, and any other source available.

A few techniques can be helpful in cases in which data and information are needed. One resource is national, regional, or state studies in which an incidence rate per thousand (or per hundred thousand) has been established. If, for example, it has been found that one out of every two marriages performed in a state will end in divorce, one can track down the average number of marriages performed in that community in a given year and calculate the number of divorces that can be expected to follow over time.

Basic to all statistical support is a knowledge of the number of people in various demographic categories (e.g., men, women, age groupings, ethnic minorities, etc.). Valuable information of this type is available in the *County and City Data Book* published by the Bureau of the Census available in the government documents section of a library. Taken from census data, this resource book includes such data categories (for both counties and cities) as ethnic breakdown, age, gender, the number of people with less than a high school education, the number of people in poverty, and other valuable information. Other resources are identified in Table 3.1.

In addition, state and/or county departments of social services, health, mental health, and corrections often collect data that can be useful in documenting the existence of social conditions or problems. Other sources include local social service agencies, United Ways, community councils, centralized data-collection resource centers, centralized information and referral agencies, law enforcement agencies, hospitals, and school district offices. The process of tracking down information is often similar to a scavenger hunt, where one clue leads to another until the point is reached at which the persons initiating change are able to make their case based on the amount and quality of support data that have been compiled.

In collecting supporting data, the change agent should think in terms of the entire "circle" of understanding the community or organizational condition. That means that data collection will not be limited to the *local* community, neighborhood, or organization that is the focus of the change effort. While

TABLE 3.1   Resources for Data Collection

1. Monthly Catalog of U. S. Government Publications
2. American Statistics Index (ASI)
3. Congressional Information Service (CIS) Index
4. U. S. Bureau of the Census. *Statistical Abstract of the United States*. Washington, D.C.: GPO.
5. U. S. Bureau of the Census. *County and City Data Book*. Washington, D.C.: GPO.
6. U. S. Bureau of the Census. *State and Metropolitan Area Data Book*. Washington, D.C.: GPO
7. U. S. Department of Health & Human Services. *Health, United States*. Hyattsville, MD: DHHS.
8. U. S. Department of Justice. *Sourcebook of Criminal Justice Statistics*. Washington, D.C.: GPO
9. *Selected Federal Periodicals*
   • *Family Economics Review*
   • *Social Security Bulletin*
   • *Public Health Reports*
   • *Children Today*

data on the smallest local units of analysis (such as the neighborhood or census tract) are certainly powerful in terms of supporting the argument that something must be done, data on the same conditions or problems at the county, state, or national levels can also be useful in comparing local data to information about these larger units.

Making the Data Meaningful for Interpretation.   Comparative data are generally more useful than a single statistic, and several techniques can be used to collect and display comparative data. These include cross-sectional analysis, time-series comparisons, and comparisons with other data units. In addition to these data displays, techniques such as standards comparisons and epidemiological analysis can be useful (Kettner, Daley, & Nichols 1985).

Cross-Sectional Analysis.   This approach focuses on a single population but provides a number of different perspectives on that population at a particular point in time. For example, a survey might focus on areas of need experienced by a particular target population and display the percentage of the population who report a problem in this area, as illustrated in Table 3.2.

As community or organizational conditions are identified, subpopulations can usually be assessed by demographic characteristics such as age, gender, ethnic minority status, and others. The most serious limitation is that a cross-sectional analysis does not reveal changes over time.

Time-Series Comparisons.   When available, data from repeated observations over time are preferred over cross-sectional analysis because they display trends. Assuming data were collected on an annual basis, a time-series com-

TABLE 3.2   An Illustration of Cross-Sectional Analysis, Examining the
Percentage of Each Population Experiencing a Problem

Variable	Percent of Population	Housing	Employment	Nutrition	Transpor-tation
Age					
0–18	19%	5%	N/A	5%	N/A
19–30	29%	14%	7%	9%	16%
31–64	39%	17%	11%	8%	19%
65+	13%	19%	33%	15%	33%
Gender					
Female	52%	5%	7%	6%	18%
Male	48%	16%	24%	11%	17%
Ethnicity					
White	78%	10%	5%	4%	7%
Asian Amer.	3%	3%	4%	5%	9%
Black	10%	17%	11%	12%	15%
Hispanic	8%	7%	10%	9%	11%
Nat. Amer.	4%	11%	23%	8%	14%

parison would look at trends in the variable(s) of interest. For example, the
number of requests for overnight stays in a homeless shelter might be displayed as shown in Table 3.3.

Statistics like these can help project need and cost into the future, based
on assumptions about trends identified through a series of observations. Comparisons between these observations can provide the change agent with valuable information. For example, they can be used to document how client need
is increasing, why additional resources are needed, and the projected dollars
necessary to fill anticipated need.

Comparison with Other Data Units.   A wealth of both regularly and spe-
cially assembled information is available for use as supporting data. For example, over the past 20 years, many federal programs have contributed to the
generation of data on rates per 1000, 10,000, or 100,000 for social, economic, and health problems. These statistics allow for comparison regardless
of the size of the city or neighborhood in question. Studies have also identified
state and local per-capita expenditures for various social and health problems.
Based on these findings, states and cities can be ranked as to the incidence and
prevalence of a problem as well as their efforts to address the problem.

TABLE 3.3   Illustration of a Time-Series Analysis Examining the Number
of Requests for Overnight Shelter by Homeless Persons

1992	1994	1996	1998
18,250	20,474	25,689	30,410

Comparisons are particularly useful in making a case that a disproportionate share of resources should go to a particularly needy community. By comparing census tracts within a county on selected variables, it becomes readily evident that problems and needs are not always equally distributed across communities and neighborhoods within the county, and therefore resources should not always be distributed on a per-capita basis.

Standards Comparisons. This technique is particularly helpful when comparative data are not available. A standard is defined as "a specification accepted by recognized authorities that is regularly and widely used and has a recognized and permanent status" (Buck et al. 1973, cited in Kettner & Martin 1987, p. 66). Standards are developed by accrediting bodies, governmental entities, or professional associations.

The Child Welfare League of America publishes comprehensive sets of standards related to community and agency programs for child abuse and neglect, adoption, and other child welfare services. Similarly, the National Council on Aging has developed case management standards. The National Association of Social Workers has developed standards for social work services in a wide variety of settings.

Where governmental units, accrediting bodies, or professional associations have defined standards, conditions considered to be below health, educational, personal care, housing, and other standards become more readily accessible as targets for change. Community leaders do not like the negative publicity that often results when their communities are described as being "below standard." These types of standards apply primarily to the quality of services being provided, and they may be more useful when applied to the identification of community or organizational problems as described in Chapters 5 and 8.

Standards of sorts may also be used to define a problem or population. For example, some cities have developed standardized criteria to define a homeless person or a gang member. Where such criteria have been defined they can be useful in interpreting existing data and compiling new data and information.

Epidemiological Analysis. This is a technique adapted from the field of public health, where an analysis of factors contributing to a disease helps to establish relationships even when a clear cause-and-effect relationship cannot be demonstrated. This approach can be applied not only to disease but to social problems as well. For example, Piven and Cloward (1971) established relationships among the variables of poverty, poor education, poor housing, and welfare dependency. While it cannot be said that any of these conditions *cause* welfare dependency, the relationship of dependency to the combination of factors is well established.

An original study of the scope of Piven and Cloward's research is beyond the expectations of most episodes of macro practice. It is mentioned here not to suggest that a social worker should attempt such studies, but so that existing studies will be recognized as viable resources. The American Public Health Association, the National Center on Child Abuse and Neglect, the American Public Welfare Association, the Urban Institute, and other such organizations have provided many sound epidemiological studies that can be used as resources by social workers.

A useful feature of epidemiological thinking is that in analyzing problems it can help avoid simplistic cause-and-effect thinking. While a single causal factor (e.g., poor education, poverty, or child abuse) may explain current problems faced by a small portion of the population, multiple factors in combination frequently help explain the problem or phenomenon for a much larger portion of the population.

Task 4: Identify Relevant Historical Incidents.   Questions to be asked for this task include:

- When was this condition, problem, or opportunity first recognized in this community or organization?
- What are the important incidents or events that have occurred from first recognition to the present time?
- What do earlier efforts to address this problem reveal?

The next task is to compile a chronology of significant events or milestones that help to understand the history of the community or organizational condition or problem. This shifts the focus to the area in Figure 3.1 where the problem and the arena overlap.

A condition or problem in any community or organization has its own history. This history can affect the ways in which people currently perceive the condition or problem. It is, therefore, important to understand how key people within the community or organization perceived the condition or problem in the past. If seen as a problem, how was it addressed? How effective were the attempts to alleviate the problem? Who were the major participants in any previous change efforts?

If one looks merely at the condition or problem as it is defined at present, much will be missed. Instead, it is crucial to determine the problem's history, particularly in terms of critical incidents that have shaped past and current perceptions of the problem. A task force might, for example, be concerned about a high dropout rate from the local high school. The following chronology of critical incidents might help them to better understand factors that influenced the origin and development of important issues in the high school over the years:

1985   Riverview High School was a predominantly lower-middle-class high school with an 82 percent graduation rate.

1987   School district boundaries were redrawn, and the student body changed. For 30 percent of its members, English was a second language.

1988   Enrollment dropped 20 percent, and the graduation rate fell to 67 percent.

1989   Riverview High School initiated a strong vocational training program designed to prepare high-school graduates for post–high-school employment; the college preparatory curriculum was de-emphasized.

1990   Enrollment increased, attendance patterns improved.

1991   Local employers hired only 32 percent of the graduates; unemployment rates among Riverview graduates one year later were as high as 37 percent.

1993   Enrollment dropped back to 1988 levels; the dropout rate hit 23 percent, its highest mark yet.

1996   Riverview High School was written up in the local newspaper as one of the ten worst schools in the state in terms of quality of education, retention rates of students, and post–high-school employment. A blue-ribbon panel was formed to make recommendations to improve the quality of education.

Tracing these historical events lends insight into some of the incidents experienced by the faculty, staff, administration, students, and families associated with Riverview High School. In this case, the task force should expect to encounter a discouraged and cynical response to any sort of a "Stay in School" campaign. The critical incidents list indicates that many of the arguments for staying in school simply did not prove true for those who graduated.

When the employment, career, and financial incentives for remaining in high school are removed, the challenge to keep students in school is greatly increased. This means that the approach to organizational change needs to be adapted in a way that is relevant and meaningful to those who are intended to be the primary beneficiaries. This has clear implications for including in the change effort those who can positively influence the employment environment for graduates.

Exploring relevant historical incidents also helps establish the credibility of the change agent. Many people are simply not open to supporting change for their communities and organizations if those organizing the change effort are perceived as being "outsiders" who have not taken the time to become familiar with what has gone on in the past.

The types of critical incidents described above are generally gleaned from interviews or discussions with long-time residents, activists, community leaders, or government employees. In tracing the history or antecedent conditions of an episode of change, what the change agent hopes to discover is: first, what happened in the past to call attention to the problem or need, and second, what was the community's (neighborhood, city, county, state, private sector) response to each emerging new problem or need?

Task 5: Identify Barriers to Problem Resolution.   Questions relevant to this task are:

- From a review of relevant literature, compilation of data, and a study of history, what appear to be the major barriers to resolving this problem?
- Which barriers, at this point, appear to be the most logical ones to be addressed in this episode of change?

When those involved in the change effort have defined the problem, completed a literature review, compiled evidence, and reviewed important historical events, they should have at least a beginning understanding of what it is that is standing in the way of change. Why has the problem persisted over time? What barriers must be dealt with in order to bring about needed changes? Preliminary identification of these barriers is a necessary step in clarifying the change effort.

Before exploring barriers, however, it is important to understand the types of barriers to be identified. When examining conditions or problems in the human services, there seems to be a strong temptation to identify lack of resources as a barrier to problem resolution. If the study is focused on an organizational problem, barriers tend to be defined in terms of a need for more staff, more equipment, expanded facilities, and so on. In defining a community problem, barriers to resolution tend to be seen in terms of lack of resources for a program—more day care slots, more training, and so on. While in many cases genuine resource deficits may exist, we caution against superficial assessments that look to dollars as the only solution to every problem. There are several reasons for a more thorough approach.

First, resources have to do with the intervention or the "solution," and they should be considered only after a specific approach has been proposed and resource issues can be addressed in detailed, not general, terms. Second, lack of resources is so universal that it is relatively meaningless as a part of problem analysis. Third, "lack of adequate resources" does not tell us what must be done in order to achieve problem resolution. The statement simply assumes that more of whatever is already being done will solve the problem. Additional resources in macro-level change can be critical to success, but the issue should be addressed later in the change process.

The types of barriers to be addressed are those fundamental factors that stand in the way of problem resolution. They are substantive factors that prevent progress toward solutions. For example, in considering what factors stand in the way of solving the problem of elder abuse, one might identify the following barriers: lack of community awareness of the problem, stress within the family, the attitudes of elderly persons toward asking for help, and other such factors. The purpose of identifying them is to help clarify the complex nature of the problem. One method useful for identifying barriers is to diagram the problem as illustrated in Table 3.4. The assumption is that if a community could eliminate all the barriers to problem resolution, then the problem would no longer exist.

Table 3.4 is a graphic representation of those factors that appear to be standing in the way of problem resolution. As newly recognized barriers emerge, they are added to the list. This becomes a centralized collection point

TABLE 3.4   Identification of Barriers to Condition Resolution

Condition Statement	Barriers	Resolution Statement
The incidence of teen suicide is increasing in Preston County	An increasing number of teens suffer from low self-esteem in Preston County	Teen suicide should be declining or non-existent in Preston County
	Many parents are only minimally involved with their teenage children	
Examples of supporting data:		
The number of suicides increased from 2 in 1990 to 7 in 1996	Teens are experiencing increased stress	
	Teen depression is increasing	
Stress-related illness in high school students increased 48% in 5 years	Many teens feel increasingly isolated & alienated from their peers	
Etc . . .	Use and abuse of drugs and alcohol is increasing among teens	
	Clues to suicide intentions are not widely recognized	

for identification of all the factors that must be addressed if the problem is to be resolved.

Identification of barriers to problem resolution is intended to help those who are exploring the need for change to focus their efforts toward removal of one or more barriers, and to recognize the scope and complexity of the problem. In most cases it is unlikely that all barriers to problem resolution will be addressed. Identification of barriers may lead to a narrower, more limited focus or it may lead to collaboration with others, with agreement that each change effort will focus on different barriers.

Task 6: Determine Whether the Condition Is a Problem.   Among questions to be asked here are:

- Given what is now known from the foregoing analysis, is it likely that the decision makers in this community or organization will consider the condition to be a problem?
- Do efforts need to be focused on convincing decision makers that the condition is a problem?

There is no precise definition of when a condition becomes a problem in terms of size, severity, or public awareness. Except in crisis situations, problems are identified and labeled gradually due to shifting perspectives, changing political agendas, or increasing awareness. Is homelessness a problem in any given community? Drug abuse? Air pollution? Crime? The answer to all these questions is, "It depends."

A condition becomes a problem when it receives enough public attention that it can no longer be ignored by community leaders, or when one or more leaders declare a condition unacceptable and decide that something must be done. For example, when a city councilperson's son is arrested for possession of heroin, that community leader may suddenly become very interested in what others have long perceived as the "drug problem." Note that people may suffer from a condition long before it is recognized as a problem. However, for the macro practitioner, recognition of the problem is important because it is only with such recognition that efforts to solve the problem can be mounted on a meaningful scale.

For the change agent, it is then important to consider the question of who will support and who will oppose the proposed change. If it is already recognized as a problem by many community or organizational leaders, or by community citizens or agency staff members, then a proposed change may be readily accepted. If not, it must first receive enough attention that decision makers cannot ignore it.

This raises pivotal questions for the change agent. Has the problem been acknowledged, and does a commitment exist to address the need? Or must efforts first be directed toward having the organization or community in some way formally acknowledge the problem and agree that change is needed? The answer will affect the immediate and long-range focus of the change effort. Ultimately, significant decision makers must be persuaded that the condition is a problem. If this cannot be done, the chances of successfully bringing about change are slim. For this reason, the focus of a change effort is sometimes shifted from the substantive change to an effort to bring attention to the problem.

Summary of Steps Involved in Understanding the Problem.   The following important points have been made so far about identifying a condition and creating an awareness that it is a problem.

1. Initiating macro-level interventions in organizations and communities begins with the identification of a condition problem.

2. For a condition to be considered a problem, some type of formal recognition is necessary. Securing this recognition may become a subsequent step in the intervention process.

3. When a condition or problem statement has been framed, relevant literature on the topic should be reviewed to gain an understanding of the concepts and issues involved.

4. Relevant data should be collected to support the contention that a problem exists and to aid in understanding its nature, size, and scope. Data displays should be carefully crafted to illustrate the perspective on the problem that the change agent wishes to convey.

5. A chronology of historical incidents can help put the current condition or problem into context and identify key participants.

6. Identification of barriers to condition or problem resolution help to make clear the scope and complexity involved in meaningful change. Identifying barriers can also increase awareness of the sources of support needed for change.

7. The purpose of this problem analysis exercise is to bring clarity to understanding the condition, to convince appropriate individuals or systems that the condition needs to be addressed, and to provide a foundation for later design of a solution or intervention.

8. By this point, the change agent should either have succeeded in convincing the appropriate individuals and groups that the condition is a problem, or the focus of the change effort should be shifted to that task.

Focus B: Understanding the Population

Problems affect people. Solutions, if they are to be effective, must reflect an understanding of the people affected. Much has been learned over the years about human growth and development. We know that the issues, concerns, and needs of adolescents, for example, are not the same as those of the elderly. Yet we sometimes make the assumption that "people are people," and that it's not really as important to understand the population as it is to understand the problem.

If we hope to understand why problems exist, we must understand the populations affected. For example, why do people commit suicide? The answer is likely very different for teenagers than it is for the elderly. How do people react to stress? The research may help us to understand that reactions can be affected by gender, ethnicity, and/or age.

In many cases a particular target population is implied or stated as a part of framing the problem. Focusing on a problem such as teen pregnancy immediately narrows the population to young women between the ages of approximately 11 and 19. Elder abuse narrows the population to people who are most likely over 65 and in a vulnerable and dependent situation. These populations lend themselves to study and understanding by conducting a review of the literature and interviewing key informants to help in understanding the local target population.

In other cases the population may not be as clearly defined. For example, an episode of change may focus on a neighborhood. In this instance, it may be necessary to identify several populations such as teens, young families, adults or elderly. When intervening at the neighborhood level, it is likely that the analysis will be more heavily focused on "arena" (to be discussed in the following chapters). However, if the needs of the target population are to be understood, a population analysis may need to be completed on several different age, gender and/or cultural groups that may exist within the neighborhood.

To conduct an analysis of the population in as efficient a manner as possible, we propose that the change agent engage in another series of tasks, which include the following: Task 7—Review the literature on the target population; Task 8—Examine relevant ethnic and gender perspectives; Task 9—Explore past experiences with the target population and problem.

Task 7: Review the Literature on the Target Population. Relevant questions are:

- What factors or characteristics gleaned from the literature on this population will be helpful in understanding the target population?
- What theoretical frameworks are useful in understanding the target population?

In Task 2 we proposed a review of the literature on the condition or problem. In many ways Task 7 may overlap with Task 2. Studies often cover both a problem and a population such as "the health needs of rural, elderly, African-American women." Literature that covers both problem and population can be doubly useful. However, it is also important that relevant literature on the population not be overlooked.

Texts on human growth and development and human behavior are frequently divided into ages and stages of life. For example, Santrock (1995) uses the following chapter headings: Beginnings, Infancy, Early Childhood, Middle and Late Childhood, Adolescence, Early Adulthood, Middle Adulthood, Late Adulthood, and Death and Dying.

Schuster and Ashburn (1992) explore biophysical, cognitive and psychosocial development at each stage of life-span development. There is a rich body of knowledge about the populations served by social workers. Understanding and applying that knowledge is as important in dealing with macro-level interventions as it is in working with individuals and families.

Identifying Relevant Theoretical Perspectives. An important part of the literature review should be devoted to identifying and applying relevant theoretical perspectives. Theories are intended to explain phenomena and to provide a framework for research and testing of hypotheses. As opposed to the random listing of facts and observations, theories allow for categorizing one's findings, making sense out of them, and turning seemingly unrelated bits of information into explanatory propositions that lead to logical, testable hypotheses.

For example, focusing on the population of high-school dropouts, one might draw on the work of B. F. Skinner (1971), Erik Erickson (1968), Carol Gilligan (1982), or Abraham Maslow (1943) to understand the behavior of the target population.

Using some of Skinner's most basic concepts such as reinforcement, extinction, or desensitization, one might examine the high-school experience for selected students. It might be hypothesized that negative reinforcements in the form of poor grades and criticism lead to discouragement and poor attendance on the part of some students. These negative responses may also extinguish certain behaviors and limit the effort a student is willing to invest in academic success. Or perhaps school disciplinary experiences such as detention, suspension, or extra assignments systematically desensitize some students to organizationally imposed sanctions. In this case, efforts would have to be expended to discover what this group of students would consider positive reinforcement, and how the academic experience could be designed so that they could achieve success.

Erickson's concept of identity might cause one to focus on the need of high-school age youth for a positive self-image. The high-school experience might then be examined to determine the degree to which it supports the development of a positive identity for some and destroys it for others. Activities would be designed to build self-esteem on the assumption that increased self-esteem will act as a motivator to academic success.

Gilligan's work raises consciousness in understanding the psychological development of women and the importance of gender on how one views the world. If dropout rates for women are related to teen pregnancy, one may want to consider the importance of gender identity. Gilligan theorizes that women seek connection and affiliation as they develop, not having to separate from the mother in the same way that boys do. Becoming pregnant, which contributes to dropping out of school, may be a young girl's way of establishing intimacy and feeling needed.

Maslow, on the other hand, would examine the phenomenon of high-school dropouts in terms of the congruence between the high-school experience and students' needs. The pertinent question would be whether the educational programs were appropriately tailored to meet the social, esteem, and fulfillment needs of students. Each level of need, once met, is no longer a motivator, so new challenges would have to be designed to achieve the goal of self-fulfillment.

Using theoretical frameworks is far more complex than illustrated here, and it is not our intent to trivialize the full depth and breadth of these explanatory theories through our brief examples. What we do hope to illustrate is that theory is an important ingredient in understanding the target population. Theoretical frameworks give the analysis internal consistency and ultimately provide a rationale for the intervention.

Explanatory theories should be selected carefully based on what fits best with the problem and population. Theories should be critically evaluated for their biases and given credibility based on how thoroughly they have been tested. Once selected as a framework for analysis, theoretical assumptions should be stated and shared with those involved in the change effort. This is intended to facilitate the achievement of a shared understanding of the problem and population(s) involved.

Task 8: Examine Relevant Ethnic and Gender Perspectives.   Questions for this task are:

- How do representatives of ethnic groups affected by this problem view the problem?
- Are there gender-related issues? Do women who are affected by this problem have a perspective that is different from men who are affected?

A full understanding of a social problem requires attention to a range of perspectives. Problems can be understood in a number of ways, including (1) experiencing the problem firsthand, (2) working closely with people who have experienced the problem, or (3) studying the literature on the problem. In considering these three approaches, it is important to distinguish between the understanding and insight gained by firsthand experience as contrasted to other methods of learning about a social problem.

When it comes to representing the perspectives of a population of people who have experienced a problem, it should be understood that those who have only secondhand experiences usually are not accepted as spokespersons by those who have direct experience with the problem. For example, people who have experienced day-to-day life on public assistance may not be willing to accept a social worker as a spokesperson to articulate their feelings and needs. Likewise, people living in a housing development may be more likely to turn to a fellow housing project resident as spokesperson. Describing the experiences that led to a posttraumatic stress disorder for a Vietnam veteran can usually be done with credibility only by someone who was there. People of an ethnic group may be able to speak for the experiences of their own group, but not for another group. One gender may not be able to represent the other with credibility. For these reasons, it is important to find spokespersons who are accepted and supported by their peers who can help to articulate the perspectives of the group(s) involved. It is also important to locate literature that will help those involved in the change effort to understand important issues and perspectives of the target population. Two especially important perspectives are those represented by culture and gender.

Understanding Cultural Perspectives.   *Culture* can be defined in many ways. One definition is "those elements of a people's history, tradition, values, and social organization that become implicitly or explicitly meaningful to the participants during an encounter" (Green 1982, p. 7). Culture is usually defined around the life experiences of people who live in close proximity to one another and pass beliefs and traditions from parent to child down through generations. *Race* is another term that is used to define unique characteristics of a population. Race can be defined as "a group of persons related by common descent, blood, or heredity" (*Webster*'s 1994, p. 1184).

A third term frequently used in connection with culture is *ethnicity*. As with culture, there are numerous definitions of ethnicity. Green (1982) suggests that there are three elements common to most definitions. First, ethnic group members share a past and related backgrounds. Second, persons who identify with ethnic groups believe that they are distinctively different from others in some important manner. Third, ethnicity becomes significant when members of a group come in contact with persons who are from different ethnic groups. Comparison is necessary because it highlights the uniqueness of one group in relation to another (Green 1982). Major ethnic groups in this country include African Americans, Hispanics, Native Americans, and Asian Americans. Each of these groups, in turn, are made up many subgroups identified by tribe or country of origin. In addition, people whose heritage is Italian, Swedish, or Polish, for example, may also fit the definition of an ethnic group. Religion is another factor that may further define a culture as with the Amish muslims or others. Members of ethnic groups in this country today often draw on customs and traditions of their culture of origin. Their perceptions and experiences can make a difference in the way a problem is perceived and understood.

Understanding Gender Perspectives.   Still another variable that must be taken into consideration in understanding the issues, needs, interests and concerns of a population is *gender*. It has been well documented (Tannen 1990) that the early childhood experiences, perceptions, and ways of viewing the world differ between boys and girls. Growing up in a household that includes both genders does not necessarily lead to cross-gender understanding. Again, a disciplined study is required, including listening to firsthand experiences and carefully reviewing relevant literature.

In the best of all possible worlds, in each episode of macro-level change, there would be a change agent available who reflects the culture, race, ethnic group, gender, age group, and life experiences of the client or target population. This is seldom the case. Social workers find themselves the focal point or conduit for concerns brought by many community people, some of whom may be clients.

If a social worker happens to be 23 years old, white or Hispanic, and working with elderly African-American people, it is incumbent upon the social worker to recognize that her experiences are not the same as those with whom she is working. Effective cross-cultural social work in this situation requires that the social worker be able to hear the voices of elderly African Americans and partner with them as they guide one another.

The Dual Perspective.   A framework helpful in understanding and dealing with the complexities of ethnicity and gender is the dual perspective. Initially

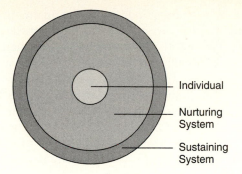

FIGURE 3.3   The Dual Perspective

[Source: Norton, D. G. *The Dual Perspective: Inclusion of Ethnic Minority Content in the Social Work Curriculum* (New York: Council on Social Work Education), 1978.]

conceptualized by Norton (1978), the dual perspective views an individual as being at the center of two surrounding systems, which Norton calls the nurturing system and the sustaining system, shown in Figure 3.3.

The center of the diagram represents the *individual.* Immediately surrounding the individual is a *nurturing system,* represented by the parenting and extended family or substitute family practices, community experiences, beliefs, values, customs, and traditions with which the individual was raised. Surrounding the nurturing system is a *sustaining system* represented by the dominant society. The sustaining system also reflects beliefs, values, customs, and traditions.

The focus of analysis for the change agent is the degree of fit between an individual's, family's, or group's nurturing system and the sustaining system within which they function. The nurturing system may, for example, support the importance of family over individual, while the sustaining system emphasizes and rewards individual competition and merit.

Sustaining systems are made up of influential and powerful people—teachers, employers, elected officials, and others. Some segments of sustaining systems may reflect racist and sexist attitudes, and they can therefore be perceived by ethnic minorities and women to represent alien and hostile environments. Yet these individuals frequently have little choice but to interact with the sustaining system environment.

For these reasons, those whose nurturing system experiences, beliefs, and values are most dissimilar to those of the sustaining system may have the most difficulty crossing cultural borders. Individuals who represent the sustaining system in local communities are frequently insensitive to cultural differences, and they assume that everyone wants (or should want) to adopt sustaining or dominant system values, beliefs, and language. This situation can set up an impasse, and it is incumbent upon the social worker to understand the nature of the impasse and to develop a basis for better mutual understanding.

It is reasonable, in attempting to improve the quality of cross-cultural and cross-gender communication, to assume that oppressed or ignored groups have a better understanding of the sustaining system than sustaining system representatives have of them. People who live within a dominant society observe and experience, on a daily basis, the values, beliefs, traditions, and language of the dominant society through personal contact, television, news-papers, and other media. The reverse is not true. Representatives of the domi-nant society do not observe and experience the values, beliefs, and traditions of non-dominant groups. Therefore, it makes sense for the social worker to concentrate on helping representatives of the dominant society to understand the needs of the client or target population.

Most programs and services, along with their underlying rationale, are designed from a sustaining or dominant perspective. Even the theories used to explain the problem and the research on which the practitioner builds hypotheses may reflect sustaining system biases. Members of diverse ethnic groups, on the other hand, may have very different perspectives of the prob-lem and how to resolve it.

Take, for example, a situation in which some of a community's elderly are experiencing a deteriorating quality of life. One culture may value the extend-ed family and wish to maintain elderly parents in the home, but most family members cannot afford the expense of taking on another dependent. Another culture may value the independence and privacy of elderly parents, but its members cannot afford to pay retirement community prices. The community's influential and powerful may believe that government should not be involved, and that decisions about aging parents should be left to adult children. It is likely that these types of perceptions will be linked to factors relating to cul-ture and/or gender and to nurturing system/sustaining system perspectives.

Resources available to the social worker in promoting better cross-cultur-al and cross-gender understanding include informal and mediating units such as self-help and voluntary associations, as well as formal organizations who represent themselves as speaking for women and cultural or ethnic groups. Whenever ethnic minorities, women, or other special population groups make up a part of the target population and are expected to benefit from the change effort, credible expertise reflecting these diverse perspectives must be sought and incorporated into the problem analysis and intervention design.

Task 9: Explore Past Experiences with the Target Population and Problem.
Relevant questions here include:

- What kinds of experiences has this population had in the past in their attempts to deal with this problem?
- How do representatives of this group perceive the sustaining system?

Finally, the change agent must compile as thorough an understanding of past experiences at the local level as possible. Has this same group or popula-tion attempted to initiate change in the past? If so, with what results? If the results were positive, why is the change effort being repeated? If the results of the past efforts were negative, what happened?

Identifying and interviewing past spokespersons for the target population and past representatives of the community or organization should aid in understanding past experiences with the target population and problem. If there have been relevant past experiences with this population, the change agent should compile a list of key actors and a chronology of interactions between the target population and community or organizational representatives leading up to the present. Findings from these interviews will help shape strategy and tactics later in the episode of change.

Summary of Steps Involved in Understanding the Population.   The following steps or tasks have been proposed as a means of understanding the population expected to benefit from the proposed change (the client population), the population that needs to change in some way for the proposed change effort to be effective (the target population), or both.

1. Complete a review of relevant literature in the interest of developing an understanding of age, cultural, gender, and client or target population perspectives.
2. Ensure that those involved in the change effort understand the important concepts and issues reflected in the literature.
3. Identify local, indigenous spokespersons who represent age, cultural, gender, and client or target-population perspectives.
4. Ensure that those involved in the change effort understand the important concepts and issues raised by local, indigenous spokespersons.
5. Develop a consensus among those involved in the change effort on the concepts and issues related to the population. The consensus should represent the best and most relevant to the current situation of what is drawn from both local people, experts, and relevant literature.

Having completed this effort to achieve the best possible understanding of the client and/or target population, those involved in the change effort turn their attention to refining the problem statement.

Focus C: Refining the Problem Statement

By this time, much data and information have been compiled on the problem and the population. The final tasks involve distilling the data and information into a focused, shared understanding of the reasons behind the continued existence of the problem.

Task 10: Speculate about the Etiology of the Problem.   Questions to be asked in connection with this task include:

- Based on the foregoing problem analysis, what seem to be the dominant themes in understanding cause-and-effect relationships?

- How should the hypothesis of etiology be framed?

Etiology is defined as "the underlying causes of a problem or disorder" (Barker 1995, p. 125). Speculating about the etiology of a problem is an attempt to arrive at an understanding of cause-and-effect relationships. As one begins to move into this territory, it is important to keep an open mind and let the data, information, and personal experiences of client/target-population representatives inform an understanding of the problem. It is highly unlikely, in analysis of social, community, and/or organizational problems, that there will be simple, linear cause-and-effect relationships. It is more likely that there will be multiple causes and that there will be multiple views on what is relevant and applicable to the current situation.

Examination of a history of the problem, current conditions, personal experiences, theory, and research on the population and the problem come together at the point at which cause-and-effect relationships are postulated. The change agent looks for patterns of events or factors that seem to be associated so that a case can be made for a working hypothesis on selected causal factors.

In many cases, alternative explanations of cause-and-effect are all logical and, in a sense, "correct," but they may apply to different subgroups of the client or target populations. For example, all the following statements are probably rational understandings about why subgroups of high-school students drop out of school:

- Some students drop out because they believe that the structure of the program and the content of the curriculum are not relevant to their needs.

- Some students drop out because of inability to handle the academic demands, even though they see relevance to their needs.

- Some students drop out because income is needed by their families and they are the only resource at the time.

- Some students drop out because they suffer discrimination and rejection from their peers and leaving the situation is a way of avoiding emotional pain.

- Some students drop out because there is such intense discord in their home and family lives that they are incapable of dealing with the added stress of academic demands.

The decision that must then be made is not one of choosing the "correct" perspective on etiology, but rather on selecting the subgroup(s) to be addressed. As with many (probably all) client/target populations and problems, one understanding of etiology and one intervention does not fit all. There are multiple rational explanations, and ultimately one or more must be selected to serve as a framework for understanding the problem and the population.

Task 11: Refine the Problem Statement.   The principle question to be asked in connection with this task is:

• How should the problem statement be framed?

When the above activities have been accomplished, the *working draft* of the condition statement can be refined into a problem statement. A simple, clear statement that includes a target population, boundary, and problem is most appropriate. Explanatory statements or supportive documentation may follow, but the statement should provide a consensus position for all those who are expected to support the change effort. The following might be used in the high-school-dropout example: "Dropouts in the Washington, Lincoln, and Jefferson attendance areas of the Preston City school district have been increasing steadily over the past five years and have reached a level that is becoming a cause of serious concern to the citizens of this community."

A brief position statement might then be developed to include an overview of relevant historical critical incidents, data that reveal trends over time and comparisons to other schools and districts, and a brief overview of what are considered to be the major causes, as gleaned from the study of the problem and the population. The problem statement and position statement then serve as a focal point around which a support system will be built.

Summary of Steps in Refining the Problem Statement.   The following steps or tasks complete the problem identification and analysis phase of a macro-level change episode:

1. Review the major concepts, issues, and perspectives identified in Focus A: Understanding the Problem.
2. Review the major concepts, issues, and perspectives identified in Focus B: Understanding the Population.
3. Bring these together by developing a shared understanding of the cause-and-effect relationships underlying the problem.
4. Prepare a refined problem statement together with a backup position statement. These will be used to develop a shared understanding of the major concepts, issues, and perspectives related to the social, community, or organizational problem.

SUMMARY

This chapter has proposed a method for understanding the problems and populations affected by macro-level change in organizations and communities. The method begins with a thorough examination of the current condition in the organization or community that has led to the perception that a problem exists. Condition is seen as a more neutral term; its use recognizes that not everyone agrees on the existence of a problem (or negatively defined condition). Someone must first identify the negatives that make the condition a cause for concern. This is accomplished by developing a clear statement of the condition, by collecting data and information about the condition, by reviewing the literature on the condition and the population(s) affected, and by identifying barriers to resolution.

A thorough analysis of all data and information gained about the condition/problem and population leads to a refinement of the problem statement, an identification of important statistical data supporting the existence of the problem, and a highlighting of factors that help to explain the etiology of the problem. Once a consensus is achieved on these issues (or concurrently with this achievement), an analysis of community and/or relevant organization(s) is undertaken. These topics will be covered in the next chapters of this book.

REFERENCES

Barker, R. L. (1995) The Social work dictionary. Washington, DC: NASW Press.

Erickson, E. (1968) *Identity, youth and crisis.* New York: Norton.

Gilligan, C. (1982) *In a different voice.* Cambridge, MA: Harvard University Press.

Green, J. W. (1982) *Cultural awareness in the human services.* Englewood Cliffs, NJ: Prentice-Hall.

Kettner, P. M., J. M. Daley, and A. W. Nichols. (1985) Initiating Change in organizations and communities. Monterey, CA: Brooks/Cole.

Kettner, P. M., and L. L. Martin. (1987) *Purchase of service contracting.* Newbury Park, CA: Sage.

Maslow, A. (1943) A theory of motivation. *Psychological Review, 50:* 370–96

Norton, D. G. (1978) *The dual perspective: Inclusion of ethnic minority content in the social work curriculum.* New York: Council on Social Work Education.

Piven, F., and R. Cloward. (1971) *Regulating the poor: The functions of public welfare.* New York: Pantheon.

Santrock, J. (1995) *Life-span development.* Madison, WI: Brown & Benchmark.

Schuster, C., and S. Ashburn. (1992) *The process of human development: A holistic life-span approach.* Philadelphia: J. B. Lippincott.

Skinner, B. (1971) *Beyond freedom and dignity.* New York: Knopf.

Tannen, D. (1990) *You just don't understand.* New York: Ballantine.

Webster's encyclopedic unabridged dictionary of the English language. (1994) New York: Gramercy.

SUGGESTED READINGS

Ashford, J. B., and LeCroy, C. W. (1997) *Human behavior in the social environment: A multidimensional perspective.* Pacific Grove, CA: Brooks-Cole.

Fellin, P. (1995) *The community and the social worker.* Itasca, IL: F. E. Peacock.

Jacobs, C., and Bowles, D. (1988) *Ethnicity and race: Critical concepts in social work.* Silver Spring, MD: National Association of Social Workers.

Jansson, B. (1994) *Social policy: From theory to policy practice.* Pacific Grove, CA: Brooks-Cole.

Kettner, P. M., Moroney R. M., and Martin, L. (1990) *Designing and managing programs: An effectiveness-based approach.* Newbury Park, CA: Sage.

Locke, D. (1992) *Increasing multicultural understanding: A comprehensive model.* Newbury Park, CA: Sage.

Martin, E., and Martin J. (1995) *Social work and the black experience.* Washington, DC: NASW Press.

Rothman, J., J. L. Erlich, and J. E. Tropman. (1995) *Strategies of community intervention* (5th ed.). Itasca, IL: F. E. Peacock.

Sotomayor, M. (1991) *Empowering Hispanic families: A critical issue for the '90s.* Milwaukee, WI: Family Service America.

Tropman, J. E., Erlich, J. L., and Rothman, J., eds. (1995) *Tactics and techniques of community intervention* (3rd ed.). Itasca, IL: F. E. Peacock.

APPENDIX

Framework for Understanding the Problem and the Target Population

FOCUS A: UNDERSTANDING THE PROBLEM

Task 1: Identify the Community or Organizational Condition

- What is the difference between a condition and a problem?
- What does this community or organization consider to be its priority problems?
- In approaching an episode of change, how should the condition statement be framed?

Task 2: Review the Literature on the Condition, Problem, or Opportunity

- What literature is considered key to understanding the condition, problem, or opportunity?
- What frameworks are useful in understanding the condition, problem, or opportunity?

Task 3: Collect Supporting Data

- What data are most useful in describing the condition, problem, or opportunity?
- Where can useful data and information be found?
- How should data be displayed in order to make the case for change clearly and concisely?

Task 4: Identify Relevant Historical Incidents

- When was this condition, problem, or opportunity first recognized in this community or organization?

- What are the important incidents or events that have occurred from first recognition to the present time?
- What do earlier efforts to address this problem reveal?

Task 5: Identify Barriers to Problem Resolution

- From a review of relevant literature, compilation of data, and a study of history, what appear to be the major barriers to resolving this problem?
- Which barriers, at this point, appear to be the most logical ones to be addressed in this episode of change?

Task 6: Determine Whether the Condition Is a Problem

- Given what is now known from the foregoing analysis, is it likely that the decision makers in this community or organization will consider the condition to be a problem?
- Do efforts need to be focused on convincing decision makers that the condition is a problem?

FOCUS B: UNDERSTANDING THE POPULATION

Task 7: Review the Literature on the Target Population

- What factors or characteristics gleaned from the literature on this population will be helpful in understanding the target population?
- What theoretical frameworks are useful in understanding the target population?

Task 8: Examine Relevant Ethnic and Gender Perspectives

- How do representatives of ethnic groups affected by this problem view the problem?
- Are there gender-related issues? Do women who are affected by this problem have a perspective that is different from men who are affected?

Task 9: Explore Past Experiences with the Target Population and Problem

- What kinds of experiences has this population had in the past in their attempts to deal with this problem?
- How do representatives of this group perceive the sustaining system?

FOCUS C: REFINING THE PROBLEM STATEMENT

Task 10: Speculate about the Etiology of the Problem

- Based on the foregoing problem analysis, what seem to be the dominant themes in understanding cause-and-effect relationships?
- How should the hypothesis of etiology be framed?

Task 11: Refine the Problem Statement

- How should the problem statement be framed?

PART II

The Community as the Arena of Change

In Part I we discussed social work macro practice from values, historical, and change perspectives. We also indicated that communities and organizations are two principal macro systems with which social workers must interact. In Part II we will focus on the community as the arena of change. This section begins with a chapter on community definitions and theories. In the next chapters we propose a process for assessing communities, first from the perspective of understanding the community itself, and second from the perspective of assessing the adequacy of the community's human service system as it relates to social problems and populations in need.

CHAPTER 4

Understanding Communities

INTRODUCTION

Communities are arenas in which macro practice takes place, yet they are so diverse that no one definition or theory will capture their total essence. Terms such as *global community* or *world community* are used in contemporary society to refer to the complex array of relationships among the world's people. Yet when most of us think about communities that are important to us we usually think less globally, remembering where we grew up, identifying with

where we live today, or focusing on various relationships that transcend traditional geographical boundaries. These relationships may be bound by various
characteristics such as shared history, cultural values and traditions, concern
for common issues, and frequent communication. Many people identify with
multiple communities, thus making "the community" a misnomer. For many
of us, affiliation with more than one community is part of who we are.

Based on their life experiences, social workers will have their own perceptions of what a community is as well as their expectations of what a community should be. These perceptions and expectations will influence how they
approach work in communities that are new to them. It is important to recognize that experiences with and feelings about community as a geographic
locality vary. Some communities will be viewed nostalgically, as desirable
places, evoking warm memories. Some communities will be seen as oppressive, restrictive, or even dangerous to the people who live there as well as to
"outsiders." Sometimes these differing views will be held by different people
about the same community because every person's experience is unique. Community-based groups such as voluntary associations, gangs, and clubs may be
ways to seek community through establishing relationships that run counter
to the local culture. Some observers and analysts believe that community as a
geographically relevant concept began to erode with the emergence of suburbs
in the 1950s and 1960s (Gerloff 1992). Others see unlimited human potential
lying dormant in inner-city communities that have been rendered dependent
by the overzealous provision of services (Kretzmann & McKnight 1993). We
believe that social workers have the responsibility to recognize that community can be a powerful medium for enfranchisement and empowerment when its
potential is understood and skillfully brought to life. We also believe that
social workers must recognize that problems and needs can often be addressed
more effectively by dealing with them collectively than they can by dealing
with them individually. The major focus of this chapter will be on understanding communities from a theoretical perspective as a first step toward better
informed and more skillful community-level intervention.

Defining Community

There are many definitions of community, and we provide only a sampling
here. No matter what definition is selected, concepts such as "space," "people," "interaction," and "shared identity" are often repeated over and over
again. As early as the 1950s one scholar identified over 90 discrete definitions
of community in use within the social science literature (Hillery 1955).

Regardless of the changes to be made in community arenas, the social
worker will want to be fully aware of how persons affected by the change
define and perceive their communities. The social worker must understand
alternative perspectives, recognize the assumptions and values that undergird
these views, and understand how differing perspectives influence change
opportunities. It is also important to recognize that even persons within the

same community will differ in their perspectives of what that community is about and of what changes are needed. For example, it is not unusual within the boundaries of a community for one ethnic or cultural group to believe that schools are relevant and city services adequate to meet local needs, while another ethnic or cultural group believes they are irrelevant and inadequate.

One of the most cited definitions of community was provided by Warren in 1978. Many schools of social work used Warren's book, *The Community in America,* as the basic textbook for courses with community content. Variations on his definition of community are still widely used in social work textbooks, particularly in understanding geographical communities (see for example, Fellin 1995, p. 4; Rothman, Erlich, & Tropman 1995, pp. 10–11). Warren (1978) defined community as "that combination of social units and systems that perform the major social functions" (p. 9) relevant to meeting people's needs on a local level. Community, according to Warren, means the organization of social activities that affords people access to what is necessary for day-to-day living, such as the school, the grocery store, the hospital, the church, and other such social units and systems. Generally, we think of social units as beginning with the domestic unit, extending to the neighborhood or to the voluntary association, and on to the larger community. Community may or may not have specific boundaries, but it is significant because it performs functions necessary for human survival.

Types of Communities

Fellin (1995) contends that community occurs when "a group of people form a social unit based on common location, interest, identification, culture, and/or activities" (p. 3). He then distinguishes three ways of categorizing community based on place or geographic locale, identification or interest, and personal network. We will briefly examine each category.

Geographical, spacial, or territorial communities vary in how they meet people's needs, how social interactions are patterned, and how collective identity is perceived. Local communities are often called "neighborhoods," "cities," "towns," "boroughs," "barrios," and a host of other terms. Smaller geographical spaces are nested within other communities, such as neighborhoods that are portions of towns or public housing developments within cities.

In earlier times, before people were so mobile and technology transcended space, communities were much more place-bound. Today, however, considerations of space must be juxtaposed with other ways of conceptualizing community. Whereas we may operate within geographical jurisdictions, the influences of forces beyond those imaginary boundaries are limitless.

Communities of identification and interest are not necessarily geographically based. Fellin actually refers to these as "non-place" communities, whereas other writers use names such as functional communities, relational or associational communities, communities of affiliation or affinity, and even communities of the mind. These nongeographical, or functional, communities bring people together based on "ethnicity, race, religion, lifestyle, ideology, sexual orientation, social class, and profession or type of employment" (Fellin 1995, p. 4).

Functional communities, which are examples of communities that are based on identification and interest, are formed when "people share a concern about a common issue, which ranges from advocacy for the needs of children with disabling conditions to environmental protection" (Weil & Gamble 1995, p. 583). For the social work practitioner, it is important to recognize and understand communities that are formed around shared concerns, such as abortion, gun control, and political loyalties. It is even more critical to recognize that these communities are formed around deeply held beliefs and values that may conflict with those of other communities. For example, religious communities or congregations that believe that being gay or lesbian is morally wrong may have a clash of values when encountering the gay and lesbian community. Similarly, professional communities that believe in social justice and advocacy for the poor may encounter political communities formed to reduce government spending and to terminate public assistance to those who are on welfare, regardless of need or capacity for self sufficiency. Communities of interest are becoming increasingly politically active and many people have warned of the polarizing effects of special-interest politics.

Fellin also distinguishes communities that are focused on *personal networks or an individual's membership in multiple communities*. In a complex society, people establish their own constellations of relationships based on both place and non-place. For example, a social worker is likely to be a member of the National Association of Social Workers (a nonplace community), live in a neighborhood (a place community), and have close relationships with persons scattered around the world (a personal network). Because each person will have a particular constellation of relationships, each person's definition of community will be distinctive. Often viewed as networks or webs of formal and informal resources, these relationships and what they mean to the person's "sense of community" are very important for the change agent to recognize, respect, and understand. Methods such as network analysis and ecological mapping are intended to reveal how individuals perceive their communities. For example, if people find their "sense of community" through disparate, scattered relationships that do not interface, the change agent may have difficulty mobilizing them to want to address a local community need.

Community, then, can be seen as those spaces, interactions, and identifications that people share with others in both place-specific and non–place-specific locations. The planned change model presented in later chapters will be applicable to both place and nonplace communities.

Distinguishing Community Theories and Models

No understanding of community is complete without viewing the historical distinction between Tonnies' (1887) concepts of Gemeinschaft and Gesellschaft. Gemeinschaft is roughly translated to mean community and focuses on the mutual, intimate, and common bonds that pull people together in local units. These bonds are based on caring about one another and valuing the relationships in the group in and of themselves. The group is valued whether or not they are producing a product or achieving a goal. Examples are the domestic unit, the neighborhood, and groups of friends. The focus of Gemeinschaft is on intimacy and relationship.

In contrast, Tonnies introduced the concept of Gesellschaft, roughly meaning society or association. Examples of this concept are the city or the state. Gesellschaft is an ideal type representing the more formalized relationships that are task-oriented. When Gesellschaft occurs, people formally come together to achieve a purpose, a task, or a goal. Although they may benefit from the relationships that are established, the purpose of these social interactions are to achieve some goal, produce some product, or complete some task.

Sociologists of the late 1800s viewed Gesellschaft as representing all the negative forces pulling people away from traditional communities that were built on institutions such as the family and religion. It is important to recognize, however, that the contribution of Tonnies' ideal types is to call attention to the differences between the informal and formal systems as well as to the richness of their interaction. Macro social workers will find elements of both concepts in the communities with which they work. As for Tonnies' work, it is cited in any historical work on community and became the base from which community theory emerged in the 1900s.

Warren's (1978) classic book on community synthesized community theory development prior to the early 1970s and is a valuable resource for identifying studies conducted up to that time. Warren distinguishes between community as: (1) space, (2) people, (3) shared values and institutions, (4) interaction, (5) distribution of power, and (6) social system. In the following discussion of community theory, these themes will be evident.

Theories are sets of interrelated concepts that explain how and why something works or does not work. Sociological theories of community often describe how communities function, whereas community practice models are intended to provide direction or guidance for persons wanting to change or intervene in a community arena. In the remainder of this chapter we present an overview of community theories and then identify models that have emerged from these theoretical understandings.

COMMUNITY STRUCTURE AND FUNCTION

Just as organizational theorists began to look at how organizations could be structured for maximum productivity, community theorists attempted to understand how community structure could be used to explain whether communities were functioning well. In this section we examine theoretical understandings of structure and function. We begin with the human ecology theorists who carefully examined structural patterns and relationships within place based communities.

Human Ecology Theory

In the mid-1930s a group of sociologists under the leadership of Robert E. Park at The University of Chicago examined local community spacial relationships, and out of their work emerged human ecology theory. Human ecology theory was based on plant and animal ecology. Park (1983) characterized human ecology as follows:

> Individual units of the population are involved in a process of competitive cooperation, which has given to their interrelations the character of a natural economy. To such a habitat and its inhabitants—whether plant, animal, or human—the ecologists have applied the term community.
>
> The essential characteristics of a community, so conceived, are those of (1) a population, territorially organized, (2) more or less completely rooted in the soil it occupies, (3) its individual units living in a relationship of mutual interdependence that is symbolic rather than societal, in the sense in which that term applies to human beings. (p. 29)

The human ecologists believed that if they studied one city well enough, what they learned could be applied with appropriate modifications to other cities. Two spacial concepts, the urban zone and the central city became important elements of the ecology school. Zones were large concentric circles surrounding the central city, whereas natural areas such as neighborhoods were smaller arenas in which social relationships developed. Both zones and natural areas were changing and dynamic. However, subsequent studies in other metropolitan areas revealed just how difficult it is to generalize. Other cities did not always show the same structural patterns.

Today, ecological theorists focus on population demographics (e.g., age, gender, race), the use of physical space, and the structures and technology within communities. An ecological approach views communities as highly interdependent, teeming with changing relationships among people and institutions. "From an ecological perspective a competent community enjoys a productive balance between its inhabitants and their environment, allowing for change in an orderly, nondestructive manner and providing essential daily sustenance requirements for its citizens" (Fellin 1995, p. 11).

Recent advances in depicting geographical communities have paralleled the development of management information systems in organizations. Geographic Information Systems (GIS) use data to develop maps and graphics as tools to solve problems in local communities. Originally used for planning and development activities in environmental protection and natural resources management, this technology is being adapted for use in human service systems for research, social planning, management, and administration. For example, a study of youth gangs in Rockford, Illinois, reported in *The Journal of Community Practice* demonstrates the use of technology to analyze the structural dimensions of community in working toward change. An advisory council appointed by the mayor gathered data from multiple sources, then used a map of the area to overlap what had been found. From the police department they obtained gang members' addresses, and these were laid over a map of city blocks. On the same map schools and human service agencies were circled. Then demographic information and reported crime statistics were overlaid. The map with multiple data sources allowed the advisory group to have a visual representation for analyzing the problem.

> [The map] showed quite clearly that the areas suffering from the most gang-related crime and violence were in the southwest quadrant. In addition to suffering from poverty, low education levels, and the other demographic and social disadvantages . . . the southeast quadrant was very poorly served by schools, parks, and other recreational centers, and even by social service agencies. Overlay technique allowed [the advisory group] to demonstrate clearly the appropriate target population for improved services, and some of the area in which services should definitely be improved" (Hoefer, Hoefer, & Tobias 1994, p. 120).

Elements such as population characteristics and geographical boundaries will be part of the framework presented in Chapter 5 to encounter a local community. Recognizing how the use of physical space can enhance access or create barriers to community resources is important, particularly in communities with diverse population groups.

Community Functions

Earlier we cited Warren's definition of community, indicating that geographical communities are structured to perform certain functions for their members. Functionalism "regards social structures (definable social entities that exist in relationship to other structures) and social functions (the roles, purposes, and uses of the entities) in a given social system as inextricably intertwined" (Harrison 1995, p. 556). What this means is that *structures* such as schools, churches, or political entities are intertwined with *functions* such as teaching, providing leadership, or advocating for change. Harrison would take the position that understanding community would require analysis of structures and function *together*, not as separate entities.

Warren (1978), on the other hand, uses community *function* as the framework for analysis. He identified five functions performed by locality-relevant communities:

- production, distribution, consumption
- socialization
- social control
- social participation
- mutual support

Production, distribution, and consumption functions are community activities designed to meet peoples' material needs, including the most basic requirements of food, clothing, shelter, and the like. While there may have been a time when a family could produce all it consumed, those times are long since past. People today are interdependent for such basic needs as food, clothing, shelter, medical care, sanitation, employment, transportation, recreation, and other goods and services. The generally accepted medium of exchange for these goods and services is money. Money, therefore, becomes an important factor in defining the limits of consumption, and comes into consideration in most, if not all community change efforts.

A second function of community is *socialization* to the prevailing norms, traditions, and values of those with whom people interact. Young people growing up in severely deprived communities will develop value perspectives different from those growing up in affluent communities, for example. Socialization guides attitudinal development, and these attitudes and perceptions influence how people view themselves, others, and their interpersonal rights and responsibilities. To understand an individual or a population, it is important to understand the norms, traditions, and values of the community or communities in which socialization has occurred.

Social control is the process by which community members ensure compliance with norms and values by establishing laws, rules, and regulations, and by ensuring their enforcement. Social control is a function performed by institutions representing various sectors such as government, education, religion, and social services. Many social workers serve in practice settings in which they constantly strive to achieve a balance between their dual roles as helpers and agents of social control. Schools, correctional institutions, probation and parole offices, and employment and training programs are just a few examples of such settings.

Other settings and programs deal with more subtle forms of control such as patterns of service distribution and eligibility criteria that govern access to resources on the part of vulnerable groups. For example, case managers often find they must deny services when faced with limited resources. Sensitivity to these limitations may spur the practitioner to work toward change, only to discover that key policy makers prefer to restrain recipients of aid rather than provide the level of assistance really needed to combat identified problems. Recognizing how social control is manifested in social welfare policies, programs, organizations, and communities can be disillusioning, but it is necessary for understanding the structure and process of service delivery.

Social participation includes interaction with others in community groups, associations, and organizations. Communities provide an outlet for people to express their social needs and interests as well as opportunities to build natural helping and support networks. People are assumed to need some form of social outlet. Some find this outlet through local churches, some in civic organizations, and some in informal neighborhood groups. Understanding the opportunities and patterns of social participation for a target population is helpful in assessing the extent to which a community is meeting the needs of its members.

Mutual support is the function that families, friends, neighbors, volunteers, and professionals carry out in communities when they care for the sick, the unemployed, and the distressed. Most helping professions and government-sponsored programs developed in response to the inability of other social institutions (i.e., domestic units, churches, civic organizations) to meet the mutual-support needs of community members. As society grew more complex and the supportive capacity of traditional institutions such as families and neighbors was increasingly strained, professions were established to address the resulting unmet needs. Some observers believe that the service mentality developed by government and the helping professions has undermined the mutual support function in neighborhoods and communities, and has weakened the capacity for collective community problem solving (Kretzmann & McKnight 1993).

When Community Functions Fail

The above five functions, according to Warren (1978), define the purpose of a community. If all functions were performed in a given community in a manner that met the needs of all its members, (that is if all consumption, socialization, social control, social participation, and mutual support needs were met in a healthy, positive, and constructive manner), then the existing natural structures of that community would represent all the resources needed to nurture and care for its members.

However, such an "ideal" community is rarely found. Some religious communities in rural areas have been able to fulfill most of these functions in a way that precluded the need for intervention and change, but these are clearly exceptions. It is far more common to find that these functions are carried out in a way that falls short of meeting the needs of at least some community members. There may be inadequate resources for distribution and consumption, or they may be distributed unevenly. Socialization may be to a set of values supported by some community members but not others. The social control function may not operate in a fair and evenhanded manner for all. Social participation opportunities may be severely limited for some. Mutual support functions may be undermined by a dominant value system that places a premium on rugged individualism. In short, communities can be considered "healthy" or "unhealthy," "functional" or "dysfunctional," and "competent" or "incompetent" based on their ability to meet community needs, and this may be particularly true for oppressed target populations within their boundaries. We hasten to say that rarely do we find a community that can be labeled so easily one way or another. Most communities are somewhere along a continuum between the sets of terms stated above.

Building on Warren's work, Pantoja and Perry (1992) provide a working model of community development and restoration. Citing production, distribution, and consumption as the economic functional area on which all other functions are dependent, they list: socialization, social control, social placement (participation), mutual support, defense, and communication. Defense and communication are added to Warren's list.

Defense is the way in which the community takes care of and protects its members. This function becomes very important in communities that are unsafe and dangerous. Some communities have even been labeled "defended communities" in that they have to focus a great deal of effort on looking after their members. This function is relevant to nonplace communities as well. For example, the function of defense is critical for those persons who are gay or lesbian since there are groups within the larger society that may seek to do them harm. Similarly, people of color in various communities have had to support one another in defending themselves against the violence of racial hatred.

Communication includes the use of a common language and symbols to express ideas. Although communication may have been assumed as part of all the functions originally identified by Warren, its identification as a separate function in contemporary society is very important. For example, the importance of language has been the subject of much debate over political correctness as well as English-only initiatives in various states. Written communication has been revolutionized through the use of electronic mail and the ability to communicate across entire continents with the push of a computer key. Communication is a function that serves as a glue to hold people together, whether it is "verbal, written, pictorial [or an] expression through sound" (Pantoja & Perry 1992, p. 230).

The assumption underlying the identification of functions is that communities serve the needs of members by performing these functions well. Conversely, when communities are dysfunctional (Pantoja & Perry 1992) or incompetent (Fellin 1995), then people suffer and change needs to occur. According to Pantoja and Perry's model, it is when the economic function breaks down that dysfunctional communities occur. Without a stable economic base the other functions, which are supportive, deteriorate or are impaired. Therefore, it is important for the social worker to carefully assess how communities are functioning and how the needs of people are or are not being addressed.

Functional definitions and understandings of community can also be useful in communities that are not geographically specific. For example, some people may have their communication needs met by keeping in touch with persons in different geographical areas. It is not unusual to have adult children of elderly parents who live miles apart calling daily to check on how their parents are doing. In professional communities, long distance communication is carried out through telephone, fax, or e-mail on a regular basis. This assumes that people have access to the technology that facilitates this communication. For many persons these options are not available, and this raises questions about the competence of the community to meet members' needs (Fellin 1995).

Community Systems Theory

The concepts of structure and function, addressed in the previous sections, are also relevant to social systems theory. We now turn to the concept of social system as it applies to community.

Warren (1978) contended that social systems theory held great promise for understanding communities. He built on the work of Talcott Parsons, a sociologist who was known for defining the characteristics of social systems. He also built on the work of others who described how community systems would differ from the groups and formal organizations to which systems theory had previously been applied. Warren contended that a community is not just one system but a system of systems in which all types of formal and informal groups and individuals interact. Given the diversity among groups and subgroups, communities have a broad range of structural and functional possibilities which do not conform to a centralized goal. The beauty of understanding a community system is that it is a complex arena in which multiple groups with differing values can exist simultaneously. Warren defined a social system as:

> a structural organization of the interaction of units that endures through time. It has both external and internal aspects relating the system to its environment and its units to each other. It can be distinguished from its surrounding environment, performing a function called boundary maintenance. It tends to maintain an equilibrium in the sense that it adapts to changes from outside the system in such a way as to minimize the impact of the change on the organizational structure and to regularize the subsequent relationships. (Warren 1978, p. 138)

Several elements of Warren's definition are critical for understanding the community as a practice arena. His contention that a system endures through time speaks to the "sense of community" discussed earlier. Social work practitioners will work with groups that are committed to maintaining their communities and are grieving over the loss of what their communities used to be. For example, the physical land and the interactions that occurred on that land may render it sacred to Native American clients. Similarly, an elderly widow who has lived on the same street corner for 60 years may hesitate to move even when increasing crime threatens her physical safety.

Warren also identifies the structure of internal and external patterns, which he labels vertical and horizontal community linkages. Vertical linkages connect community units (people, groups, organizations) to units outside the community. These linkages are exemplified by human service agencies with headquarters outside the community, by local chapters connected with state and national umbrella organizations, and by public agencies having a central office outside the community from which they receive instruction. Horizontal connections occur within the same geographical space or locality. For example, the local nursing home may work with the neighborhood school to develop an intergenerational program for residents and children. By distinguishing between types of relationships, Warren acknowledged the complex array of possible relationships within the community and to the larger society.

Boundary maintenance is also part of systems theory. Establishing boundaries is critical to system survival. If boundaries become blurred or indistinguishable, then the community as a spacial set of relationships will become

less viable. Macro practitioners will witness the struggle for boundary maintenance in their work with communities. For example, the residents in a neighborhood that has been separated by a new highway system will face major
changes in how they view their community. The annexation of a portion of the
county into the city limits will bring protesters to city hall. The reexamination
of a planning and service area that changes who an agency can serve may
mean that clients formerly considered part of one's community will no longer
be eligible for service.

Systems theory, as applied to community, recognizes the importance of formal groups and organizations. For example, the relationship between the county health department and the public school is acknowledged as a horizontal
linkage. However, it is equally important to recognize and acknowledge informal linkages. For example, the social support that a female caregiver of an aged
parent receives from other caregivers may not be formalized or highly visible in
the community. Yet this linkage is vital to whether caregivers will be able to
continue the caregiving role. Systems thinking, therefore, is value-based thinking in that what is selected for consideration will determine what is considered
important. Since communities are complex, thinking of them as social systems
involves balancing a number of variables that are in dynamic interaction.

COMMUNITY PEOPLE, VALUES, AND INTERACTIONS

Parallel to the focus on space, structure, function, and systems is an interest in
how people behave in communities, how they understand and find meaning in
relationships, and what values guide their actions. There are many ways to
examine these aspects of community, and we will touch upon only a few ways
here. However, suggested readings listed at the end of the chapter provide
additional resources for the interested reader.

Beginning with rural communities and then expanding to urban environments, early anthropologists and sociologists explored how people related to one
another. The Lynds' 1929 study of Middletown and its 1937 follow-up provided a
cultural anthropological view of a small American city (Lynd & Lynd 1929;
1937). The study of Plainville, Illinois (a fictitious name), was similar to the Lynds'
approach (West 1945). Early studies were based on the assumption that rural
communities were able to maintain traditional values whereas cities were moving
closer to a mass society orientation in which competing values made life more
complex. We often hear these same distinctions and concerns expressed today.

Anthropologists attempted to understand the daily lives of people, their
behavior patterns and their belief systems. What emerged from these and other case studies was a recognition of the deeply held values that are inherent in
community life.

Community as Collective Identity

Clark (1973) proposes stepping back from the structural approaches to community and looking at the psychological ties that bind people in a community.

He proposes that community is indeed a sense of solidarity based on psychological identification with others. Going beyond social interactions, community is deep seated in a sense of "we-ness" that can be either place-specific or can transcend place. This sociopsychological perspective (Martinez-Brawley 1995) complements the structural approach to community in that it focuses on the meaning or "sense of community" that people feel in relationship to others.

A subcategory of collective identity or interpersonal communities is the therapeutic community that some sociologists and social workers view with skepticism. In therapeutic communities, the purpose of coming together is for the good of the individual so that he or she can be better, feel better, or do better. This quest for individualistic self-actualization carried to extremes can undermine the very concept of community as a collective notion. Leading writers have questioned "if psychological sophistication has not been bought at the price of moral impoverishment" (Bellah, Madsen, Sullivan, Swidler, & Tipton 1985, p. 139), and others call for a sense of collectivism and community as a basis for social work practice (Specht & Courtney 1994). The proliferation in the number of self-help groups is an example of how therapeutic collectivities develop around common concerns.

Cohen (1985) views the community as ripe with symbols, values, and ideologies that people have in common with one another but which also distinguish people from those who hold different beliefs. For example, the colors that a youth wears may symbolize certain values not easily recognized to someone who is not part of a particular culture. Yet wearing those colors into another community in which those colors are viewed as hostile can incite a gang war.

This relational view of community implies boundaries that are not necessarily tied to place. Boundaries may be physical, but they may also be racial, ethnic, linguistic, or religious. Boundaries may be perceptual and may even vary among those who are part of the same relational community, just as persons who are not part of that community will perceive boundaries differently. Cohen (1985) explains that it is not the clarity of boundaries that are important (for they are always changing), but it is "the symbolic aspect of community boundary" (p. 12) that is most crucial. For example, even though people may move out of a local community, the key phrases and words that they used with others will remain as symbols of their close relationship. Similarly, when a disabled person moves into a long-term care facility the ties that are maintained with persons outside the home become symbolic of returning home.

Unlike the functionalist perspective on community that focuses on culture as the integrating force that binds people together, Cohen suggests that "the commonality which is found in community need not be uniformity. It does not clone behavior or ideas. It is a commonality of forms (ways of behaving) whose content (meanings) may vary considerably among its members. The triumph of community is to so contain this variety that its inherent discordance does not subvert the apparent coherence which is expressed by its boundaries" (p. 20). Another way of expressing this perspective is that the secret of the successful community is to find unity amid diversity.

COMMUNITY POWER, POLITICS, AND CHANGE

Given the diversity within communities, the focus of much of the community literature has been on community building and creating bonds among people. However, it is vitally important to recognize political and social dynamics within communities as powerful forces that can be oppressive as well as supportive.

In Chapter 3 we introduced a framework called the dual perspective, which viewed the individual in a nurturing system that functions within the context of a larger sustaining system. The nurturing system is made up of those traditions and informal relationships in which the individual feels most comfortable. The sustaining system is made up of traditions, beliefs, values, and practices of the dominant society. This framework is important in understanding how communities contain built-in conflicts. Persons who experience divergence between nurturing and sustaining systems will be aware of community politics, power, and change as part of their daily experience. On the other hand, if there is congruence between nurturing and sustaining systems, then there may be a false sense that communities are benign or supportive of all their members.

To illustrate how norms of community are often taken for granted, Stanfield (1993) points to the importance of civic responsibility and civic cultures in African-American traditions. Historically, these traditions have been supported by institutions such as "civic associations, fraternal orders, and churches rather than businesses and finance institutions" (p. 137). While European American communities have prided themselves on a civic culture rooted in production, distribution, and consumption (the economic function of community), African-American communities have been traditionally excluded from full participation in the dominant institutions within local communities. In addition, Stanfield points out that African American communities are not just formed in response to oppression, but they are based on unique cultural attributes that find expression through the development of community.

Since civic society is treasured by dominant groups because it reflects the hallowed traditions of those in power, those same persons in power will resist the development of civil rights associations and other organizations that are dedicated to changing the status quo through political and economic empowerment. Stanfield (1993) indicates that it is critical to revise sociological concepts that are based on viewing community as grounded in structural-functionalism and social processes such as socialization. This orientation, he says, is based on a "monocultural system perspective" which views American society from a singular value perspective in which conflict is deviant. As long as there are set ways or familiar approaches to understanding community, associations and institutions created by population groups that do not conform to these accepted standards will be perceived as underdeveloped, dysfunctional, and pathological.

Understanding the politics of different communities is critical to social workers as they interact with diverse groups. For example, the meaning of volunteerism in traditional American communities translates to a formalized process in which volunteers are organized and coordinated. Stanfield (1993) points out that volunteerism in African-American communities is so integral a part of the informal nature of caring that it becomes a way of life. Yet, there is no calculation of in-kind contributions or records of volunteer time in this latter definition of volunteerism. It is not captured in anyone's log or volunteer record book. Put simply, it does not exist because it cannot be defined as "volunteerism" in traditional communities in America.

Another example of communities that do not conform to dominant criteria is provided by Kayal (1991) in his study of Gay Men's Health Crisis in New York City. Kayal analyzes how volunteerism among those in the AIDS community became absolutely necessary at a time when government support was not forthcoming. He explains how "the gay community's response to AIDS represents yet another chapter in the long American tradition of voluntary problem solving on the local level. For this reason, those most at risk were expected, even forced, to take on the burden themselves of responding to AIDS with any magnanimity, virtually alone." (p. 307) We could identify many more examples of groups that have formed locally, have responded to problems, but whose work has often not been recognized or valued within traditional understandings of community. Because social workers advocate with and for these groups, conflict is inevitable when intervening through macro practice.

Politics cannot be ignored as a part of community understanding. Feminist writers have long declared that the personal is political, indicating that every action or inaction that one takes is a political statement (Bricker-Jenkins & Hooyman 1986). We point to multiple examples of various interest groups, some more formalized than others, interacting within local communities. A political economy perspective recognizes this interplay of interest groups competing for resources within the community.

Neo-Marxist theory views social services as serving a social control function, as providing just enough resources to keep the voices of dissent from becoming louder, and in maintaining the status quo (Hasenfeld 1983). Understanding power and politics as part of community dynamics is critical to macro intervention.

CONTEMPORARY COMMUNITY THEORY AND PRACTICE

In the 1950s and 1960s sociological interest in and research on communities suffered a decline. It was assumed that mass society had replaced the concept of community (Lyon 1987), giving in to the fears that Tonnies' Gesellschaft had overwhelmed Gemeinschaft. During the past three decades there has been a nagging fear among many writers, theorists, and citizens that community has been lost and that there must be a search to regain, revitalize, and reinforce community. This fear has been magnified in national, state, and local politics as persons campaigning for public office have reinforced the importance of decentralizing government, returning control to local communities, and reestablishing family values. "Community lost" has been a theme in the popular media when people use words like "helplessness" and "disempowerment" to describe their feelings about what is happening to community life.

Putting this in perspective, however, these concerns have waxed and waned since the Industrial Revolution. Hunter (1993) points out that, "For decades, social analysts have described the disappearance of the local community in modern society, and social pundits have decried the concomitant social decay, decadence, and deviance" (p. 121). He goes on to say that a number of researchers have reminded us of the resilience of the informal relationships and structures that have maintained human relationships even prior to the advent of modern society. What is hopeful about Hunter's reminder is that he recognizes and validates what was once viewed as nonrational, short-lived, unimportant, and invisible. The relationships that women with children have formed in local neighborhoods, the plethora of self-help groups that have emerged in the past decades, the nurturing systems of racial and ethnic minorities, the voluntary associations to which people flocked, the efforts of natural helpers, and the human bonds that transcend time and space maintain semblances of community when the formal structures suffer crises in credibility, integrity, and financial viability. Essentially, Hunter declares that those linkages that we so carefully delineated as "micro" and "macro" are intricately interwoven so that if one works with individuals one will by definition have to understand community.

In the mid-1980s and into the 1990s, community scholars regained what we believe to be a more balanced perspective, indicating that both mass society and community are relevant concepts. Communities, like people, have great resilience (Lyon 1987). Of particular relevance is the rapidly increasing literature on the communal nature of people (see for example, Lohmann 1992).

The communitarian movement, postmodernism, and feminist theory converge to provide a new era for how we look at communities, organizations, and societies. Communitarianism, spawned by concerns about weakening communities in American society, appeals to people from diverse political persuasions (Harrison 1995). Arguing that the common good must be reconsidered, the communitarian movement proposes renewed community development efforts. Viewing social policies as critical to how people work together in community, principles focus on the collective rather than the individual. A leading advocate of the communitarian movement, Etzioni (1993) explains the return to local control and responsibility:

> The government should step in only to the extent that other social subsystems fail, rather than seek to replace them. . . . [A]t the same time vulnerable communities should be able to draw on the more endowed communities when they are truly unable to deal, on their own, with social duties thrust upon them. (p. 260)

Whereas theories of community provide an understanding for why communities do what they do, community action and community development writers seek to prescribe how change can occur in communities. Numerous community practice models have been and are being used by social workers to effect community change. These models are heavily grounded in systems and ecological language.

Community Practice Models

By now it should be clear that there are multiple theoretical perspectives emerging as this book is being written. Approaches to understanding communities, much less practicing in communities, are far from refined. There are multiple ways of viewing community, just as there are different and often conflicting views on how to proceed with social change. Marie Weil, Editor of the *Journal of Community Practice,* opened the first issue in 1994 with a call for clarity in connecting theory with reality. At this point, there is much room for theory development, based on what social work practitioners learn. Our advice to the reader is to recognize the complexity of community relationships and dynamics, and attempt to look at communities from different perspectives rather than to search for one integrated way. There are many ways to approach community, and practice models reflect those possibilities.

Weil and Gamble (1995) provide an overview of the community practice models used by social workers. Eight basic models are identified:

- neighborhood and community organizing
- organizing functional communities
- community social and economic development
- social planning
- program development and community liaison
- political and social action
- coalitions
- social movements

Each of these models are described and placed in a matrix according to the following comparative characteristics: desired outcome, system targeted for change, primary constituency, scope of concern, and social work roles (p. 581) (Table 4.1).

What these models reflect are the many different ways in which social workers engage in community work. They range from grass roots community organizing in which social workers participate with indigenous groups to make change, all the way to social movements that occur across geographical communities. Social movements, such as the Disability Movement (Mayerson 1993) or the Gay and Lesbian Movement (Adam 1995), are usually broad-based. They transcend geography, and often may include a wide range of people and perspectives. Social movements remind us of Warren's distinction

TABLE 4.1 Current Models of Community Practice for Social Work

Comparative Characteristics	Models							
	Neighborhood and Community Organizing	Organizing Functional Communities	Community Social and Economic Development	Social Planning	Program Development and Community Liaison	Political and Social Action	Coalitions	Social Movements
Desired outcome	Develop capacity of members to organize; change the impact of citywide planning and external development	Action for social justice focused on advocacy and on changing behaviors and attitudes; may also provide service	Initiate development plans from a grass-roots perspective; prepare citizens to make use of social and economic investments	Citywide or regional proposals for action by elected body or human services planning councils	Expansion or redirection of agency program to improve community service effectiveness; organize new service	Action for social justice focused on changing policy or policy makers	Build a multiorganizational power base large enough to influence program direction or draw down resources	Action for social justice that provides a new paradigm for a particular population group or issue
System targeted for change	Municipal government; external developers; community members	General public; government institutions	Banks; foundations; external developers; community citizens	Perspectives of community leaders; perspectives of human services leaders	Funders of agency programs; beneficiaries of agency services	Voting public; elected officials; inactive/potential participants	Elected officials; foundations; government institutions	General public; political systems
Primary constituency	Residents of neighborhood, parish, or rural county	Like-minded people in a community, region, nation, or across the globe	Low-income, marginalized, or oppressed population groups in a city or region	Elected officials; social agencies and interagency organizations	Agency board or administrators; community representatives	Citizens in a particular political jurisdiction	Organizations that have a stake in that particular issue	Leaders and organizations able to create new visions and images

TABLE 4.1   Current Models of Community Practice for Social Work   *continued*

	Models							
Comparative Characteristics	Neighborhood and Community Organizing	Organizing Functional Communities	Community Social and Economic Development	Social Planning	Program Development and Community Liaison	Political and Social Action	Coalitions	Social Movements
Scope of concern	Quality of life in the geographic area	Advocacy for particular issue or population	Income, resource, and social support development, improved basic education and leadership skills	Integration of social needs into geographic planning in public arena; human services network coordination	Service development for a specific population	Building political power; institutional change	Specified issue related to social need or concern	Social justice within society
Social work roles	Organizer Teacher Coach Facilitator	Organizer Advocate Writer/ communicator Facilitator	Negotiator Promoter Teacher Planner Manager	Researcher Proposal writer Communicator Manager	Spokesperson Planner Manager Proposal writer	Advocate Organizer Researcher Candidate	Mediator Negotiator Spokesperson	Advocate Facilitator

Source: Weil, M., and D. N. Gamble. (1995) Community practice models. In *The Encyclopedia of Social Work* (19th ed., 1: 577–93). Washington, DC: National Association of Social Workers. Reprinted with permission from NASW.

between vertical and horizontal relationships because they often connect people from multiple communities (vertical) as well as develop local chapters
(horizontal) (Jansson 1994).

A major concern is that the reader should recognize that there is not one
way or a "right" way to categorize models, strategies, and tactics. Planned
community change is a mixture of various approaches, based on careful assessment of the situation to be changed. It is critical also to recognize that since situations and problems are constantly evolving, social workers must be flexible
in altering their direction as new information emerges and reassessment occurs.

In addition, Rothman (1995) builds on the three community practice
models he originally developed in 1968, and he proposes a multi-modal
approach. His three intervention approaches are locality development, social
planning/policy, and social action. The goal of *locality development* is to
develop "community capacity and integration" through self-help, based on
the assumption that broad cross sections of the community need to engage in
problem solving. Empowerment in this mode occurs through collaborative
efforts and informed decision-making by community residents. The more
task-oriented goal of *social planning/policy* is to problem solve "with regard
to substantive community problems." Whereas locality development is more
process oriented, social planning/policy engages participants in an interaction
designed to address substantive social problems with the hope of empowering
consumers by hearing their needs and making them more informed in "their
service choices." The goal of *social action* is both process and task oriented in
that participants seek to shift "power relationship and resources" in order to
effect "institutional change." Beneficiaries of this type intervention are often
perceived to be victims of an oppressive power structure, and empowerment is
achieved when beneficiaries feel a sense of mastery in influencing community
decision-making. Rothman provides a chart that displays these three
approaches by selected practice variables (pp. 44–45). He is quick to point out
that these models are "ideal types" and that there are multiple ways in which
they can interrelate and overlap.

Community Strengths

We want to leave the reader with a contemporary perspective that we believe
is important if one is to use the various community practice models that are
available effectively. This is the strengths perspective as presented by Saleeby
(1996). Whereas communities may not be as functional or competent as we
would like, social work practitioners must be careful to assess the strengths
within the communities with which they work. Whereas one may be addressing horrible social problems such as homelessness and violence, it becomes too
easy to write off entire communities as pathological and beyond assistance.
Saleeby reminds us of words like "empowerment," "resilience," and "membership" that can lift and inspire. *Empowerment* means assisting communities
in recognizing the resources they have. *Resilience* is the potential that comes
from the energy and skill of ongoing problem-solving. *Membership* reminds

us that being a member of a community carries with it civic and moral strength. It is with a strengths perspective that we hope the reader will approach the next chapters, in which frameworks for analyzing communities and community service systems are provided.

SUMMARY

This chapter provided a very general overview of community theory and practice models used by social workers. There are multiple definitions and types of communities. Three types were briefly examined: (1) geographical, spacial, or territorial; (2) communities of identification and interest; and (3) personal networks or an individual membership in multiple communities. The planned change model presented in later chapters will be applicable to both these place and nonplace communities.

An overview of community theory revealed that community structure and function has dominated how communities are viewed. The human ecology theory, originating with the work of Robert E. Park, views communities as highly interdependent and changing. Five community functions were identified by Warren: (1) production, distribution, and consumption; (2) socialization; (3) social control; (4) social participation; and (5) mutual support. Pantoja and Perry added two additional functions: (6) defense and (7) communication. According to their approach, it is when the economic function breaks down that dysfunctional communities occur. Under structure and functional approaches, community systems theory was introduced.

Community people, values, and interactions include the human behavior within communities studied by early anthropologists and sociologists. The emergence of community as collective identity reveals that communities are ripe with symbols, values, and ideologies that people hold in common.

Community power, politics, and change are hallmarks of social work practice. Social workers often view communities as political arenas in which the power of dominant groups necessitates a change so that underserved population needs can be addressed. Understanding the politics of different communities is critical to social workers as they interact with diverse groups.

Finally, contemporary community theory and practice revealed a new interest in rethinking the value of community as an arena for future study. Various practice models were presented as a way to introduce the reader to the multiple strategies used to foster community change. We ended with a note about approaching community change using a strengths perspective.

REFERENCES

Adam, B. D. (1995) *The rise of a gay and lesbian movement*. New York: Twayne.
Bellah, R. N., R. Madsen, W. M. Sullivan, A. Swidler, and S.M. Tipton. (1985) *Habits of the heart: Individualism and commitment in American life*. New York: Harper & Row.

Bricker-Jenkins, M., and N. R. Hooyman. (1986) *Not for women only.* Silver Spring, MD: National Association of Social Workers.

Clark, D. C. (1973) The concept of community: a reexamination. *Sociological Review,* 21: 397–416.

Cohen, A. P. (1985) *The symbolic construction of community.* London: Routledge & Kegan Paul.

Etzioni, A. (1993) *The spirit of community: Rights, responsibilities, and the communitarian agenda.* New York: Crown.

Fellin, P. (1995) The Community and the Social Worker (2nd edition). Itasca, IL: F. E. Peacock.

Gerloff, R. (1992) Rediscovering the village. *Utne Reader,* 93–100.

Harrison, W. D. (1995) Community development. In *The Encyclopedia of Social Work* (19th ed., 1: 555–62). Washington, DC: National Association of Social Workers.

Hasenfeld, Y. (1983) *Human service organizations.* Englewood Cliffs, NJ: Prentice-Hall.

Hillery, G. (1955) Definitions of community: Areas of agreement. *Rural Sociology,* 20: 779–91.

Hoefer, R., R. M. Hoefer, and R. A. Tobias. (1994) Geographic information systems and human services. *Journal of Community Practice, 1*(3): 113–27.

Hunter, A. (1993) National federations: the role of voluntary organizations in linking macro and micro orders in civil society. *Nonprofit and Voluntary Sector Quarterly, 22*(2): 121–36.

Jansson, B. S. (1994) *Social policy: From theory to policy practice.* Pacific Grove, CA: Brooks/Cole.

Kayal, P. M. (1991) Gay AIDS voluntarism as political activity. *Nonprofit and Voluntary Sector Quarterly, 20*(3): 289–312.

Kretzmann, J. P., and J. L. McKnight. (1993) *Building communities from the inside out.* Evanston, IL: Northwestern University, Center for Urban Affairs and Policy Research.

Lohmann, R. A. (1992) *The commons.* San Francisco: Jossey-Bass.

Lynd, R. S., and H. M. Lynd. (1929) *Middletown: a study in contemporary American culture.* New York: Harcourt & Brace.

Lynd, R. S., and H. M. Lynd. (1937) *Middletown in transition: a study in cultural conflicts.* New York: Harcourt & Brace.

Lyon, L. (1987) *The community in urban society.* Philadelphia: Temple University Press.

Martinez-Brawley, E. E. (1995) Community. In *Encyclopedia of Social Work,* (19th ed., 1: 539–48). Washington, DC: National Association of Social Workers.

Mayerson, A. (1993) The history of the ADA: A movement perspective. In L. O. Gostin and H. A. Beyer, eds., *Implementing the Americans with Disabilities Act: Rights and responsibilities of all Americans* (pp. 17–24). Baltimore: Paul H. Brookes.

Pantoja, A., and W. Perry. (1992) Community development and restoration: a perspective. In F. G. Rivera and J. L. Erlich, eds., *Community organizing in a diverse society* (pp. 223–49). Boston: Allyn & Bacon.

Park, R. E. (1983) Human ecology. In R. L. Warren and L. Lyon, eds., *New perspectives on the American community* (pp. 27–36). Homewood, IL: Dorsey Press.

Rothman, J. (1995) Approaches to community intervention. In J. Rothman, J. L. Erlich, and J. E. Tropman, eds., *Strategies for community intervention* (5th ed., pp. 26–63). Itasca, IL: F.E. Peacock.

Rothman, F., J. L. Erlich, and J. E. Tropman, eds. *Strategies for community intervention* (5th ed.). Itasca, IL: F. E. Peacock.

Saleeby, D. (1996) The strengths perspective in social work practice: Extensions and cautions. *Social Work, 41*(3): 296–305.

Specht, H., and M. Courtney. (1994) *Unfaithful angels.* New York: Free Press.

Stanfield, J. H. (1993) African American traditions of civic responsibility. *Nonprofit and Voluntary Sector Quarterly, 22*(2): 137–53.

Tonnies, F. (1987/1957) *Community and society* (Gemeinschaft und Gesellschaft) (C.P. Loomis, trans., ed.). East Lansing: Michigan State University Press. (Original work published 1887).

Warren, R. L. (1978) *The community in America* (3rd ed.). Chicago: Rand McNally.

Weil, M., and D. N. Gamble. (1995) Community practice models. In *The Encyclopedia of Social Work* (19th ed., 1: 577–93). Washington, DC: National Association of Social Workers.

West, J. (1945) *Plainville, U.S.A.* New York: Columbia University Press.

SUGGESTED READINGS

Alcorn, S., and J. D. Morrison. (1994) Community planning that is "caught" and "taught": Experiential learning from town meetings. *Journal of Community Practice, 1*(4): 27–43.

Bailey, D., and K. M. Koney. (1995) Community-based consortia: One model for creation and development. *Journal of Community Practice, 2*(1): 21–42.

Coulton, C. J. (1996) Poverty, work, and community: A Research Agenda for an era of diminishing federal responsibility. *Social Work, 41*(5): 509–19.

Figueira-McDonough, J. (1995) Community organization and the underclass: Exploring new practice directions. *Social Service Review, 69*(1): 57–85.

Gutierrez, L. M., and E. A. Lewis. (1994) Community organizing with women of color: A feminist approach. *Journal of Community Practice, 1*(2): 23–44.

Hummon, D. M. (1990) *Commonplaces: community ideology and identity in American culture.* Albany: State University of New York.

Inglehart, A. P., and R. M. Becerra. (1995) *Social services and the ethnic community.* Boston: Allyn & Bacon.

Mancoske, R. J., and J. M. Hunzeker (1994) Advocating for community services coordination: An empowerment perspective for planning AIDS services. *Journal of Community Practice, 1*(3): 49–58.

Mary, N. L. (1994) Social work, economic conversion, and community practice: Where are the social workers? *Journal of Community Practice, 1*(4): 7–25.

Mizrahi, T., and J. D. Morrison, eds. (1993) *Community organization and social administration: Advances, trends and emerging principles.* New York: Haworth.

Odendahl, T., and M. O'Neill, eds. (1994) *Women and power in the nonprofit sector.* San Francisco: Jossey-Bass.

Perlmutter, F. D., ed. (1994) *Women and social change.* Washington, DC: National Association of Social Workers.

Rosenthal, S. J., and J. M. Cairns. (1994) Child abuse prevention: The community as co-worker. *Journal of Community Practice, 1*(4): 45–61.

Weil, M. O. (1996) Community building: Building community practice. *Social Work, 41*(5): 481–499.

CHAPTER 5

Understanding and Analyzing Community Strengths and Problems

Setting out to understand a community is a major undertaking. Often long-time residents will comment, "I've lived here for 40 years and I still don't understand this town!" How, then, can a student or practitioner hope to understand something as complex as a community, much less propose ways to change it?

First, it should be made clear that there is no one accepted, orderly, systematic method that allows one to understand all the elements that go into making up a community. Understanding, for the macro practitioner, means gathering as much data and information as possible in a narrowly focused area of interest or concern, within the time frame allotted, and making the best informed decisions the information will allow.

There are three reasons why macro practitioners need a systematic approach to conceptualizing a community, its strengths, and social problems. First, the person-in-environment view is critical to professional social work practice. The community in which one lives has a lot to do with who one is, the problems one faces, and resources available to deal with these problems. Professional social work prescriptions may not be feasible or realistic without an understanding of these community influences. The framework presented here for understanding community is designed to assist in conceptualizing the environment within which clients experience hope and draw strength, as well as face oppression and frustration.

Second, community-level macro change requires an understanding of the history and development of a community as well as an analysis of its current status and subgroups. Without this knowledge, the practitioner has a limited grasp of the breadth and depth of values, attitudes, and traditions and their significance in either maintaining the status quo or allowing for change.

Third, communities constantly change. Individuals and groups move into power, economic structures change, sources of funding change, and citizens' roles change. A framework for understanding and analyzing community can be helpful in recognizing and interpreting these changes.

TWO COMMUNITY VIGNETTES

Vignette 1: Canyon City

Located in the western United States, Canyon City had a population of 60,000 people in 1970. Twenty-five years later Canyon City had grown to 250,000 and was continuing to grow when other major cities had long since declined. Because the city was populated by many persons who had moved to the western Sunbelt to follow job opportunities, many of its residents were not native to the area. Census data indicated that 20 percent of Canyon City's population were Hispanic, 60 percent were White not of Hispanic origin, 10 percent were Native American, 5 percent were African American, and another 5 percent were Asian American.

Encountering the Community.   A recent social work graduate took a position in a multiservice agency in Canyon City. One of her tasks was to develop a program to address the needs of battered women in the community. Data from the police department and various other sources revealed a high incidence of domestic violence within the community relative to other communities of similar size. The social worker was new to Canyon City, having lived in another part of the country most of her life. She viewed this chance to understand and analyze the community with great anticipation.

She began her work by talking with a number of police officers, social workers, medical personnel, and others who had expertise in domestic violence. Through these contacts, she was able to locate a few women who were willing to talk with her confidentially about their situations. She learned that each woman perceived the situation somewhat differently. Based on numerous conversations she found that there was a general sense of isolation within the community, that neighbors did not always tend to know one another and that newcomers felt it was hard to become part of the community. Given the transient nature of the community and its rapid growth, this was not surprising. It was soon clear that people tended to focus on the problems and to talk about how awful the situation was. She had to probe for information on community strengths.

The strengths of Canyon City were many. First, community members seemed willing to acknowledge the problem and were anxious to address it. She encountered few people who denied that something needed to be done. Second, there was diversity within the community that made for a rich mix of customs, traditions, and values. Third, there were several women's groups in Canyon City who were willing to volunteer their efforts to whatever program was developed. Fourth, a foundation was willing to fund a well-designed project.

Narrowing the Focus.   In the course of collecting data and defining boundaries, the social worker determined that the problem of domestic violence was being addressed in several pockets of the community. There were three battered women's shelters within the city, but they served only a part of the entire community. A counseling service for persons dealing with domestic violence was available, but only to those who could afford the service. It became clear that persons who were not being served by the shelters and the counseling service were primarily Hispanic women. She began to narrow her focus to address their needs.

The social worker had to be careful to recognize the diverse cultural traditions and beliefs of this target population. There were a number of models for developing shelters, safe homes, and services for white middle-class women, but few that focused on women of color. The social worker found that Hispanic women in the community often provided shelter for one another but that this imposed an excessive financial burden upon these women. She began to talk with Hispanic women about how to design a program that would be sensitive and relevant to identified needs.

In the process she also discovered additional community strengths. There was a strong sense of community among many Hispanic women who had lived in the area most of their lives. There were informal associations of women that were not identified in any listings of services or programs because they were not as formalized as other groups. This informal network was a source of pride in the community, yet these relationships were not recognized in Canyon City as a whole. Two Hispanic churches had identified domestic violence as their theme for the coming year and were willing to work with the social worker and her agency. A support group for women of color had been meeting in one of the churches for several years.

Mobilizing Resources.   In a period of several weeks, the social worker had realized that there were more resources in the community than she had originally anticipated. However, she had also discovered that there were definite locations of power. Community leaders among the women of color were not visible in the larger community, and had often felt invisible in the decision-making process. Within her own agency, she found that members of the Board of Directors were not certain they wanted to focus on women of color because they had originally identified the problems of all women in the community. The foundation was willing to fund a project that would focus on Hispanic women's needs, but their board members wanted to be assured that the funds would be used to do something "innovative" rather than duplicating an existing model. They also were willing to fund the project only if it would be self-sufficient within three years. The women's shelters that were already open were cautious about supporting the new program concept for fear that it might call attention to their failure to serve many women of color in the past. The women's support group in the local church was concerned that they would lose their focus and become part of a bigger project that would take them away from their feeling of closeness and intimacy.

It was the social worker's job to continue to collect information and to determine the project's feasibility. Although it was time consuming, she continued to hear the perspectives of various women who had been battered and to include them in the development of a community project.

Vignette 2: Lakeside

Lakeside was a planned community developed in the 1930s. The downtown area was built around a small lake, surrounded by weeping willow trees. The Baptist, Methodist, and Presbyterian churches sat side by side along the lake front, forming what was known as "church circle." Each of the Protestant denominations had a children's home, and the Methodist Home for Orphaned Children built in 1902 was a local landmark.

The population in Lakeside during the 1930s was approximately 20,000 people. The majority of employees worked for a major office products manufacturing company, making Lakeside "a company town." There were other businesses in town that manufactured paper, building supplies, and various other products.

Major Changes Occur.   By the 1970s Lakeside had grown to 35,000 persons and the community was going through a number of changes. Many residents had moved to various suburbs outside the downtown area and had taken jobs in a larger city nearby, creating problems for the economic base of the town. The various manufacturing companies had experienced occasional layoffs that made community residents feel uncertain about job security and advancement.

Several public housing developments for elderly and disabled persons had been built downtown. The Methodist Children's Home began targeting services to the elderly as well as to children, since orphans were few in number but the number of older persons was increasing.

Whereas Lakeside had been a haven for Protestant families and diversity had been limited, the population was changing. In 1930 only one Catholic church and one Jewish synagogue were located in Lakeside. In 1975 there was a mosque, two AME Zion churches, and a number of splinter groups had formed from the mainline churches on "church circle". In 1930, 20 percent of the downtown population was African American. By 1975, African Americans comprised 60 percent of the downtown population. The "church circle" remained a centerpiece in the community around the lake, but many of the members commuted to houses of worship from outside the city limits.

How Things Had Changed.   One social worker at the Methodist Home was assigned to work with older persons and persons with disabilities in Lakeside. She found that the three public housing developments in Lakeside housed many of her clients. The target population, however, was very diverse in terms of age, disability, and race. Elderly residents ranged in age from 60 to 105. However, persons with disabilities ranged in age from 25 to 95. Fifty-five percent of the public housing community was African American, with only 2 percent Hispanic and 43% white.

Many of the residents had lived in Lakeside all their lives and knew many of the other residents. Also, there was a large senior citizens center housed in an old department store that had moved to the mall. Many of the residents had family in the area and felt "connected" with that region of the country.

The social worker was pleased to learn about these strengths, but she was also aware of the problems that had emerged in Lakeside. There was a definite sense of racial tension in the town. There was also tension between the old-old and young persons with disabilities who were living in the same apartment buildings. Older clients complained about loud music and partying at all hours of the night. Younger persons were frustrated at "being forced" to live with old people. The major stores in the downtown area had been vacated and mobile community members shopped in the mall. Persons without transportation, however, walked to the remaining few stores downtown, where prices were high and bargains were few. Getting Social Security Checks cashed at the one downtown grocery store meant paying a three-dollar fee for cashing privileges.

Amid these tensions and concerns had arisen a tremendous amount of fear. Two older women who lived alone had been murdered in the past two months, and now a third female victim had just been found. In a small community, this was the "talk of the town," and no one felt safe anymore. Elderly women who lived in the downtown area were being cautioned to keep their doors locked at all times, not to let strangers in, and to call 911 if they had any reason to be suspicious of anyone. A neighborhood crime watch association had been organized and volunteer escorts were available in the evening hours for anyone having to go out alone. The police department had contacted the social worker so that they could work together, and the senior center was holding self-defense classes. The social worker heard older residents complain over and over again that Lakeside just wasn't the community they had known.

Communities change, and it is not unusual for residents to grieve over the loss of what has been. Some changes are planned, such as the deliberate attempts in Vignette 1 to develop a project that would address the needs of Hispanic women who have been abused. Other changes are unplanned, such as the way in which the "planned" community of Lakeside's downtown area changed.

The two vignettes offer a glimpse at what social workers in community practice arenas experience. In Canyon City, the social worker encountered a growing city with much diversity. In Lakeside the social worker found a city that was no longer vital and growing. However, both discovered strengths and problems, tensions and frustrations. Both found that the inclusion of multiple perspectives was important but complicated the analysis. For example, in Vignette 1 the social worker had to deal with the power dynamics between a possible funding source, local women's shelters that were already established, and Hispanic women whose voices were not always heard. In Vignette 2 the social worker encountered racial as well as intergenerational tensions among residents of downtown public housing developments.

Each vignette requires asking many questions in order to know how to intervene. This chapter provides questions with which one might begin to conceptualize communities like Canyon City and Lakeside from the perspective of the target populations served.

A FRAMEWORK FOR CONCEPTUALIZING COMMUNITY

A first step toward understanding community is creating a framework that will help in comparing elements in one community with elements in another. Some communities are larger than others, some have different ethnic make-ups, some are wealthier than others.

In searching for a framework to help understand community, we turn to Warren (1978), who proposes that communities can be better understood if selected community variables are analyzed. Building on his work, we have identified eight tasks that comprise a four-step framework to be used in understanding and analyzing a community. In subsequent chapters, we will present methods for planning changes based on this understanding. This framework is shown in Table 5.1.

Focus A: Identifying Target Populations

Many approaches to community analysis propose that the community be understood in its totality to the greatest extent possible before intervention is planned. We propose, instead, that the definition of community be narrowed by first selecting a target population, and that the community be understood from the perspective of the concerns and needs of that population. The target population is defined as those individuals, families, and/or groups who are experiencing a problem or need and for whose benefit some type of community change is being considered.

The choice of a particular target population is a choice of values. In every community there are multiple groups with varying needs. Therefore, the social worker must realize that in focusing on one target population, he or she is making a choice to examine the community from a specific perspective. It will be important, then, to go back and look at the community again from the perspective of more than one target population so that a richer understanding can develop. For example, existing reports on community issues and populations may predetermine what target group the practitioner will serve, with only limited opportunity to familiarize oneself with other community needs and concerns.

We suggest that a community be analyzed and understood from this limited perspective because (1) practically speaking people who become involved in community change are generally people with full-time jobs and other responsibilities, and it is not unusual that macro-level intervention responsibilities are added on top of those jobs; and (2) there is a limit to the amount of

TABLE 5.1   The Community Encounter Framework

	Focus	Variable		Task
A.	Identifying the Target Population	People	1.	To understand characteristics of target population members and their perceptions of the community.
B.	Determining Community Characteristics	Space	2.	To identify geographic boundaries of the community toward which a change effort is to be targeted.
		Social Problems	3.	To establish a profile of problems affecting the target population within the community.
		Values	4.	To observe and understand dominant values affecting the target population within the community.
C.	Recognizing Differences	Oppression	5.	To recognize ways in which the target population has been formally or covertly restricted by powerful persons and/or institutions.
		Discrimination	6.	To assess evidence that the target population has been subjected to discrimination in the community.
D.	Identifying Structure	Power	7.	To recognize stakeholders and where power is located in addressing target population needs.
		Resources	8.	To inventory resource availability in relation to target population needs within the community.
		Patterns of Community Control and Citizen Participation	9.	To determine who provides and who controls resource delivery to the target population within the community.

information that can be used in macro-level interventions. In short, we do not disagree with those who suggest that, in the ideal, everything possible should be known and understood about a community. We are simply suggesting that, with limited time and resources, responsible change efforts can be initiated by narrowing the parameters of community analysis.

Identifying a population in need can, in itself, be complex because none of us is a part of only one community. Community can be defined in terms of ethnicity (e.g., the Latino community), religion (e.g., the Catholic community), commitment to a position (e.g., the pro-choice community), profession (e.g., the social work community), avocational interest (e.g., recreational and sports enthusiasts), and many other designations. Each of us are part of many different communities at the same time.

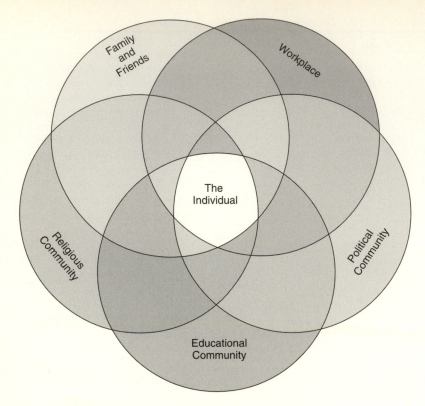

FIGURE 5.1   The Individual Within the Community

We recognize that there are differences in urban, suburban, and rural communities and that this approach may be difficult in a rural community where members of the target population are geographically dispersed. We also caution the reader not to assume that the target population can be disengaged or isolated from the larger community, even though one may focus on the target population in order to manage this complex undertaking. In fact, members of the target population may already feel isolated from the larger community. Certainly, we do not want to reinforce this sense of isolation.

Viewed graphically, a community would look like a series of overlapping circles. As an individual, any person from a community, pictured graphically, might look like a circle subdivided into many different reference groups, as illustrated in Figure 5.1.

By beginning with a population in need, we are suggesting that a person attempting to understand a community first identify the population of focus. This begins a narrowing-down process. Initial definitions of population can be broad, with the understanding that the more precise the definition selected, the more feasible a full understanding of the community context for this population.

For example, issues surrounding alcoholism prompt a concern for macro-level change, the population of focus for a particular community analysis could be "people with alcohol problems who live in Riverdale County" or it could be "ethnic minority women alcoholics who have been convicted of driving while intoxicated within the past two years in Riverdale County." One is more inclusive, the other more focused. It is probably advisable, at this early stage, that a broader definition be adopted, with an understanding that it will become more precise as a clearer understanding of needed change emerges.

Once a population has been identified and the definition appropriately narrowed, all other dimensions of the community are explored and examined from the perspective of that population. For each dimension to be explored, we will identify a task intended to bring focus to the collection of data and information. We will next focus on questions to be asked about the population. Finally, we will propose some questions to be asked about a community that will aid in understanding each dimension and in comparing it to other communities. Although this framework contains a number of tasks, the process of analyzing any community requires the social worker to go back and forth, returning to refine previous tasks as new information is gathered. The social worker is urged to use the framework as an interactive and iterative guide rather than a rigid formula for approaching community.

Task 1: *Understand Characteristics of Target Population Members.*
Questions to be asked for this task include:

- What is known about the history of the target population in this community?
- How many persons comprise the target population, and what are their relevant characteristics?
- How do persons in the target population perceive their needs?
- How do persons in the target population perceive their community and its responsiveness to their needs?

In their book on community organization, Brager, Specht, and Torczyner (1987) remind us that:

> Demographic differences [do not] exhaust the variations among subgroups of the poor. Although attitudinal differences are more difficult to define and identify, a wide diversity of world views exists even within demographically homogenous populations. Thus, some poor are more alienated than others, some more upwardly aspiring, and some angrier. Where they fall on these dimensions has a bearing on how they will respond to particular efforts to involve them in organizing projects. (p. 60)

It is precisely these shades of difference about the target population that the macro practitioner is attempting to understand. The study usually begins with an examination of available demographic data. Basic to any understanding is analysis of socioeconomic status, age, race, and gender by census tract. It is important to identify areas of poverty and high need and to determine whether the target population is heavily concentrated in these areas or is spread across an entire county.

In addition to gathering statistics, it is important also to talk with people who understand its history, as perceived by the target population. Bellah, Madsen, Sullivan, Swidler, and Tipton (1985) explain why this is important:

> A community is a group of people who are socially interdependent, who participate together in discussion and decision-making, and who share certain practices that both define the community and are nurtured by it. Such a community is not quickly formed. It almost always has a history and so is also a community of memory, defined in part by its past and its memory of its past. (p. 313)

Examining the characteristics of the target population and identifying where they are located, together with gathering information from the perspective of people in the target population, completes the first task in the community encounter.

The following questions can be helpful in collecting and using data and information:

1. What are the key demographic characteristics of the target population, and how do they compare to the demographic profile of the various political subdivisions (e.g., city, county, state, whichever is relevant) within which the community is located? Key demographic characteristics should include at least socioeconomic-status variables, race, gender, and age, by census tract.
2. Generally, how do people in this target population (and others close to them) perceive their concerns, problems, issues, and/or needs? Do they tend to see them in terms of a need for empowerment, freedom from oppression? In terms of access to opportunity, removal of barriers? In terms of a need for resources? In terms of protection? In terms of a need for services?
3. Generally, how do people in this target population perceive the community's responsiveness to their concerns, problems, issues, and/or needs?

Focus B: Determining Community Characteristics

Size is an important characteristic of a community, and it can be assessed in a number of ways. Size can be calculated in terms of the amount of space covered, by the number of people living within its boundaries, or both. It is an important characteristic for the macro practitioner because geographical boundaries established for macro-level interventions can range from neighborhood to county and even larger. Clearly, the size of the community as defined will affect the nature of the macro-level analysis, and ultimately the intervention.

Task 2: Identify Community Boundaries.   Among the questions to be asked for this task are:

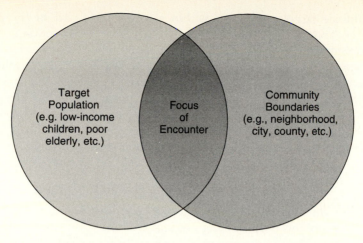

FIGURE 5.2   **Setting Parameters for the Community Encounter**

- What are the geographical boundaries within which intervention on behalf of the target population will occur?
- Where are members of the target population located within the geographical boundaries?
- What physical or social barriers exist for the target population?
- How compatible are jurisdictional boundaries of health and human service programs that serve the target population?

Space is the distance or area covered by a community. It is one dimension of a community's size. Focusing on space allows the practitioner to establish manageable boundaries. If resources are available to focus on the entire city or county, then these may be appropriate boundaries in that instance. If, however, the effort is to be undertaken by a small committee of volunteers who have limited time and resources available, then one may decide to focus the encounter on a limited part of the city in which there appears to be the greatest need for intervention.

Establishing boundaries for macro-level intervention, therefore, is initially done by focusing on a target population and is further refined by selecting a geographical boundary. For most initial macro-level interventions we recommend beginning one's understanding of community by limiting boundaries to county or its equivalent, and focusing down from that level to more limited boundaries if appropriate. This is in no way intended to indicate that intervention at state, regional, or national levels is not appropriate. It is simply to recognize that, for the vast majority of interventions, a level of county or smaller will be most relevant.

Figure 5.2 illustrates the boundary-setting process. Knowing that one cannot address all target population needs within large arenas, the encounter focuses on the target population within a manageable part of the broader community. This becomes the focus of the macro-level intervention.

A community may be a small section of the inner city or a fairly large expanse encompassing scattered farms in a rural area. For example, community as space is applicable to barrios in which groups of Hispanic people reside within a larger metropolitan area. Spatial concepts of community are also relevant in less population-dense areas but may be more difficult to determine. This was pointed out by a Navajo social worker who explained how difficult it was to determine spatial boundaries on a reservation. There were no street systems, property information and signs indicating county lines, or well-defined human service areas.

Another characteristic important in understanding community as space is jurisdictional units established by various government agencies for planning and service-provision purposes (e.g., school districts or mental health catchment areas). Since the macro practitioner's focus is typically limited to a designated geographical area, mapping overlapping jurisdictional units can be important and useful. For example, a change agent may be working with people in a particular county to establish a prenatal health care campaign for pregnant teens, only to discover that he or she is dealing with representatives from county and multiple city governments. Establishing who is responsible within what geographical domain can be extremely important politically. Similarly, the practitioner hired by a mental health clinic may find that the clinic's geographical boundaries overlap parts of three school districts, requiring letters of agreement with multiple school boards. It pays to know the geographical parameters of various institutional units within the community of focus.

A third characteristic related to space and helpful in understanding target populations is that of service accessibility. If health and human service organizations are scattered across a broad area and there is limited public or other transportation, consumers may find that they are simply not able to make use of existing services. Centrally located multiservice centers, on the other hand, may make problems much more manageable.

To gain a better understanding of community as space, it may be helpful to attempt to answer the following questions:

- Is the target population highly concentrated or scattered through identified community boundaries?
- What jurisdictional boundaries overlap within the community?
- How accessible are services for the target population?

Task 3: Profile Social Problems.   Important questions include:

- What are the major social problems affecting the target population within this community?
- Are there subgroups of the target population who are experiencing major social problems?

- What data are available on the identified social problems, and how are available data used within the community?
- Who collects the data, and is this an ongoing process?

Macro-level interventions tend to be conceptualized and organized around a selected population and a specific problem they are experiencing. For example, a social worker might discover a lack of child-care options for teen parents who wish to return to school, or an increasing problem of malnutrition among isolated elderly, or a community made up primarily of African Americans and Latinos who believe their requests are not receiving a fair hearing by the city council.

This is not to indicate, however, that any target population experiences only one problem at any one time. If one is to understand a target population, we propose that one must understand as much as possible about the social problems they experience. Do people in this population tend to have limited or adequate financial resources? Are transportation options limited? Is unemployment a prevalent problem? How widespread is drug or alcohol abuse?

Understanding social problems helps in two ways: (1) it enables the macro practitioner to appreciate the full range of difficulties experienced by the target population, thereby helping to prioritize needs, and (2) it should help in proposing more realistic solutions. For example, sometimes a transportation need must be addressed before a service can be offered.

Social problems are negatively labeled conditions recognized by community residents. Identified social problems will vary by community and by target population. Sometimes there are conditions that exist that have not been labeled as a problem. It may be the social worker's task to bring these conditions to the attention of people in power so that they are recognized as social problems. This is not always easy because some community residents may have a great deal invested in denying that there is a problem.

The purpose of establishing a profile is to understand conditions affecting the target population. This requires both direct contact and library research. Direct contact with people who can articulate the problems and needs of the target population gives the practitioner a first-person interpretation of issues. Library research adds theoretical knowledge about identified social problems, as well as practice and research findings based on the experiences of others with the same or similar populations and problems.

We cannot emphasize strongly enough the importance of original, indigenous, authoritative sources in understanding a target population. Populations must be understood in terms of their diversity. In family practice, for example, the meaning of family—of husband-wife relationships, of parent-child relationships, of aging grandparent roles—may differ from one culture to the next. Similarly, the ways in which members of the gay and lesbian community define family may depart radically from traditional community values. A target population will not be adequately understood if these potentially widely divergent views are not taken into consideration.

Once major social problems defined by community members have been identified, one can begin to determine their incidence and prevalence. "Incidence refers to the actual occurrence of a phenomenon during a time period." For example, 15 students may have been arrested for drug use in the local high school in the most recent academic year. "Prevalence refers to the number of cases or instances of a phenomenon existing in a community group at a given time" (Kettner, Daley, & Nichols 1985, p. 72). For example, current estimates indicate that drug use among teenagers is as high as 50 percent.

Social-indicator data may be helpful in gaining a broad overview of social problems at the national, regional, state, and local levels. In this way the community's social problems can be comparatively assessed. Other professionals in the community, or at the county or state levels, can also be valuable sources of information. They may have firsthand experience with the target population, or their organizations may have conducted surveys or collected statistics on specific social problems. The local public, college, or university library may also provide many documents valuable in understanding local problems and needs. Accessing information electronically via the Internet is important as well.

Pursuing answers to the following questions will aid in understanding the major social problems experienced by the target population:

1. What data sources are available to aid in understanding a community's social problems?
2. What are the major social problems affecting the target population as perceived by their spokespersons?
3. To what extent are they interconnected? Must some be solved before others can be addressed?

Task 4: Understand Dominant Values   Questions to be asked for this task include:

- What cultural values, traditions, or beliefs are important to the target population?
- What are the predominant values that affect the target population within the community?
- What groups and individuals espouse these values, and who opposes them?
- What are the value conflicts surrounding the target population?

Another variable to be considered in attempting to understand a community is values. *Values* are strongly held beliefs, and *community values* are those beliefs that are strongly held by persons who make up the community. These values are often reinforced by the associations and organizations with which community residents affiliate.

The idea of shared values requires refinement in today's changing world. At one time, communities without divisions of labor may have been more likely to have shared value systems. As people specialized, community members had limited understanding of what other persons in the community did for a living. In addition, differentiation of interests and associations occurred as society shifted from primary groups (face-to-face groups such as families and neighbors) to secondary groups (more formalized groups and organizations). Local associations became chapters of national organizations, tying their members into an extracommunity network. Technological advances made it possible to maintain contact with others who were geographically dispersed. Given these changes, one must take care not to assume a single, common, shared value system in contemporary communities. Also, the social worker must not assume that members of the target population have equal access to these advances in technology.

Depending on the selected target population, practitioners will find a host of value perspectives. For example, if the target population is people with AIDS, some persons in the community will feel strongly that they deserve the best possible care and comfort, while others will react in fear, not wanting people with AIDS in their local acute and long-term care facilities. Similarly, if the target population is pregnant teens, value conflicts may arise between community residents who believe that teens should be given contraceptive information and those who believe that this information will only encourage sexual activity.

Jansson (1988) states that "value clarification lies at the heart of social welfare" (p. 6). He identifies five moral issues that drive decision making. Applied to the target population within a local community, the following questions arise:

1. Should the target population receive services, and on what terms?
2. For what needs and problems is the community responsible, and what target population needs should receive priority?
3. What strategies should be used to address specific target population problems?
4. Should the community give preferential assistance or treatment to the target population?
5. Should the community use its resources to address target population needs?

These five value-clarification questions may be answered differently depending on the population targeted within the community. This series of questions implies that some populations may be valued more than others—that some persons may be perceived as "deserving" and others as "undeserving." Whereas there may be an outcry to treat drug-addicted infants, their addicted mothers may be treated with disdain. Whereas homeless families may be perceived as "down on their luck," homeless alcoholics may be seen as "bringing this upon themselves."

Depending on the target population group, there may be subgroups within the larger whole that are viewed differently. Recognition of the importance of diversity will lead the macro practitioner to check carefully the values of each ethnic or racial group affected, the possible different perspectives of women and men, and younger and older adults in the target population, and the perspectives of representatives of gay and lesbian groups, if they are affected by the change. It is far wiser to take the time to be inclusive of a wide range of values than to find out, too late, that a change effort is not working because differing perspectives were overlooked. Change agents should go into this value-clarification exercise understanding that they may not always like what is discovered about community values, but struggling with value conflicts will give the change agent some understanding of how much the community is committed to addressing the needs of the target population.

As one begins to form an understanding of major community-value perspectives, one must take care to recognize the fit (or lack of fit) between target population perspectives and dominant community perspectives. Are target population perspectives taken into consideration when decisions are made that affect them? Recognizing value differences and power discrepancies is an important part of the community-analysis process.

Answering the following questions may help in understanding community values and the potential for conflict:

1. How do people in, and close to, the target population perceive the etiology of their current problems?
2. What are alternative perspectives on the etiology of these current problems?
3. Which perspectives are held by community leaders?
4. How widespread is the support for target population perspectives?
5. How do people in this community feel about giving and receiving help?
6. What are the predominant shared perspectives in this community on inclusion of the target population in decisions that affect them?

Focus C: Recognizing Differences

Up to this point we have examined two areas of focus relevant to understanding communities: identifying target populations and determining community characteristics. We turn now to a third area of focus: recognizing differences. No matter what target population one identifies, there will be differences between this population and other groups within the community. There will also be differences within the target population. Potential differences include culture, race, ethnicity, gender, age, and a host of other factors.

The "dynamics of difference" (Cross, Bazron, Dennis, & Isaacs 1989, p. 20) may involve cross-cultural exchanges, in which groups with diverse histories and values interact. There is always room for misunderstanding and misinterpretation when this occurs. "Both will bring culturally-prescribed patterns of communication, etiquette, and problem-solving. Both may bring stereotypes or underlying feelings about serving or being served by someone who is 'different'" (Cross et al. 1989, p. 20). For example, professionals who serve the elderly may rationalize why they do not serve many Hispanic clients by stereotyping Hispanic families as taking care of their own, and therefore needing few formal services. This oversimplification may ignore the fact that one fourth of the Hispanic families in a local community are poor, and caring for an older family member is a tremendous financial burden. It also ignores the fact that all Hispanic elderly do not have other family members residing in the community.

Differences may be subtle or taken for granted, yet they may influence the way in which members of the target population communicate with one another and with other groups. Feminist writers encourage the recognition of gender differences in psychological development (Gilligan 1982), in interpreting the world (Belenky, Clinchy, Goldberger, & Tarule 1986), and in communication (Tannen 1990). Tannen's research indicates that men and women speak in separate dialects or "genderlects" that comprise "cross cultural communication" (p. 18). For example, a male social worker was assessing a community's responsiveness to single mothers with young children. He attended several support groups for the target population and was frustrated that all they did was talk without coming to a consensus on what they wanted from the larger community. He assessed part of the problem as an unwillingness on the part of the target population to face up to their problems and to work on solutions. The women in the support group, however, felt that this was an opportunity to process their thoughts and feelings. They did not view the group as a place to raise problems for immediate resolution. The group was a place to make connections and to achieve intimacy.

Task 5: Identify Formal and Covert Mechanisms of Oppression. Among the questions to be asked are:

- What differences are observed among members of the target population?
- What differences are observed between members of the target population and other groups within the community?
- How are target population differences viewed by the larger community?
- Is the target population oppressed because of these differences?
- What target population strengths can be identified, and how might these strengths contribute to empowerment?

Oppression is "the social act of placing severe restrictions on a group or institution. Typically, a government or political organization that is in power places these restrictions formally or covertly on oppressed groups so that they may be exploited and less able to compete with other social groups" (Barker 1995, p. 265). Oppression focuses on differences, the assumption being that some group is lesser than, not as good as, or less worthy than others.

Some people are uncomfortable with differences, and because they assume that one way must be better than another they look on differences as a problem to be solved. An alternative perspective is that differences reflect a variety of ways to view the world, to believe, and to behave. Social workers can employ differences as potential strengths within a target population, but they must remember that differences often include alternative definitions of a successful outcome. For example, in the women's group described above, the social worker was frustrated because he believed the group members were not solving their problems. For the members, however, the group itself was something of a solution. It provided a forum in which single mothers could share their concerns and find understanding and support. This forum could, in turn, serve as a foundation on which additional solutions might be built.

Areas around which oppression often occurs are gender, race, ethnicity, sexual orientation, age, and disability. Depending on the target population, all of the resulting "-isms" or selected ones may be relevant. In many cases, the target population may be defined as persons affected by one or more of the "-isms."

Sexism is discrimination based on attitudes and assumptions about gender. Often these attitudes become barriers to community participation even though they are subtle and difficult to identify. They exist in the values, norms, and traditions of a society to be translated into local community activities. For example, as children are socialized in their educational and familial roles they are given messages regarding what is considered appropriate for women and men. Bricker-Jenkins and Hooyman (1986) propose that patriarchy within the community be examined. They suggest that the recording of history and the establishment of myths that set direction for succeeding generations are parts of a patriarchal system in which experiences of women tend to be devalued as subordinate to those of their male colleagues.

The devaluation of the homemaker role may also be an important form of sexism. Many women feel compelled to enter the workplace, not so much by economic pressures, but by societal pressures. So much of one's identity is derived from work, yet women's housework, volunteering, childbearing, child rearing, and caregiving (eg, elderly parents) are not considered economically productive (Waring 1988).

Access to employment and services may, in some instances, limit opportunities for women. For example, women may be limited to homemaker roles because work opportunities are not readily available close to home. Lack of services such as day care and transportation may limit access to employment. Inadequate transportation systems within the community may require women to transport children, limiting their abilities to be engaged in some types of employment as well as other pursuits in which they may have an interest (Fellin 1995). Groups such as the displaced homemakers' network or public offices that deal with equal employment opportunity complaints may be able to help in understanding gender-based practices that affect the target population.

Clearly the most serious type of oppression against women is violence. Statistics on violence against women and resources to deal with this problem are available from such organizations as women's support groups, women's centers, or shelters for battered women (Kasper & Aponte 1996).

Racism is stereotyping and generalizing about people based on the physiological characteristics of their racial group. Ethnic groups share a common language, customs, history, culture, race, religion, or origin. *Ethnocentrism* implies that one's own ethnic group is superior to others (Barker 1995).

The terms *ghetto* and *barrio* are important in understanding racial and ethnic communities. Choldin (1985) defines *ghetto* as a "bounded geographical residential area in which a defined racial or ethnic group is forced to live" (p. 236). *Barrio* describes neighborhoods with large proportions of Hispanic people. Within the ghetto and barrio, residents develop their own culturally driven interactions and ways of looking at the larger society. In many large cities, ethnic communities are named according to the group that occupies that portion of the city—the Polish community, for example (Fellin 1995).

Barrera, Munoz, and Ornelas (1972) view the barrio as an internal colony. "To be colonized means to be affected in every aspect of one's life: political, economic, social, cultural, and psychological" (p. 467). The internal colony is based on four interrelated concepts: (1) forced entry, (2) cultural impact, (3) external administration, and (4) racism.

Forced entry implies that the colonized group has no choice in being a part of the dominant society. Because of this involuntary process, the cultural impact of the dominant culture transforms and destroys indigenous values and the ways of responding. *External administration* speaks to the management of the colonized group by the dominant group, based on a racist perspective that assumes the superiority of the managers. Barrera et al. reject the possibility of assimilation into the larger society because they believe that trading the Chicano culture for the dominant society would result in a bland, consumer-oriented replacement of a rich tradition.

The target population may encompass one or more racial or ethnic groups. Information on such factors as rates of employment, educational achievement, and socioeconomic status within these subgroups is important to understanding effects of institutional racism. Involvement of persons from different groups within the target population in decision-making roles is an important indicator of sensitivity to ethnic and cultural issues. Service to people from diverse ethnicities in the target population proportionate to their numbers in the community is another.

Homophobia is a term used to describe irrational fears held by people toward others who have a same-gender sexual orientation. Homophobia, in the extreme, has taken the form of "gay bashing," a practice of physically beating gay men. In other forms, homophobia results in job discrimination, ridicule, and ostracizing. Like all prejudices (literally, "prejudgments"), homophobia blinds those afflicted with it to individual qualities of lesbian women and gay men and causes them to be perceived only in the context of their sexual orientation.

Ageism is stereotyping and generalizing about people because of their age, and *ableism* is discrimination against those who are not considered physically or functionally able to perform as well as others.

Although older persons are often perceived as being too physically or mentally limited to engage in ongoing community activities, only 5 percent of persons over 65 are institutionalized and an additional 12 percent need some in-home care (Rabin & Stockton 1987, p. 156). Clearly, however, the vast majority are capable of self-sufficiency and productive lives, yet they may be excluded from employment and from playing an important role in the community because of perceptions about their abilities. The same treatment is often experienced by people of any age who have physical or functional limitations.

If age or disability is relevant to understanding the target population, statistics on the numbers and age ranges of those persons in the community should be compiled. How many persons are frail elderly (85+)? How many persons are physically disabled, and what types of disabilities have been documented? Is there adequate access to services that engage persons with disabilities in active community roles—transportation and outreach, for example? Are there support services (e.g., nutrition programs, homemaker, respite) that sustain these persons and their caregivers?

Gathering data in response to the following questions will help in understanding the impact of discrimination on selected subpopulations of the target population:

1. What percentage of the target population are people of color, ethnic group members, women, gay or lesbian, older persons, or persons with disabilities?
2. What do available data and information indicate about quality-of-life factors as they affect people of color as compared with other community members? Women as compared with men? Homosexual or bisexual as compared with heterosexual? Elderly or disabled as compared with younger or persons without disabilities?
3. To what extent are the perspectives of people of color, women, gays and lesbians, older persons, and persons with disabilities sought in decisions affecting the target population?

Task 6: Identify Evidence of Discrimination.   The two key questions to be asked for this task are:

• Are there barriers that inhibit the target population from becoming fully integrated into the community?
• What forms of discrimination are experienced by the target population within the community?

Identifying value conflicts is critical to recognizing oppression and discrimination. Values may be based on prejudices, prejudgements that community residents have about the target group that are not grounded in systematic evidence. The issue of systematic evidence is one that needs to be treated with a great deal of care and sensitivity. Many people still believe that every individual essentially controls his or her own destiny, and that hard work and persistence will overcome any barrier or limitation. This belief is reinforced when severely disabled persons accomplish incredible physical feats or severely deprived persons make it to the top.

These accomplishments become "evidence" for local, state, and national leaders that those who need help are simply not trying hard enough. People who hold this belief look at what they consider to be systematic evidence and deny that their beliefs are prejudices. What is overlooked here, however, is generations of differential treatment that have made it difficult for people of color, for women, for persons with physical and developmental disabilities, and others to have equal access to economic resources and self-sufficiency. So, for example, when a job is available and a homeless person chooses not to take it, one person will see that as evidence that he is lazy while another will recognize it as a response to a lifetime of hopeless, discouraging, dead-end jobs. For some, the pain of life on the street is less than the pain of hopelessness in their share of the workplace.

Prejudices are intimately tied to values and may affect how a person feels. Discrimination is acting out those prejudices. These actions can be observed in the differences in quality of life between the target population and the rest of the community.

For example, existing data indicate that, "most of the elderly poor are female (72%) and either black (40%) or Hispanic (26%).... To be old, female, nonwhite, and living alone is to bear the heaviest burden of all. An astonishing 55% of that multimarked contingent lives *below* the poverty level" (Margolis 1990, p. 10). This is the type of evidence that points to generations of blocked opportunities, discrimination, and neglect. Serious damage is done to the fabric of the country, and therefore to the fabric of its communities, when any group of people is discriminated against as a whole category, when an individual is treated only as a member of a group, and when individual differences are disregarded. To many who are victims of this attitude, the message is that it doesn't matter how hard they work, how honest and law-abiding they are, how much they play by the rules; they can never escape discrimination and oppression because they are lifetime members of the group.

Recognizing discriminatory behavior is important in assessing the community. These questions may assist in the process:

1. What barriers have been identified that inhibit the target population from being a part of the larger community?
2. What community groups, organizations, rules, procedures, or policies discriminate for or against the target population?

Focus D: Identifying Structure

The fourth area of focus in the pursuit of understanding a community is structure. Its purpose is to ground the macro practitioner in recognizing the distribution of power, the provision and allocation of resources, and the patterns of service distribution that affect the target population within the community.

Task 7: Recognize Locations of Power.   Central questions to be asked include:

- What are the primary sources of funding (both local and extracommunity) for health and human services designed for the target population within the community?
- Are there strong leaders within the segment of the health and human service community that serves the target population?
- What type of community power structure influences the service-delivery network designed for the target population?

Originally primary groups, composed of families, friends, and neighbors performed the functions necessary for community survival. Gradually, business and government have assumed many of these functions. The most obvious change occurred during the New Deal era in the mid-1930s when government reluctantly responded to the social welfare needs of a post-Depression society. At that time, the balance between public and private service provision shifted, with public dollars taking over an increasing share of human service funding.

Urbanization and industrialization have also greatly affected the social, political, and economic structures of this country. One of the major areas of impact, noted by Warren (1978), was the separation of a person's working life from where he or she lives. Because of this change, people who hold power change, depending on the way in which a community is defined.

As local and extracommunity ties have expanded, so has bureaucratization and its accompanying impersonalization. Bureaucratic structures are usually adopted by government, business, and voluntary organizations as size of population served increases. Funding patterns can lead to power brokers external to the community. Major sources of funding for local service efforts imply the ability to influence and direct provider decisions in regard to target population needs. For example, the specialized volunteer-run community-based agency that once served the neighborhood may have been transformed into a multiservice agency with many paid staff. This means that there may be a number of new leaders within the health and human service system, all representing different sectors of the economy. In addition, the larger multiservice organization may have multiple funding sources, including federal, state, and local government funds, United Way, private contributions, and fees. Each source must be satisfied that its expectations are being met.

Viewing the community from a power perspective requires identifying the formal and informal leaders within a community. It also means examining their effectiveness in getting things done. Assessing the political climate requires reading local newspapers and talking with local community leaders to determine top-priority issues competing for funding. If a legislative change is needed, it is necessary to identify who may be willing to take the lead on issues affecting the target population.

Community power has been viewed from three perspectives: (1) an elitist structure, (2) a pluralist structure, and (3) an amorphous structure. An elitist approach assumes that a small number of people have disproportionate power in various community sectors. A pluralist perspective implies that as issues change, various interest groups and shifting coalitions arise. This perspective may be increasing as more and more special-interest groups develop within the local community. The amorphous structure implies no persistent pattern of power relationships within the community (Meenaghan, Washington, & Ryan 1982).

Gaining a growing understanding of the community's power dynamics will enable the practitioner to evaluate the community on these questions:

1. Who are the major community leaders who will respond to concerns of the target population?
2. Who are the major community leaders who will oppose requests from the target population?
3. What public and private resources are available to deal with target population needs?
4. What individuals or groups control the resources required to bring about needed changes for the target population?

Task 8: Determine Resource Availability.   Among the questions to be asked are:

- What are the existing community agencies and groups currently seen as major service providers to the target population?
- What are the major funding sources for services to the target population?
- What nonmonetary resources are needed and available?

Also related to community structure is the issue of available resources. Communities can be described as resource-rich or resource-poor when it comes to providing for the needs of the target population. While it is important to consider resources in connection with power, as discussed above, it is also important to compile information on resources so that appropriate sources will be targeted in pursuit of community change.

There are many types of resources to consider. Resources may be very tangible, such as a welfare check, or highly symbolic, such as caring or social support. Resources can be grouped into six categories: love, status, information, money, goods, and services (Specht 1986). Most early community encounters will focus heavily upon the more concrete resources that are exchanged (money, goods, and services) because tangible resources are easier to define and observe. However, as the professional becomes more actively engaged in community practice, there will be more and more opportunities to learn about the more symbolic exchanges (love, status, and information) that are equally important to members of the target population.

Resources may be available from a number of different domains. King and Mayers (1984) developed guidelines for community assessment designed for use in analyzing community resources for minority elderly. Their framework, presented as Table 5.2, is a tool that may be helpful in examining community resources for selected target populations. It suggests that, in assessing community resources available to a particular population, a number of

TABLE 5.2   Guidelines for Community Assessment

1. Target population groups
   a. Age distribution
   b. Socioeconomic, ethnic, and religious characteristics
   c. Organizational and political affiliations
2. Health resources (hospitals; district health centers; dental, mental health, and other specialized outpatient clinics, etc.)
   a. Service policies, practices, and limitations
   b. Admission practices (eligibility and waiting list)
   c. Distance from community
3. Welfare resources (human services, food stamps, senior citizens' centers)
   a. Service policies, practices, limitations
   b. Admission practices (eligibility, waiting lists, dropout after intake, short-term services, etc.)
   c. Distance from community
4. Educational resources (public schools, community and four-year colleges, other educational institutions)
   a. Admission policies, practices, limitations
   b. Program offerings
   c. Fees and payment procedures
   d. Locations
5. Housing resources (public and private)
   a. Condition of housing stock
   b. Availability of housing units
   c. Public housing policies affecting senior citizens
   d. Tenant involvement in policy determination
6. Recreational facilities (public and private)
   a. Senior centers
   b. Parks, clubs, sporting outlets
   c. Special services for older people
7. Additional resources
   a. Courts and criminal justice systems
   b. Consumer affairs and citizen protection advocates (public and private non-profit)

Source: King, S. W., and Mayers, R. S. (1984). A course syllabus on developing self-help groups among minority elderly. In J. S. McNeil and S.W. King, eds. *Guidelines for developing mental health and minority aging curriculum with a focus on self-help groups.* Publication supported by National Institute on Mental Health Grant #MH 15944-04 pp. 8–9.
Reprinted with permission from Dr. John S. McNeil, School of Social Work, University of Texas at Austin.

domains be explored (e.g., health, welfare, education, etc.). Within each domain, questions of policy, practice, eligibility, location and participation must be addressed in order to determine how available each resource is to the target population.

For example, if the target population is low-income children, resources to be explored would include child welfare services, day-care services, the educational system, and others. How effective are these systems in meeting the needs of the community's children and satisfying the expectations of the community? If the target population is low-income families, a thorough analysis would require exploration of the services designed to meet basic needs of food, clothing, shelter, and health care.

The major focus of the macro practitioner, however, will in most instances be the formal health and human service network that serves the target population. Formal government service systems as currently designed in most communities in the 1990s, however, operate in close cooperation with a whole network of nonprofit community organizations. For example, a child and family agency may provide counseling funded by local government, child welfare services under contract with state government, federally funded congregate meals, and home-delivered meals through private contributions and a grant from a religious denomination.

Having examined the resources available to the target population, those involved in community analysis should attempt to address the following questions:

1. What resources are available from the following systems:
   - Health
   - Welfare
   - Education
   - Housing
   - Recreation
   - Employment
   - Business
   - Religion
   - Others
2. What factors affect how the target population accesses and utilizes resources within the community?

Task 9: Identify Patterns of Resource Control and Service Delivery.

Questions to be asked relative to this task include:
- What groups and associations advocate for and provide assistance to the target population?
- How is resource distribution to the target population influenced by interaction within the community?
- How is resource distribution to the target population influenced by extracommunity forces?

In 1954 the urban renewal program acknowledged the importance of participation by persons affected by change within the community. Administrative regulations required that "citizen participation" be incorporated into planning in order to legitimize change efforts and to change citizen attitudes. During the 1960s citizen participation took on new meaning. The War on Poverty programs were some of the first to mandate that consumer groups should have a voice in planning. Agencies created by the Community Action Program (CAP) were fundamental in including the poor in community decision making. Attempts to phase out CAP agencies under the Nixon administration failed because constituents had become too strong and CAP agencies were closely aligned with local government. These poverty programs institutionalized citizen participation as a legitimate means of involving community people in mutual aid exchanges initiated by the federal government (Burke 1968). In recent years, requirements for participation have weakened or disappeared along with the traditional poverty programs. Depending on the target population, the practitioner may find varying degrees of citizen participation efforts influencing patterns of service distribution within the community.

When assessing patterns and levels of participation, it is important that the macro practitioner distinguish between citizen and consumer-client participation. There are many citizens who, for reasons of altruism and conviction, are committed to fight for the rights of the poor and oppressed. They bring a certain perspective to the discussion, and make a contribution to constructive change in communities. However, it should not be assumed that interested citizen advocates represent the same perspective as the persons directly affected by the problem. Representatives of the target population should, whenever possible, be sought out to represent themselves in their own words; it should not be left to professionals and other concerned citizens to speak for them.

When dealing with the question of control over service availability to a target population, there can be both intracommunity and extracommunity sources of control. In practice, external and internal patterned interactions tend to develop as community units work together (Fellin 1995). Examples of extracommunity sources of control are county, state and federal government funding of community-based health clinics. Resources are typically allocated through contracts that include regulations and expectations. Various human service agencies within the local community, then, interact with these extracommunity public entities. Relationships internal to a community have an important part in linking community subsystems together. Organizations with similar interests often form loosely knit federations to accomplish certain functions where there are common interests. For example, several women's groups may form a coalition to establish a battered women's shelter.

Not only are there horizontal relationships that tie one to local informal and formal groups and organizations within the community, there are also numerous vertical ties that transcend geographical boundaries. Local community autonomy may be reduced as extracommunity forces influence what one does and how one thinks. The importance of extracommunity forces on the target population within the local community must be considered in order to understand service distribution patterns. On the other hand, extracommunity forces may actually strengthen communities by providing more options and additional resources.

How powerful the controlling entities become in a community often depends on the extent of citizen participation. Burke (1968) describes five citizen participation roles:

1. Review and comment
2. Consultation
3. Advisory
4. Shared decision making
5. Controlled decision making

One role is to review proposals for change within communities. This review process may be carried out in committee meetings, through requests for feedback from selected individuals, or through public hearings. It is a very limited role, and comments may or may not be incorporated. Consultation involves giving opinions on the change when asked. An advisory role usually involves a formal ongoing mechanism such as a United Way advisory council or planning committee, the purpose of which is to react to all factors affecting the target population. While advisory committees do not have the power of policy boards, they can have a strong voice because of their access to decision makers.

Shared decision making is clearly a stronger role than advising, and places citizens and consumers in roles in which they can, in collaboration with community leaders and professionals, affect decisions. Finally, controlled decision making places citizens and consumers in positions of power over decisions such as policy statements, review boards, or membership on boards of directors. These types of positions allow for the greatest amount of control by citizens and consumers. For example, a consumer who serves on the governing board of a family service agency may convince other board members that quality day-care services for single mothers should be a top agency priority.

One cannot assume that citizen participation automatically goes hand in hand with changes practitioners initiate within the community. The concept of citizen participation is essential to democracy, but it will often involve groups who disagree with one another. Just as citizens may comprise the local board of Planned Parenthood, there are citizens who believe that some of the services offered by this agency are morally wrong. Whenever interested citizens and consumers participate in community activities, these types of clashes in perspective should be expected.

A review of the following questions will be helpful in assessing control and citizen participation in a community:

1. What organizations internal to the community exercise control over decision making for services to the target population?
2. What organizations external to the community exercise control?
3. What limits are placed on services to the target population, and who establishes these limits?
4. What roles do citizens and consumers play in the control of services to the target population?

SUMMARY

We began this chapter by discussing three reasons why macro practitioners need a framework for assessing communities. First, social work in general and macro practice in particular require an orientation toward the person-in-environment perspective. In this chapter, the community in which the target population functions comprises the environment. Second, communities change and professionals need a framework for understanding these changes. We have discussed nine tasks that provide insight into how the target population is served within the community. Third, macro-level change requires an understanding of the history and development of a community as well as an analysis of its current status.

The community encounter provides one method of analyzing what has occurred and is occurring within the designated arena. Skilled macro practice requires (1) focused and precise data collection, (2) analysis of historical trends, and (3) a thorough understanding of qualitative elements that reflect human experiences, interactions, and relationships.

REFERENCES

Barker, R. L. (1995) *The social work dictionary*. Washington, DC: National Association of Social Workers.

Barrera, M., C. Munoz, and C. Ornelas. (1972) The barrio as an internal colony. *Urban Affairs Annual Review, 6*: 480–98.

Belenky, M. F., B. M. Clinchy, N. R. Goldberger, and J. M. Tarule. (1986) *Women's ways of knowing*. New York: Basic Books.

Bellah, R. N., R. Madsen, W. M. Sullivan, A. Swidler, and S. M. Tipton. (1985) *Habits of the heart: Individualism and commitment in American life*. New York: Harper & Row.

Brager, G., H. Specht, and J. L. Torczyner. (1987) *Community organizing*. New York: Columbia University Press.

Bricker-Jenkins, M., and N. R. Hooyman, eds. (1986) *Not for women only*. Silver Spring, MD: National Association of Social Workers.

Burke, E. M. (1968) Citizen participation strategies. *Journal of the American Institute of Planners, 34*(5): 293.

Choldin, H. M. (1985) *Cities and suburbs*. New York: McGraw-Hill.

Cross, T. L., B. J. Bazron, K. W. Dennis, and M. R. Isaacs. (1989) *Towards a culturally competent system of care*. Washington, DC: Georgetown University Child Development Center.

Fellin, P. (1995) *The community and the social worker*. Itasca, IL: Peacock.

Gilligan, C. (1982) *In a different voice*. Cambridge, MA: Harvard University Press.

Jansson, B. S. (1988) *The reluctant welfare state: A history of American social welfare policies*. Belmont, CA: Wadsworth.

Kasper, B., and C. I. Aponte. (1996) Women, violence and fear: One community's experience. *Affilia, 11*(2): 179–94.

Kettner, P. M., J. M. Daley, and A. W. Nichols. (1985) *Initiating change in organizations and communities*. Monterey, CA: Brooks/Cole.

King, S. W., and R. S. Mayers. (1984) A course syllabus on developing self-help groups among minority elderly. In J. S. McNeil and S. W. King, eds., *Guidelines for developing mental health and minority aging curriculum with a focus on self-help groups*. Publication Supported by National Institute Mental Health Grant #MH 15944-04.

Margolis, R. J. (1990) *Risking old age in America*. Boulder, CO: Westview Press.

Meenaghan, T., R. O. Washington, and R. M. Ryan. (1982) *Macro practice in the human services*. New York: Free Press.

Rabin, D. L., and P. Stockton. (1987) *Long-term care for the elderly: A factbook*. Oxford: Oxford University Press.

Specht, H. (1986) Social support, social networks, social exchange, and social work practice. *Social Service Review, 60*(2): 218–40.

Tannen, D. (1990) *You just don't understand*. New York: Williams Morrow.

Waring, M. (1988) *If women counted*. San Francisco: Harper & Row.

Warren, R. L. (1978) *The community in America* (3rd ed.). Chicago: Rand McNally.

SUGGESTED READINGS

Benedict, A., J. Shaw, and L. G. Rivlin. (1992) Attitudes toward homeless persons of those attending New York City community board meetings. *Nonprofit and Voluntary Sector Quarterly, 21*(1): 69–80.

Castex, G. M. (1994) Providing services to Hispanic/Latino populations: Profiles in diversity. *Social Work, 39*: 288–96.

Checkoway, B. (1991) Neighborhood needs and organizational resources: New lessons from Detroit. *Nonprofit and Voluntary Sector Quarterly, 20*(2): 173–89.

Cuba, L., and D. Hummon. (1993) A place to call home: Identification with dwelling, community, and region. *The Sociological Quarterly, 34*(1): 111–31.

Figueira-McDonough, J. (1991) Community structure and delinquency: A typology. *Social Service Review, 65*(1): 68–91.

Figueira-McDonough, J. (1995) Community organization and the underclass: Exploring new practice directions. *Social Service Review, 69*(1): 57–85.

Lazzari, M. M., H. R. Ford, and K. J. Haughey. (1996) Making a difference: Women of action in the community. *Social Work, 41*(2): 197–205.

Lee, J. A. B. (1994) *The empowerment approach to social work practice*. New York: Columbia University Press.

McLaughlin, M., M. Irby, and J. Langman. (1994) *Urban sanctuaries: Neighborhood organizations in the lives and futures of inner city youth*. San Francisco: Jossey-Bass.

Oropesa, S. R. (1995) The ironies of human resource mobilization by neighborhood associations. *Nonprofit and Voluntary Sector Quarterly, 24*(3): 235–52.

Parsons, R. J., and E. O. Cox. (1994) *Empowerment-oriented social work practice with the elderly*. Pacific Grove, CA: Brooks/Cole.

Rivera, F. G., and J. L. Erlich. (1992) *Community organizing in a diverse society*. Boston: Allyn & Bacon.

Rousseau, M. (1991) *Community: the tie that binds*. New York: University Press of America.

Saleeby, D. (1996) The strengths perspective in social work practice: extensions and cautions. *Social Work, 41*(3): 296–305.

APPENDIX

Framework for Conceptualizing Community

FOCUS A: IDENTIFYING TARGET POPULATIONS

Task 1: Understand Characteristics of Target Population Members

- What is known about the history of the target population in this community?
- How many persons comprise the target population, and what are their relevant characteristics?
- How do persons in the target population perceive their needs?
- How do persons in the target population perceive their community and its responsiveness to their needs?

FOCUS B: DETERMINING COMMUNITY CHARACTERISTICS

Task 2: Identify Community Boundaries

- What are the geographical boundaries within which intervention on behalf of the target population will occur?
- Where are members of the target population located within the geographical boundaries?
- What physical or social barriers exist for the target population?
- How compatible are jurisdictional boundaries of health and human service programs that serve the target population?

Task 3: Profile Social Problems

- What are the major social problems affecting the target population within this community?
- Are there subgroups of the target population who are experiencing major social problems?

- What data are available on the identified social problems, and how are available data used within the community?
- Who collects the data, and is this an ongoing process?

Task 4: Understand Dominant Values

- What cultural values, traditions, or beliefs are important to the target population?
- What are the predominant values that affect the target population within the community?
- What groups and individuals espouse these values and who opposes them?
- What are the value conflicts surrounding the target population?

FOCUS C: RECOGNIZING DIFFERENCES

Task 5: Identify Formal and Covert Mechanisms of Oppression

- What differences are observed among members of the target population?
- What differences are observed between members of the target population and other groups within the community?
- How are target population differences viewed by the larger community?
- Is the target population oppressed because of these differences?
- What target population strengths can be identified, and how might these strengths contribute to empowerment?

Task 6: Identify Evidence of Discrimination

- Are there barriers that inhibit the target population from becoming fully integrated into the community?
- What forms of discrimination are experienced by the target population within the community?

FOCUS D: IDENTIFYING STRUCTURE

Task 7: Recognize Locations of Power

- What are the primary sources of funding (both local and extracommunity) for health and human services designed for the target population within the community?
- Are there strong leaders within the segment of the health and human service community that serves the target population?

- What type of community power structure influences the service-delivery network designed for the target population?

Task 8: Determine Resource Availability

- What are the existing community agencies and groups currently seen as major service providers to the target population?
- What are the major funding sources for services to the target population?
- What nonmonetary resources are needed and available?

Task 9: Identify Patterns of Resource Control and Service Delivery

- What groups and associations advocate for and provide assistance to the target population?
- How is resource distribution to the target population influenced by interaction within the community?
- How is resource distribution to the target population influenced by extra-community forces?

CHAPTER 6

Understanding a Community Human Service System

In any situation in which an assessment is called for, whether it be an assessment of an individual, a family, or an entire community, it is helpful to use a framework. A framework aids in identifying each of the variables to be examined, just as was done in the previous chapter. In this chapter we will propose a conceptual approach intended to permit a student or practitioner to examine a constellation of services within a given locale to determine adequacy of existing resources to deal with current or projected levels of need.

While we will use the term human service *system* to describe the focus of the assessment, we caution students and practitioners not to place too much emphasis or credence in this term. There is rarely a master plan. Human service systems are generally made up of loosely related or unrelated client-serving programs operating under a variety of auspices, rather than clearly planned parts that come together into a comprehensive whole. We will attempt to present a framework for assessing the extent to which this network of existing resources is capable of meeting need.

A FRAMEWORK FOR ANALYZING COMMUNITY HUMAN SERVICE SYSTEMS

We approach the assessment of a community's existing human service system with several assumptions, as follows: (1) that an entire human service system in most communities is too complex to analyze as a whole, and therefore services must be assessed for a specified target population, (2) that a community's human service system should be assessed and evaluated in relation to the extent to which it meets the needs of its people, and (3) that the needs of people in a community should be examined not only in terms of individual need, but also in terms of collective need.

Following these assumptions, we propose a framework for analyzing and evaluating a community's human service system. The tasks that comprise this framework are shown in Table 6.1.

Focus A: Understanding Need

Task 1: Identify the Target Population.   Questions to be asked in relation to this task include:

- What target populations have been identified as being in need of services within the community, and how are they categorized?
- What target population will be the focus of this assessment?

TABLE 6.1   Framework for Assessing Community Human Service Systems

Focus	Tasks
A. Understanding need	1. Identify the target population
	2. Define continuum of need
	3. Assess target population needs
	4. Identify collective community needs
B. Identifying auspices or sponsoring organizations	5. Examine informal service-delivery units
	6. Examine mediating service-delivery units
	7. Examine formal service-delivery units
C. Determining systemic competence	8. Determine linkages between units

- What priority is given to the needs of the target population in this community?

People who are identified as being in a target population are consumers of services, and ideally the services provided are designed to meet their needs. However, it is important to recognize that people's needs are always changing. This requires a human service system that has flexibility to respond to changing needs. Gonzalez, Gonzalez, Freeman, and Howard-Pitney (1991) remind us that even cultural identity changes. "One can always expect to find both change and diversity within any community. In fact, even a community that appears to represent one culture or cultural group will actually be quite mixed, demonstrating a range of behaviors and beliefs that are common to that culture" (p. 2). Because the characteristics of community residents vary, there may be subgroups that require special attention. For example, if a community has a high proportion of retirees, one can expect that many of the services will address the needs of older people. If services are not available, the delivery system may not be adequately addressing community needs.

For the sake of discussion, consider the following seven target populations. They are frequently used for planning purposes, and funding tends to be clustered around these categories:

- Children
- Youth
- Families
- Older adults
- Adults
- Developmentally disabled persons
- Physically/mentally disabled persons

Obviously, these groups are neither exhaustive nor mutually exclusive. In addition, they do not specify the many subgroups that fall within each category. For example, if the target population is children, it is important to recognize that children come from families of all socioeconomic statuses, racial and ethnic groups, and locations within a community.

Although we have identified seven categories of people who may have some common characteristics and needs, individual communities will have their own definitions of target populations. How does the community categorize client groups for planning purposes? Local and regional planning agencies, United Ways, community councils, and associations of agencies often produce agreed-upon classification schemes for data collection and planning purposes. Regardless of existing categories, it is ultimately the task of the individual or group doing the community assessment to define the target population.

Task 2: Define a Continuum of Need.   The main question related to this task is:

- How can target population needs be conceptualized so that a determination can be made about the extent to which they are (or are not) being met?

Need is a concept that has been defined in a number of ways. Meenaghan, Washington, and Ryan (1982) define need as "any identifiable condition that limits a person as an individual or a family member in meeting his or her full potential" (p. 168). They go on to identify four ways in which needs are quantified:

1. The need represents an identified social, economic, or health-related problem of individuals and/or families.
2. The problem affects categories of individuals (or families) with similar characteristics.
3. Persons affected may be located in a defined geographic area.
4. The identified problem may be directly addressed by some current or future service that may be provided by an organization or individual.

Abraham Maslow developed a hierarchical framework for understanding lower- and higher-level needs. Maslow's hierarchy of needs moves from the most basic survival or physiological needs to the next higher level of safety and security needs, to social or belonging needs, to esteem or ego needs, and finally to the highest level of self-actualization needs, as depicted in Figure 6.1.

Maslow hypothesized that lower-level needs must be addressed before an individual can move on to the next level. At any point at which a lower-level need is not being met, one regresses down the hierarchy to satisfy that unmet need. Lower-level needs usually require a more immediate response, thus having high urgency.

This framework can be useful in rank ordering and assessing the needs of a target population and using this understanding of needs to assess adequacy of services. The assessment task is one of defining more specifically the problems faced by the target population at each level and identifying the extent of met and unmet need in relation to each problem. For example, for the target population of the elderly, problems can be defined as follows:

Survival Needs

- Some elderly are malnourished;
- Some elderly are not able to meet their daily personal needs/perform basic activities of daily living;
- Some elderly have no place to live, etc.

Safety and Security Needs

- Some elderly are abused;
- Some elderly are neglected;
- Some elderly are victims of crime, etc.

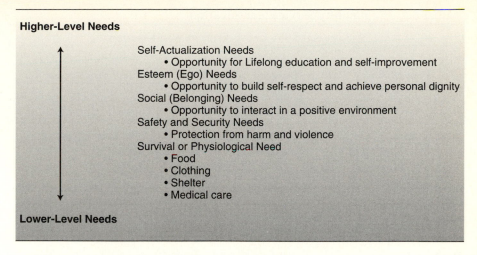

Higher-Level Needs

Self-Actualization Needs
• Opportunity for Lifelong education and self-improvement
Esteem (Ego) Needs
• Opportunity to build self-respect and achieve personal dignity
Social (Belonging) Needs
• Opportunity to interact in a positive environment
Safety and Security Needs
• Protection from harm and violence
Survival or Physiological Need
• Food
• Clothing
• Shelter
• Medical care

Lower-Level Needs

FIGURE 6.1   Maslow's Hierarchy of Needs

Table 6.2 illustrates an approach to identifying needs and resources for widows aged 85+ living alone in the hypothetical community of West Kingston. It allows the practitioner to use the hierarchy of needs concept to assess what services are available within the local community. By categorizing these services according to Maslow's framework, priority services that address the survival or safety and security needs of this vulnerable target population can be identified. Whereas medical and personal care services appear to be available in this community, transportation and in-home services are very limited, if they exist at all. For elderly widows living alone in Kingston, therefore, a crisis would most likely be handled in an institutional setting because there would be limited services available to them in their homes. Similarly, if they required a more sheltered environment, a variety of housing options would not be available in Kingston. The hierarchy-of-needs framework, therefore, allows the practitioner to identify needs in order of urgency as well as potential gaps in available services for the target population.

Pantoja and Perry (1992) view the "nature of the human person [and] his/her dimensions and the needs these create" (p. 229) in discussing a community development perspective. They begin, as does Maslow, with basic biological needs such as food, rest, and medicine. They then discuss the need for love and belonging (a second level of biological need); for groups and relationships, particularly in times of emergency (social); for self-expression through symbols such as art and language (cultural); for learning from the past (historical); for the use of power (political); for viewing the past, present, and future through action, words, and movement (creative/spiritual); and for explana-

TABLE 6.2   **Community Service Identification**

	Widows Aged 85+ Living Alone in West Kingston	
Type of Need	Services Typically Designed to Meet Need	Services Available in This Community
Self actualization needs	Educational programs Volunteer opportunities	Available at Kingston Senior Center
Esteem needs	Support groups Psychosocial counseling Mental health centers	Two support groups Mental health center has limited services
Social needs	Recreational and social groups Senior centers Home visitors	One senior center
Safety and security needs	Emergency response system Adult family homes Congregate care facilities Senior housing Continuing care retirement communities Wellness clinics Telephone contact	No emergency system Three unlicensed homes One congregate facility No senior housing No retirement community Public health department has wellness clinic Church runs telephone reassurance program
Survival needs	Home delivered meals Senior discounts Mobile meals Transportation Homemaker Home health Personal care Medical care	Limited delivered meals program 20 mobile meals slots No bus system, one senior van available One licensed homemaker program No home health provider Two licensed personal care agencies One community hospital and one nursing home

tions that connect what happens in one's world through investigation and experimentation (intellectual).

Task 3: Assess Target Population Needs.   Under this task the key question is:

- What are feasible and appropriate ways to find out how many people are in need in each of the areas of need identified as relevant to this target population?

Eight general methods of approaching a needs assessment have been discussed in the literature. They include (1) *general population surveys,* which consist of interviews with a sample of community residents; (2) *target population surveys,* which interview members of a select group; (3) *service provider surveys,* which interview the groups and organizations that serve the target population within the community; (4) *key informant surveys,* which focus on knowledgeable and influential community residents; (5) *secondary data analysis* of existing statistics on the target population; (6) review of *social indicators* such as income or occupational levels of the target population; (7) administrative or managerial *record review;* and (8) review of *information from other agencies* (Meenaghan et al. 1982).

The preferred approach in assessing need for a particular population is to use existing data. Original data collection is expensive and time consuming, and is usually beyond the scope of the macro practitioner unless a particular change effort has widespread community and financial backing. Table 6.3 summarizes the advantages and disadvantages of using each approach.

Ideally the macro practitioner would like to know (1) the number of people in the target population who are experiencing each problem, and (2) the number of people that can be served using existing resources. The first number minus the second number represents the community's unmet need. Unmet need, inadequately met need, or inappropriately met need are frequently the focus of macro-level change efforts.

With special population groups that require multiple services, classification schemes are often based on the concept of a continuum of care. A continuum of care consists of a broad menu of services from which items can be selected to address the specific needs of certain individuals or groups. Conceivably, each menu will vary based on what is needed for the target population served. Table 6.4 provides one way of classifying continuum of care services for persons who require long-term care.

Task 4: Identify Collective Community Needs.   Questions to be asked include:

- Are there needs in this community that require something other than a human service response?
- What data support the existence of these needs?
- How are these needs expressed by the people of this community?

While understanding need and examining community responses to each level are important tasks in conceptualizing a hierarchy, this is not enough. Need is an elusive and complex concept and must be understood from a variety of perspectives.

Needs are experienced at the simplest level by individuals who require some type of response. A hungry person needs food; an unemployed person needs a job. If there are resources to meet these needs, the needy person is matched up with the resources and the need is met.

TABLE 6.3   Needs Assessment Methods: Advantages and Disadvantages

Method	Description	Advantages	Disadvantages
General population surveys	Interviews with community residents	Provides broad overview of needs	Requires great time and expense
Target-population surveys	Interviews with a select group	Obtains data directly from target population	Often difficult to locate survey respondents Is time consuming and costly
Service provider surveys	Interviews with providers that service target population	Gives perspective from those who serve the target group	Providers may be professionally biased
Key informant surveys	Interviews with knowledgeable/ influential residents	Provides a community leaders' perspective	Community leaders may represent power structure, but may not represent target population
Secondary data analysis	Analyzing existing data	Data are already collected and usually accessible	Analysis is restricted by what data were collected
Social indicators	Reviews of data such as income, age, occupation, etc.	Data are available and provide broad overview of community	Indicators do not provide detailed information
Record Review	Review administrative/ managerial documentation	Provides insights into major issues and concerns	Is subjective and may be difficult to access
Information from other agencies	Review any other data from county, state, local agencies	May provide new information not available elsewhere	May be difficult to locate

What we have discussed thus far in this chapter is really individual need experienced by many people. When one person is hungry it is an individual problem. When hundreds of people are hungry and the community is not prepared to feed them, it becomes a social problem. When needs clearly outstrip resources, it is a community-wide problem and may require a human service response. More food banks, more homeless shelters, and more employment training services may be needed. It is important to note, however, that just

TABLE 6.4   Continuum of Long-Term Care Services by Category

In-home services
  Outreach
  Information and referral
  Comprehensive geriatric assessment
  Emergency response system
  Companionship/friendly visiting
  Telephone reassurance
  Caregiver respite services
  Homemaker and chore services
  Household repair services
  Personal care
  Home delivered meals
  Home health
  In-home high-technology therapy
  Hospice

Community-based services
  Case management
  Transportation
  Senior centers
  Senior discount programs
  Recreational activities
  Caregiver support groups
  Self-help groups
  Counseling
  Foster homes
  Adult care homes
  Shared housing
  Congregate housing
  Wellness and health promotion clinics
  Geriatric assessment clinics
  Physician services
  Adult day care
  Mental health clinics
  Outpatient clinics

Institutional services
  Alcohol and drug treatment
  Rehabilitation
  Psychiatric care
  Swing beds
  Skilled nursing care
  Extended care

because social workers believe that a community should respond to a problem does not mean that this belief will be shared by everyone in that community.

There is yet another perspective on need that should be understood by the macro practitioner. It is a need that requires something other than a human service response. It may even require some fundamental redesign of structures and systems. As discussed in the previous chapter, structure and power are important variables for community analysis. When a whole community suffers from inferior housing, transportation, or schools, or from an inadequate economic base, these problems may be more than simply individual problems on a large scale. They should be understood as collective needs.

It is an assumption in the social work field that communities need adequately functioning basic systems to achieve at least a minimally acceptable quality of life. They need an economic base that will produce jobs and income. They need affordable housing, adequate transportation, sound community health practices, protection from disease, good quality and relevant education for their children, protection from harm and violence, and freedom to pursue obligations and interests without fear. When these conditions are absent, a service response (more money, more resources, more social consensus, greater tolerance of differences of any kind) may provide temporary relief without dealing with fundamental structural problems.

The long-term need may be for collective empowerment, a collective sense of dignity, full participation in decisions that affect the lives of people in the community, self-direction, and self-control. Assessing collective need requires an understanding of the history and development of the community, an ability to compare economic data and social problem data to other surrounding communities, and a sensitivity to the needs and aspirations of those who live in the community. Collective need may also have to be addressed at another level, such as the state legislature or U.S. Congress. The focus can remain on the local community and actions can be taken locally, but the point of intervention may be outside the community.

When collective need for empowerment, participation, control and other such factors is identified or expressed, the role of the macro practitioner is different from the role taken when the need is for a human service response. These roles will be discussed in Part IV of this book.

Focus B: Identifying Auspices or Sponsoring Organizations

In assessing and understanding a community's human service system, it is important to examine the sponsoring unit or organization. Table 6.5 identifies the types of units that should be considered when assessing service provision in a community. These units, taken together, comprise the total health and human service delivery system within the community, and they operate interdependently. A given community, depending on availability of resources, may emphasize the provision of services through one set of units more than another. For example, in a resource-poor community, reliance on informal units may be a necessity until publicly funded formal services can be obtained. However, in all communities elements of informal, mediating, and formal ser-

TABLE 6.5   Units within the Health and Human Service Delivery System

Informal units
  Household units
  Neighborhood groups
Mediating units
  Self-help groups
  Voluntary associations
Formal units
  Voluntary agencies
  Public agencies
  Profit agencies

vice units will be found. The astute practitioner will carefully assess all avenues of service delivery for the target population.

Task 5: Examine Informal Service-Delivery Units.   Questions to be asked here include:

- What informal units would typically assist the target population within a local community?
- What importance does the household unit have to the target population within this community?
- What importance do natural support systems or social networks have to the target population within this community?
- What informal units are actively engaged in service delivery to the target population within this community?
- Is race, ethnicity, or gender a factor in the provision of informal services and support?

Informal units are those that are not publicly incorporated as legal entities to deliver health and human services (e.g. relatives, neighbors, fictive kin). Often, these units have not been recognized for their importance in the service delivery system, whereas they in fact perform a vast assortment of mutual support tasks. They include the household unit, and natural support systems and social networks.

Household Units.   The household unit consists of those persons who reside within a common dwelling, whether they consider themselves families, significant others, friends, partners, or roommates. "The concept of the family is roughly equivalent to the household, but in recent decades more and more people have lived together in dwelling units without being related, making household a more broadly useful term" (Smith 1991, p. 138). Service provision in this unit generally takes the form of caregiving and tends to fall heavily on women in our society. The potential for caregiver burden or strain suggests that mutual support provided by the informal system may require assistance from others within the community. Respite services are often needed in the interest of sustaining the physical and mental well-being of the caregiver.

In assessing the extent of service provided in household units within a given community one should look for indicators of what is happening within private dwellings for the target population. For example, are identified caregivers within the community overburdened? Is there an identified need for respite services for caregivers of the physically disabled, developmentally disabled, elderly, and/or young children? Are requests for live-ins and shared housing increasing? Answers to these and related questions will aid in the process of assessing the domestic dwelling as a service-delivery unit.

Of particular concern is identifying the importance of the household unit for the target population. For example, if the target population is frail widows living alone, the household unit does not contain others who can assist. Not only are caregivers not available, but formerly active older women may suddenly find themselves alone after years of providing care to children and spouses. On the other hand, target populations such as inner-city children, who often live in crowded households where privacy is limited and tension is high, may draw support from siblings, peers, and parents. Respite for single mothers may be difficult to locate, and poverty may have reduced opportunities and life choices. Yet the household unit can be a critical source of support for these children, fragile as it may be. Recognizing the household unit as a source of community strength and developing services to support this unit can produce a double benefit in strengthening families and reducing the need for other support services.

Natural Support Systems and Social Networks.   Often an unstructured, informal approach to mutual support will evolve as natural or social support systems develop. Most people are part of social networks, but this in itself does not constitute a natural support system. A natural support system, according to McIntyre (1986), exists when resources have actually been exchanged.

The existence of natural support systems have been recognized for years. Recent studies and an emphasis on informal support have prompted a more intense examination, particularly among people of color and aging populations (Specht 1986).

Because networks do not have established boundaries and depend on interaction between informal individuals and groups, they are likely to extend beyond the local community. Mutual support tasks may be provided by geographically dispersed, as well as geographically close, network members. Dispersed networks will depend on linkages such as transportation systems and telephones, and may therefore be vulnerable in times of crisis. Balgopal (1988) explains the importance of social networks:

Social networks such as kin, friends, neighbors, and coworkers are supportive environmental resources that function as important instruments of help, especially during times of crisis. Social networks provide emotional resources and strength for meeting the need of human relatedness, recognition, and affirmation. They also serve as mutual aid systems for the exchange of resources such as money, emotional support, housing, and child care. Well-developed social networks often consciously and purposefully serve as helpers to families in crisis, making it unnecessary for these families to resort to institutionalized services through publicly and privately supported health and welfare agencies. The concept of a family's social network emphasizes the idea of the family with multiple affiliations, some of which overlap and some of which do not, as well as the idea of the family as an active selector, manipulator, and creator of its environment. (p. 18)

Within the local community there are indicators of the extent of informal neighborhood groups and support systems. Neighborhood associations, child-care exchanges, and neighbor-to-neighbor interaction are all indicators of the extent of support available within this unit.

The significance of natural support systems and social networks will depend on the target population. Networks that advocate for and provide ongoing support for the target population should be identified as a part of the human service system.

Task 6: Examine Mediating Service-Delivery Units.   Questions relevant to this task are:

- What mediating units would typically assist the target population within a local community?
- What self-help groups are available to the target population within this community?
- What voluntary associations have members from, or take an interest in, the target population within this community?
- What mediating units are actively engaged in service delivery to the target population within this community?

Self-Help Groups.   Self-help groups are one of the fastest-growing elements of community support. They have been formed to deal with a variety of personal and social problems and needs including bereavement and loss, depression, parenting, and many other issues. A number of self-help groups (probably the best known being Alcoholics Anonymous) have formed national and international chapters and are recognized vehicles of service delivery.

Hutcheson and Dominguez (1986) acknowledge the importance of ethnic self-help groups in their research on Hispanics. Because language and cultural barriers can occur for ethnic populations, self-help groups assist in maintaining community identity and involvement.

Self-help groups are often viewed as being compatible with a feminist perspective as well. Such groups are directed at widows, women who have been exploited or abused, and caregivers. Mutual support provided through self-help groups may assist in protecting the mental and physical health of caregivers.

Depending on the target population identified, self-help groups may be more or less important. For example, groups that already have access to the service system and its resources may find them less necessary, while populations that are struggling to have their needs recognized may find them extremely helpful in supporting their efforts.

Voluntary Associations.   Voluntary associations often serve as a bridge between the informal and formal components of a human service system. *Voluntary association* is defined as "a structured group whose members have united for the purpose of advancing an interest or achieving some social purpose. Theirs is a clear aim toward a chosen form of 'social betterment'" (Van Til 1988, p. 8). Community groups such as neighborhood associations or local churches fall within this category. Similar to self-help groups, voluntary associations vary in their degree of formalization. Since they are membership groups, a dues structure will often be in place. Therefore, their boundaries become more clearly defined than informal groups in terms of those who are paying members and those who are not.

Voluntary associations have several characteristics. Members share a sense of community, which provides a collective identity. Social status may be enhanced by membership; social control may be exercised over members. A function of the association may be to enhance the well-being of its members in a supportive manner. If the association is strong, it may serve as a powerful force to nonmembers. This influence may be positive or negative (Williams & Williams 1984). For example, associations such as the Ku Klux Klan are powerful yet destructive forces within certain communities.

Voluntary associations are a study in inclusiveness as well as exclusiveness. Williams and Williams (1984) discuss the importance of the black church in the development and growth of mutual aid societies. Historically, many mainstream activities beyond the church were closed to blacks who migrated to urban centers. "Blacks organized voluntary associations in the church in such forms as sick and burial societies, economic self-help groups, mission societies, and various secret and fraternal orders" (Williams & Williams 1984, p. 21). Voluntary associations within the black church became an adaptive mechanism to deal with discrimination. Numerous studies report higher participation rates of blacks in voluntary associations than for any other groups (Florin, Jones, & Wanderman 1986). In fact, ethnic groups, lesbians and gays, and other oppressed people may generally use informal and mediating units to a larger degree than other populations. Neighborhood groups, self-help groups, and voluntary associations serve as a means of mutual support, as a place for clarifying perspectives, and as a focal point for action. In some cases these activities lead to recognition and wider support, and to improved access to the existing formal units of human service delivery in a community.

In assessing available services for a target population it is important that the macro practitioner identify voluntary associations. Churches, unions, and professional groups are all potential sources of support for the target population. They may not be listed in human service directories, yet they may be the first source to which some people turn when in need (Wineberg 1992).

Task 7: Examine Formal Service-Delivery Units.   Questions to be asked here include:

- What nonprofit agencies deliver services to the target population within this community?
- What public agencies deliver services to the target population within this community?
- What for-profit agencies deliver services to the target population within this community?
- Are there differences in service delivery across formal units that appear to be based on race or ethnicity, gender, sexual orientation, disability, age or religion?

In this section, we are concerned with formal vehicles of health and human service delivery. Although these service providers are interconnected in numerous ways, we shall examine them according to three types of auspice:

- Nonprofit
- Public (governmental)
- For-profit (commercial)

Nonprofit Agencies.   As voluntary associations become more formalized, they may become incorporated as nonprofit agencies, recognized as publicly chartered tax-free organizations (Van Til 1988). There are many types of nonprofit agencies, but here we will focus on nonprofit human service agencies, defined by Kramer (1981) as: "those [organizations] that are essentially bureaucratic in structure, governed by an elected volunteer board of directors, [and] employing professional or volunteer staff to provide a continuing human service to a clientele in the community" (p. 9).

Nonprofit agencies are formal vehicles of health and human service delivery. They are often viewed traditionally within local communities as the agency of choice—a voluntary initiative that targets a specialized clientele. This traditional view is based on the early welfare system in this country, which arose from a profusion of agencies sponsored by various religious and secular groups.

Recent figures indicate that health services accounted for 51 percent of the total annual funds available to all organizations in the nonprofit sector in

1992 (Hodgkinson & Weitzman 1996). The category of health service providers includes mostly hospitals, nursing and personal-care facilities, and outpatient care and allied services. Human service organizations, which provide social and legal services other than health care, account for about 11 percent of total annual funds in the nonprofit sector. However, the 54,783 such agencies is almost double the number of nonprofit health care organizations (Hodgkinson & Weitzman 1996).

Nonprofit agencies receive funds from donations, payments from clients or their insurers, payments from government agencies, or monies from other sources such as private or public grants. However, government funding has fluctuated in its availability over time, and charitable contributions as a percentage of personal income have been declining since the 1960s. As a result, the funding base of nonprofit human service organizations has changed considerably. In 1977, for example, charitable contributions made up 32 percent of the budget of these organizations, whereas in 1992 this figure had dropped to 20 percent. Meanwhile, over the same period the percentage of funds garnered from client payments for services rose from 10 percent to 18 percent (Hodgkinson & Weitzman 1996). The largest share of these organizations' budgets still comes from government payments, but this percentage declined moderately from 54 percent in 1977 to 50 percent in 1992. Accordingly, nonprofit agencies are in most cases not largely charitably funded organizations but fee-for-service providers whose principal consumers are the government and individual clients.

Nonprofit agencies provide many different services within local communities. While all nonprofit agencies using government funding serve clients without regard to race or gender, a growing number of agencies are specifically designed to serve the special needs of ethnic communities and families, women who are victims of discrimination and/or violence, and other groups underserved by more traditional agencies. The macro practitioner should identify which nonprofit agencies serve the target population and whether they have particular service emphases.

Public Agencies.   The public sector consists of federal, state, regional, county, and city government entities. When the mutual support function is performed by government, it is referred to as social welfare. The U.S. social welfare system has been described as a "patchwork quilt," which "does not represent a coordinated, comprehensive, integrated, and nonredundant series of social welfare services; instead, it is a helter-skelter mix of programs and policies that defy a systematic understanding of the welfare state" (Karger & Stoesz 1990, p. 167).

By the time federal programs are operationalized within the local community, they have usually gone through several levels of bureaucracy. Depending on the structure, which will vary by program type, there may be several extra-community levels through which dollars have flowed. There may be regional as well as state mandates, rules, regulations, and procedures that instruct local providers regarding what they can and cannot do. Local decision making and autonomy will vary depending on the policies that drive a particular program. In short, extracommunity sources have a definite influence on the local delivery of public services.

In assessing a community's human service system, it is important to gain knowledge about policies and programs that affect the target population. For example, working with the elderly means that one must be familiar with the Older Americans Act. Familiarity with the Older Americans Act tells us that there is a designated state unit on aging in every state and a network of area agencies on aging (AAAs). Every state must have a three- to five-year plan for services to the elderly, and each AAA must have a more localized plan. Therefore, every community within the United States will be included in a plan that addresses the needs of the elderly. Experience suggests that this does not mean that every community *meets* the needs of their elderly members. Resources will be limited and the actual carrying out of the plan will include the use of Older Americans Act dollars, in partnership with other public and private initiatives. In addition, many communities have waiting lists for services, and state commitments to carrying out the objectives of the federal legislation vary.

If one's target population is single mothers receiving Aid to Families with Dependent Children (AFDC), the social worker will need to know that states vary regarding what income is counted against benefits received. States also establish their own needs standard for families in that state. Therefore, although AFDC is a large public assistance program developed at the federal level, state-level decisions influence what benefits families will receive. To be effective, the social worker will need to understand how federal and state governments interact and how community attitudes toward AFDC recipients influence clients.

In assessing the distribution of public resources across an entire community, including the funding and charge or mandate of social service programs, it is important once again to examine community practices from the perspective of special populations. Voluntary associations often serve as advocates for their members and have had varying degrees of success in influencing the allocation of resources. In many communities the elderly have been highly successful in these efforts, but attention to the needs of children varies. Ethnic groups have exercised increasing political power over the past few decades, but still find, in many communities, that their interests and needs are considered a low priority. Lesbian and gay groups have increasingly taken up causes such as funding for AIDS research and have participated in the political arena to influence allocation of resources, but they still face widespread discrimination.

Understanding the political system within the community is a challenge. In the United States, jurisdiction over health and human service programs is "distributed across municipal, county, state, and federal governments, in addition to specialized governmental units such as school districts, housing authorities, and regional and metropolitan governments" (Brager, Specht, & Torczyner 1987, p. 20).

Assessing the public sector requires stamina. Not only are there federal statutes, regulations, administrative rules, and funding formulae to contend with, but there are state and local laws and funding procedures to identify. Professional colleagues, however, can provide perspectives on types of services and whether government is truly addressing the needs of the target population. For example, for macro practitioners working in a public housing development, social workers in other developments will be helpful in interpreting how regulations assist as well as constrain their efforts. Locating colleagues in similar settings is important to developing a professional support system to aid in coping with public policies, procedures, and rules.

For-Profit Agencies.   In the past, the for-profit or commercial sector assumed a lesser role in providing mutual support within the community than either the nonprofit or public sector. However, this does not discount the role corporate foundations have played in funding programs that benefit local communities or the many corporations that have provided employee benefits addressing health, human service, and retirement needs. Indeed, a growing number of social workers are involved in the corporate workplace through employee assistance programs (EAPs). These programs have developed as corporations realize that productive employees are those who are supported in all aspects of their lives (Abramovitz & Epstein 1983). In an aging society, some large corporations have created eldercare support networks for employees caring for aged parents.

In the past decade, the actual delivery of health and human services has been increasingly carried out by for-profit corporations. For example, the majority of nursing homes are now for-profit organizations (Margolis 1990, p. 154). According to Gronbjerg (1987), the entry of proprietary or for-profit organizations into any given service area is marked by a cooling effect on the relationship between the public and nonprofit sectors. Because proprietary organizations tend to dominate within the economy, patterns of interaction shift.

These shifting patterns were first noticed in the health care arena, when proprietary hospitals began competing with traditional nonprofit providers. Marmor, Schlesinger, and Smithey (1987) explain this shift in terms of a life-cycle model involving these steps:

1. A new service is developed by nonprofit agencies.
2. The service is broadly accepted.
3. Use in the proprietary sector increases.
4. Policy makers become concerned about those unable to pay for this service.

First, a new service is developed through technical or social innovation. Typically, these efforts are initiated by nonprofit agencies because new services are normally expensive and require subsidization from private or public sources. Second, once the service is well received, broad acceptance follows. Third, interest from the proprietary sector is sparked and proprietary organizations enter the arena, competing with the nonprofit providers. In efforts to keep up with the competition, nonprofit providers begin behaving much like their for-profit competitors. Last, policy makers become concerned about those persons who cannot pay for the service because both profit and nonprofit organizations are competing for those who can pay. If the service is important enough, the public sector will finance the poor and uninsured, "which in turn tends to reduce the importance of charitable provision of care by private nonprofit agencies" (p. 229). Inevitably, some consumers fall into the gaps—not being able to purchase the service themselves, but not qualifying under the strict eligibility criteria set for public subsidy. This life-cycle model reflects patterns identified in the health care field, as proprietary corporations have begun competing with nonprofit organizations in the community.

Public financing of health care through private mechanisms was only the beginning. Stoesz (1988) tells us more:

> By the 1980s, human service corporations had established prominence in child care, ambulatory health care, substance abuse and psychiatric care, home care, and life care. Increasingly, proprietary firms obtained funds for facilities through commercial loans or sales of stock and met ongoing costs by charging fees to individuals, companies, and nongovernmental third parties. Insofar as resources for human service corporations were not provided by the state, firms were free to function independently of the government. (pp. 54–5)

As profit-making corporations bid for public contracts, competition with nonprofit organizations increases. Fifteen years ago our discussion of the health and human service systems would have focused almost entirely on the government and nonprofit sectors and their partnership. Today, as we approach the 21st century, the term *mixed economy*, including government, nonprofit, and for-profit services is clearly a more accurate description.

Given the complexity of the formal service-delivery system, the purpose of this assessment is to gain a better understanding of what organizations are providing services to the target population in this community. Having a general idea of what nonprofit, public, and for-profit agencies are available leads to an examination of how they work together.

Focus C: Determining Systemic Competence

Knowing what agencies are available does not go far enough. It is important for the macro practitioner to know whether or not those agencies actually work together so that target groups do not fall through gaps in the service-delivery system. The next two tasks in the assessment process thus examine the linkages that are evident to the practitioner and require a judgment as to whether these interacting units truly comprise a system that is responsive to multiple needs.

Task 8: Determine Linkages between Units.   Questions to be asked are:

TABLE 6.6   Five Levels of Interaction Leading to Improved Programming

Level of Interaction	Type of Interaction
Communication	Verbal, written, or other forms of communication limited to sharing information or ideas between organizations. Includes consultation.
Cooperation	Two or more separate organizations plan and implement independent programs, but all work toward similar, non-conflicting goals. The organizations share information but act on it independently. Organizations advertise for each other and try to avoid unnecessary duplication of services.
Coordination	Two or more separate organizations work together to plan programs and ensure that they interact smoothly and avoid conflict, waste, and unnecessary duplication of services. Organizations share information, advertise for each other, and make referrals to each other.
Collaboration	Two or more separate organizations join together to provide a single program or service. Each organization maintains its own identity but resources are jointly shared.
Confederation	Two or more organizations merge to provide programs or services. None of the participating organizations maintains a separate identity or separate resources.

Source: Tobin, S. S., Ellor, J. W., and Anderson-Ray, S. (1986). *Enabling the elderly: Religious institutions within the community service system.* New York: State University of New York Press. Reprinted with Permission from State University of New York Press.

- How are the various types of service units generally connected within a community?
- What are the established linkages between units that serve the target population within *this* community?
- Where are linkages between service units obviously needed, but not currently established?
- Are the interests of people of color, women, gays and lesbians, and other oppressed groups represented in the network established through linkages between units?

If there are multiple agencies with overlapping relationships and numerous types of services, is there a glue that holds the community delivery system together? Certainly there may be competition among units, but there will also be connections. Just as the individual is embedded in a social network, so are the group and organizational units within the community. These relational patterns may change over time.

Tobin, Ellor, and Anderson-Ray (1986) identify five levels of interaction between human service agencies within the community. Table 6.6 provides an overview of their interactional types.

Communication. Communication can be formal or informal. Information and referral exemplifies formal communication that happens between units on a daily basis. Communication designed to increase interagency information and understanding may be enhanced through the use of brochures, pamphlets, and media. Informal communication occurs between units as groups meet to discuss community issues or staff talk about their programs at conferences. Although communication is assumed to occur, breakdowns in the delivery system often happen because this process of sharing information across units is not nurtured. Often, written agreements are developed as a reminder of the importance of constant communication as staff change within organizations and new groups are formed within the community.

Cooperation. Cooperation occurs when units within the community agree to work toward similar goals. A local private children's day-care center may work closely with a public human service agency. Both want to provide support for single mothers with young children, yet these units provide different resources. Social workers at the day-care center meet with staff at the human service agency once a month to discuss common concerns and to maintain a sense of continuity for mothers who are clients of both agencies. If the target population is single mothers, the practitioner needs to know that these linkages are established.

Corporate volunteerism represents a cooperative linkage between the for-profit and nonprofit sectors. The Levi Strauss Company provides an example. In communities throughout the United States in which Levi Strauss factories are located, there are community involvement teams. In one southeastern city, the company encouraged its employees to become actively involved with a multicounty nonprofit home aide service for elderly and physically disabled persons. Employees donated time to painting and repairing the homes of older shut-ins, as well as provided friendly visits to the agency's clients. If the target population is older widows, the social worker needs to know that the corporate sector is willing to address client needs.

The concept of corporate volunteerism is manifested in a number of ways. A business may subsidize their employees by giving them release time to do community service work. Other companies will loan employees to human service agencies for a specified period of time so that the expertise required for a project can be provided at no cost to the agency. As employees near retirement, the for-profit sector often provides preretirement training in which volunteer opportunities post retirement are presented. In this way, the for-profit sector actually performs a recruitment function for the nonprofit service-delivery system.

The interchange between the for-profit and nonprofit sectors also occurs in the form of corporate cash and in-kind contributions. Computer manufacturers may donate hardware to a local service agency, assisting in computerizing its information system. Restaurants donate food to homeless shelters. A local for-profit nursing home may open its doors to older community residents who live alone in a large metropolitan area during a time of anxiety over a crime wave. Hotels provide emergency housing after natural disasters. In this community, what cooperative efforts exist between service units within different sectors that focus on the target population's needs? Are race, ethnicity, gender, or sexual orientation factors that need to be taken into consideration in assessing service system interactions? Are any of these interests left out when they should be included?

Coordination.   Coordination implies a concerted effort to work together. Often separate units will draft agreements that outline ways in which coordination will occur.

In a continuum-of-care system that attempts to address the needs of such populations as older persons, those with disabilities, or AIDS victims within the community, coordination is necessary. As consumers exit the acute-care hospital, discharge planners work to develop a care plan. This requires knowledge of and close coordination with local service providers. Service plans often include a package to support the client's needs—mobile meals, visiting nurses, and homemaker services. Depending on the level of disability and length of time expected for recovery, this service plan may make the difference between returning home or convalescing in a long-term care facility. Extensive coordination is required.

The growth of case management within local communities reflects the need for interunit oversight as consumers receive services from multiple units. Case management programs attempt to provide a coordination function so that service delivery flows between informal and formal providers of care. Where there are case managers serving the target population it is useful to learn how they view the relationships between service units that serve the target population and where they see gaps.

Collaboration.   Collaboration implies the concept of a joint venture. Joint ventures are agreements in which two or more units within the community agree to set up a new program or service. This usually occurs when no one separate unit within the community is able or willing to establish the new venture alone.

For example, a local senior citizens center identified the need for repair services for many of its participants. Because older persons tend to own older homes, repairs were often needed. The center did not have the resources to begin this program alone, but by working with a community action agency, a home repair service was sponsored jointly by the center and the agency. Eventually, the home repair service became a separate unit, incorporated as a nonprofit organization.

Coalition building is another form of collaboration. A coalition is a loosely developed association of constituent groups and organizations, each of whose primary identification is outside the coalition. For example, historically, state coalitions were formed as part of the National Health Care Campaign. Community organizations, voluntary associations, public agencies, and interested individuals joined forces to work toward a common goal—health care for all citizens. In coming together, a new voluntary association was formed. Even though the diverse members of this coalition represented various interests across community units, their collaboration on health care concerns provided a strong and focused network for change. In some communities, agencies created to serve the needs of a special population collaborate to assess need, to examine the fit between needs and services, and to present a united front and a stronger voice in pursuing funding for programs.

Albrecht and Brewer (1990) call for change agents within communities to move beyond coalition building, which is often temporary, and toward building alliances. The "concept of alliance as a new level of commitment that is longer-standing, deeper, and built upon more trusting political relationships" requires asking questions such as "Who sets the agenda? What are the power differentials? What different skills do we bring to the table? What different visions of social change do we have? And what different leadership styles do we use and do we value?" (p. 4)

In this community what coalitions are focused on target population needs? How active are coalitions in advocating for change? Are there joint ventures (new programs) developed by two or more service units? Are there coalitions that are moving toward building long-term alliances?

Confederation.   Units within the community may actually merge, often when one or both units becomes unable to function autonomously. A horizontal merger occurs, for example, when two mental health centers consolidate into a single organization. A vertical merger occurs when a hospital absorbs a home health provider. A conglomerate merger occurs when units within the community form a confederation of multiple smaller units under a large umbrella agency. These actions are generally limited to nongovernmental agencies.

Agency interaction inevitably involves competition and conflict. Change agents learn to cope with competition and conflict on a regular basis. These types of interactions will be discussed in Part III of this book.

Overall, the above tasks may be approached as a series of general questions to be applied to the task of assessing community services in a community. These include:

1. Is the community generally sensitive to the needs of the target population?
2. Are target population needs adequately assessed in this community?
3. Is there a "continuum of care" concept or framework that guides service planning and funding for target population needs?
4. How adequate is funding to meet target population needs in the community?
5. Are services appropriately located for target group accessibility?
6. What is the degree of cooperation, collaboration, and competition in providing services to the target population?

7. What gaps in services and problems affecting the target population have been identified in the process of conducting this assessment?
8. How does the race or ethnicity, gender, or sexual orientation of the target population, or some people in the population, affect the need for and provision of services?

SUMMARY

In this chapter we presented a framework for assessing a community's human service system. The assessment process begins with the definition of a target population, whose needs must then be conceptualized in a hierarchy according to their urgency. Following this, the human service response is explored and collective needs are considered. Sources of help are then addressed, including informal sources such as households and social networks and mediating sources such as self-help groups and voluntary associations. Formal sources of services include nonprofit, public, and for-profit providers, and both the nature and orientation of services may differ in important ways across these auspices. Determining the competence of these systems in combining to meet needs in an effective way is the final consideration.

Based on data and information accumulated in the process of assessing a community's human service system, the macro practitioner must finally exercise professional judgment in evaluating the adequacy of resources devoted to the target population within the community. If the assessment has been thorough and productive, the practitioner will have gained enough understanding of what occurs within the community to identify and begin assessing needed change on behalf of the target population.

REFERENCES

Abramovitz, M., and I. Epstein. (1983) The politics of privatization: Industrial social work and private enterprise. *Urban and Social Change Review, 16*(1): 13–9.

Albrecht, L., and R. M. Brewer. (1990) *Bridges of power: Women's multicultural alliances.* Philadelphia: New Society.

Balgopal, P. R. (1988) Social networks and Asian Indian families. In C. Jacobs and D. D. Bowles, eds., *Ethnicity and race: Critical concepts in social work* (pp. 18–33). Silver Spring, MD: National Association of Social Workers.

Brager, G., H. Specht, and J. L. Torczyner. (1987) *Community organizing.* New York: Columbia University Press.

Florin, P., E. Jones, and A. Wandersman. (1986) Black participation in voluntary associations. *Journal of Voluntary Action Research, 15*(1): 65–86.

Gonzalez, V. M., J. T. Gonzalez, V. Freeman, and B. Howard-Pitney. (1991) *Health promotion in diverse cultural communities.* Palo Alto, CA: Health Promotion Resource Center.

Grønbjerg, K. (1987) Patterns of institutional relations in the welfare state: Public mandates and the nonprofit sector. *Journal of Voluntary Action Research, 16:* 64–80.

Hodgkinson, V., and M. S. Weitzman. (1996) *Nonprofit almanac: Dimensions of the independent sector 1996–1997*. Washington, DC: The Independent Sector.

Hutcheson, J. D., and L. H. Dominguez. (1986) Ethnic self-help organizations in non-barrio settings: Community identity and voluntary action. *Journal of Voluntary Action Research, 15*(4): 13–22.

Karger, H. J., and D. Stoesz. (1990) *American social welfare policy*. New York: Longman.

Kramer, R. M. (1981) *Voluntary agencies in the welfare state*. Berkeley: University of California Press.

Margolis, R. J. (1990) *Risking old age in America*. Boulder, CO: Westview Press.

Marmor, T. R., M. Schlesinger, and R. W. Smithey. (1987) Nonprofit organizations and health care. In W. W. Powell, ed., *The nonprofit sector* (pp. 221–39). New Haven, CT: Yale University Press.

McIntyre, E. L. G. (1986) Social networks: Potential for practice. *Social Work, 31*(6): 421–6.

Meenaghan, T. M., R. O. Washington, and R. M. Ryan. (1982) *Macro practice in the human services*. New York: Free Press.

Pantoja, A., and W. Perry. (1992) Community development and restoration: A perspective. In F. G. Rivera and J. L. Erlich, eds., *Community organizing in a diverse society* (pp. 223–49). Boston: Allyn & Bacon.

Smith, D. H. (1991) Four sectors or five? Retaining the member-benefit sector. *Nonprofit and Voluntary Sector Quarterly, 20*(2): 137–50.

Specht, H. (1986) Social support, social networks, social exchange, and social work practice. *Social Service Review, 60*(2): 218–40.

Stoesz, D. (1988) Human service corporations and the welfare state. *Society, 25*(5): 53–8.

Tobin, S. S., J. W. Ellor, and S. Anderson-Ray. (1986) *Enabling the elderly: Religious institutions within the community service system*. New York: State University of New York Press.

Van Til, J. (1988) *Mapping the third sector: Voluntarism in a changing social economy*. New York: The Foundation Center.

Williams, C., and H. B. Williams. (1984) Contemporary voluntary associations in the urban black church: The development and growth of mutual aid societies. *Journal of Voluntary Action Research, 13*(4): 19–30.

Wineberg, R. J. (1992) Local human services provision by religious congregations. *Nonprofit and Voluntary Sector Quarterly, 21*(2): 107–18.

SUGGESTED READINGS

Browdie, R. (1992) Ethical issues in case management from a political and systems perspective. *Journal of Case Management, 1*(3): 87–9.

Damron-Rodriguez, J. (1993) Case management in two long-term care populations: A synthesis of research. *Journal of Case Management, 2*(4): 125–9.

Dinerman, M. (1992) Managing the maze: Case management and service delivery. *Administration in Social Work, 16*(1): 1–9.

Fabricant, M. B., and S. Burghardt. (1992) *The welfare state crisis and the transformation of social service work*. Armonk, NY: M.E. Sharpe.

Falik, M., D. Lipson, D. Lewis-Idema, C. Ulmer, K. Kaplan, G. Robinson, E. Hickey, and R. Veiga. (1993) Case management for special populations: Moving beyond categorical distinctions. *Journal of Case Management, 2*(2): 39–45.

Fatout, M., and S. R. Rose. (1995) *Task groups in the social services.* Thousand Oaks, CA: Sage.

Fiene, J. I., and P. A. Taylor. (1991) Serving rural families of developmentally disabled children: A case management model. *Social Work, 36*(4): 323–7.

Gidron, B., and Y. Hasenfeld. (1994) Human service organizations and self-help groups: Can they collaborate? *Nonprofit Management & Leadership, 5*(2): 159–72.

Inglehart, A. P., and R. M. Becerra. (1995) *Social services and the ethnic community.* Boston: Allyn & Bacon.

Mitzrahi, T., and J. D. Morrison. (1993) *Community organization and social administration: Advances, trends, and emerging principles.* New York: Haworth.

Moore, S. (1992) Case management and the integration of services: How service delivery systems shape case management. *Social Work, 37*(5): 418–23.

Netting, F. E. (1992) Case management: Service or symptom. *Social Work, 37*(2): 160–4.

Nishimoto, R., M. Weil, and K. S. Thiel. (1991) A service tracking and referral form to monitor the receipt of services in a case management program. *Administration in Social Work, 15*(3): 33–47.

Osborne, S. P., and M. Tricker. (1994) Local development agencies: Supporting voluntary action. *Nonprofit Management & Leadership, 5*(1): 37–51.

Rose, S. M., and V. L. Moore. (1995) Case management. *Encyclopedia of Social Work,* (19th ed., 1: 335–40). Washington, DC: National Association of Social Workers.

Salamon, L. M. (1992) *America's nonprofit sector: A primer.* New York: The Foundation Center.

Scott, J. T. (1995) Some thoughts on theory development in the voluntary and nonprofit sector. *Nonprofit and Voluntary Sector Quarterly, 24*(1): 31–40.

Wehmeyer, M. L. (1993) Sounding a certain trumpet: Case management as a catalyst for the empowerment of people with developmental disabilities. *Journal of Case Management, 2*(1): 14–8.

Wineburg, R. J. (1993) Social policy, community service development and religious organizations. *Nonprofit Management & Leadership, 3*(3): 283–97.

APPENDIX

Framework for Analyzing Community Human Service Systems

FOCUS A: UNDERSTANDING NEED

Task 1: Identify the Target Population

- What target populations have been identified as being in need of services within the community, and how are they categorized?
- What target population will be the focus of this assessment?
- What priority is given to the needs of the target population in this community?

Task 2: Define a Continuum of Need

- How can target population needs be conceptualized so that a determination can be made about the extent to which they are (or are not) being met?

Task 3: Assess Target Population Needs

- What are feasible and appropriate ways to find out how many people are in need in each of the areas of need identified as relevant to this target population?

Task 4: Identify Collective Community Needs

- Are there needs in this community that require something other than a human service response?
- What data support the existence of these needs?
- How are these needs expressed by the people of this community?

FOCUS B: IDENTIFYING AUSPICES OR SPONSORING ORGANIZATIONS

Task 5: Examine Informal Service-Delivery Units

- What informal units would typically assist the target population within a local community?
- What importance does the household unit have to the target population within this community?
- What importance do natural support and social networks have to the target population within this community?
- What informal units are actively engaged in service delivery to the target population within this community?
- Is race, ethnicity, or gender a factor in the provision of informal services and support?

Task 6: Examine Mediating Service-Delivery Units

- What mediating units would typically assist the target population within a local community?
- What self-help groups are available to the target population within this community?
- What voluntary associations have members from, or take an interest in, the target population within this community?
- What mediating units are actively engaged in service delivery to the target population within this community?

Task 7: Examine Formal Service-Delivery Units

- What nonprofit agencies deliver services to the target population within this community?
- What public agencies deliver services to the target population within this community?
- What for-profit agencies deliver services to the target population within this community?
- Are there differences in service delivery across formal units that appear to be based on race or ethnicity, gender, sexual orientation, disability, age or religion?

FOCUS C: DETERMINING SYSTEMIC COMPETENCE

Task 8: Determine Linkages between Units

- How are the various types of service units generally connected within a community?
- What are the established linkages between units that serve the target population within *this* community?
- Where are linkages between service units obviously needed, but not currently established?
- Are the interests of people of color, women, gays and lesbians, and other oppressed groups represented in the network established through linkages between units?

PART III

The Organization as the Arena of Change

*P*art II addressed communities as the focus of planned change. Communities are important arenas of practice for social workers because they have such a major influence on the lives of clients and they establish a context within which human service organizations function. In Part III, we will discuss organizations as another important form of macro system in which social workers operate. Chapter 7 begins with a review of the considerable theoretical literature that exists concerning organizations. This review is intended to promote an understanding of how and why organizations function the way they do. Chapter 8 focuses specifically on human service organizations and attempts to identify the major areas in which organizational problems have been identified and solutions proposed.

CHAPTER 7

Understanding Organizations

Overview

INTRODUCTION

Ours is a society of organizations. Whether they are large or small, formally or informally structured, it is organizations that carry out the basic functions of society. As noted in previous chapters, prior to the industrial revolution most individuals lived in rural, agrarian settings in which they were personally responsible for meeting their fundamental needs. People built their own houses, drew their own water, grew their own food, and made their own clothes. In modern times, however, the vast majority of our population lives in large, complex, urban and suburban communities, where people's needs are met by specialized organizations—supermarkets, restaurants, department stores, municipal utilities, construction companies, schools, social welfare institutions, and many others.

Organizations also constitute the building blocks of larger macro systems, and individuals engage their society through these organizations. Communities are critical societal units, yet individuals tend not to interact directly with their community but with organizations that comprise the community. In fact, communities often can be understood not just as masses of individuals but as networks of organizations. Communities provide the superstructure within which organizations interact, but it is organizations that carry out most of the essential community functions that we described in Chapter 4. As sociologist Talcott Parsons notes, "the development of organizations is the principal mechanism by which, in a highly differentiated society, it is possible to 'get things done,' to achieve goals beyond the reach of the individual" (1960, p. 41). Macro practice that involves working with communities inevitably requires an understanding of organizations as well.

Of still further importance is the fact that most social workers (as well as most members of society as a whole) carry out their jobs from within organizations. In organizations other than the workplace, individuals usually have a consumer-provider relationship, and they are free to turn to alternative organizations if the relationship is unsatisfactory. The place of work, however, represents a different type of relationship that is not as easily terminated, and the need for a paycheck may force the individual to maintain a far-from-satisfactory relationship with the organization.

A social worker in a human service agency may not only be tied to the organization as his/her source of income, but it may also be an agency that does not function well. Over time, organizations may stagnate, lose sight of their mission and goals, and begin to provide services that are unhelpful or even harmful to clients. This can occur because of inadequate resources, poor leadership, poor planning, inappropriate procedures or structures, or a combination of these factors. Social workers in these agencies may have the option to leave, but doing so creates other dilemmas. We believe that professional social workers have an obligation to attempt to correct problems in their organizations for the benefit of both their clients and themselves. Just as agencies can lose a sense of mission and direction, so too can they regain it. The path to change begins with an understanding of the organization itself—its history, its underlying theoretical principles and assumptions, and the causes of its current problems. The major focus of this chapter will be on understanding organizations in general through review of a rich and varied theoretical literature. In the next chapter we will address the special case of human service organizations, where most social workers serve.

Defining Organizations

Organizations will be defined here as collectives of individuals gathered together to serve a particular purpose. The key word in this definition is *purpose*. Parsons (1960) contends that, "*primacy of orientation to the attainment of a specific goal* is the defining characteristic of an organization which distinguishes it from other types of social systems" (p. 17).

As noted above, the kinds of goals that people may organize themselves to achieve span the full range of human needs, from obtaining basic necessities to achieving growth of the self. Goals may focus on production and profitability, as is usually the case in profit-making enterprises, or, as in human service agencies, the goal may be to improve the quality of life of persons outside the organization. In each case, the organization exists because, as a collective, it makes possible the accomplishment of tasks that could be completed either not as well or not at all by a single individual.

As we discussed in Chapter 2, today's society has been made possible in large measure by the rise of an "organizationalized" social structure. This point is expressed well by Etzioni (1964) in the introduction to his classic book on modern organizations:

> We are born in organizations, educated by organizations, and most of us spend much of our lives working for organizations. We spend much of our leisure time paying, playing, and praying in organizations. Most of us will die in an organization, and when the time comes for burial, the largest organization of all—the state—must grant official permission. (p. 1)

The ubiquity of organizations is certainly true in human services as well. As social workers, our roles within, interactions with, and attempts to manipulate organizations define much of what we do.

Clients often come to us seeking help because they are not able to obtain help from organizations that are critical to their survival or quality of life. In turn, the resources we attempt to gain for these clients usually come from still other organizations. For example, consider the basic social work function of case management that was mentioned in Chapter 6. Barker (1995) defines case management as:

> [a] procedure to plan, seek, and monitor services from different social agencies and staff on behalf of a client. . . . The procedure makes it possible for many social workers in the agency, or different agencies, to coordinate their efforts to serve a given client through professional teamwork, thus expanding the range of needed service offered. Case management may involve monitoring the progress of a client whose needs require the services of several professionals, agencies, health care facilities, and human service programs. (p. 47)

Thus, social work practice, beginning with this fundamental role, requires considerable effort spanning many different agencies and service systems. Social workers with little or no idea of how organizations operate, how they interact, or how they can be influenced and changed from both outside and inside are likely to be severely limited in their effectiveness.

The following is an introduction to organizations as societal units that social workers must both work in and work with in order to do their jobs. Our review will by no means be complete, as there is such a large body of theory and research on organizations that full coverage of it is well beyond the scope of this book. Instead, we will present a brief review of the most important schools of thought concerning organizations, including a brief review of the main tenets of each school, and the strengths and weaknesses of each.

Distinguishing Organizational Theories

In our discussion, we will examine ways of understanding organizations that have been proposed by various theorists, proceeding in a roughly chronological order. An important distinction that we will make will be between *descriptive* and *prescriptive* schools of thought. Descriptive approaches are intended to provide a means of analyzing organizations in terms of certain characteristics or procedures. They often reflect a sociological approach to organizations, which has as its goal the understanding of organizations as social phenomena. In contrast, prescriptive approaches are designed specifically as "how-to" guides, and their goal is to help build better organizations. Not surprisingly, since managers usually play important roles in deciding how to build and operate an organization, most prescriptive organization theories are part of the literature on management and leadership.

Table 7.1 illustrates other distinctions between various schools of thought about organizations that will be covered. These distinctions are shown partly in terms of key concepts associated with each school. Also illustrated are distinctions relating to whether each particular theory approaches organizations as *open systems* or *closed systems*. Open-system perspectives are concerned with how organizations are influenced by interactions with their environ-

TABLE 7.1 Comparative Dimensions of Key Organizational Theories

	Dimensions	
Theory (Theorist)	Key Concepts	Conception of Organization in Environment
Bureaucracy (Weber)	Structure Hierarchy	Closed system
Scientific and Universalistic Management (Taylor; Fayol)	Efficiency Measurement	Closed
Human Relations (Mayo)	Social rewards Informal structure	Closed
Management by Objectives (Drucker)	Setting goals and objectives	Closed
Organizational Goals (Michels; Selznick)	Goal displacement Natural systems	Closed
Decision Making (Simon; March)	Bounded rationality Satisficing	Closed
Open Systems (Katz and Kahn)	Systems theory Inputs/outputs	Open
Contingency Theory (Burns and Stalker; Morse and Lorsch; Thompson)	Environmental constraints Task environment	(Varies)
Power and Politics (Pfeffer; Wamsley and Zald)	Political economy	Open
Organizational Culture (Schein)	Artifacts, values, beliefs	Closed
Theory Z (Ouchi)	Quality circles Team orientation	Closed
"In Search of Excellence" (Peters and Waterman)	Worker involvement Consumer focus	Open
Managing Diversity (Thomas)	Empowerment of employees	Open
Total Quality Management (Deming)	Consumer/quality orientation Process focus	Open

ments, while closed-system approaches are more concerned with internal structures and processes.

BUREAUCRACY AND ORGANIZATIONAL STRUCTURE

Organizational structure refers to the way relationships are constituted among persons within an organization. As we discussed earlier, one of the advantages of organizations is that individuals working in concert can often accomplish much more than the same number of individuals working independently. The reason for this is the coordination of organizational members' activities such that the work of each enhances that of the others. Organizational structure is the means by which this coordination is achieved.

Even in informal task groups, members usually do not all attempt to do the same activities. Instead, they divide among themselves the responsibilities for diverse tasks. Members also have varying skills and interests, and the process of dividing up specific tasks usually takes this into account. Finally, to ensure that each person's activities are both appropriate to reaching the goal and supportive of other members' efforts, at least one individual in the organization usually takes on a management role. These aspects of organizational functioning, including task specialization, matching of person and position, and leadership, are among a group of structural characteristics that are common to virtually all organizations and that provide a means by which they may be analyzed and understood.

The most important conceptual work on organizational structure remains that of German sociologist Max Weber. Weber coined the term *bureaucracy* and applied it to a particular form of organization. The bureaucracy is an *ideal type,* meaning that it is a pure conceptual construct, and it is unlikely that any organization fits perfectly with all the characteristics of a bureaucracy. The bureaucracy typifies descriptive organizational theories in that it provides a model against which organizations can be compared, after which they can be described in terms of the extent to which they fit this model. It is also important to note that Weber did not necessarily intend the bureaucratic model to serve as some sort of goal toward which organizations should strive. Instead, he designed it as a theoretical tool to assist in understanding organizational structure and how organizations vary from one to the next.

The following is a list of characteristics of the bureaucracy adapted from Weber (1947) and subsequent summaries of his work (Rogers 1975). The characteristics include:

1. Positions in the organization are grouped into a clearly defined hierarchy.
2. Job candidates are selected on the basis of their technical qualifications.
3. Each position has a defined sphere of competence. In a hospital, for example, a physician has exclusive authority to prescribe medications but a financial officer determines the vendor, quantity of bulk purchases, etc.

4. Positions reflect a high degree of specialization based on expert training.
5. Positions typically demand the full working capacity (i.e., full-time employment) of their holders.
6. Positions are career-oriented. There is a system of promotion according to seniority or achievement, Promotion is dependent on the judgment of superiors.
7. Rules of procedure are outlined for rational coordination of activities.
8. A central system of records is maintained to summarize the activities of the organization.
9. Impersonality governs relationships between organizational members.
10. Distinctions are drawn between private and public lives and positions of members.

Weber was interested in this organizational model because he believed it reflected a change in the values of society as a whole. Indeed, his work began with a more general concern about the way power is legitimized in social relations—why people consent to do the will of others. He used *authority* as the term for power wielded with the consent of those being led, and he identified three major forms of such authority:

1. *Traditional authority:* the right to govern bestowed by the people on kings, emperors, popes, and other patrimonial leaders. This type of authority rests in the ruler's claim to historic or ancestral rights of control, thus it is associated with long-lasting systems and can be passed from generation to generation of rulers.
2. *Charismatic authority:* dominance exercised by an individual through extraordinary personal heroism, piety, fanaticism, martial skill, or other traits. Systems based on this type of authority tend to be unstable and transitional.
3. *Rational/legal authority:* power assigned on the basis of the ability to achieve instrumental goals. This type of authority derives from the legitimacy given to rational rules and processes and from expertise rather than authoritarianism.

Bureaucracies are the embodiment of rational/legal authority, and the fact that they have become the dominant organizational model reflects societal movement away from systems based on traditional or charismatic authority.

Strengths and Weaknesses.   Bureaucratic organization is designed to bring about the accomplishment of specific instrumental tasks, and its focus is on maximizing the *efficiency* with which this is done. Weber argues:

> The decisive reason for the advance of bureaucracy has always been its purely technical superiority over any other form of organization. The fully developed bureaucratic mechanism compares with other organizations exactly as does the machine with the non-mechanical modes of production. (1946, p. 214)

As the bureaucracy evolved, this technical superiority helped to bring about the industrial revolution and the immense growth in size and complexity of manufacturing, distribution, and other commercial firms. It also furthered the rise of vast governmental institutions, ranging from the military to a broad range of public welfare organizations responsible for income maintenance, child welfare, mental health, corrections, and other services. In particular, bureaucratic organization helped these institutions carry out their tasks in greater quantity than was possible before. Consider the number of people served by governmental organizations providing Social Security payments, Medicare, and other large-scale social programs. These agencies are not simply larger than the social service organizations that preceded them; they are clearly more bureaucratic in their organization.

In some ways, the practice of social work functions in a manner consistent with specific characteristics of bureaucracies. For example, the profession tends to support a high degree of specialization based on professional training and practice expertise. Assigning individuals to specific jobs and organizational levels on the basis of this expertise is also considered a part of good practice. Social workers tend to be career-oriented, and in most human service organizations the accumulation of experience and expertise is rewarded by favoring more senior persons for promotion. Finally, the profession subscribes to the belief that people's abilities on the job should count for more than who they know or how well liked they are, and fame or fortune outside the organization should not count for more than their competence on the job. In other words, though we do not often think of it in such terms, social workers and the organizations they customarily work in are like many others in modern society in their adherence to the above principles.

Still, bureaucratic agencies often conjure up images of vast, impersonal, monolithic organizations that are anything but efficient. They and other organizations go out of their way to avoid being described as *bureaucracies,* and this term has become one that in everyday usage is almost unfailingly negative. Why is this so? Weber certainly did not believe the bureaucracy was a model for poor organization, and research has shown that bureaucratic organization and structure can indeed contribute to greater productivity and efficiency.

The answer is somewhat complex but important. As the bureaucracy has become more prevalent, it has shown both its good and bad sides. For example, the machinelike qualities to which Weber calls attention may be consummately well suited to manufacturing firms but can also be disastrous in organizations (such as human service agencies) in which the goal is to meet unique needs of individuals. Indeed, many theorists subsequent to Weber have explored ways in which characteristics of the bureaucracy actually undermine its presumed strengths.

One example of these problems is offered by Merton (1952) in his study of the experiences of individuals working within bureaucracies. He found that over time, workers' concern for completing the key instrumental activities of their jobs was gradually replaced with a concern for meeting the procedural and paperwork requirements of the bureaucracy, regardless of whether the basic job was done. Merton called this the "bureaucratic personality." He also coined the term *trained incapacity* to describe the ways in which bureaucratic personalities become incapable of meeting the real needs of the people they were intended to serve. These behaviors are often considered an inevitable consequence of tightly structured chains of command and expectations for unthinking compliance with rules. Most important, he believed these behaviors develop from individuals' realization that their own interests were best served not by doing the job well but by doing it "by the book."

A great deal of contemporary organizational thought has addressed ways such as these in which bureaucracies fall short of their goal of maximal organizational functioning. In particular, various schools of thought have addressed aspects of complex organizations that extend beyond the bureaucracy's emphasis on structural characteristics. As will be seen, many of these aspects were examined specifically from the perspective of how the bureaucratic model fails to account for their importance. Among these are organizational goals, decision-making process, technology, and the role of the individual within the organization.

There is also an argument to be made that ethnic minorities and women have been disadvantaged in bureaucratically structured organizations. "It should be no surprise that feminists have asserted that bureaucracies have a male orientation and a male bias" (Kelly 1991, p. 97). As employees are promoted through lower and middle levels to upper-level administrative positions, there has been a tendency for white males to dominate the highest levels. This phenomenon has been referred to as the "glass ceiling." Women and minorities can reach a level at which they have a close-up view of functioning at the top, but they often cannot reach the top because those who select for top positions seemingly value sameness and fear diversity.

MANAGEMENT THEORIES

Scientific and Universalistic Management

One of the earliest and most important schools of thought on the management of tasks and functions in the workplace was the work of Frederick Taylor, an American industrialist and educator whose main works appeared in the first two decades of this century. Taylor had experience as both a laborer and a mechanical engineer, and he was primarily concerned with management techniques that would lead to increased productivity. He believed that many organizational problems were tied to misunderstandings between managers and workers. Managers thought that workers were lazy and unmotivated, and they also mistakenly believed they understood workers' jobs. Workers thought that managers cared only about exploiting workers, not about productivity.

To solve these problems, Taylor developed what came to be known as *scientific management,* which derives its name from his emphasis on the need for managers to conduct scientific analyses of the workplace (1947). One of the first steps is to complete a careful study of the work itself, commonly by identifying the best worker and studying that person. The goal is to find the optimal way of doing a job—in Taylor's words the "one best way"—to develop the best possible tools for completing it, fit workers' abilities and interests to particular job assignments, and find the level of production the average worker can sustain.

Following this, a critical step is then to provide incentives to workers to increase productivity. Taylor's favorite tool for this was the piece-rate wage, in which workers are paid for each unit they produce. In this manner, more units are produced, unit cost is reduced, organizational productivity and profitability are enhanced, and workers earn more.

Taylor was seeking above all an industrial workplace in which the traditional animosity between management and labor could be overcome by a recognition of the mutual aims of each. His points in this regard were summarized by George (1968, p. 89) as follows:

1. The objective of good management is to pay high wages and have low unit production costs.
2. To achieve this objective management has to apply scientific methods of research and experiment . . . in order to formulate principles and standard processes which would allow for control of the manufacturing operations.
3. Employees have to be scientifically placed in jobs where materials and working conditions are scientifically selected so that standards can be met.
4. Employees should be scientifically and precisely trained to improve their skill in performing a job so that the standard of output can be met.
5. An air of close and friendly cooperation has to be cultivated between management and workers in order to ensure the continuance of a psychological environment that would make possible the application of the other principles.

As can be seen from these principles, Taylor's interests were as much in the area of organizational psychology as in traditional management theory. Subsequent to his work, other writers focused more narrowly on Taylor's concern with maximizing organizational productivity and began to ask whether broader principles could be identified that encapsulated the ideals of rational management. They eventually became known as the *universalistic management* theorists. One of the best known of this group was French industrialist Henri Fayol, whose writings focused on specifying the structural attributes of organizations that managers should develop and promote. Scott (1981) condenses Fayol's central ideas into the following six principles:

1. *Scalar principle*—calls for a hierarchical structure with a pyramid-shaped chain of command.
2. *Unity of command principle*—specifies that each person should have only one immediate supervisor.

3. *Span of control principle*—limits a supervisor's number of subordinates to a manageable number, usually no more than six to eight.
4. *Exception principle*—specifies that subordinates are responsible for routine matters covered by standard rules, leaving the supervisor responsible for exceptional circumstances not covered by these rules.
5. *Departmentalization principle*—incorporates a strong emphasis on division of labor within the organization, and specifies that similar functions should be grouped together (e.g., functions that are similar in terms of purpose, process, clientele, or location).
6. *Line-staff principle*—distinguishes between line functions, which are those most central to completion of basic organizational activities, and staff functions, which are primarily supportive or advisory.

Though somewhat broader in scope, the outcomes intended from the application of these principles were similar to the goals of scientific management. These included stability, predictability (especially with respect to the manufacturing process), and maximum individual productivity. Also, though these writers were prescriptive management theorists, whereas Weber was a descriptive sociological observer, it is not difficult to see that a manager adhering to the above principles would tend to create an organization that strongly reflects many of the characteristics of the bureaucracy.

Strengths and Weaknesses.   The works of both Taylor and Fayol were subsequently criticized for what Mouzelis (1967) termed a "technicist" bias; that is, that both writers tended to treat workers as little more than cogs in a wheel. No two people, and no two workers, are exactly alike, thus the "one best way" of doing a job may also be unique to the person doing it. In fact, forcing a similar approach on a different worker may decrease both productivity and worker satisfaction. Also, because these approaches addressed means for increasing the output of workers, they were subjected to considerable criticism (especially by writers in the labor movement) for allegedly assisting in the exploitation of workers by management.

Because both Taylor and Fayol were interested primarily in industrial organizations, their work was generally deemed to have little applicability to human service organizations during the first few decades in which social work began drawing on management theories. For example, the predominant approach to allocating work responsibility followed that of physicians, assigning "cases" or clients to social workers who acted on a very loosely structured mandate to employ their professional skill to meet client needs. As a result, the focus of scientific and universalistic management on precision, measurement, and specialization of function fit poorly with this type of job design.

However, during the past decade, social work has begun to adopt a more "scientific" approach to practice. In many areas of specialization, procedures and protocols specify parameters for professional activity in certain types of cases. Also, in the interest of improving practice, a great deal of emphasis has been placed on conducting formal research on clients in one's own caseload, often through the use of single-subject designs. Similarly, requirements for outcome evaluation have placed more rigorous demands on the design of interventions and the measurement of success. Though these trends do not necessarily embrace the more mechanistic aspects of Taylor's notions, they do echo his concern for organizational operations that are based on the most careful possible analysis of the work itself.

Human Relations

As the field of organizational management and analysis grew, the works of Taylor, Weber, and others were criticized for their focus on rational, structural approaches to understanding organizations. The earliest of these criticisms addressed Taylor's assumptions concerning factors that motivate organizational actors. In particular, they took issue with the notion that workers are oriented to the instrumental goals of the organization and respond most readily to material rewards (e.g., piece-rate wages) that are designed to further those goals. One such group began with the intention of testing Taylor's principles concerning productivity enhancement. Eventually, however, its members concluded that organizations must be viewed as social institutions, and it is social factors—friendship, belongingness, and group solidarity—that are most important in both understanding and affecting the behavior of organizational actors.

Often referred to as the human relations school, this view had its origins in the well-known Hawthorne studies conducted in the 1920s. Experimenters placed a group of workers in a special room and then varied the intensity of the lighting and other environmental factors to observe its effect on productivity. The greater the intensity of lighting, the more productivity increased. When the researchers had clearly established the positive correlation between increased lighting and productivity, they attempted to confirm their findings by reducing the lighting, expecting to find reduced productivity. Instead, productivity continued to increase even in very dim lighting. The researchers concluded that the cause of the increase in productivity was *social factors*. Workers appeared not to respond to the lighting but instead to the fact that they were members of a group to which they wanted to contribute their best effort, and it was this sense of social responsibility that prompted improved performance.

Subsequent experiments on the effect of social factors in organizations (including many from the burgeoning field of industrial psychology) examined more general questions concerning the behavior of groups. Etzioni (1964) summarizes the basic tenets of the human relations approach that developed from these findings:

1. *"The level of production is set by social norms, not by physiological capacities"* (p. 34).
2. *"Non-economic rewards and sanctions significantly affect the behavior of the workers and largely limit the effect of economic incentive plans"* (p. 34). A number of studies found that workers who were capable of

producing more would often not do so. The reason seemed to be that they were unwilling to exceed what the group as a whole was able to do, even if this meant a reduction in their earnings.

3. *"[W]orkers do not act or react as individuals but as members of groups"* (p. 35). For example, attempts by management to influence workers' behavior can sometimes be more successful if targeted toward the group as a whole rather than at individuals (who would be unwilling to change unless accompanied by group members).

4. The role of leadership is important in understanding social forces in organizations, and this leadership may be either formal or informal. The importance of informal leadership is that it influences behavior in ways that can either amplify or negate formal leadership acting through established organizational structures. In addition, democratic leadership is more effective in eliciting cooperation and willingness to change than more authoritarian forms.

The prescriptive lessons to be drawn from these tenets include the idea that organizational actors are more likely to draw satisfaction from social relationships within the organization than from its instrumental activities. Also important is the notion that workers' willingness to follow management comes from willingness to follow members of the work group. As a result, the key to making effective changes in organizational operations lies not in rules and formal structure but in the quality of personal affiliations and the coherence of informal structures. Managers who succeed in increasing productivity are most likely to be those who are responsive to the social needs of workers.

Strengths and Weaknesses.   No viewpoint fails to generate dissent, and in this case criticisms of the human relations school tend to fall into two major categories. First, a number of writers have raised concerns about the methodological soundness of some of the research on which these views are based. For example, the original Hawthorne experiments have gained a somewhat infamous place in the history of research methodology. The so-called Hawthorne effect refers to the fact that experimental subjects may perform in certain ways simply because of the knowledge that they are being studied. In other words, the workers in the Hawthorne plant may have raised production not because of lighting levels or a sense of group solidarity but because of self-consciousness about being in an experiment. Other critics have argued that the design of these studies was such that expectations about economic incentives might still have influenced the subjects, further undermining the supposed importance of social factors (Sykes 1965).

A second line of criticism argues that it is possible not only to underestimate but also to overestimate the importance of social factors in organizations. For example, various research has indicated that informal organizational structures may not be as prevalent or powerful as the human relations writers suggest, that democratic leadership is not always associated with greater productivity or worker satisfaction, and that economic benefits *are* of primary importance to many employees. Moreover, Landsberger (1958) argued that this school's emphasis on worker contentedness at the expense of economic rewards could foster an administrative model that is even more manipulative and paternalistic than might be the case with scientific management.

Still, the human relation theorists have had an important impact on organizational thinking. With respect to management practice, their views have provided a humanizing counterbalance to the very formalized approach of other management theories. They have also had an impact on descriptive approaches, serving as a reminder of how the needs and interests of individual employees can be critical determinants of organizational behavior.

The title *human relations* has been somewhat misleading to students of organizational theory. For example, ask any group of social work students to choose their favorite organizational or management theory and a sizable number will likely select the human relations school. It has a nice ring to it—human relations—that suggests a real concern for human beings. However, it is interesting to note that some critics of management theories place human relations theory, along with scientific and universalistic management, among those that tend to dehumanize, oppress, and exploit workers. Indeed, human relations theory, like all other management theories to that point, concentrated power and decision making at the top. It was never intended to empower employees or assist them in gaining genuine participation in the running of the organization. If people were treated more humanely under human relations management, it was because managers believed that this would lead to greater productivity. It was not necessarily because of any sincere concern for the employee or effort to create a more democratic workplace.

The practice of dealing with people on the basis of their perceived personal/social relationships within the workplace is another phenomenon that may well have disadvantaged women and minority employees over the years. Networking in organizations has been credited with identifying and securing jobs and promotions for people. Women and minorities however, have often been excluded from important networks that control these rewards.

Later theories would develop around genuine empowerment for employees, but human relations management eventually died out as an approach to running an organization when it was recognized that a happy workforce was not necessarily a productive workforce, and other variables began to enter the equation. Nevertheless, the lessons of the Hawthorne studies—the importance of teamwork, cooperation, leadership and positive attention from management—should not be lost on executives and staff of human service organizations today.

Theory X and Theory Y

Later writers drew on the work of human relations theorists but altered many of their tenets and incorporated them into more general theoretical frameworks of human motivation. One example is Douglas McGregor (1960), who adopted Maslow's hierarchy of needs as a basis of understanding workers' actions. For McGregor, organizational actors were not simply social beings but *self-actualizing* beings whose ultimate goal in organizations is to meet these higher-order needs. To illustrate this point, he identified two contrasting approaches to management which he labeled "Theory X" and "Theory Y." *Theory X* is an amalgamation of traditional approaches to management such as that of Taylor, Weber, and even Mayo, which, McGregor argued, begin with certain propositions about human nature. These include:

1. The average human being has an inherent dislike of work and will avoid it if he [or she] can. (p. 33)
2. Because of this human characteristic of dislike of work, most people must be coerced, controlled, directed, threatened with punishment to get them to put forth adequate effort toward the achievement of organizational objectives . . . .
3. The average human being prefers to be directed, wishes to avoid responsibility, has relatively little ambition, wants security above all. (p. 34)

These assumptions lead to what McGregor sees as the domineering, oppressive aspects of Theory X management.

In contrast, *Theory Y* assumes that the task of management is to recognize workers' higher-order needs and design organizations that allow them to achieve these needs. Its assumptions are that:

1. The expenditure of physical and mental effort in work is as natural as play or rest . . . .
2. External control and the threat of punishment are not the only means for bringing about effort toward organizational objectives. [People] will exercise self-direction and self-control in the service of objectives to which [they] are committed.
3. Commitment to objectives is a function of the rewards associated with their achievement . . . .
4. The average human being learns, under proper conditions, not only to accept but to seek responsibility . . . .
5. The capacity to exercise a relatively high degree of imagination, ingenuity, and creativity in the solution of organizational problems is widely, not narrowly, distributed in the population.
6. [In modern organizations] the intellectual potentialities of the average human being are only partly utilized. (pp. 47–8)

The critical feature of this model was its break from the management-dominated approach of previous theories in favor of a genuine transfer of decision-making power to lower-level actors.

Strengths and Weaknesses.   McGregor's analysis was supported by the research of Frederick Herzberg (1966). Herzberg studied motivation among employees and divided motivational elements into two categories: extrinsic factors and intrinsic factors. Factors extrinsic to the job included considerations such as wages, hours, working conditions, and benefits. Intrinsic factors were those that had to do with the actual conduct of the work at hand. Herzberg discovered that, in the long run, extrinsic factors tend to keep down the levels of dissatisfaction with the job, but they do not motivate workers to work harder. Only intrinsic factors, such as the ability to use one's own creativity and problem-solving capabilities, actually motivated employees to work harder and become more productive.

On the other hand, results of other studies indicated that there were limits to how loosely structured an organization's operations could become and still function effectively. For example, Morse and Lorsch (1970) found that organizations in which tasks were loosely defined and variable appeared to fit well with the tenets of Theory Y. However, those in which tasks were predictable, repetitive, and required great precision functioned better when organized according to principles that McGregor categorized as Theory X management. The importance for social work is that its tasks are often loosely defined and apparently better suited to Theory Y management, yet many human service organizations are still managed with a Theory X mentality. These views will be discussed in greater length later, but one of their key points was that no single management model applies equally well across all types of organizations.

Management by Objectives (MBO)

Fundamental to the conceptualization and functioning of an organization is *purpose,* a commonly shared understanding of the reason for existence of the organization. In most cases, purpose has to do with productivity and profit. Taylor, Weber, and Mayo each stressed a different approach to achievement of purpose, but all agreed that an understanding of purpose was basic to the construction of a theory of organizational management.

One management theorist, Peter Drucker (1954), proposed a somewhat different approach to organizational management. Drucker suggested that organizational goals and objectives be used in a rational way by making them the central construct around which organizational life would function. In other words, instead of focusing on structure or precision or efficiency and hoping for an increase in productivity and profit, Drucker proposed beginning with the desired outcome and working backward to structure organizational effort to achieve that outcome. Termed "management by objective" (MBO), the process involves both short-range and long-range strategic planning, and it is through this planning process that the organizational structures and procedures necessary to achieve an outcome are established.

Drucker identifies several elements of MBO's strategic planning process. *Expectations* are the hoped-for outcomes, and an example might be the addition of a new service or client population in an agency, or it might be an improvement of some specified amount in the number of clients served or results of their services (e.g., an increase of 25% in client satisfaction over current levels). *Objectives* are means of achieving expectations, such as the steps that would be taken to add or improve programs. *Assumptions* reflect what is presumed about how meeting the objectives will achieve expectations (e.g., that the use of better service techniques will improve outcomes).

Other elements in the process include consideration of *alternative courses of action,* such as the costs and benefits of taking no action. Also, the plan must take into account what Drucker terms the *decision structure,* which represents the constraints that exist on how much the plan can do, and the *impact stage,* which addresses costs associated with implementing the plan and limitations it may place on other initiatives or operations. Finally, once implemented a plan will have *results,* and in essence the success of an MBO process is measured by the extent to which actual outcomes match the original expectations.

Strengths and Weaknesses.   One major advantage of MBO comes in its emphasis on producing clear statements, made available to all employees, about expectations for the coming year. Techniques are also developed for breaking goals and objectives into tasks, and for monitoring progress throughout the year. This type of activity tends to improve collaboration and cooperative activity.

On the other hand, MBO adopts a very particularistic approach to management, which some critics have argued tends to concentrate attention on the trees rather than on the forest. In other words, management requires large-scale strategic thinking in addition to small-scale tactical thinking, yet MBO may tend to focus more attention on the latter. Another criticism is that, while there is something admirable about being so clear and direct about organizational expectations, the concept of building organizational life around goals and objectives has its drawbacks. As we will see in the next section, organizational goals often change, and the stated goals of an organization can be subverted in the interest of promoting unstated goals.

Still, many human service agencies, both public and private, have adopted various aspects of MBO in their planning systems over the past three decades. Most state agencies still require the development of an annual plan in which goals and objectives in each programmatic area are made explicit. While many other theoretical concepts and perspectives permeate the management perspectives of the 1990s, MBO has clearly made its contributions. Among the most significant has been the focus on *outcomes* for programs and organizations. Social work as a profession has been very concerned with *process* in the development of its practice approaches over the years. MBO, together with the emphasis on accountability, emphasizes the importance of program outcomes for clients as a major focus in determining funding and program continuation.

MBO has also served to make program planning more proactive. Prior to the use of goals and objectives, results were something that organizations hoped for but that did not drive their structure and procedures. Now many human service organizations consciously pursue achievements that clearly benefit clients. In some instances this has served to guide allocation of resources, and has provided a focus for monitoring and evaluation efforts. So, while the full thrust of MBO as a theory of management has diminished over the years, many of the techniques still serve human service organizations very well.

ORGANIZATIONAL GOALS AND THE NATURAL-SYSTEM PERSPECTIVE

One theme made explicit in Drucker's MBO model is the assumption that organizations should be directed by rational actions designed to achieve certain goals. This assumption began to be questioned by writers concerned about whether rational, goal-directed, formalized structures are the best way of serving organizational goals, and indeed whether these goals provide a clear direction in which to go. In fact, the idea that the goals of an organization and its members could gradually change had been present in organizational literature for some time.

For example, in the early 1900s Robert Michels examined political parties as examples of large modern organizations (1949, originally published in 1915). He documented the rise of oligarchies, or small groups of key decision makers, within these parties. The results suggested that these and other organizations had identifiable life cycles that go through the following steps:

1. The organization develops a formal structure.
2. The original leaders move into positions at the upper levels of the hierarchy.
3. These individuals discover the personal advantages of having such positions.
4. They begin to make more conservative decisions that might not advance their original cause as forcefully as before but that are less likely to jeopardize their own security or that of the organization.
5. Eventually, the organization's political goals are pushed aside and it becomes primarily a tool for achieving the personal goals of upper-level administrators.

Michels called this the "Iron Rule of Oligarchy," based on his conclusion that it is an unavoidable fate of large organizations that adopt bureaucratic approaches to structuring themselves.

Philip Selznick (1949) found yet another such mechanism in his classic study of the early years of the Tennessee Valley Authority (TVA). The TVA was a creation of the New Deal era, and its goal was to promote economic development in the poverty-stricken Tennessee River valley through an ambitious mix of public works projects and grass-roots organizing. With its enormous scope and rather vague goals, it became essential for the organization to delegate decision making to subunits responsible for particular projects in local areas. In this way, its aims became vulnerable to *cooptation* by existing local authorities whose involvement brought needed power and influence but whose own goals began to turn the TVA's subunits in new and unintended directions. Eventually, the TVA became, in many ways, merely a structure for serving the specific goals defined by the interests of local units. Selznick (1957) refers to this as the process of *institutionalization* of the organization. By this he means that organizations can take on a life of their own that may have more to do with the interests of their own participants than with the instrumental goals the organization is supposedly serving.

Other writers refer to this more generally as the process of *goal displacement,* and mechanisms such as cooptation, the growth of oligarchies, and the development of the bureaucratic personality are all means by which organizational goals can be displaced. In Selznick's view, the consistency with which these processes appeared in formal organizations argued against theories (such as Weber's) that seek to describe organizations as rational systems. Instead, Selznick believed the better analogy was that of the organization as a *natural system,* one that is similar in key aspects to a biological organism. The most important of these aspects is the system's awareness of its own self-interest. Just as the prime motivation of an organism is to protect itself, an organization's principal goal often is to maintain its own functioning. This means that predicting an organization's behavior on the basis of what it will do to survive may often be more accurate than predictions based on its expected use of rational approaches to meeting task goals. Etzioni (1964) identifies this in terms of the distinction between organizations' *real* goals and *stated* goals. In situations in which both cannot be served simultaneously, it is real goals (e.g., self-preservation) that almost always determine eventual actions.

Strengths and Weaknesses. Recognition of the importance of organizational goals, particularly survival goals, has proved to be an important contribution to the development of organizational and management theory. Moreover, these views have had considerable influence on the study of human service organizations, such as David Sills' well-known 1957 study of the March of Dimes. Organized originally to unify the efforts of volunteers attempting to raise money for polio research, the March of Dimes became one of the vanguard organizations in the fight against polio nationwide. These efforts were eventually successful, in that funding from the March of Dimes provided part of the support for Jonas Salk's development of the first polio vaccine. This and subsequent vaccines proved to be so effective that polio eventually became a rare medical problem, meaning that the activities of the March of Dimes were no longer needed. Since it had been successful in achieving its goal, the organization could simply have disbanded, but it did not. Instead, it adopted a whole new cause—birth defects—and its efforts shifted toward solving this new problem.

Sills points out that this is exactly the behavior that would be predicted by the natural-system model. That is, the survival imperative prevails even if it means the system must alter its original reason for existence. The result is not necessarily bad, as can be argued in this case, in which an experienced organization took up the cause of a new social need. However, as we will review at greater length in the next chapter, survival goals can also lead to the abandonment of client services, thus the recognition of the role of these goals remains an important component in organizational analyses.

DECISION MAKING

Other writers continued their efforts to explain organizations as rational systems, but this work began to focus on assessing the limits of organizational rationality. One of the most prominent of these writers is Herbert Simon, whose wide-ranging work eventually earned him a Nobel Prize in economics, and who undertook the study of organizational behavior via the process of organizational decision making (1957).

Simon began by changing the primary unit of analysis from the organization as a whole to individuals within the organization. More specifically, he was interested in individual *decisions* about organizational matters. He had been influenced by the growing body of psychological research and was particularly drawn to behaviorist views about the importance of stimulus-response connections as explanations for human behavior. He believed organizations can be conceptualized as aggregations of individuals' decisions within the organization, and organizational decision making can be viewed as a behavior that occurs in response to certain stimuli.

March and Simon (1958) argued that the key to understanding organizational decisions is understanding that there are constraints that limit decision making. They termed this phenomenon *bounded rationality,* and identified three major categories of constraints:

1. habits, abilities, and other personal characteristics that individuals bring with them into the decision-making process and that influence their actions in certain ways irrespective of the circumstances surrounding a specific decision;
2. "motivations, values, and loyalties [whereby] an individual's strong identification with a certain group whose values diverge from organisational values might limit the individual's rational behavior" (Mouzelis 1967, p. 124); and
3. the inability of the decision maker to know either all the variables that might influence the decision or all possible consequences of the decision.

Because all decisions carry some measure of risk, the process of decision making in organizations may therefore be thought of as a sort of risk-management process. The goal of the decision maker is not necessarily to achieve a "perfect" outcome, because this may never be possible. Instead, the decision maker seeks to reduce uncertainty as much as possible in order to make a decision that provides a reasonable likelihood of achieving an acceptable outcome. March and Simon called this *satisficing,* and they argued that understanding how satisfactory outcomes are pursued via decisions made in the context of bounded rationality is key to understanding organizations.

Subsequent works expanded on these ideas in several directions. For example, Cyert and March (1963) suggested that decision making in aggregate is a process of bargaining between individuals and units having different views and goals. The eventual actions of the organization can be understood as the outcome of these ongoing negotiations among organizational members. Later, March and Olsen (1976) proposed a "garbage can" analogy to describe the rather chaotic process in which decisions emerge from a mixture of people, problems, ideas, and "choice opportunities" that is unique to every organization and situation. This approach assumes that rationality plays a relatively minor role in these situations; instead, the process of interaction among these various elements is the primary determinant of the eventual decisions.

Strengths and Weaknesses.   One aspect of decision-making theory that has had considerable impact on organizational analysis is its concern with the nature and quality of information available to decision makers. This concern generally coincided with the advent of computers, and it has played a part in the rapid growth of interest in information management in organizations. The basic idea is that information systems, augmented by the unique data processing capabilities of computers, can be used to reduce the uncertainty that decision makers must confront and increase the likelihood that they will make effective decisions.

On the other hand, as a means of understanding organizations, the decision-making approach has a number of limitations. For example, in a critique of March and Simon's work, Blau and Scott (1962) argue that the model focuses too narrowly on formal decision making, ignoring the interpersonal aspects of organizations and the influence that informal structures can have on decisions that are made. Champion (1975) also notes that little attention is paid to situations in which a particular individual may not seek overall rationality but personal or local-unit gain. Most important, the decision-making model has been criticized for its focus on internal factors that lead to particular decisions. This emphasis ignores the fact that often it is influences *external* to the organization that are most important in both eliciting and determining a decision. In fact, growing attention toward the importance of external factors provided the impetus for the next important developments in organizational theory.

ORGANIZATIONS AS OPEN SYSTEMS

Understanding Open Systems

In learning about practice with individual clients, most social workers are introduced to systems theory. This approach is based on the work of biologist

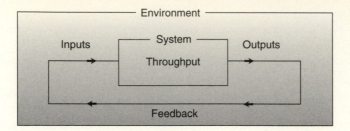

FIGURE 7.1   The Open Systems Model

Ludwig von Bertalanffy, who believed that lessons from fields such as ecology, which concerns organisms' interdependence with their surroundings, provide a basis for conceptualizing other phenomena as systems engaged in environmental interactions (1950). Via this model, individual clients are viewed not merely as isolated entities that are driven primarily by internal psychological processes. Instead they are seen as social beings whose personalities and behaviors can be analyzed in terms of their constant interaction with the world around them. As *open systems,* clients both give to and draw from elements external to themselves. The key to understanding clients lies in this ongoing process of exchange with critical elements (e.g., culture, community, family, etc.) that comprise their personal environment. Beginning in the 1960s, a group of writers argued that organizations can be understood in similar ways.

One influential example was the work of Katz and Kahn (1966), who used von Bertalanffy's ideas to lay the groundwork for an open-systems view of organizations. They began by arguing that previous writers had analyzed organizations as though they were closed systems whose functioning could be understood entirely through study of their internal structure and processes. Katz and Kahn considered this a naive view, arguing that organizations must be understood as open systems that "maintain themselves through constant commerce with the environment, i.e., a continuous inflow and outflow of energy through permeable boundaries" (p. 17). Simply examining internal aspects of an organization—its structure, management style, goals, etc.—was in their view insufficient to understanding it. Instead, organizations must be understood as systems existing within a particular environment, in large part defined by the process of exchange in which they act on and respond to their environments.

As illustrated in Figure 7.1, systems are comprised of collections of constituent parts (whether cells comprising an organism or people comprising an organization) that receive *inputs,* operate on them through some sort of process (called the *throughput*) and produce *outputs.* In human service agencies, inputs include resources vital to the agency, such as funding, staff, facilities, and services provided by other agencies in their organizational environment. Clients are important inputs, as are the types and severity of the problems for which they are seeking help. More subtle but also critical are inputs such as values, expectations, and ideas that are held by community members, funding agencies, regulatory bodies, and other segments of the environment.

Throughput involves the services provided by the agency—often referred to as its *technology*—and the way it is structured to apply this technology to the inputs it receives. Outputs refer to the organization's products. In industrial firms this is usually some sort of material object; in social work agencies it is the completion of a service to a client. As we will discuss, the important aspect of service output is often defined as an *outcome,* which is a measure of a quality-of-life change (improvement, no change, or deterioration) on the part of a client.

Another key element of many open systems is a *feedback* mechanism, which is a defining characteristic of what are called "cybernetic systems." Cybernetic systems are self-correcting systems that are able to act on information from their surroundings, interpret the data, and adjust their functioning accordingly. Biological organisms are examples of cybernetic systems, in that they adapt themselves to changing conditions in their environments. Organizations are also cybernetic systems, and it is virtually impossible to envision one that could survive without gathering information from and taking steps to adjust to conditions in its environment. For example, manufacturers must constantly adjust to changing markets for their goods, and their survival often depends on the ability to adjust quickly by increasing output of fast-selling items and decreasing or changing products that are not selling well. Likewise, human service agencies must be providing needed and relevant services or they will go out of business. This process of receiving feedback from the environment and making adaptations to fit external conditions is at the heart of the open-systems approach to understanding organizations.

Contingency Theory

Partly in response to the apparent soundness of open-systems thinking and partly because of doubts about management theories that promoted a single model of management for all organizations, a new outlook began to take shape in the 1960s. The underlying premise was that different organizational styles may be entirely appropriate due to the particular circumstances each organization faces. Known generally as *contingency theory,* this approach can be boiled down to three basic tenets. The first two, proposed by Galbraith (1973), summarize criticisms of both earlier management theorists and the decision-making model:

1. There is no one best way to organize.
2. Any way of organizing is not equally effective. (p. 2)

To these, Scott (1981), adds a third principle that incorporates the open-systems perspective:

3. The best way to organize depends on the nature of the environment to which the organization must relate. (p. 114)

The unifying theme across all these principles is that the nature of the organization and its management scheme are contingent upon a variety of factors that are unique to that organization. For example, managing a human service agency in the same way as an auto-assembly plant may not help it to achieve maximum productivity.

Morse and Lorsch (1970) took issue with McGregor's notion that a decentralized, humanistic management model is the preferred approach across virtually all organizations. Their research findings showed that, to the contrary, high organizational effectiveness and a strong sense of personal competence could be found in organizations with relatively rigid rules and structure. Similarly, these measures were low in some organizations having a loose structure and a great deal of individual autonomy. The key contingency to which their results pointed was the nature of organizational tasks. Manufacturing organizations with very predictable tasks fared best with a tightly controlled structure. Those with less-predictable tasks (in this case a research and development role) appeared to be much better suited to a loose structure and management style.

A typology of these differences was proposed by Burns and Stalker (1961), who described distinctions between two primary forms of management systems—*mechanistic* and *organic*. Mechanistic management systems, which reflect both the characteristics of bureaucracies as described by Weber and the managerial techniques laid out by Taylor, are associated with organizations existing in relatively stable environments. Organic forms occur in unstable environments in which the inputs are unpredictable and thus the organization's viability depends on its capacity to respond in ways that are not rigidly restrained by formal rules and structures. Table 7.2 compares and contrasts the characteristics of organic and mechanistic organizations.

Lawrence and Lorsch (1967) echoed these themes, arguing that the tenets of earlier schools of thought apply more or less well to a particular organization according to the characteristics of its environment at the time. In particular, they called attention to the importance of stable versus changing environments as the critical contingency on which an analysis of organizational structure and management should rest. For example, they noted that "in simplified terms, the classical [e.g., Weberian] theory tends to hold in more stable environments, while the human relations theory is more appropriate to dynamic situations" (p. 183).

Also, incorporating some of the notions of the decision-making approach, Lawrence and Lorsch focused on the importance of certainty versus uncertainty in determining organizational actions, but in this case the unit of analysis was organizational units rather than individual decision makers, and uncertainty was considered as a characteristic applying to the organizational environment rather than to individual decisions. Stable environments allow for greater certainty in structuring operations, thus a human service agency that deals mainly with particular clients having a particular problem (such as a

TABLE 7.2 Elements of Mechanistic versus Organic Organizations

Variable	Mechanistic Organization	Organic Organization
Focus of work	Completion of discrete tasks	Contribution to overall result
Responsibility for integrating work	Supervisor of each level	Shared within level, across units
Responsibility for problem-solving	Limited to precise obligations set out for each position	Owned by affected individual; cannot be shirked as "out of my area."
Structure of control and authority	Hierarchic	Networked
Location of knowledge, information	Concentrated at top	Expertise and need for information assumed to exist at various levels
Character of organizational structure	Rigid; accountability rests with individual	Fluid; accountability is shared by group
Content of communication	Instructions, decisions	Information, advice
Direction of communication	Vertical, between supervisor and subordinate	Lateral and also across ranks
Expected loyalty	To supervisor, unit	To technology, outcome

Source: Adapted from Burns, T., and Stalker, G. M. (1961) *The management of innovation.* London: Tavistock.

food bank) may be expected to be characterized by fairly routinized operations and formal structure. Conversely, organizations that deal with a wide variety of clients and unpredictable client problems (such as a counseling agency) can be expected to be structured loosely and have a much less "by-the-book" approach to operational rules.

In his classic 1967 book *Organizations in Action,* James Thompson echoed the argument that the key issue in organization/environment interactions is the degree of *uncertainty* in the environment. Thompson contended that organizations seek predictability in the environment because this allows the ongoing operation of rational structures. However, as Simon and others point out, the environment is never perfectly predictable. Accordingly, the organization that structures itself too rigidly will not last long. The goal is to

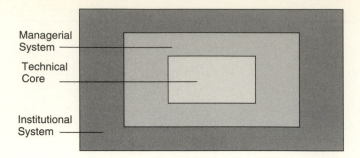

FIGURE 7.2   Thompson's Organizational Model

be able to respond to changes in the environment to ensure organizational survival.

Thompson focused considerable attention on the nature of the organization's technology. As illustrated in Figure 7.2, he described three levels of organizational functioning: (1) the technical core, (2) the managerial system, and (3) the institutional system. The *technical core* includes the structures and processes within the organization's boundaries that allow it to carry out the principal functions for which the organization was created (i.e., the structure and processes that go into the assembly of a product or the delivery of a service). Theoretically, the technical core works best when allowed to do the same thing in the same way; that is, when environmental inputs never vary. However, since the environment is constantly changing, the rational organization seeks to accommodate to environmental variations while still protecting its most vital elements, thus ensuring survival. The *managerial system* includes those structures and processes that manage the work of the technical core. The *institutional system* deals with interactions between the organization and the environment.

The means by which an organization structures itself to achieve this balance is at the heart of Thompson's analytical model. He argues that this is a rational process designed to maintain organizational viability. Specifically, he hypothesizes that adaptive responses fall into a three-part sequence: (1) actions to protect the technical core of the organization; (2) actions to acquire power over the task environment; and (3) actions to absorb important elements of the environment by changing organizational domains. Actions to protect the technical core primarily involve responses that allow the organization to absorb necessary changes within itself, such as by increasing or decreasing output, hiring or laying off staff, or shifting resources among different internal units.

The *task environment* is the term Thompson uses to describe external organizations on which an organization depends, either as providers of needed input (money, raw materials, client referrals) or as consumers of its output. If internal responses are unsuccessful in accommodating change, Thompson says the next step is for the organization to attempt to alter its relationships with members of the task environment in such a way that it has more control over the change. Examples of this might include negotiating long-term funding agreements or arranging for regular referral of clients from another organization (e.g., a residential treatment center may become the exclusive provider of treatment for a particular school district).

Finally, if the organization cannot adapt to change by any of these methods, Thompson predicts that it will seek to incorporate into itself parts of the environment that relate to the change. For example, a human service organization dependent on providing services to substance-abusing clients that are paid for by contracts with a public agency may suddenly find itself jeopardized when governmental funding priorities shift toward prevention rather than treatment services. If a relatively small and new agency in the area appears to be in line for much of this funding, the older, larger agency may seek to merge with the smaller one in an effort to maintain its funding base by providing these new services. Because such a move involves changing at least part of the original agency's technical core, however, this type of response is likely to take place only after other adaptive strategies have been tried and proved inadequate.

Strengths and Weaknesses.   Open-systems models continue to have considerable influence on organizational analysis. The environment has come to be recognized as a critical variable in the life of every organization. This perspective has been particularly valuable in understanding human service organizations. Environmental considerations (such as procurement of funds and other resources) have always been prominent in agency concerns, and Thompson's theory has given them proper recognition. Identification of survival as the primary reason for existence of all organizations helps bring into a clearer focus the driving forces behind a good deal of organizational behavior. Thompson's postulates about techniques to protect the technical core add to our understanding of how it is that organizations survive.

Organizations' increasing attention to cultural diversity in their workforces offers an example of how Thompson's ideas can explain organizational actions. As noted earlier, an important input that organizations draw from their environments is employees who have the knowledge and skills to carry out organizational tasks. A study of employment trends called the Workforce 2000 Report (Jamieson & O'Mara, 1991) estimated that, of every 10 new employees coming into an organization in the year 2000, only 1.5 will be white males while the rest will be women and ethnic minorities. If organizations did not constantly monitor their environment and seek to adapt to its changes, it might be expected that little was being done to respond to this trend. In actuality, though, great numbers of organizations have begun adapting their technology, office locations, training procedures, and even rule of interpersonal conduct in an effort to attract, retain, and promote members of an increasingly diverse workforce.

The ideas of the contingency theorists still have certain weaknesses, however. For example, one limitation of Thompson's ideas was his caveat that the processes he described took place under "norms of rationality." By this Thompson meant that organizations that did not apply rational analytical processes in adapting to environmental change might act in unpredictable ways. The problem is that "rationality" is an elusive notion, particularly when applied to the process of reasoning that different organizations in different circumstances may need to do in order to respond to environmental turbulence. In commercial firms, for example, it may be "rational" to protect the interests of shareholders by maximizing profitability, but equally rational to keep profits and dividends modest in order to emphasize long-term investment. Similarly, actions such as stiffening eligibility criteria may be rational for a for-profit human service agency wishing to protect its earning capacity, but they may be irrational for a nonprofit agency wishing to protect its mission of serving poor clients.

Even similar organizations facing similar circumstances may choose different courses of action based on divergent interpretations of what these circumstances mean. Knowing how an organization perceives and evaluates its environment is useful in predicting how the organization will act, but there are limits to how well environments or organizational decision-making processes can be known. This means that the predictability of organizational actions will also remain limited.

CONTEMPORARY PERSPECTIVES

The history of organizational and management theory has been, in many ways, the history of a search for insights into the best ways to organize and manage—a search for the theory that will unlock the secrets of productivity. As we have attempted to illustrate in this chapter, the theme was different for each new theory. For Weber it was structure, for Taylor it was precision, for Mayo it was attentiveness to the human element, for Drucker it was a commonly shared sense of direction, for Simon it was the process of decision making, and for Thompson it was coping with environmental changes.

A major contribution of contingency theory was the introduction of the idea that no one theme or set of variables was right for every situation. For contingency theorists, when asked the question, "What is the best way to manage an organization?" the only correct answer was, "It depends." The development of contingency theory over the past few decades has focused on the question, "On what does it depend?" In short, every organization is made up of a unique mix of variables, and the position of contingency theorists is that there can be no single formula for optimal structure and management style. The direction the organization takes will depend on the nature of the organization and its expectations for productivity.

Whether or not its tenets are always accepted, it is probably fair to state that the contingency approach has been a springboard for contemporary thinking about organizational and management theories. The 1980s saw a number of alternative perspectives introduced and, while none has dominated the field, each has contributed an interesting new dimension to how organizations are understood, analyzed, managed, and led. Numerous terms are highly visible in the contemporary literature on organizations. These terms include vision, excellence, quality, culture, empowerment, diversity, and values. *Leadership* has become the word of choice over *management,* even though both are acknowledged as having their place. The following discussion will briefly introduce the reader to a sampling of the themes in recent organizational literature.

Power and Politics

Jeffrey Pfeffer (1981) argues that organizational actions are best understood in terms of power relationships and political forces. He defines *power* as the ability to influence actions and *politics* as the process whereby this influence is used. Asked where power originates, Pfeffer would explain that power is derived from an individual's position within the organization. Therefore, power and organizational structure are closely tied to one another.

To illustrate the relationship of power and organizational structure, Pfeffer compared three models of organizational analysis: (1) the bureaucratic model, (2) the rational-choice model, and (3) the political model. The *bureaucratic model* is based in the classic Weberian approach that assumes an organization is both structured and acts in a manner that maximizes its efficiency in achieving its goals. Pfeffer's criticisms of this model are essentially the same as those detailed earlier in this chapter. The *rational-choice model* derives from the work of decision-making theorists such as Simon and March. Pfeffer agreed with their points concerning the constraints that limit rational decision making. However, he noted that these models still assume that decision making is oriented toward a clear organizational goal, thus the greatest drawback to rational choice models is that "they fail to take into account the diversity of interests and goals within organizations" (p. 27). It is for this reason that Pfeffer urged the use of the *political model* of structural analysis. Its benefit is in calling attention to the manner in which organizational actions may be either instrumental (that is, serving the presumed goals of the organization as a whole) or parochial, serving the perceived self-interest of a particular individual or organizational unit. Learning how power is acquired and then used to influence decision making was for him the key to the fullest understanding of how organizations operate.

Wamsley and Zald (1976) argue that structure and process in organizations is best understood in terms of the interplay of political and economic interests both internal *and* external to the organization. *Political* means the processes by which the organization obtains power and legitimacy. *Economic* means the processes by which the organization gets resources such as clients, staff, and funding.

The goal of this *political economy* perspective is to incorporate much of the work of previous schools into a more general conceptual model. Within this model elements such as individual interests and goals, the power wielded by the holders of these interests, and environmental resources and the relative influence of those who control them are all seen to interact in a way that creates the unique character of an organization. This character is not static but changes as the political economy of the organization changes.

For an example of how these ideas build on and extend previous work, consider our earlier discussion of the weaknesses of Thompson's model. Pfeffer would argue that Thompson, in assuming that "norms of rationality" govern organizational actions, fails to account for the fact that both instrumental *and* parochial concerns are being addressed. That is, individuals who have the power to choose a particular organizational action will make their decisions based not only what is best for the organization but also what is best for themselves. Moreover, the competing self-interest of other powerful individuals within the organization and the interests of powerful organizations in the environment will also be weighed in this person's decisions. This interplay of interests is what Pfeffer as well as Wamsley and Zald refer to as the political context of organizations. Their central point is that organizational behavior can be best understood as the outcome of decisions by individuals who have acquired decision-making power, and these decisions will reflect their assessment of what is politically and economically wise for both themselves and the organization.

The topic of power has also been discussed extensively in the feminist literature, both in relationship to politics within organizations and within the larger society in general. Gottlieb (1992) calls for a reconceptualization of empowerment and politics in organizations that serve women. She explains that "Women in both corners of the service relationship are affected by the societal definitions and oppression of women, although many members of both groups avoid seeing those effects" (p. 301). Because social work is a profession a profession that has large numbers of women both as practitioners and as clients, Gottlieb encourages an increasing awareness of the political dimensions in the larger society that affect human service organizations.

Organizational Culture

The concept of *organizational culture* has had a profound influence on the development of contemporary theories. Edgar Schein (1985) defines culture as:

> a pattern of basic assumptions—invented, discovered, or developed by a given group as it learns to cope with its problems of external adaptation and internal integration—that has worked well enough to be considered valid and therefore, to be taught to new members as the correct way to perceive, think, and feel in relation to those problems. (p. 9)

Schein explains that an organizational culture develops through shared experiences. Newly formed organizations are heavily influenced by leaders who bring their perspectives to the organization and around whom assumptions and beliefs emerge. "Culture, in this sense, is a learned product of group experience and is, therefore, to be found only where there is a definable group with a significant history" (p. 7). Schein argues that leadership and culture are intimately related, and understanding what assumptions leaders bring to organizations is central to analyzing how change occurs within an agency.

The connection of leadership to organizational culture has been explored in numerous ways. Of particular interest is the rapidly expanding literature on leadership and gender:

> By 1990 an ongoing debate had developed over whether women want the same type of success as men, whether they are able to demonstrate the behavior and leadership required for modern organizations to compete at high levels, and whether successful female managers need to adopt male behavioral styles in order to lead or compete. (Kelly 1991, p. 96)

Feminist scholars have begun to analyze the processes of empowerment and collective action within organizations and the impact these processes have on changing cultural assumptions within organizations (Astin & Leland 1991). Language and communication, values, orientations toward power, perceptions of relationships, and leadership styles are fertile ground for exploration of gender and the development of organizational culture.

Organizational culture is important in understanding any organization; it is highly "visible" and "feelable" (Schein 1985, p. 24). When entering an organization, one quickly perceives that established patterns occur within that system even if they are not explicitly stated. The social worker who assumes a new place in an organization must be aware that these patterns may be so central to organizational functioning that they are taken for granted by members of that organization. When violated, members may respond emotionally because they are so invested in the "way things have always been done." It is difficult to understand how employees feel about an organization without considering the culture. Organizational culture, therefore, is much broader than looking at climate, ideology, or philosophy. It is a sense of group identity that permeates decision making and communication within the organization.

Theory Z

In the late 1970s and early 1980s attention in the United States began to be directed toward growing competition from Japan. Markets long dominated by American firms were being taken over by Japanese industries, and there was considerable curiosity about how Japanese industrial organizations had overcome their earlier reputation for poor-quality work to such an extent that Japanese manufacturing was setting worldwide standards for quality and durability.

William Ouchi attempted to capture Japanese-style management in his 1981 best-seller *Theory Z*. The message of the title was that the philosophical and theoretical principles underlying Japanese management went beyond McGregor's (1960) conceptualization of Theory Y that we discussed earlier in this chapter.

An organization in Japan, said Ouchi, is more than just a structural or goal-oriented entity as it is in America. It is a way of life. It provides lifetime employment, it is enmeshed in the social, political, and economic network of the country, and its influence spills over into other organizations such as universities and public schools, all the way down to the nursery-school level.

The basic philosophy of Japanese-style management is that involved workers are the key to increased productivity. While this may sound a bit like the human relations school, it is dramatically different. The Japanese are concerned not simply about having workers feel that their social needs are met in the workplace, but rather that workers become a demonstrable part of the process through which the organization is run. Ideas and suggestions about how to improve the organization are regularly solicited and, where feasible, implemented. One example is the *quality circle,* where employees set aside time to brainstorm about ways to improve quality and productivity.

In contrast to American organizations, Japanese organizations tend to have neither organizational charts nor written objectives. Most work is done in teams, and consensus is achieved without a designated leader. Cooperation rather than competition is sought between units. Loyalty to the organization is extremely important, and it is rewarded by loyalty to the employee.

While Japanese productivity has remained high and its products continue to set the standard for quality in many areas, experiments designed to transplant Japanese-style management to this country have met with limited success. In most cases it has been concluded that the entire philosophy is compatible with a homogenous culture like Japan's, but does not fit well with the more heterogenous and individualistic character of the American workplace. Nevertheless, some of the concepts from *Theory Z* have been incorporated into contemporary management thought, and they have had an important influence on organizational and management theory.

"In Search of Excellence"

Another important management theme in the 1980s was the "excellence" theme, developed by Thomas Peters and Robert Waterman (1982). Peters and Waterman were employees at McKinsey and Company, a management consulting firm. Concern began to grow in the firm about problems with management, and the pair became the leaders of a project on organizational effectiveness. They established a definition of what they considered to be excellent companies, and selected 62 of them for their study. They immersed themselves in the current thinking about the theory and practices of excellent companies and discovered that the dominant themes were such topics as organizational culture, a family feeling among employees, a preference for smallness, a preference for simplicity rather than complexity, and attention to individuals. In effect, they found that the prevailing management practices in these organizations focused more on the human elements emphasized by Mayo and McGregor than on the structure of the workplace as emphasized by Weber and Fayol.

While they discovered that a rational base built on collection and analysis of data is indispensable, they also concluded that analysis of data must be flexible and take into account a wide range of considerations, including the human element. Rational approaches, they determined, need to stop considering the human implementer a "necessary nuisance" and instead build on the strengths brought into the system by its employees.

Ultimately they translated their findings into eight basic principles, which have become the focal point of the "excellence approach" to organizational management:

1. *A bias for action:* a preference for doing something—anything—rather than sending a question through cycles and cycles of analyses and committee reports.
2. *Staying close to the customer:* learning preferences and catering to them.
3. *Autonomy and entrepreneurship:* breaking the corporation into small companies and encouraging them to think independently and competitively.
4. *Productivity through people:* creating in all employees the awareness that their best efforts are essential and that they will share in the rewards of the company's success.
5. *Hands-on, value-driven:* insisting that executives keep in touch with the firm's essential mission.
6. *Stick to the knitting:* remaining with the business the company knows best.
7. *Simple form, lean staff:* few administrative layers, few people at the upper levels.
8. *Simultaneous loose/tight properties:* fostering a climate where there is dedication to the central values of the company combined with tolerance for all employees who accept those values.

As the provision of human services has, over the years, moved closer and closer to a provider-consumer relationship, these principles and the findings of the Peters and Waterman study have taken on increased importance.

In 1989 Rosabeth Moss Kanter ushered in the 1990s with her book entitled *When Giants Learn to Dance.* Viewing the changes in management as a "post-entrepreneurial" revolution, Kanter concluded that "modest change everywhere in the corporation [was] becoming orthodoxy" (p. 10). Reaching beyond concepts such as "total quality" and "continuous improvement," she began to investigate not only what strategies organizations were using to solve their problems but what consequences these changes were having for those persons who were a part of these organizations. Breaking tradition with metaphors of war and sports, her book focused on whether "elephantlike" organizations heavily characterized by bureaucracy could actually learn to dance collaboratively with one another.

Emerging concerns in the 1980s carried over into the 1990s as change became a way of organizational life. Public as well as private agencies began quality improvement, quality assurance, and total-quality programs. Strategies to cope with uncertain environments were joined with encouragement for organizations to engage in flexible and collaborative relationship building in order to survive.

Managing Diversity

Roosevelt Thomas, Jr. (1991) takes a somewhat different approach to managing the workforce of the 1990s. He identifies diversity as the key variable affecting productivity, and sees effective management of diverse populations as a critical skill. He identifies three trends that, he believes, will dictate the need for dealing with a more diverse workforce:

1. American corporations must now do business in a global market that has become intensely competitive.
2. The makeup of the U.S. workforce is changing dramatically as it becomes more diverse.
3. The "melting pot" concept is becoming less applicable. Instead, individuals have begun to emphasize and take pride in differences.

In order to remain competitive, Thomas believes that American organizations will have to learn how to draw on the creative resources represented in a workforce made up of Asian Americans, African Americans, Latinos, Anglos, and other races, as well as a more even mix of males and females. To accomplish this objective, he proposes an analytical framework for understanding organizational culture that breaks diversity down into three phases: (1) affirmative action, (2) valuing differences, and (3) managing diversity.

Affirmative action refers to programs and efforts designed to bring ethnic minorities and women into the organization. The focus is on recruitment efforts, and success is measured by the numbers and percentages of minorities recruited and retained in the organization. Thomas sees affirmative action as a temporary step in moving the organization toward managing diversity.

Valuing differences focuses on enhancing interpersonal relationships among individuals. Much of the responsibility for these efforts falls on staff training and personnel development, with the objective of fostering acceptance and mutual respect across racial and gender lines, enhancing understanding of differences, assisting participants with understanding their own feelings and attitudes toward differences, and enhancing working relationships among people who are different.

Managing diversity, which is Thomas's vision, refers to a complete evaluation of the organization as a system to determine if it is as effective and productive as it can be and needs to be in an increasingly competitive environment. If the system is not effective, and if it is not prepared to deal with a diverse work force, Thomas suggests it may need to undertake a long-term strategy to modify the core culture. This requires a full understanding of the existing culture and a planned transition to a new culture in which an environment is created that supports full utilization of a diverse work force. This requires a mind set that recognizes and values differences among all employees, including white males, and searches for opportunities to tap the reservoir of talent and strength represented in a diverse staff.

Thomas cites a number of major American corporations that have undertaken the challenge to change their organizational culture and increase productivity and competitiveness by effectively managing diversity. While most human service organizations have had a diverse workforce for several decades, a thorough understanding of Thomas's conceptual framework would very likely lead many to the conclusion that they have not moved much beyond the phase of affirmative action, and that they have much to learn about valuing differences and eventually managing diversity well.

Total Quality Management (TQM)

Organizations in the commercial sector, especially manufacturing firms, began recognizing in the 1980s that one problem they faced in competing against foreign businesses was that American-made goods were no longer perceived by consumers as being of dependably high quality. As we noted in our discussion of Theory Z, this spurred intense interest in management practices of foreign firms, particularly Japanese firms that had gained a reputation for both competitive prices and superior quality. Ironically, the search led to the work of American writers such as W. Edwards Deming who had begun in the 1950s to assist the Japanese in developing quality-oriented administrative strategies. Another American, Arnold Feigenbaum, first coined the term *total quality* to describe the major thrust of this approach (1991), but its central principles were set out earlier in a summary published by Deming in 1982. The movement quickly became known as total quality management, or TQM.

As its name suggests, TQM places the quality of organizational outputs (whether goods or services) at the focal point of all operations. Management is charged with the responsibility for creating both structures and procedures within the organization that will continually reinforce this goal. Table 7.3 presents a typology by Martin (1993) that lists principles of TQM in comparison with traditional management approaches.

While some of the principles listed in the table are unique to TQM, others represent an embrace of preceding schools of thought. For example, Schmidt and Finnigan (1992) note that TQM adopts McGregor's view (from Theory Y) that workers obtain satisfaction from doing their job productively if they

TABLE 7.3   Comparison of Traditional American Management Principles with TQM Management Principles

Traditional American Management Principles	Total Quality Management (TQM) Principles
The organization has multiple competing goals.	Quality is the primary organizational goal.
Financial concerns drive the organization.	Customer satisfaction drives the organization.
Management and professionals determine what quality is.	Customers determine what quality is.
The focus is on the status quo—"If it ain't broke, don't fix it."	The focus is on continuous improvement—"Unattended systems tend to run down."
Change is abrupt and is accomplished by champions battling the bureaucracy.	Change is continuous and is accomplished by teamwork.
Employees and department compete with each other.	Employees and departments cooperate with each other.
Decisions are based on "gut feelings." It is better to do something than to do nothing.	Decisions are based on data analysis. It is better to do nothing than to do something wrong.
Employee training is considered a luxury and a cost.	Employee training is considered essential and an investment.
Organizational communication is primarily top-down.	Organizational communication is top-down, down-up, and sideways.
Contractors are encouraged to compete with each other on the basis of price.	Long-term relationships are developed with contractors who deliver quality products and services.

Source: Martin, L. L. (1993) *Total quality management in human service organizations.* Thousand Oaks, CA: Sage.

Reprinted with permission from Sage Publications.

are allowed discretion and influence in determining how the job is to be done. TQM is also favorable to the use of quality circles and other team-building approaches described by writers such as Ouchi or Peters and Waterman, and it is favorable to the promotion of an organizational culture to which staff can become attached. At the same time, however, TQM specifically rejects other organizational approaches. Among these are bureaucratic (rule-oriented) structure and theories (such as those of some open-systems advocates) that seek to achieve organizational stability and predictability, which TQM principles view as threats to ongoing quality improvement. In particular, Saylor (1996) notes that TQM is incompatible with the principles of management by objectives (MBO). This is because TQM is oriented to customer satisfaction, which is considered a moving target and demands a continual *process* orientation to anticipate and adapt to new customer needs. MBO, he argues, focuses on achieving static *outcomes* that may ignore the changing needs of customers and can lead the organization into passivity or outdatedness.

Because TQM has its origins in commercial manufacturing firms, its applicability to human service organizations in the public or private sectors may be questioned. However, interesting historical precursors exist regarding its use in social work agencies, and guidelines are now being proposed for applying specific principles of TQM in these organizations. One forerunner of TQM in social work is the effectiveness-driven management movement, which calls for administrative approaches that orient the organization toward meeting client needs (Patti 1985; Rapp & Poertner 1992). More recently, Moore and Kelly (1996) have argued that "TQM is a useful tool despite the fact that social and public services organizations are not prepared to implement it in its most orthodox form" (p. 33). Among the elements of TQM they believe can be adopted by human service agencies are (1) the use of quality circles to improve staff involvement and make services more relevant, (2) the use of careful measurement practices to monitor whether consumer needs are being met, (3) hiring and training staff in ways that ensure frontline staff have both the skills and interests necessary for their jobs, and (4) management staff that can define a quality orientation and move the organization toward that goal.

Summary and Analysis of Contemporary Theories

The perspectives discussed above come together in some interesting ways. Clearly, one trend coming out of the 1980s was the move toward a better, more thorough understanding of organizational culture. Often this begins with an identification of the locus or centers of power and an understanding of the effectiveness of various individuals or groups in exercising political and leadership skills. These factors, together with others identified by Schein, make up what has come to be understood as organizational culture, a powerful and sometimes seemingly intractable force for continuation of "business as usual."

An increasingly powerful factor in the development and evolution of organizational cultures will be the diversity of the workforce. Despite the current debate over affirmative action and methods by which opportunities can be equalized across gender and racial groups, it is manifestly clear that both workers and administrators of the future will be much more diverse than in the past. This means that organizations will need to continuously address the question of whether their structures and procedures are compatible with the diversity of their workforce, and whether they are positioned to use this diversity in ways that benefit both the organization and its individual members.

Finally, the notion of quality may become the criterion for designing structures and processes as well as for evaluating organizational success. Whether this will bring about genuine change, however, may be largely dependent on how "quality" is defined. In his discussion of goal displacement in organizations, Selznick (1949) argued that one starting point for the process is "unanalyzed abstractions," which are touted by management as being noble goals but which may have little real meaning in practice. (References by politicians to powerful but often vague symbols such as "freedom" or "patriotism" are examples of such abstractions). If "quality" becomes merely another unanalyzed abstraction it is likely to have little long-term effect on organizations.

Still, advocates of the approaches suggested by Ouchi, Peters and Waterman, and Deming all argue that they represent truly new ideas due to their emphasis on *process* rather than exclusively on outcomes. Through this process orientation, they argue, fundamental changes can occur in the way organizations work. Such changes might include increased involvement by line staff in the design of procedures and services. They might also include a definition of quality operations that effectively incorporates workforce diversity as an organizational resource.

Or, finally, it may be seen that no "one-size-fits-all" approach to organizing will be found. In Burns and Stalker's language, we may find that some organizations must indeed move away from a mechanistic structure and design toward a more organic approach. For others, however, it may be found preferable to avoid entrepreneurial, laissez-faire styles of management in favor of more circumscribed, even mechanistic approaches. As contingency theorists are fond of saying, "It depends." The most useful organizational and management theories and approaches for human service agencies in the 1990s and beyond will depend on such factors as mission; objectives; target population served; personal, family and social problems addressed; the types of people employed; the state of the art of treatment or intervention; the clarity of outcome expectations; and other such variables. All things considered, what faces us is an exciting scenario for application of new knowledge and discovery of new approaches to understanding and managing organizations, particularly those in which social workers operate.

SUMMARY

The goal of this chapter has been to introduce theoretical notions about organizations and to begin tying these notions to the task of understanding organizations in which most social workers practice. These theories and perspectives can be understood partly in terms of the way they differ among themselves (Table 7.1). Some theories (such as scientific management and the human relations school) are prescriptive models, meaning that they provide guidelines on how to organize. In contrast, descriptive theories (such as the bureaucracy and the decision-making model) offer conceptual strategies for analyzing organizations and their operations.

These theories can also be distinguished according to their approach to explaining organizational behavior. Some theories assume a rational model in which behavior is seen as the result of logical decision making oriented toward the instrumental goals of the organization. Other theories employ a natural systems approach, in which the organization is seen as being analogous to a biological organism and its behavior as responding to basic concerns for survival and self-maintenance.

Another way organizational theories differ involves whether they adopt a closed- or open-systems perspective on the role of the organizations' environments. Closed-systems approaches implicitly focus on internal structure and process in organizations and tend to direct little or no attention to the role of the environment. By comparison, open-systems models emphasize organizations' dependence on their environment and adopt analytical strategies that view internal structure and process as the product of interactions with the environment.

Each theory we have reviewed can also be understood in terms of one of a small group of organization variables toward which it tends to direct attention. These variables include structure (the bureaucracy), productivity and the role of management (scientific and universalistic management), social interactions and self-actualization (human relations and Theory Y), organizational goals (the institutional school and management by objectives), strategic choice (the decision-making model), environmental interactions (contingency theory), the exercise of power and political influence (the political economy model), organizational culture, and quality of output (TQM). As is often the case with theory-building in many different arenas, many of the models have developed out of criticisms of earlier works that have directed attention in new and fruitful directions. Nonetheless, even the earliest of these theories still has some validity, and the critical task in an organizational analysis is to glean from these various models the ideas that best explain the particular organization being addressed.

As we will see, organizational analysis in human service organizations has already produced a substantial body of literature that can be very helpful to macro practice. Chapter 8 will review this literature and discuss means for applying it to specific problems that may arise in human service organizations.

REFERENCES

Astin, H. S., & Leland, C. (1991) *Women of influence, women of vision: A cross-generational study of leaders and social change.* San Francisco, CA: Jossey-Bass.

Barker, R. L. (1995) *The social work dictionary* (3rd ed.). Washington, D.C.: National Association of Social Workers.

Blau, P. M., and Scott, W. R. (1962) *Formal organizations.* San Francisco: Chandler.

Burns, T., and Stalker, G. M. (1961) *The management of innovation.* London: Tavistock.

Champion, D. J. (1975) *The sociology of organizations.* New York: McGraw-Hill.

Cyert, R. M., and March, J. G. (1963) *A behavioral theory of the firm.* Englewood Cliffs, NJ: Prentice-Hall.

Deming, W. E. (1982) Out of the crisis. Cambridge: Massachusetts Institute of Technology, Center for Advanced Engineering Study.

Drucker, P. F. (1954) *The practice of management.* New York: Harper.

Etzioni, A. (1964) *Modern organizations.* Englewood Cliffs, NJ: Prentice-Hall.

Feigenbaum, A. V. (1991) *Total quality control.* New York: McGraw-Hill.

Galbraith J. R. (1973) *Designing complex organizations.* Reading, MA: Addison-Wesley.

George, C. S. Jr. (1968) *The history of management thought.* Englewood Cliffs, NJ: Prentice-Hall.

Gottlieb, N. (1992) *Empowerment, political analyses, and services for women.* In Hasenfeld, Y., ed. Human services as complex organizations (pp. 301–19) Newbury Park, CA: Sage. Herzberg, F. (1966) *Work and the nature of man.* Cleveland: World.

Jamieson, D., and O'Mara, J. (1991) *Managing workforce 2000: Gaining the diversity advantage.* San Francisco: Jossey-Bass.

Kanter, R. M. (1989) *When giants learn to dance.* New York: Simon & Schuster.

Katz, D., and Kahn, R. L. (1966) *The social psychology of organizations.* New York: Wiley.

Kelly, R. M. (1991) *The gendered economy: Work, careers, and success.* Newbury Park, CA: Sage.

Landsberger, H. A. (1958) *Hawthorne revisited.* Ithaca, NY: Cornell University Press.

Lawrence, P. R., and Lorsch, J. W. (1967) *Organization and environment: Managing differentiation and integration.* Boston: Graduate School of Business Administration, Harvard University.

March, J. G., and Olsen, J. P. (1976) *Ambiguity and choice in organizations.* Bergen, Norway: Universitetsforlaget.

March, J. G., and Simon, H. A. (1958) *Organizations.* New York: John Wiley.

Martin, L. L. (1993) *Total quality management in human service organizations.* Thousand Oaks, CA: Sage.

McGregor, D. (1960) *The human side of enterprise.* New York: McGraw-Hill.

Merton, R. K. (1952) Bureaucratic structure and personality. In Merton, R. K., Gray, A. P., Hockey, B., & Selvin, H. C., eds. *Reader in bureaucracy* (pp. 261–372). Glencoe, IL: Free Press.

Michels, R. (1949) *Political parties* (Paul, E., & Paul, C., trans.) Glencoe, IL: Free Press. (First published in 1915.)

Moore, S. T., and Kelly, M. J. (1996) Quality now: Moving human services organizations toward a consumer orientation to service quality. *Social Work, 41*(1), 33–40.

Morse, J. J., and Lorsch, J. W. (1970) Beyond Theory Y. *Harvard Business Review, 45,* 61–8.

Mouzelis, N. P. (1967) *Organization and bureaucracy.* London: Routledge & Kegan Paul.

Ouchi, W. (1981) *Theory Z: How American business can meet the Japanese challenge.* Reading, MA: Addison-Wesley.

Parsons, T. (1960) *Structure and process in modern societies.* Glencoe, IL: Free Press.

Patti, R. (1985) In search of purpose for social welfare administration. *Administration in Social Work, 9*(3), 1–14.

Peters, T. J., and Waterman, R. H. (1982) *In search of excellence: Lessons from America's best-run companies.* New York: Harper & Row.

Pfeffer, J. (1981) *Power in organizations.* Marshfield, MA: Pitman.

Rapp, C. A., and Poertner, J. (1992) *Social administration: A client-centered approach.* New York: Longman.

Rogers, R. E. (1975) *Organizational theory.* Boston: Allyn & Bacon.

Saylor, J. H. (1996) *TQM simplified: A practical guide* (2nd ed.). New York: McGraw-Hill.

Schein, E. H. (1985) *Organizational culture and leadership.* San Francisco: Jossey-Bass.

Schmidt, W. H., and Finnigan, J. P. (1992) *The race without a finish line: America's quest for total quality.* San Francisco: Jossey-Bass.

Scott, W. R. (1981) *Organizations: Rational, natural, and open Systems.* Englewood Cliffs, NJ: Prentice-Hall.

Selznick, P. (1949) *TVA and the grass roots.* Berkeley: University of California Press.

Selznick, P. (1957) *Leadership in administration.* New York: Harper & Row.

Sills, D. L. (1957) *The volunteers.* New York: Free Press.

Simon, H. A. (1957) *Administrative behavior* (2nd ed.). New York: Macmillan.

Sykes, A. J. M. (1965) Economic interests and the Hawthorne researchers: A comment. *Human Relations, 18,* 253–63.

Taylor, F. W. (1947) *Scientific management.* New York: Harper & Row.

Thomas, R. R., Jr. (1991) *Beyond race and gender: Unleashing the power of your total work force by managing diversity.* New York: AMACOM.

Thompson, J. D. (1967) *Organizations in action.* New York: McGraw-Hill.

von Bertalanffy, L. (1950) An outline of general system theory. *British Journal for the Philosophy of Science, 1*(2), 493–512.

Wamsley, G. L., and Zald, M. N. (1976) *The political economy of public organizations.* Bloomington: Indiana University Press.

Weber, M. (1946) *From Max Weber: Essays in sociology* (Gerth, H. H., and Mills, C. W., trans.) New York: Oxford University Press.

Weber, M. (1947) *The theory of social and economic organization* (Henderson, A. M., and Parsons T., trans.) New York: Macmillan. (First published in 1924).

SUGGESTED READINGS

Ahrne, G. (1990) *Agency and organization: Towards an organizational theory of society.* Newbury Park, CA: Sage.

Banner, D. K., and T. E. Gagne (1995) *Designing effective organizations: Traditional and transformational views.* Thousand Oaks, CA: Sage.

Bedeian, A. G. (1984) *Organizations: Theory and analysis* (2nd ed.). Chicago: Dryden Press.

Clegg, S. (1990) *Modern organizations: Organizational studies in the postmodern world.* London: Sage.

Golembiewski, R. T. (1995) *Managing diversity in organizations.* Tuscaloosa: University of Alabama Press.

Hage, J. (1980) *Theories of organizations: Form, process, and transformation.* New York: Wiley.

March, J. S., and H. A. Simon (1990) *Organizations* (2nd ed.). Cambridge, MA: Blackwell.

Matteson, M. T., and J. M. Ivancevich (1981) *Management classics*. Glenview, IL: Scott, Foresman.

McWhinney, W. (1992) *Paths of change: Strategic choices for organizations and society*. Newbury Park, CA: Sage.

Pasmore, W. A. (1988) *Designing effective organizations: The sociotechnical systems perspective*. New York: Wiley.

Roberts, K. H. (1993) *New challenges to understanding organizations*. New York: Macmillan.

Shafritz, J. M., and J. S. Ott (1992) *Classics of organizational theory* (3rd ed.). Belmont, CA: Wadsworth.

CHAPTER 8

Analyzing Human Service Organizations

Overview

Having reviewed in the previous chapter a variety of approaches to understanding organizations in general, we now turn our attention specifically to human service organizations, in which most social workers are employed. These agencies have unique characteristics that distinguish them from other organizational types and that social workers must understand in order to employ their macro-practice skills effectively. However, the distinguishing features of these agencies are not always clear-cut, thus we begin with a discussion of how human service organizations are defined.

In an earlier chapter, we quoted a definition of human service organizations as "the vast array of formal organizations that have as their stated purpose enhancement of the social, emotional, physical, and/or intellectual well-being of some component of the population" (Brager & Holloway 1978, p. 2). This definition provides a starting point, but it leaves some troubling questions. For example, manufacturing firms increase the well-being of the population by creating desirable products, but does this make them human service organizations? Also, any number of groups ranging from political lobbying firms to the Ku Klux Klan seek to promote what they perceive to be the well-being of some component of the population, but does this make them human service organizations? Hasenfeld (1983) addresses this question in part by noting that human service organizations "work directly with and on people whose attributes they attempt to shape. People are, in a sense, their 'raw material'" (p. 1). In other words, human service organizations operate in some way on people themselves, and though they may distribute or even produce certain goods (as in a food bank or housing cooperative) their focus is on improving the quality of life of their constituents, consumers, or clients.

However, many kinds of organizations work with or on people, and service providers from boutiques to barber shops to bistros are carefully designed to enhance at least the perceived well-being of their clients. Are these human service organizations? Hasenfeld addresses this point in the second part of his definition, which specifies that human service organizations "are mandated—and thus justify their existence—to protect and to promote the welfare of the people they serve" (p. 1). In other words, these organizations are expected to conform to societal expectations (both implicit and explicit) that services are provided to their constituents in a way that also promotes the overall welfare of the public. Agencies whose activities cannot be legitimized in the context of these expectations cannot be considered human service organizations.

A large variety of organizations may still be encompassed within this definition, and to make sense of this diversity the most important consideration is the auspice, or sectoral location, of the agency. As we discussed in Chapter 6, human service agencies may be classified as one of three types, corresponding to the three major sectors of the economy: public, nonprofit, or for-profit. These are important distinctions because the mission, service orientation, and nature of practice within an organization vary considerably across these types. Though for-profit agencies are growing in importance as employers of social workers, public bureaucracies and nonprofit agencies remain the most common practice venues. The following vignettes illustrate the issues and problems encountered by social workers in public and nonprofit agencies.

TWO VIGNETTES OF HUMAN SERVICE ORGANIZATIONS

Vignette 1 focuses on a large public agency and its development. Problems and issues illustrated include the growth of bureaucracy, hierarchical structure, the role of elected officials, frustrations over slow change processes, limited creative application, and barriers to client services.

Our second vignette describes a medium-sized nonprofit agency established at the turn of the century. As times change, the organization grows through the receipt of government grants and contracts. Issues related to working with boards of directors and sponsoring groups, attempts to address the needs of multiple constituencies in an increasingly regulated environment, and the use of volunteers are presented.

We hope that these vignettes will set the stage for how a social worker can begin to analyze what is happening in diverse human service organizations. Immediately following the vignettes we will briefly discuss the issues raised, after which we will present a framework for analyzing human service organizations.

Vignette 1: Canyon County Department of Child Welfare

Creating a Dynamic Organization.   Canyon County Department of Child Welfare had, for a long time, considered itself a unique and innovative organization. Created in the early 1960s, its initial years of development came during a time when national attention was focused on the development of high-quality human service programs designed to address client needs and community problems. The director of child welfare was hired as a result of a national search. She had built a strong reputation in a northeastern state as a person who ran successful programs and was well liked by the community, her staff, and clients alike.

She took the job because she was excited by the challenge of building a department from scratch with more-than-adequate resources made available from federal, state, and county governments. She hired people who, like herself, were committed to teamwork, to collaboration, and to problem solving. Middle managers and supervisors were people with many years of experience, most of whom had MSW degrees; line workers tended to be recent graduates of MSW programs. The director stressed high energy, enthusiasm, collaboration, mutual support, morale, and competence in her hiring interviews.

During the 1960s and 1970s, the Canyon County Department of Child Welfare built a reputation for providing high-quality services, for a high rate of success, and for an extremely positive work environment. It was an organization other counties looked to for leadership in dealing with emerging problems of the time—child abuse and neglect, family violence, drug and alcohol abuse, and other family-related problems.

Dismantling a Dynamic Organization.   Toward the end of the 1970s, two things happened to change the direction of the department. First, as a county in a state with the fastest-growing population in the country, the population of Canyon County doubled in size during the 1970s. Increasing fiscal and political conservatism influenced decisions of the county board of supervisors, and the child welfare budget became the focal point of a major budget reduction effort. Second, the director reached retirement age.

The board of supervisors used this opportunity to appoint a person who had spent his career in the insurance industry. They saw this as their opportunity to introduce some "hard-headed business practices" into the running of human service programs. Because of its strong national reputation, employment by the Canyon County Child Welfare Department served as a solid reference and made an individual highly marketable in other counties and states. Many managers and supervisors took advantage of other employment opportunities, and their positions were filled by people who had political connections to the board or to the director. The team approach that had dominated for two decades was replaced by a more rigid bureaucratic structure, and collegial practices were replaced by strictly enforced administrative policies.

By the end of the 1980s, the department bore little resemblance to the one that had built such a strong reputation during the 1970s. The most noticeable change was in the structure of the organization. The organizational chart reflected clearly defined work units, with reporting lines from entry level all the way through to the director. Standardized workloads were assigned regardless of the difficulty or complexity of cases. Specialization was eliminated. Likewise, employee-oriented efforts such as job rotation, job sharing, and flex-time were eliminated.

Involvement of the County Board.   The members of the county board of supervisors began to experience mounting complaints about the child welfare department. Child abuse and neglect reports went uninvestigated. Annual reports revealed a steady decline in the successful resolution of problems for families served by the department. A consultant was hired to do an organizational analysis and to make recommendations to the board of supervisors.

The consultant found little personal involvement in organizational objectives. Line staff felt that their opinions did not matter, so they either kept comments to themselves or complained to colleagues. When problems were identified, little effort was expended to analyze them or to propose solutions. Most staff members believed that success was defined in terms of adherence to policies and procedures. Ambitious staff members who hoped for successful careers in the department became experts on existing policy, not on understanding problem families or on professional practice with families as the previous staff had done.

For those who were hired into management positions, the emphasis was on control. Virtually all decisions about cases had to pass through and be signed by a supervisor and a program manager. Managers felt that staff ignored their efforts to enforce policies and procedures, especially when it came to keeping paperwork up to date. Conflict was mostly covert and managed by office politics. A personal relationship with the director or deputy director was perceived as being more important than a problem or issue faced by the organization.

Vignette 2: Lakeside Family Services

Historical Development.   Lakeside Family Services Agency was originally incorporated as the Methodist Home for Orphaned Children in 1902. Begun by the Methodist Church, this home served children with no living relatives. Situated on a large parcel of donated land on the outskirts of a metropolitan area, the home was the site of many church gatherings as well as fund-raising events over the years. Volunteers from the church and community were part of almost every activity at the home.

During the 1920s the home was the recipient of generous contributions from wealthy church and civic-minded leaders, and in the 1930s it became a Red Feather Agency. The Red Feather fund-raising campaign was the forerunner of what was now the local United Way. As campaign contributions increased, so did the scope of the home. By the mid-1940s, the home had expanded to include services for unwed mothers and family counseling, and had hired several professionally trained social workers.

Originally, the fifteen-member voluntary board of directors was elected by the Annual Conference of the Methodist Church. The bylaws specified that at least 75 percentage of board members must be members of the church and that the executive director should also be a member. Although it was not required, the majority of staff were church members and there was an active volunteer auxiliary of over 100 persons.

Major Changes Occur.   During the 1960s, the board engaged in a number of controversial meetings to determine the future of the home. Not only had service needs changed, but there were fewer and fewer orphans. The United Way was putting pressure on the home to merge with two other family service agencies in the same city. The percentage of the home's budget that came from the Methodist Church was getting smaller, even though actual dollar amounts increased each year. Several board members were encouraging the home to rethink its mission and to actively seek state and federal funding. By 1970, after a decade of controversy, the home changed its name to Lakeside Family Services Agency, disaffiliated from the Methodist Church, and became a major nonprofit provider of government contract services to children, families, and the aged. The agency relocated and the church-owned property on which the home stood reverted back to the church. Lakeside remained a United Way agency, and its funding allocations increased yearly. By 1980, however, a majority of the agency's budget (70%) came from government contracts and grants.

The remnant of the board that had supported these changes in the agency's mission, funding, and structure were joined by persons carefully selected for their expertise in fund raising and politics. They chose an executive director with an MSW and hired a director of development.

The agency was structured into three program components: (1) children's services, (2) family services, and (3) aging services. Each program component received government contracts, as well as United Way funds and private contributions, and within each component there was service diversification. For example, aging services included homemaker/chore services, home health, and adult day care.

Program directors began complaining that contract dollars never truly covered the full cost of services and that state and federal regulations were restricting their ability to provide adequate care to their respective clientele. The executive director searched for strategies to deal with these complaints and spent a great deal of time conferring with directors of other nonprofit organizations.

The Search for Strategies.   The 1980s witnessed a period of government retrenchment. Lakeside Family Services experienced cutbacks in two of its program areas. When the executive director talked with other providers, she perceived a new sense of competitiveness that she had not sensed before. When staff suggested the use of volunteers to help keep services going, the executive director realized that the previously active volunteer pool of earlier days had not been nurtured and maintained. In fact, only the aging-services program was using volunteers—in this case to do home visits to frail elderly. Even this use was limited, because the volunteers' activities were carefully structured and greatly limited by state service specifications. At the executive director's request, the board approved a fee-for-service schedule and instructed the director of development to create a plan for recruiting fee-paying clients. Staff were angered by the agency's new focus on private fee payers when they could not serve those persons they considered in greatest need. In 1990, the agency was in great financial difficulty. In desperation, the executive director began unsuccessful negotiations with United Methodist Church officials to see if they would be interested in taking the agency back under their wing.

It is not unusual for organizations, over time, to exhibit the symptoms of unhealthy behavior described in Vignettes 1 and 2. When this happens, it is often tempting to opt for a seemingly simple solution like changing the director in Vignette 1 or attracting more paying clients in Vignette 2. However, cultural change in organizations usually occurs over a long period of time. Attitudes and behaviors tend to permeate all levels of staff, so a simple change in the organization rarely solves all problems.

The two vignettes differ in that one agency is public and exists because of a government mandate, whereas the other evolved in the private nonprofit sector. However, there are a number of parallels. Both organizations developed in growth climates, only to face severe financial and political constraints in recent years. Whereas Canyon County became more bureaucratic, Lakeside became more professionalized. Just as rigid rules developed within Canyon County, Lakeside experienced the constraints of state and federal regulations when they began receiving more and more government monies. Both organizations searched for answers to complex problems that could not be easily solved. In this chapter, we propose a method of conducting organizational analyses that will enable practitioners to understand more fully what is happening in organizations like Canyon County and Lakeside.

FRAMEWORK FOR ORGANIZATIONAL ANALYSIS

The framework we propose for use in analyzing organizations is presented in the form of tasks to be completed and questions to be asked within each task. While no listing of tasks could be comprehensive for every type of organization, we will attempt to cover the major elements and considerations as they relate to human service organizations. Hasenfeld (1995) identifies a framework for analyzing a human service agency that examines (1) the agency and interorganizational relationships, and (2) the functioning of the organization itself. The framework recommended here uses a similar "road map" in directing the organizational analysis.

Completion of the tasks associated with assessing agency-environment relationships and identifying selected elements of the organization is intended to lead to a more complete and accurate understanding of the organization as a whole. It is expected that this, in turn, will facilitate change efforts. Table 8.1 provides an overview of the framework.

Focus A: Identifying the Agency's Task Environment and Assessing Relationships

Identifying the Agency's Task Environment.   The process of using the framework in Table 8.1 may be thought of as collecting information in relation to organizational boundaries (see Figure 8.1).

The framework proposes (1) *identification* of the significant elements of an organization's environment and *assessment* of organization/environment relationships; and (2) *understanding* the internal workings of the organization.

TABLE 8.1   Framework for Assessing Organizations

Focus	Tasks
A. Identifying the Agency's Task Environment and Assessing Relationships	1. Identify sources of cash and noncash revenues
	2. Assess relationships with revenue sources
	3. Identify client population and referral sources
	4. Assess agency's relationship to client population and referral sources
	5. Identify other important organizations in the task environment
	6. Assess agency's relationships to other important organizations in the task environment
B. Analyzing the Organization	7. Identify corporate authority and mission
	8. Understand administration, management, and leadership style
	9. Understand organizational and program structure
	10. Assess the organization's programs and services
	11. Assess personnel policies, procedures, and practices
	12. Assess adequacy of technical resources and systems

To understand considerations external to the organization, we will use the concept of task environment to describe the critical elements of an organization's environment. These critical elements provide the organization with its raw materials and resources (e.g., clients, revenues) and impose certain constraints.

As noted in our review of the work of James Thompson (1967) in Chapter 7, the task environment consists of elements outside an organization that enable it to operate and that set the basic context for these operations. Thompson notes that, as originally defined by Dill (1958), the task environment includes four key components: (1) customers (both distributors and users); (2) suppliers of materials, labor, capital, equipment, and work space; (3) competitors for both markets and resources; and (4) regulatory groups, including governmental agencies, unions, and interfirm associations (pp. 27–8) (see Figure 8.2).

Hasenfeld (1995) identifies three components including (1) a generalized agency environment (organizations, entities and systems important to the

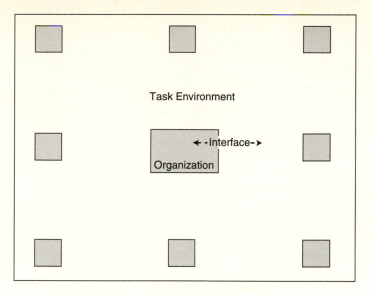

FIGURE 8.1   Organization, Task Environment, and Interface

agency), (2) market relations with entities that receive an agency's outputs and with those offering complementary or competing services, and (3) regulatory groups. Martin (1980) identifies the many environmental entities important to human service organizations. The most critical of these elements are:

- Funding sources
- Sources of noncash revenues

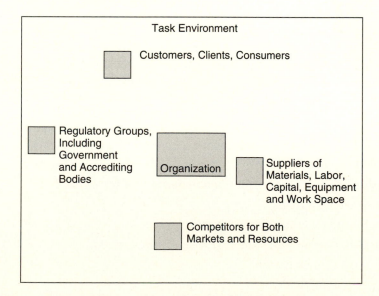

FIGURE 8.2   Typical Task Environment for an Organization

- Clients and client sources
- Other constituents

We will draw on the above work and will distill Martin's four elements into three (funding and noncash revenue sources; clients and client sources, and other constituents, including regulatory groups). We will then use them as a guide for the questions to be asked in analyzing an organization's task environment.

Recognizing the Dynamics of Agency/Environment Relationships.

Having identified important elements of the task environment of human service organizations, an equally important concern is the way in which organizations interact with these elements. Based on organizational theory and subsequent research growing out of open-systems models, two concepts appear to be critical in analyzing these dynamics: (1) resource dependence and (2) domain setting. These concepts provide the basis of a discussion of human service organizations' interactions with their environments.

Task 1: Identify Sources of Cash and Noncash Revenues.

Cash Revenues.   Questions to be asked with regard to cash revenues include:

- What are the agency's funding sources?
- How much and what percentage of the agency's total funds are received from each source?

A cynical variation on the "Golden Rule" states that "the one who has the gold makes the rules." Unfortunately, there is an undeniable element of truth to this statement when applied to many circumstances, including the operation of most organizations. Understanding how a particular agency is financed is often the key to understanding the agency itself. However, this process can be difficult in light of the fact that modern human service organizations typically obtain funds from a multitude of sources. Moreover, most organizations do not tend to make detailed funding information readily available except in cases where public funds are used and budget documents are, by law, considered public records.

A first step in analyzing organizational funding is to determine the sources from which funds come. The following list identifies major sources of revenue for human service organizations.

Major Revenue Sources for Human Service Organizations
- Government funds
  - Direct government appropriation
  - Government purchase-of-service contract funds
  - Government grants
  - Matching funds

- Tax benefits
- Donated funds
  - Direct charitable contributions (from individuals, groups, and associations such as religious groups)
  - Indirect contributions (e.g., through United Way)
  - Private grants (e.g., foundation monies)
  - Endowments
- Fees for service
  - Direct payments from clients
  - Payments from third parties (e.g., private or public insurers)
- Other agency income
  - Investments (e.g., interest, dividends, royalties)
  - Profit-making subsidiaries
  - Fund raising events and appeals

As might be expected, the sources of its funds greatly influence an organization's flexibility in how it responds to proposed change. Governmental agencies that depend totally on direct appropriations are likely to have most of their activities rigidly specified by public policy. Nonprofit agencies tend to receive funds from a greater variety of sources and thus may have greater flexibility, but even donated funds usually come with some strings attached. For-profit agencies that depend on paying clients also have greater flexibility than public agencies, but their decision making is guided foremost by the requirement that they produce returns for their investors.

Direct appropriations are virtually the exclusive source of revenues for organizations at the federal level. This source is also primary for many state, county, and local agencies, but these organizations also make use of a mixture of funds from higher levels of government. In general, the lower the level of government, the larger the number of funding sources from which organizations at that level are likely to draw revenues. Among the most important mechanisms for dissemination are block grants (lump-sum appropriations in which specific allocations are left to local governments), matching funds (which, for example, provide a certain amount of federal funds for each dollar expended by state-level agencies), and grant programs in which funds are targeted for a specific use and are restricted to that program. In the vignette regarding Canyon County earlier in this chapter, the Child Welfare Department was funded solely by government funds.

Nonprofit agencies, like Lakeside Family Services in Vignette 2, tend to have an even greater range of funding sources. Moreover, though by definition these are the agencies toward which charitable contributions are targeted, such contributions make up only a small portion of the annual budget of most nonprofit agencies. The most recent figures available show that in 1992, nonprofit organizations garnered an average of 18 percent of their funds from charitable contributions (down from 26 percent in 1977), 39 percent from dues, fees, and charges, 31 percent from government sources (up from 27 percent in 1977), and 11 percent from other sources (Hodgkinson & Weitzman 1996).

In a study that focused specifically on nonprofit human service organizations, we found the average distribution across funding sources was 34 percent from government contracts, 33 percent from charitable donations, 13 percent from client fees, 10 percent from public grants, 5 percent from private grants, and 5 percent from other sources (McMurtry, Netting, & Kettner 1991). Government contract funds are those in which a nonprofit or for-profit agency contracts with a public agency to provide specific services to specific clients. Combining these funds with those received via public grants—the average agency in this study drew almost half (44%) of its funds from government sources—and some agencies reported receiving all their funds from these sources. This suggests that many human services agencies, though nominally part of the nonprofit sector, may be more accurately viewed as quasi-public agencies. Important elements of the task environments of these organizations will thus be the public agencies that establish contract expectations and reimbursement rates.

For-profit firms are a growing arena for social work practice, and among such organizations as hospitals and nursing homes they are major service providers. In fact, Stoesz (1988) notes that as early as 1985 two hospital corporations each had revenues exceeding all charitable contributions collected nationwide by the United Way that year. Other areas in which large human service corporations are developing include child care, home-based nursing care, and corrections. Also, private counseling firms, though traditionally small in scale, are a part of this sector. All these organizations share a predominant reliance on fee-for-service revenues.

Sometimes the fees are paid directly by the agency's clients. However, most clients' fees are paid by other organizations, thus individual consumers tend to be a less important part of the task environment of private agencies than insurance companies and other third-party payers who establish policies and rates for reimbursement. For example, a for-profit counseling agency may draw a majority of its clients from the employee assistance program of a near-by manufacturing plant; thus, relationships with the manufacturer will likely be the paramount environmental consideration for this firm.

In general, a critical point in understanding funding sources is that most funds come with strings attached, and decisions on how to spend them may rest much more with the funding agency than with the recipient. This means, using governmental organizations as an example, that a county agency that appears to be subject to local decision-making processes may in fact be more accurately viewed as a local extension of the state agency that provides the bulk of its funds. A change episode that attempted to influence the use of these funds would thus be likely to succeed only if the persons seeking change recognized that decision-making power over the funds rested with organizations in the agency's task environment rather than inside its own boundaries.

The number of sources from which an agency's funds are drawn is also a key consideration. Somewhat paradoxically, an agency with many funding sources often has greater autonomy and flexibility than one with few because the loss of any single source might not jeopardize the overall viability of the organization. On the other hand, the greater the number of funding sources, the more complex the agency's operations become. With each new source comes another layer of regulatory constraints, program diversity, and account-ability expectations. Whereas the agency with a single funding source may risk becoming rigid and highly specialized, the agency with many sources may have difficulty defining and focusing on its mission.

Noncash Revenues.   Questions to be asked with regard to noncash revenues include:

- Does the organization use volunteers? If yes, how many and for what purposes?
- What material, in-kind resources (e.g., food, clothing, physical facilities, etc.) does the organization receive?
- What tax benefits does the organization receive?

In considering resources, it is also important to keep in mind that actual dollars coming into a human service organization are not the only form of resources. Many other assets on which agencies rely are not as obvious as cash revenues but may be equally important. Three such assets are volunteers, material resources, and tax benefits.

Volunteers.   Volunteers have traditionally been a mainstay of human service or-ganizations. As noted in Chapter 2, the entire nonprofit human service sector originated with the activities of individual volunteers who began to work together in order to organize their efforts better. In the Lakeside vignette presented earlier in this chapter, volunteers were critical to the organization's early development. Today, the contribution of these individuals to human service organizations is enormous. Hodgkinson and Weitzman (1996) summarize these contributions:

> In 1994, 48 percent of all American adults volunteered at an average rate of 4 hours per week ... [which totals] 89 million adults contributing over 19 billion hours. In terms of full-time equivalent employment, this translated into 8.8 mil-lion full-time employees whose assigned value was $182 billion. (p. 13)

About 13 percent of all volunteer time was devoted to organizations con-cerned with health, and about 12 percent was spent in other types of human service organizations.

Volunteers perform many different roles in human service agencies. Non-profit agencies may rely heavily on professional staff to deliver services. One important role that volunteers play is service on boards of directors. Volun-teers also contribute time to public and for-profit agencies. For example, a large for-profit corporation may allow its workers release time to volunteer for a human service project or a government department may recruit volun-teers to work with its staff. In settings such as hospitals, hospices, and nursing homes, volunteers perform numerous duties such as delivering patient mail, friendly visiting, telephone reassurance, and assisting at mealtime.

In-Kind Contributions. A second type of resource is contributions of material goods. Examples are food, clothing, physical facilities, real estate, vehicles, and a wide variety of household and office materials. In some cases these goods are provided for use directly by the agency, in other cases they are donated for the purpose of resale in order to generate cash revenues, and in still other cases they simply pass through the agency for distribution directly to clients. In each circumstance, though, the total value of these resources to organizations is again substantial. Though specific figures are difficult to obtain, one example of the magnitude of this source of income is deductions on individual and income taxes claimed for noncash charitable contributions. In 1993, almost 14 million individual filers claimed noncash charitable contributions, the monetary value of which totaled more than $15.2 billion dollars (Internal Revenue Service 1995).

Tax Benefits. Tax benefits are particularly important for private, nonprofit human service organizations. Indeed, one defining characteristic of nonprofit agencies is an official designation as a charitable organization under section 501(c)(3) of federal Internal Revenue Service regulations. Meeting the requirements of this section allows nonprofit agencies to avoid income taxes that for-profit firms must pay, and this can be a critical benefit in service arenas such as health care, where nonprofit and for-profit hospitals often engage in intense competition for patients and physicians. Tax laws are also important in terms of their effects on other revenue sources, particularly charitable contributions. For example, Karger and Stoesz (1990) note that the Tax Reform Act of 1986 may have reduced contributions to nonprofit agencies by limiting tax breaks for contributors to those who itemize deductions on their tax returns. Still, tax deductions claimed for cash contributions totaled more than $120 billion in 1993 (Internal Revenue Service 1995), and it is likely that this source of funds for human service organizations would drop precipitously if tax laws were changed to make charitable contributions no longer deductible.

Noncash resources are important considerations in an organizational analysis because an agency's behaviors may be understood as efforts to acquire and protect these assets. For example, an organization that relies heavily on volunteers may seek to protect this resource even if in so doing it comes into conflict with the interests of professional staff. Similarly, the structure of an agency may be adapted to take advantage of one of these resources, as with the growing number of nonprofit agencies that are raising funds by collecting donated material goods and reselling them through thrift stores. On the other hand, attention to noncash resources may also be important in initiating change efforts. For example, some organizational problems are often left unaddressed due to pessimism about the ability to raise funds to add or augment services, and a change agent's awareness of the possibilities posed by the use of noncash resources may be a key to overcoming this barrier.

TABLE 8.2   Tool for Assessing Cash and Noncash Resources

List Relevant Funding Sources	% of Revenue	Flexibility in Using Resources
Contract with state department of social services	26	Low
Client fees	22	High
Charitable donations	14	High
Government grant	8	Low
Other		

List Noncash Revenues	Describe
Volunteers	9 board of directors
	33 respite care for foster parents
	12 transportation providers
In-kind	1 van
	1 branch office
Tax benefits	$120,000 annually in savings from nonprofit status

Using a tool such as the one depicted in Table 8.2 can be helpful in assessing the status of cash and noncash resources for an organization.

Task 2: Assess Relationship with Revenue Sources.   The main question to be asked in relation to this task is:

- What is the quality of the relationship between funding sources and the agency?

Resource dependence means that because organizations are open systems, they must rely on elements in their environment in order to obtain resources necessary for survival. Because of this dependence, organizations try to establish relationships that minimize uncertainty regarding the availability of these resources. Relationships with elements of the task environment are based on exchanges (e.g., of funds, clients, or services), and exchanges are always reciprocal to some degree (Thompson 1967). An exchange may be a more or less equal one that benefits both organizations and in which each member holds roughly equal power. Other exchanges, however, may be dramatically unequal.

The dynamics of client selection can be better understood in terms of resource dependence. As we noted, the resource-dependence model posits that external bodies upon which an organization depends for vital resources are often more powerful determinants of organizational actions than internal factors (Pfeffer & Salancik 1978). Within this model, clients can be seen as simply one of a variety of resources for which agencies compete.

Cash funding, for better or for worse, is central to the consideration of resources. The extent and consequences of external control are affected both by the source of funds and the circumstances of the agency acquiring them. For example, Hardina (1990) studied the funding base of 53 organizations to determine the relationship between client's access to service and an agency's relative reliance on various funding sources. Her results showed that agencies restricted to grass-roots funding (primarily local donations) were less able than those who drew funds from outside the community to establish and maintain reliable service availability. In general, the greater the variety of funding, the greater the fiscal health and service flexibility of the organization. The exception was government funds, which were found to limit service flexibility and client self-help, stiffen eligibility requirements, and reduce citizen participation.

Wardell (1988) developed a set of four propositions embodying the dynamics of both resource dependency and domain setting in his study of Youth Advocate Programs in Pennsylvania:

1. An organization's survival is a function of its ability to learn and adapt to changing environmental contingencies.
2. The degree of an organization's dependence on some element of its task environment is (1) directly related to the organization's need for resources which that element can provide, and (2) inversely related to the ability of other elements to provide the same resource.
3. Organizations which are perceived as threatening to an existing organizational configuration will evoke defensive reactions by established local organizations.
4. The persistence (or survival) of an organization over time is directly related to the degree of formalization it attains in exchange agreements with other organizations constituting its task environment. (pp. 92–3)

A tool such as the one depicted in Table 8.3 can be helpful in assessing an agency's relationship with revenue sources.

Task 3: Identify Client Population and Referral Sources.   Questions to be asked in this area include:

- What client groups does this organization serve?
- What are the demographic characteristics of clients?
- What percentages of clients pay full fees, partial fees, or no fees, or are covered by contract revenues?
- What are the major sources of client referrals?

Understanding a client population begins with identifying the problems and needs they are experiencing and the services that are being provided. Programs and services provided by a human service organization should be seen as responses to community need. When a community suffers from a problem of dependent, abused, and neglected children, for example, child welfare agencies respond by providing both in-home and out-of-home services.

TABLE 8.3   Assessing the Relationship to Funding Sources

List Relevant Funding Sources	Describe Nature of Communication, Length of Relationship, Changes in Funding
Contract with state department of social services	Quarterly site visits; have contracted for 12 years; funding has always stayed steady or increased
Client fees	Most clients are seen on a weekly basis; they either pay directly or through their insurance plan; client fees have declined 2 percent in the past three years
Charitable donations	Largest donations come from church groups; agency staff visit church representatives once a year; donations have increased 3.5 percent in the past year

In attempting to understand a client population as a part of the task environment, it is important to understand: (1) what problems are being addressed (e.g., family violence, depression, homelessness), (2) clients' perspectives on the etiology (cause-and-effect relationships) of the problem, (3) various community perspectives on the etiology of the problem, and (4) how well client and community needs and expectations are being addressed.

This assessment requires some background research and data collection, probably through interviews with key informants. Findings will provide the change agent with a sense of how relevant, important, and valued this agency is to both the client population and the community.

A second approach to understanding the client population is to produce a demographic profile. This profile typically includes such factors as age, gender, cultural/ethnic group, marital status, educational background, and other important variables. It is important to understand the degree of demographic homogeneity or diversity, and to compare client demographics to those of the population in need. This comparison will provide a basis for understanding the quality of agency/community relationships. For example, how an agency is perceived by the African-American community or by the gay/lesbian community in terms of meeting their needs can be critical in terms of future agency appeals for funding or other types of support.

A third important variable in understanding the client population is the financial relationship between client and agency. In commercial firms, customers are those who purchase goods or services, thus the organization carefully designs its outputs to meet the needs of this group. In human service agencies, those who pay for services often are not the same as those who receive them. This is an important distinction, and for our purposes we will define the clients of human service organizations as those who are direct recipients of services.

Within this definition, clients can be divided into two groups. In the first group are those who are able to pay the agency (either personally or through third-party reimbursement) at least as much as their services cost. Paying clients are important resources that agencies both seek to attract and are most likely to serve. Revenues from paying clients are typically used to offset the cost of serving nonpaying clients in a nonprofit agency.

The second group consists of persons who are able to pay only part or none of the cost of their services (Netting, McMurtry, Kettner, & Jones-McClintic 1990). Revenues for serving these clients must be generated from other sources(e.g., through fund raising, profits earned from serving paying clients, or other means).

Because clients are central to every agency's mission and function, referral sources are important elements in the task environments of human service organizations. Formal and informal referral arrangements among agencies for exchange of clients form the basis for interactions that are often viewed with equal importance as relationships with funding sources. Residential treatment centers, for example, rely on referrals from public agencies, school districts and nonprofit agencies to keep their beds full.

A tool such as the one depicted in Table 8.4 can be helpful in identifying client population and referral sources.

Task 4: Assess the Agency's Relationship to Client Population and Referral Sources.   Among the questions to be asked here are:

- What is the organization's domain (specifically, for what types of expertise is the agency recognized?)
- Does the agency claim a larger domain than it serves?
- Does demand for services outstrip supply, or is there unused capacity?
- What types of clients does the organization refuse (e.g., are there disproportionate numbers of poor, elderly, person of color, women, persons with disabilities, gays/lesbians, or other groups that are typically underserved?

A useful concept for understanding agency-client-community relationships, taken from the systems framework is the notion of organizational domain (Levine & White 1961). A domain refers to what the organization does and who it serves, and it is the means by which the organization establishes its role or niche within its environment.

Domain setting refers to the process by which organizations establish their domains among others within their task environment. One part of the process is domain legitimation, whereby the organization wins acknowledgment of claims it makes as to its sphere of activities and expertise. Legitimation is not always immediately forthcoming, and there is usually a disparity

TABLE 8.4   Identifying Client Populations and Referral Sources

List Client Groups Served

1. Couples/individuals relinquishing children
2. Couples wanting to adopt
3. Foster parent applicants
4. Foster parents
5. Individuals in need of personal counseling
6. Families in need of counseling
7. Drug abusers

Demographic Makeup of Client Population

Age	%	Ethnicity	%	Gender	%	Fees	%
Under 20	5	American Indian	3	Female	64	Full pay	26
20–29	15	African American	14	Male	36	Some pay	38
30–39	22	Asian American	4			No pay	15
40–49	29	Hispanic	19			Contract	21
50–59	19	White	60				
60–69	8	Other					
70+	2						

Referral Sources	%
Physicians and clinics	15
Attorneys	26
School counselors	18
Clergy	22
Social service agencies	19

between what an organization says are its boundaries, the claimed domain, and what these boundaries actually are—the de facto domain (Greenley & Kirk 1973).

Claims regarding domains tend to evolve along with circumstances in the environment. Specifically, agencies seek to take advantage of available resources, and most are constantly adjusting their domains as a means of doing so. Funding trends in Washington, D.C., and state capitols are followed, and agencies may attempt to compete for funds in areas where they have no real expertise or experience.

From a resource standpoint, clients can be viewed as either assets or liabilities by an agency, depending on whether they fit within the organization's domain and whether they can pay for services. Recognizing this dynamic, a longstanding concern relative to agencies' relationships with clients is whether certain groups of clients, especially the most needy, are being excluded from access to services (Cloward & Epstein 1965). Results of a variety of studies over the past 20 years suggest this may indeed be the case.

In an early study, Kirk and Greenley (1974) examined clients' efforts to obtain services. Their results showed that only 47 of every 100 clients were served by the first two agencies they visited; the rest were either rejected or referred at least twice. In a companion piece, Greenley and Kirk (1973) analyzed the dynamics of these outcomes and identified domain selection as a key factor. Because most agencies had larger claimed domains than de facto domains, they attracted clients that they were unable to serve. Nevertheless, this disparity was apparently seen as desirable by many agencies, since it afforded them the opportunity to "cream" the best-fitting clients who could pay and to refer or reject the remainder.

In addition, important distinctions appeared between agencies in terms of boundary control, meaning the ability of the agency to reject clients that it did not wish to serve. Agencies with high boundary control (usually for-profit and prestigious nonprofit organizations) were those most likely to engage in creaming, leaving clients who were rejected to seek out agencies with low boundary control. This resulted in the clients with the greatest difficulties and the least ability to pay being directed to agencies that were already the most overcrowded and had the fewest available resources (Greenley & Kirk 1973).

As a general rule, boundary control is highest in for-profit organizations, where the primary goal is making a profit, and lowest in governmental organizations, which are intended to provide the "safety net" for clients who cannot obtain services elsewhere. However, since the early 1980s governmental policies have tended to accelerate existing trends toward shifting a greater burden of services to the private sector. The presumption has been that private sector organizations can provide services more efficiently and effectively than large governmental bureaucracies, and that, in the case of nonprofit organizations, they can also draw on their traditional commitments to the poor to ensure that these clients are served.

Unfortunately, a number of studies suggest that this trend has often led to service reductions or restrictions, particularly on the part of nonprofit agencies. Among the reasons for these cutbacks have been changes in governmental rules (Berg & Wright 1981) and delays in reimbursement for contract services (Kramer & Grossman 1987). Grønbjerg (1990) studied the effects of changing governmental policies on nonprofit agencies in the Chicago area. She argues that services often diminished because these policies misunderstood the nature of the private sector, noting:

> these [policies] were unrealistic because only a few nonprofit organizations focus on the poor and their problems, and relatively few made significant efforts to move in that direction during the early to mid-1980s. Nonprofit organizations are not as responsive to the poor as public stereotypes might suggest, probably because they have enough to do without focusing on the poor and their difficult problems. [The policies] falsely assumed that nonprofit organizations have a strong commitment to the poor that is independent of the incentives provided by government funding. (pp. 228–9)

TABLE 8.5   **Assessing Relationships with Clients and Referral Sources**

Client Population	Supply vs. Demand	Unserved/Underserved
Adoptive couples/ children available	5 couples for every child available	Special needs children
Foster homes/ children in need	1.5 children in need for every home available	Special needs children
Families in need of counseling	2 to 3-week waiting list	Non-English-speaking families
Drug abusers	3-month waiting list	Poor, no pay, low pay, uninsured

The important point is that human service agencies adjust their boundaries according to a wide range of factors, and a misunderstanding of these may lead to critical service gaps. One key criterion in boundary setting is the nature of the clients themselves, and being poor or having complex, long-standing problems are characteristics that simultaneously increase the level of need yet, ironically, decrease the likelihood of being served.

A tool such as the one depicted in Table 8.5 can be helpful in assessing the agency's relationship to client populations and referral sources.

Task 5: Identify Other Important Organizations in the Task Environment. Questions to be asked include:

- What state and federal regulatory bodies oversee programs provided by this organization?
- With what government agencies does this organization contract for service provision?
- What professional associations, labor unions, or accrediting bodies influence agency operations?
- What are the perceptions of the "general public" in terms of the relevance, value, and quality of agency services?

Within an organization's task environment are groups that do not necessarily provide resources but that set the context in which the agency operates. One example is regulatory bodies that are responsible for setting the boundaries of acceptable service practices. Many of these are governmental licensing agencies that inspect and certify both the physical environment and services of certain organizations (e.g, nursing homes, child-caring institutions, residential treatment facilities, etc.). Others are government contracting agencies that often require provider agencies to conform to detailed procedural guidelines in order to be reimbursed for the services they deliver. Still others are local, state, and federal revenue departments that levy taxes and monitor financial accounting procedures. Extensive accounting and funding-usage requirements are also imposed by nongovernmental funding sources such as the United Way.

Organizations such as professional associations, labor unions, and accrediting bodies also help to establish the regulatory boundaries of practice. However, their influence may be exerted through individuals within the organization rather than on the organization as a whole. For example, standards established in the National Association of Social Workers (NASW) Code of Ethics and for members of the Academy of Certified Social Workers (ACSW) govern the activities of staff who are members of these bodies. State licensing bodies impose similar constraints, and organizations with a high proportion of employees who meet these requirements may function differently than those with relatively few. Accrediting bodies such as the Joint Commission on Accreditation of Health Care Organizations (JCAHO) have the power to determine whether organizations will be allowed to continue in an accredited status. Loss of this status can influence funding, referrals, and even continuation as a viable organization.

The "general public" is another part of this set of constituents. By their nature, human service organizations are dependent on some form of social sanction for their activities, and loss of public support may jeopardize their existence. Unfortunately, views of members of the general public are not always apparent. Moreover, public opinion is seldom unanimous. Organizations must determine which of a typically wide variety of expressed views represents the predominant attitude.

Within the task environment, public opinion is often conveyed through a bewildering diversity of elements. These include elected representatives, interest and advocacy groups, civic organizations, and others. In addition, funding sources are indirect but nonetheless important indicators of public views. Patterns in the ebb and flow of charitable donations, for example, suggest both general levels of public concern and particular problems toward which this concern is directed (as do the priorities of private foundations). Finally, mass media outlets are critical purveyors of public attitudes, though by their nature they often emphasize the most extreme rather than the most typical opinions.

Child protective services provide an example of the relationship between agencies, public opinion, and mass media (as both a carrier and shaper of public opinion). Deciding whether to remove an at-risk child from his or her home involves a delicate balancing act between concern for the child's well-being and concern for parental rights. In one well-publicized case in Washington state, for example, the fatal abuse of a child led to public outcry, which in turn resulted in legislative changes that instructed protective service workers to favor the safety of the child in such decisions. However, publicity on cases in other locations has featured allegations of "child-snatching" by protective service workers, which in turn led to legislative imposition of stricter guidelines governing the removal of children.

TABLE 8.6 Identifying Other Important Organizations

Other Important Organizations	Programs Affected
Regulatory	
State department of child welfare	Day care
County health department	Day care
Contracts	
State department of	Respite care
developmental disabilities	Vocational training
Professional associations	
National Association of Social Workers	Individual and family counseling
American Psychological Association	
Accreditation	
Council on Accreditation	Individual and family counseling
General public	
Media accounts (past 3 years)	Drug and alcohol programs
Advocacy groups	

The point is that public opinion is dynamic rather than static, and similar agencies at different times or in different places may encounter very divergent public attitudes and expectations. Identifying the task environment is therefore an ongoing process as new groups develop and as public attitudes change. A tool such as the one depicted in Table 8.6 can be useful in identifying other important organizations in the agency's task environment.

Task 6: Assess the Agency's Relationship to Other Important Organizations in the Task Environment. Questions to be asked include:

- What other agencies provide the same services to the same clientele as this organization?
- With whom does the organization compete?
- With whom does the organization cooperate? Is the organization part of a coalition or an alliance?
- How is the organization perceived by regulatory bodies, government contracting agencies, professional organizations, accrediting bodies, and the general public in relation to its peers and competitors?

One further element of the environment that also plays a role in these dynamics is other service providers. Relationships between agencies within each others' task environments can be competitive, cooperative, or a mixture of the two, depending on the circumstances.

In Chapter 6, Table 6.6 delineated five levels of interaction leading to improved programming. These levels were communication, cooperation, coordination, collaboration, and confederation. These levels can be used to assess how a human service organization relates to other members of its task environment.

Competitive relationships characterize circumstances in which two or more agencies seek the same resources (clients, funds, volunteers, etc.) from the same sources. Increasingly, this competition takes place between nonprofit and for-profit agencies, and the competition targets fee-for-service and contract-eligible clients. Nonprofit agencies also compete among themselves for charitable donations and for government and private foundation grants. For example, McMurtry et al. (1991), found that nonprofit agencies reported competition for both funds and clients to have risen during the previous three years, with the greatest source of competition being other nonprofit organizations rather than for-profit agencies.

Competition is not the exclusive approach, however. Cooperative arrangements are also common, as in the case of referral agreements between agencies, which are used as a means of exchanging clients that do not fit the referring agency but are considered resources by the agency to whom they are referred. More generally, agencies have also developed large-scale coalition-building efforts designed to improve their ability to advocate for particular client needs (Weisner 1983). Others have developed community-oriented cooperative arrangements to ensure more complete service coverage within particular areas (Merritt & Neugeboren 1990). Factors contributing to this behavior include community awareness of service needs, resource scarcity, and the capacity of local governments to coordinate these arrangements.

The final assessment of agency-community relationships, then, has to do with how the agency is perceived in relation to its peers and competitors. How do the regulatory agencies, accrediting bodies, government contracting agencies, professional associations, the media, and the general public perceive this organization? Is it seen as a valued part of a community service network? Or is it seen as self-serving and unconcerned about its community? Assessing these perceptions assumes that the agency has some sort of a "track record" in the community, and that key informants are willing to share perceptions of how the agency fits into the overall community service network.

A tool such as the one depicted in Table 8.7 can be useful in assessing relationships to other important organizations in the agency's task environment.

Focus B: Analyzing the Organization

Analysis of organizations, like analysis of communities, requires a breakdown of a large, complex entity into elements. The objective is to be able to identify the points or locations within the organization that help to explain organizational strengths and to understand its weaknesses or problem areas. Each element must be understood in terms of how it relates or does not relate to identified problem(s), and to understand how interactions between and among elements support or fail to support the continuation of problem(s).

TABLE 8.7   Describe Relationship with Other Service Providers

Other Agencies Providing Service	Relationship
State Department of Child Welfare	Collaborative
Central City Family Services	Competitive
Counseling Advocates, Inc.	Competitive
New Foundations	Collaborative
Baptist Family Services	Collaborative
Etc . . .	

For an illustration of organizational analysis, let us return to the examples of the Canyon County Department of Child Welfare and Lakeside Family Services Agency used at the beginning of this chapter. When an organization such as Canyon County is experiencing problems in productivity, in quality of client service, in morale, and in worker-management relationships, it would not be unusual for the county board of supervisors to hire a management consultant to do an analysis of the department. Similarly, in a nonprofit organization such as Lakeside that has become more professional, has become dependent on government funds, whose mission has evolved, and which is now experiencing cutbacks in funding, a consultant is often hired to analyze the organization and recommend strategies needed to become economically self-sufficient.

It is possible that consultants, after interviewing representative staff, consumers, board members, and others would be able to document all the problems identified above, would pose some reasons for existence of the problems (working hypotheses), and would recommend some solutions or remedies. Using such an approach, consultants are often misled into recommending short-term solutions such as staff development and training, employee incentive programs, morale-building activities such as social events, relationship-building activities between management and staff, attempts to humanize the chief executive officer, and other such activities. These kinds of undertakings rarely solve the kinds of fundamental problems that necessitated the use of a management consultant in the first place.

An alternative approach to organizational analysis would be to conduct a systematic examination of a number of organizational elements. These elements might include: (1) organizational mission; (2) organizational structure, including location, management, staffing and workload of programs and services; (3) goals and objectives of programs; (4) adequacy of funding; (5) personnel policies and practices; (6) management style; (7) problem solving and communication patterns; and other such elements.

Within each element one could examine ideal models or optimal levels of functioning as illustrated in current theoretical or research literature. From the ideal, one would then move to an examination of data and documentation that depict the actual situation, and finally to an examination of the gaps between ideal and real. The attempt is to put one's finger on the underlying cause(s) as precisely as possible in the interest of solving long-term problems and avoiding dealing merely with symptoms.

In this section we propose a framework for analysis that identifies elements to be examined within the organization, that explores relevant theoretical frameworks, that identifies the questions to be answered, and that proposes data and documentation to be collected or examined.

The elements to be examined include:

1. Corporate authority and mission;
2. Administrative, management, and leadership style;
3. Organizational and program structure;
4. Planning, delivery, and evaluation of programs and services;
5. Personnel policies and practices;
6. Adequacy of technology and resources.

Task 7: Identify Corporate Authority and Mission.   Major questions to be asked under this task are:

- What is the basis for and extent of the organization's corporate authority?

- What is its mission?

- Is the organization operating in a manner that is consistent with its authority and mission?

- To what extent is the mission supported by staff who perform different roles within the organization?

- Are policies and procedures consistent with mission and authority?

Basic to understanding any organization is understanding its domain, as described earlier in this chapter. Examining corporate authority involves an attempt to understand the legal basis on which the organization operates. If the organization is public (governmental), its legal basis is established in statute or executive order. If it is not public, its legal basis rests in articles of incorporation. In some situations it can be important to examine these documents firsthand rather than accept secondary interpretations. There have been instances in which organizations are incorporated for one purpose, and perhaps even funded through a trust that specifies that purpose, such as the running of an orphanage as in the example of Lakeside Family Services. Over the years new populations and services are added to the mission, such as services to pregnant teens. It is possible that such expansion can reach the point at which an agency begins operating outside of its legally authorized area.

A statement of mission establishes the problems or needs to be addressed, the populations to be served, and the client outcomes (in general terms) expected. Mission statements are relatively permanent expressions of the reason for existence of an organization, and they are not expected to change unless the fundamental reason for existence of the organization changes. Lack of clarity in a mission statement or differences between mission and organizational activity can be indicators of problem areas. For example, Lakeside Fam-

TABLE 8.8   Assessing Corporate Authority and Mission

Checklist	Yes	No
1. Are articles of incorporation on file?	____	____
2. Is there a written set of bylaws?	____	____
3. Are board members and agency director familiar with bylaws?	____	____
4. Is there a mission statement?	____	____
5. Is it one page or less?	____	____
6. Does it make a statement about expected client outcomes?	____	____
7. Are staff aware of, and do they practice in accordance with the mission statement?	____	____

ily Services is a prime candidate for reexamining its original mission established in the early 1900s when the agency was an orphanage. If this organization has not revised its mission, it may find that its stated reason for existence does not accurately reflect what it actually does. Rethinking the mission and what the organization wants to be may begin the process of redirecting the agency.

Peters and Waterman (1982) are unequivocal in their commitment to the notion of shared vision as integral to the success of an organization. Without some common understanding of mission and direction there will inevitably be individuals and groups working at cross purposes. With a shared vision, there may still be differences about strategies, but there will be commitment to the same ends or outcomes.

Some of the more important documentation and data sources to be examined in understanding corporate authority and mission might include:

1. Articles of incorporation, statutes, or executive orders;
2. Mission statement;
3. Bylaws of the organization;
4. Minutes of selected board meetings;
5. Interviews with selected administrators, managers, and staff.

A tool such as the one depicted in Table 8.8 can be useful in assessing the agency's corporate authority and mission.

Task 8: Understand Administration, Management and Leadership Style.
Questions to be asked include:

- How is the workplace organized and work allocated?
- Is appropriate authority and information passed on along with responsibility?
- How close is supervision and what, exactly, is supervised? Is it tasks, is it functions, or is it the employee?
- How are decisions made? Is information solicited from those affected?

- Do employees feel valued at every level? Do they believe they are making a contribution to the success of the organization?
- How is conflict handled?

A wealth of literature exists concerning approaches to administration, management, and leadership. Miles (1975) classifies managerial theories or models into one of three categories: (1) the traditional model, (2) the human relations model, and (3) the human resources model.

The traditional model is characterized by very close supervision of work, control of subordinates, breaking work down into simple tasks that are easily learned, and establishing detailed work routines. Similar to McGregor's characterization of "Theory X," the assumptions are that people inherently dislike work, that they are not self-motivated or self-directed, and that they do it only because they need the money. The traditional model would include such theorists as Weber, Taylor, and others committed to the basic tenets of bureaucracy or scientific management (as discussed in Chapter 7).

The human relations model is characterized by efforts on the part of management to make each worker feel useful and important. Management is open to feedback, and subordinates are allowed to exercise some self-direction on routine matters. Assumptions are that people want to feel useful and important, that they have a need to belong, and that these needs are more important than money in motivating people to work. Theories that support the human relations model would include Mayo's human relations theory, as well as many of the theorists who expanded on Mayo's work and focused on employee motivation.

The human resources model is characterized by a focus on the use of untapped resources that exist within employees. The manager is expected to create an environment in which all members may contribute to the limits of their abilities. Full participation is encouraged on all matters, and self-direction and self-control are supported and promoted. Assumptions are that work means a great deal more than merely earning a paycheck. It is an important part of people's lives, and they want to contribute to the success of the total work effort. Furthermore, people are assumed to be creative, resourceful, and capable of contributing a great deal more when they are unrestricted by the constraints of the traditional or the human relations models. The theories that support the human resources model are drawn essentially from the work on contingency theory (Burns & Stalker 1961) and well supported by a number of contemporary authors (Peters & Waterman 1982).

This philosophy of management is important to understand because it affects so many facets of organizational life. It can affect, for example, whether adult protective service workers are allowed merely to collect facts from a battered elderly person and then turn to a supervisor who will direct the next steps, or whether they are allowed to use professional judgment to intervene as they see fit.

TABLE 8.9   Assessing Leadership and Management Style

	Management Only	Input Allowed but Ignored	Input Solicited and Used	Group Consensus, Full Participation
1. How are organizational goals established?	_____	_____	_____	_____
2. What is the climate for supporting the achievement of goals?	_____	_____	_____	_____
3. Where are program-level decisions made?	_____	_____	_____	_____
4. How does information flow throughout the organization?	_____	_____	_____	_____
5. Who has involvement in providing feedback about performance?	_____	_____	_____	_____

Some of the more important documents and data sources to be examined to understand organizational administration, management, and leadership style might include:

1. Job description of the chief executive officer (CEO) and other staff in positions of leadership.
2. Interviews with board members (if the agency is private) or the person to whom the CEO is accountable (if the agency is public) to determine their expectations of the CEO.
3. Criteria used for performance evaluation of the CEO and other staff in positions of leadership.
4. An interview with the CEO to determine expectations for other staff in positions of leadership.
5. Organizational chart.
6. Interviews with staff in various roles to determine perceptions about the job, the workplace, supervision, and administration.

A tool such as the one depicted in Table 8.9 can be useful in assessing the agency's management and leadership style.

Task 9: Understand Organizational and Program Structure.   Major questions to be asked include:

- What are the major departmental or program units on the organizational chart?

- What is the rationale for the existing organizational structure?
- Is this the most logical structure? Is it consistent with and supportive of the mission?
- Is supervision logical and capable of performing expected functions? Are staff capable of performing expected functions?
- Is there an informal organization (people who carry authority because they are respected by staff, and thus exert influence) that is different from those in formally designated positions of authority?

When we think of organizational structure we tend to think of an organizational chart with boxes and lines indicating a hierarchy from the highest level down through entry-level positions. The chart helps us to understand who reports to whom, who is responsible for what divisions of the organization, and how the chain of command proceeds from bottom to top.

This system, of course, is patterned after the bureaucratic model described by Weber (1946). This model of organizational structure is used widely because it is easy to understand and apply, it ensures that everyone has one and only one supervisor, and it provides for lines of communication, exercise of authority, performance evaluation, discipline, and the many other functions necessary to the running of an organization.

However, there are many critics of bureaucracy and many who believe that it is not the best structure for human service agencies, for a number of reasons. Critics argue that bureaucratic structure causes problems in human service organizations because such standardized techniques work well only in predictable circumstances, whereas individual clients and their problems are unique. Rules that govern the production process in manufacturing enterprises, for example, may be helpful in ensuring consistent quality of the product, but in a human service organization these rules may serve only to constrain workers' ability to exercise professional judgment.

A number of terms have been used to describe the dysfunctions of bureaucracies. Merton (1952) uses the term *learned incompetence* to signify the performance of employees who rely so heavily on a policy manual to make their decisions that they are unable to think logically or creatively about the problems clients bring to the agency.

Lipsky (1984) uses the term *bureaucratic disentitlement* to describe situations in which clients fail to receive benefits or services to which they are entitled due to decisions that are based on internal organizational considerations rather than service needs. Hasenfeld (1983) calls attention to *goal displacement,* which describes the tendency of organizations to lose sight of organizational mission and goals and to focus on the concerns of units and subunits within the organization. Still, Etzioni (1964) argues that bureaucratic structure both persists and expands because its highly rational

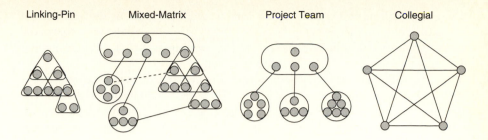

Linking-Pin	Mixed-Matrix	Project Team	Collegial

Stable	ENVIRONMENT	Turbulent
Fixed	GOALS	Ambiguous
Standardized	TECHNOLOGY	Unprogrammed

FIGURE 8.3   Human Resources Structures and Environmental Conditions

(This figure is based on a diagram developed by Rober Biller.)

[Source: Miles, R. *Theories of Management: Implications for Organizational Behavior and Development* (New York: McGraw-Hill, 1978), p. 91.] Reprinted with permission from McGraw-Hill.

approach to structuring complex systems leads to greater efficiency and predictability.

Contingency theorists, in addressing the question of what organizational structure is best, contend that it depends on what it is that the organization is expected to produce. Morse and Lorsch (1970) demonstrated that higher productivity in one type of organization (a container-manufacturing plant) was achieved through a traditional structure with clearly defined roles, responsibilities, and lines of supervision. Another type of organization (a research lab) achieved higher productivity through a very loose structure, which allowed researchers maximum flexibility to carry out their own work unfettered by rules, regulations, and supervision. Alternative structures are depicted in Figure 8.3.

Miles (1975) proposes several alternatives to bureaucratic structure. One option, adapted from the work of Likert (1961), is called a linking-pin structure. In this type of organization, rigid lines of reporting and one-on-one relationships are abandoned in favor of placing an emphasis on work units. One or more persons within a work unit are then selected to play a linking role to other work units, in which collaboration is important. By serving as a fully functioning participant in both units, persons in the linking role are able to facilitate better communication and working relationships than are possible through the traditional structure.

Another option is matrix structure, where supervision is assigned to a function rather than to a person. Under this type of structure, staff are likely to have more than one supervisor, and constant communication is a necessity. A matrix management structure might be used in a ward of a mental hospital, where supervision of a social worker with an MSW degree for the activities of the ward falls to the designated ward supervisor who may be a registered nurse, while supervision of professional functioning and performance evaluation falls to a senior-level MSW social worker.

Still another structure is the project team structure, in which teams working on the same effort take responsibility for different functions and work relatively independently. For example, in starting up a community project, one team might conduct a needs assessment, another explore funding, another handle incorporation responsibilities, and another secure a facility. Work is coordinated by a committee of team leaders to ensure that the project teams are headed in the same direction and that their efforts are oriented toward a common end.

A final structural option proposed by Miles is the collegial structure. In this type of organization, individual professionals operate relatively independently and come together only in circumstances in which their work overlaps. A medical clinic would be a good example. Five physicians may collaborate on the purchase of a building and equipment and the hiring of receptionists and nursing staff. No single individual has more authority than any other. Each generates her or his own income. Each operates as an entrepreneur, except in situations in which the functioning of the organization requires overlap.

Probably no single organizational structure could be said to be superior to another as applied to the field of human services. For large public agencies, some type of bureaucratic structure will probably be required because of sheer size and accountability considerations. For a small, community-based agency, a collegial model may work very effectively. Much will depend on the mission, purpose, and goals of the organization, the services provided, and the expectations for accountability.

A related issue has to do with staff competence and preparation for the roles they fill and responsibilities they carry. The field of human services encompasses a wide range of specializations, including, but not limited to mental health, drug and alcohol abuse, developmental disabilities, child welfare, services to the aging, residential treatment for a variety of populations, adult and juvenile corrections, services to special populations, and many others.

Each organization providing direct services within these fields employs people from a wide variety of disciplines. These may include social work, counseling, psychology, child care, nursing and other health professions, education, and others. Support services may also be provided by people from diverse fields such as accounting, management, public relations, and fund raising.

The important issue in examining professional competence is the organization's standards governing job expectations, hiring, performance, supervision, and evaluation of performance. What, for example, are the educational requirements for each position? Does the organization adhere to these requirements? What experience is required? What licenses or certifications are necessary?

In the early work on job performance, both Taylor (1947) and Weber (1946) emphasized the importance of clearly defined job expectations, workers who were well prepared to perform expected functions, supervision, performance evaluation, and feedback to improve performance. Taylor, of course, focused his efforts on what would be considered essentially assembly-line technologies. Weber's work is more applicable to the definition, supervision, and evaluation of professional functions.

Miles (1975) refers to this issue as job design. He points out that in organizations where the prevailing management philosophy comes from the traditional model, jobs are designed in a manner that permits only the carrying out of routine physical and mental tasks. Sometimes this type of job design is appropriate when the work is something like forms completion or data processing. However, when complex professional responsibilities are assigned, the staff member has professional training and yet the staff member is allowed to perform only routine tasks, conflicts will eventually emerge.

Operating under a human relations philosophy, while it sounds more employee-oriented, can be deceptive. Constraints are often the same as those under the traditional model. The only differences are that a concern is expressed for the human needs of the employee, such as the desire for self-esteem. Teamwork may be emphasized in order to support employee needs for belonging, but the fundamental approach to job design still focuses on carrying out routine physical and mental tasks.

Job design under the human resources model is more complex. In this type of organization employees are involved with management in joint goal setting. Work is performed under conditions of self-direction and self-control. Data and information generated about individual performance and program performance are shared with the employee in the interest of promoting professional growth and development. This type of job design, while ideal for the experienced employee with professional education, may be inappropriate for positions in which the job requires more task definition and supervision.

Documentation and data to be examined in order to understand organizational structure might include:

1. Organizational chart;
2. Job descriptions;
3. Relevant policy and procedure manuals;
4. Interviews with selected administrators, managers staff, and representatives of each discipline.

A tool such as the one depicted in Table 8.10 can be useful in assessing the appropriateness of organization and program structure.

Task 10: Assess the Organization's Programs and Services.   Questions to be asked in relation to this task are:

- What programs and services are offered?
- Are the services consistent with the goals and objectives of the program?

TABLE 8.10   Assessing Organizational and Program Structure

	Total Organization	Program A	Program B	Program C
1. Would you describe the structure as rigid or flexible?	____	____	____	____
2. Is the structure appropriate to the needs of the organization or program?	____	____	____	____
3. Is communication primarily top down, or in all directions?	____	____	____	____
4. Are staff competent to do the jobs expected of them?	____	____	____	____
5. Is supervision appropriate to the need?	____	____	____	____

- Are staffing patterns appropriate to the services to be provided? Are workload expectations reasonable given expectations for achievement with each client and within each service and program?
- Is there a common understanding among management and line staff within each program about problems to be addressed, populations to be served, services to be provided, and client outcomes to be achieved?
- Are there established standards for quality of services?

Central to understanding every human service organization is assessing indicators of efficiency, effectiveness and quality that reflect a commitment to providing the best services possible at the lowest cost. Recent government initiatives (often referred to as "reinventing government" or as "performance measurement") make it clear that new standards will be established and agency performance will be monitored and evaluated for all organizations using government funding (Martin & Kettner 1996). These standards will encompass efficiency accountability, quality accountability and effectiveness accountability. *Efficiency accountability* focuses on the ratio of outputs to inputs or, more specifically, the ratio of volume of service provided to dollars expended. If Agency ABC provides 1000 hours of counseling at a cost of $75,000 and Agency XYZ provides 1000 hours of counseling at a cost of $100,000, Agency ABC is determined to be more efficient.

Quality accountability focuses on the provision of services and differentiates between organizations that meet a quality standard and those that do not. For example, using "timeliness" as a quality standard, an organization would be required to monitor and distinguish between services that were provided in a timely manner (e.g., within 10 minutes of the time of appointment), and those that were not.

Assessing quality can make an important contribution to understanding human service organizations. Most people have experienced the uncertainty of entering an unfamiliar organization and immediately sensing dynamics that are not easily interpreted. For example, a social work intern described her feelings about entering a particular nursing home for the first time. She stated that she did "not feel good about it" but when questioned about what that meant, she was at a loss for words to describe why she felt this way.

Several weeks later she was able to identify reasons for her concern. The nursing home's odor; the observed interactions between staff and residents; the receptionist's lack of interest in greeting visitors; the arrangement of furniture in the lobby in a way that was not conducive to interaction; the fact that residents were lined up in hallways; and the staff's discouragement of residents who wanted to bring personal possessions into the home were problematic for her. These elements began to paint a picture of an organization that did not fully value its residents, staff, or visitors.

These types of concerns do not always surface when evaluating efficiency, productivity, or effectiveness. However, identifying quality standards and using them as a basis for evaluating the service quality directly addresses these concerns. Some of the quality indicators used by organizations to evaluate quality include: accessibility, assurance, communication, competence, conformity, courtesy, deficiency, durability, empathy, humaneness, performance, reliability, responsiveness, security, and tangibles (Martin 1993).

Effectiveness accountability focuses on the results, effects, and accomplishments of human service programs. Some of the central questions for all human service organizations in the 1990s and beyond include: (1) Are clients any better off after coming to this organization than they were before they came? and (2) Do programs and services offered resolve the client problems they are funded to address?

These questions need to be dealt with in the context of understanding what goes into the planning, delivery, and evaluation of programs. A complete program should include a problem analysis, goals and objectives, program and service design, a data collection and management information system, and a plan for evaluation (Kettner, Moroney, & Martin 1990). Written plans provide the blueprints for programs and services and also serve as standards against which programs, when implemented, can be evaluated.

Each program should be based on a clear understanding of the problems it is intended to address and the populations it is intended to serve. It is not unusual to find that in some longstanding programs there has been a shift in emphasis over the years. For example, a program that was designed to deal with drug abuse may have begun with an emphasis on detoxification and long term intensive therapy, later shifting to provision of methadone, and finally to intensive self-help groups. Each of these emphases stems from a different understanding of the etiology of the problem and requires a different working

TABLE 8.11   Assessing Efficiency, Quality, and Effectiveness

	Program A	Program B	Program C
1. Does each program specify and monitor measures for efficiency (e.g., productivity per worker)?	_____	_____	_____
2. Does each program specify and monitor quality measures (e.g., reliability/consistency of services)?	_____	_____	_____
3. Does each program specify and monitor client outcomes (e.g., standardized scales that measure severity of problems before and after treatment)?	_____	_____	_____

hypothesis. These changes, in turn, may lead to changes in the population served, resources, patterns of staffing, and methods of evaluating effectiveness. These changes should be made consciously, not through "drift," and written program plans should reflect the intended changes.

Some of the more important documents and data sources to be examined to understand the planning, delivery, and evaluation of programs and services might include:

1. Program plans;
2. Organizational charts;
3. Roster of staff and job descriptions;
4. Annual reports of programs and services;
5. Needs assessment surveys;
6. Evaluation findings, including client satisfaction surveys;
7. Case records.

A tool such as the one depicted in Table 8.11 can be useful in assessing the agency's programs and services.

Task 11: Assess Personnel Policies, Procedures, and Practices.   Questions to be asked here include:

- Is there a written human resources plan?
- Is there a job analysis for each position?
- Is there a plan for recruitment and selection?
- Is there a plan for enhancing agency diversity?
- Is there a plan for staff development and training?
- Is there a performance evaluation system in place?
- Are there written procedures for employee termination?

Most organizations go to great lengths to ensure that their equipment will be in good working order. They purchase maintenance contracts for their photocopy machines, computers, printers, vehicles, and anything else that needs to be in good running order. Unfortunately, not all organizations invest the same level of concern or resources in their employees. And yet employees have a variety of needs to be met if they are to function at their optimal levels of productivity. Perhaps one way to understand how effectively an organization is addressing its personnel needs is to understand how an "ideal" personnel system might function.

One approach recommended in the literature to ensure that personnel needs and issues are properly addressed is to develop a human resources plan (Schmidt, Riggar, Crimando, & Bordieri 1992). Overall agency planning is referred to as "strategic planning"; it focuses on establishing goals, processes, and actions that determine future agency directions. Once future directions are established, they form the basis for human resource planning—the forecasting of personnel needs to implement the mission. The significance of a human resources plan is that it is critical to the success of an organization that new employees be brought on board in an orderly, systematic manner that maximizes the likelihood that they will be successful and productive during their tenure at the agency.

Basic to a human resources plan is a job analysis. "Job analysis identifies those tasks a job entails and determines the relationships between and among positions. It also specifies the qualifications of positions" (Schmidt et al. 1992, p. 31). A job analysis becomes the basis for writing a job description, which in turn establishes the organizing theme for the components of the human resources plan: recruitment, selection, orientation, supervision, training and development, performance appraisal, and, if necessary, termination.

The process of job analysis involves the gathering, evaluating, and recording of accurate, objective, and complete information about a given position from a variety of sources (Malinowski 1981). It begins with an itemization of tasks that are carried out by those who hold a particular job. For each task or group of tasks, the job analyst must identify methods or techniques for carrying out the task(s), knowledge and skills needed, and the results expected. The resulting product provides a complete understanding of the requirements and expectations associated with a particular job. From this document, a briefer, more concise job description is developed.

Once job qualifications and expectations are understood, the next step is to design a recruitment and selection plan. Effective recruitment requires a strategy, including selection of the recruitment territory (local, statewide, or national), consideration of labor market conditions, determination of recruitment audience and the intensity of search and recruiting efforts. These decisions are crucial to successful staffing, since employee selection can be made only from the pool of applicants generated by the recruitment strategy. This is a critical point, at which the agency needs to assess the diversity of its staff

and give special attention to recruitment of people from various ethnic backgrounds as well as women, gays and lesbians, or older and/or disabled
employees, to ensure a diverse and representative staff.

Selection involves a three-stage process. Recruitment typically produces
applications, including resumes. In the first stage, resumes and letters of reference are reviewed to eliminate applicants who are not qualified or not a good
fit for organizational needs. In the second stage, those with the highest qualifications are further narrowed down to a short list, usually a maximum of three
to five applicants. In the third stage, those on the short list are interviewed. A
job offer is then made to one of those interviewed. Screening criteria and interview questions are developed ahead of time so that they match the qualifications and job expectations established in the job analysis.

Upon being hired, the new employee is provided a complete orientation to
the job, the workplace, and the community. Upon completion of orientation, a
plan for supervision, training, and development is initiated. This approach is
intended to ensure a smooth entry into the job and to provide the information,
the knowledge, and the resources necessary for successful and productive
employment.

In order to ensure that employee performance is appropriately monitored
and evaluated, a well-designed personnel or human resources system will have
a performance-appraisal system based, again, on the job analysis. Tasks identified in the job analysis should be used as a basis for designing the performance-appraisal instrument. This will ensure that the job, as described at the
point of recruitment and hiring is the same job for which orientation and
training have been provided, and is the same job on which the employee is
evaluated. Criteria and procedures for performance evaluation should always
be specified ahead of time, in writing. In a well-designed performance evaluation system, it is rare that employees are surprised by the written evaluation.

Finally, it is advisable, as part of the personnel system, to include policy
and procedures for termination. These may include establishing legitimate reasons for termination, and a series of interviews or activities that are undertak-
en during the process. Involuntary termination may be the result of a series of
poor performance evaluations or it may be based on a single incident. In any
case, the agency will be much more likely to avoid extended grievances and lit-
igation when policies and procedures are clearly spelled out in writing.

In assessing a particular agency's effectiveness in the area of personnel
policies and procedures, these are the types of elements one would want to
examine. Helpful and informative documents for conducting the assessment
would include:

1. Manual of personnel policies and procedures;
2. Copy of a human resources plan, including affirmative action/equal
   employment opportunity plans;
3. Job analysis and job descriptions;
4. Recruitment and selection procedures;
5. Staff development and training plan;

TABLE 8.12   Assessing an Organization's Personnel or Human Resources System

A. Does the organization have a job analysis for each position within the agency that includes the following?

Responsibilities and Tasks	Methods	Knowledge and Skill	Results
Counseling			
1. Counsel individuals	One-on-one	Human behavior;	Client
2. Counsel families	Family treatment	group and family	develops
3. Lead groups	Group treatment	dynamics; under-	independent
4. Consult with self- help groups	Occasional group meetings	stand professional role	living and social skills

B. Is this job analysis consistent with the following?
    1. The job description
    2. The recruitment and selection plan (or procedures)
    3. The plan or practices relative to hiring a diverse workforce.
    4. Staff development and training plans or activities
    5. Performance evaluation criteria
    6. Plans for involuntary termination

    6. Performance evaluation forms;
    7. Statistics on absenteeism, turnover, usage of sick leave;
    8. Grievances and complaints filed with the human resources department;
    9. Interviews with representative staff who perform different roles.

Tools such as the one depicted in Table 8.12 can be useful in assessing the quality of an organization's personnel or human resources system.

Task 12: Assess Adequacy of Technical Resources and Systems.   Among the questions to be asked here are:

- Are program staff involved in a meaningful way in providing budgetary input? Do they get useful feedback about expenditures and unit costs during the year?

- Do program staff use budget data as a measure by which they attempt to improve efficiency?

- Do resources appear to be adequate to achieve stated program goals and objectives?

This task encompasses (1) budgetary management and (2) assessment of facilities, equipment, and computers. Additional questions arise that are specific to these two categories.

Budget Management.   Relevant questions to be asked include:

- What type of budgeting system is used by the agency?

- How are unit costs calculated? Do staff understand the meaning of unit costs? How are they used?

Budgeting and budget management is often an activity left to upper administration and treated as though line staff, first-line supervisors, and other people involved in service delivery need not be involved. Good financial management practices, quite to the contrary, involve all levels of staff. Fiscal soundness and budgeting practices affect programs and services in a profound way. To put it simply, organizations cannot run without money. Yet, good financial management practices would dictate that programs and services drive the budget, not the other way around.

For many years human service agencies were limited to a very simplified type of budgeting, called "line-item budgeting." This involved identifying expenditure categories and estimating the number of dollars that would be needed to cover all expenses in each category for one year. Categories typically included personnel; operating expenses such as rent, utilities, supplies, and travel; and other such items.

In recent literature, more sophisticated budgeting techniques have been developed for application to human service agencies (Lohmann 1980; Kettner et al. 1990). These techniques, referred to as functional budgeting and program budgeting, are based on program planning and budgeting systems (PPBS) (Lee & Johnson 1973). Both approaches to budgeting operate within the conceptual framework of programs. Both produce cost and expenditure data in relation to programs rather than in relation to the entire agency. Functional and program budgeting techniques produce data such as total program costs, cost per unit of service, cost per output (client completion of program or service), and cost per outcome (the cost of producing measurable change in a client's quality of life).

These data become increasingly important in an environment of intense competition for scarce and diminishing resources. In the same manner that individuals shop for the best buy with their own personal purchases, government contracting agencies—in competitive environments—shop for the lowest unit cost. Organizations that do not have the type of budgeting system or data base that permits calculation of unit costs increasingly find themselves at a distinct disadvantage in a competitive market.

Some of the more important documentation and data sources to be examined in order to understand the agency's approach to financial management and accountability might include:

1. Annual reports;
2. Audit reports;
3. A cost allocation plan;
4. Program goals and objectives;
5. Community-wide comparative studies of unit costs;
6. Interviews with all levels of program staff.

Assessment of facilities, equipment, and computers.   Questions to be asked are:

- Is the physical work environment attractive and conducive to high productivity? Do employees feel that they have enough space?
- Have problems been identified with current facilities and equipment? Is there a plan to address the problems and to fund solutions?
- Are there conditions related to facilities or equipment (especially computers) that appear to act as barriers to productivity or work flow?
- Does the agency have a computerized record-keeping and management information system that includes client data?
- Is the agency able to produce data that will answer important questions about clients, programs, and services?

Considerations in the areas of facilities include adequacy of space, physical condition and maintenance of facilities, and geographical location of agency and branches. The important points are that offices and work space allotted to personnel are suited to the needs and resources of the agency and provide as pleasant a work environment as possible for staff. Plans for renovation and expansion should be in place and appropriate to reasonable expectations for growth.

Equipment analysis should include an assessment of computer availability to staff. Agencies that use computers only for word processing and billing, with no plans to build and maintain a client data system, are in jeopardy of becoming obsolete very quickly as demands for data outstrip their ability to compile data and information by hand.

The type of client records kept is often determined by the reporting requirements of funding sources. However, agencies that collect only the data necessary to satisfy demands of funding sources are limiting their ability to make good use of client, program, and funding data to improve the quality of services and the efficiency of agency operations. A management information system that incorporates data about clients, services provided, evaluation of services, cost of services, and other such relevant data is invaluable in this era of data-based decision making. Software is available that will permit aggregation of data by caseworker, by unit, by program, or by agency. The organization that builds such an information system is in a much better position to compete successfully into the next century.

Tools such as the one depicted in Table 8.13 can be useful in assessing the adequacy of technical resources and systems.

SUMMARY

In order to really understand an organization, with all its strengths and weaknesses, one would have to spend years analyzing documents and talking to people familiar with the organization. However, an overview of selected elements of the organization and its relationships to its environment can provide a necessary basis for understanding why certain problems may exist, as well as possible clues as to how they may be resolved.

TABLE 8.13   Assessing Adequacy of Technical Systems and Resources

	Staff Input into Decisions?	Feedback to Staff After Decisions Are Made?
1. Budget-preparation process	____	____
2. Designing the management information system	____	____
3. Collecting client data	____	____
4. Designing/decorating the office spaces	____	____
5. Allocation of computer resources	____	____

In this chapter we have proposed that understanding an organization includes two parts: (1) identifying the task environment and understanding the relationship of the organization to the significant elements of the task environment and (2) understanding the inner workings of the organization itself.

Significant elements of the task environment include funding sources and those who contribute noncash resources, clients and referral sources, and other important organizations such as regulating and accrediting bodies. Strong and positive relationships with these entities make an important contribution to the overall strength and stability of the agency.

Assessing the internal functioning of the organization includes understanding components such as corporate authority and mission; management and leadership style; organizational and program structure; agency measures of efficiency, quality, and effectiveness; personnel policies and practices; and adequacy of resources.

Using the tools provided in this chapter should enable a student or beginning practitioner to better understand the organizational context within which problems are identified and changes are proposed.

REFERENCES

Berg, W. E., and R. Wright. (1981) Goal displacement in social work programs. *Administration in Social Work,* 20: 25–39.

Brager, G., and S. Holloway. (1978) *Changing human service organizations: Politics and practice.* New York: Free Press.

Burns, T., and G. M. Stalker. (1961) *The management of innovation.* London: Tavistock.

Cloward, R. A., and I. Epstein. (1965) Private social welfare's disengagement from the poor. In M. N. Zald, ed., *Social welfare institutions* (pp. 623–44). New York: Wiley.

Dill, W. R. (1958) Environment as an influence on managerial autonomy. *Administrative Science Quarterly,* 2(1), 409–43.

Etzioni, A. (1964) *Modern organizations.* Englewood Cliffs, NJ: Prentice Hall.

Greenley, J. R., and S. A. Kirk. (1973) Organizational characteristics of agencies and the distribution of services to applicants. *Journal of Health and Social Behavior, 14,* 70–9.

Grønbjerg, K. A. (1990) Poverty and nonprofit organizations. *Social Services Review, 64*(2), 208–43.

Hardina, D. (1990) The effect of funding sources on client access to services. *Administration in Social Work, 14*(3), 33–46.

Hasenfeld, Y. (1983) *Human service organizations.* Englewood Cliffs, NJ: Prentice-Hall.

Hasenfeld, Y. (1995) Analyzing the human service agency. In J. Tropman, J. L. Erlich, and J. Rothman, eds., *Tactics and techniques of community intervention.* Itasca, IL: F. E. Peacock.

Hodgkinson, V. A., and M. S. Weitzman. (1996) *Nonprofit Almanac: Dimensions of the Independent sector 1996–1997.* Washington, DC: The Independent Sector.

Internal Revenue Service, Statistics of Income Division. (1995) *Statistics of Income—1993, Individual Income Tax Returns* (publication no. 1304) Washington, DC: Author.

Karger, H. J., and D. Stoesz.(1990) *American social welfare policy: A structural approach.* New York: Longman.

Kettner, P. M., R. M. Moroney, and L. L. Martin. (1990) *Designing and managing programs: An effectiveness-based approach.* Newbury Park, CA: Sage.

Kirk, S. A., and J. R. Greenley. (1974) Denying or delivering services? *Social Work, 19*(4), 439–47.

Kramer, R., and B. Grossman. (1987) Contracting for social services. *Social Service Review, 61*(1), 32–55.

Lee, R. D., and R. W. Johnson. (1973) *Public budgeting systems.* Baltimore: University Park Press.

Levine, S., and P. E. White. (1961) Exchange as a conceptual framework for the study of interorganizational relationships. *Administrative Science Quarterly, 5,* 583–601.

Likert, R. (1961) *New patterns of management.* New York: McGraw-Hill.

Lipsky, M. (1984) Bureaucratic disentitlement in social welfare programs. *Social Service Review, 58*(1), 3–27.

Lohmann, R. (1980) Financial management and social administration. In F. D. Perlmutter and S. Slavin, eds., *Leadership in social administration.* Philadelphia: Temple University Press.

Malinowski, F. A. (1981) Job selection using task analysis. *Personnel Journal, 60*(4), 288–91.

Martin, L. L. (1993) *Total quality management in human service organizations.* Newbury Park, CA: Sage.

Martin, P. Y. (1980) Multiple constituencies, dominant societal values, and the human service administrator. *Administration in Social Work, 4*(2), 15–27.

Martin, L. L., and P. M. Kettner (1996) *Measuring the performance of human service programs.* Newbury Park, CA: Sage.

McMurtry, S. L., F. E. Netting, and P. M. Kettner. (1991) How nonprofits adapt to a stringent environment. *Nonprofit Management and Leadership, 1*(3), 235–52.

Merritt, J., and B. Neugeboren. (1990) Factors affecting agency capacity for inter-organizational coordination. *Administration in Social Work, 14*(4), 73–85.

Merton, R. K. (1952) Bureaucratic structure and personality. In R. K. Merton, A. P. Gray, B. Hockey, and H. C. Selvin, eds., *Reader in bureaucracy* (pp. 261–372). Glencoe, IL: Free Press.

Miles, R. E. (1975) *Theories of management: Implications for organizational behavior and development.* New York: McGraw-Hill.

Morse, J. J., and J. W. Lorsch. (1970) Beyond theory Y. *Harvard Business Review, 48,* 61–8.

Netting, F. E., S. L. McMurtry, P. M. Kettner, and S. Jones-McClintic. (1990) Privatization and its impact on nonprofit service providers. *Nonprofit and Voluntary Sector Quarterly, 19*(1), 33–46.

Peters, T. J., and R. H. Waterman. (1982) *In search of excellence: Lessons from America's best-run companies.* New York: Harper & Row.

Pfeffer, J., and G. R. Salancik. (1978) *The external control of organizations: A resource dependent perspective.* New York: Harper & Row.

Schmidt, M. J., T. F. Riggar, W. Crimando, and J. E. Bordieri. (1992) *Staffing for success.* Newbury Park, CA: Sage.

Stoesz, D. (1988) Human service corporations and the welfare state. *Society, 25*(5), 53–8.

Taylor, F. W. (1947) *Scientific management.* New York: Harper & Row.

Thomas, R. R. (1991) *Beyond race and gender.* New York: AMACOM.

Thompson, J. D. (1967) *Organizations in action.* New York: McGraw-Hill.

Wardell, P. J. (1988) The implications of changing interorganizational relationships and resource constraints for human services survival: A case study. *Administration in Social Work, 12*(1), 89–105.

Weber, M. (1946) *From Max Weber: Essays in sociology.* (H. H. Gerth and C. W. Mills, trans.) Oxford, England: Oxford University Press.

Weisner, S. (1983) Fighting back: A critical analysis of coalition building in the human services. *Social Service Review, 57*(2), 291–306.

SUGGESTED READINGS

Adler, P. T. (1990) Improving staff salaries through performance based compensation. *Administration and Policy in Mental Health, 18,* 123–5.

Auslander, G. K., and M. E. Cohen. (1992) Issues in the development of social work information systems: The case of hospital social work departments. *Administration in Social Work, 16*(2), 73–88.

Cox, T. (1994) *Cultural diversity in organizations.* San Francisco: Berrett-Koehler.

Dattalo, P. (1994) Perceived continuing education needs of licensed clinical social workers. *Journal of Social Work Education, 30*(2), 217–27.

Ewalt, P. L. (1991) Trends affecting recruitment and retention of social work staff in human service agencies. *Social Work, 36,* 214–7.

Ezell, M. (1993) Gender similarities of social work managers. *Administration in Social Work, 17,* 39–57.

Gowdy, E. A., and E. M. Freeman. (1993) Program supervision: Facilitating staff participation in program analysis, planning, and change. *Administration in Social Work, 17,* 59–79.

Kagle, J. D. (1993) Record keeping: Directions for the 1990s. *Social Work, 38*(2), 190–6.

Packard, T. (1993) Managers' and workers' views of the dimensions of participation in organizational decision-making. *Administration in Social Work, 17,* 53–65.

Zunz, S. J. (1991) Gender-related issues in the career development of social work managers. *Affilia: Journal of Women and Social Work, 6,* 39–52.

APPENDIX

Framework for Analyzing a Human Service Organization

FOCUS A: IDENTIFYING THE AGENCY'S TASK ENVIRONMENT AND ASSESSING RELATIONSHIPS

Task 1: Identify Sources of Cash and Noncash Revenues

Cash Revenues

- What are the agency's funding sources?
- How much and what percentage of funds are received from each source?

Noncash Revenues

- Does the organization use volunteers? If yes, how many and for what purposes?
- What material, in-kind resources (e.g., food, clothing, physical facilities, etc.) does the organization receive?
- What tax benefits does the organization receive?

Task 2: Assess Relationships with Revenue Sources

- What is the quality of the relationship between funding sources and the agency?

Task 3: Identify Client Population and Referral Sources

- What client groups does this organization serve?
- What are the demographic characteristics of clients?
- What percentages of clients pay full fees, partial fees, no fees, or are covered by contract revenues?
- What are the major sources of client referrals?

Task 4: Assess the Agency's Relationship to Client Population and Referral Sources

- What is the organization's domain (specifically, for what types of expertise is the agency recognized)?
- Does the agency claim a larger domain than it serves?
- Does demand for services outstrip supply or is there unused capacity?
- What types of clients does the organization refuse (e.g., are there disproportionate numbers of poor, elderly, persons of color, women, persons with disabilities, gays/lesbians, or other groups that are typically underserved)?

Task 5: Identify Other Important Organizations in the Task Environment

- What state and federal regulatory bodies oversee programs provided by this organization?
- With what government agencies does this organization contract for service provision?
- What professional associations, labor unions, or accrediting bodies influence agency operations?
- What are the perceptions of the "general public" in terms of the relevance, value, and quality of agency services?

Task 6: Assess the Agency's Relationship to Other Important Organizations in the Task Environment

- What other agencies provide the same services to the same clientele as this organization?
- With whom does the organization compete?
- With whom does the organization cooperate? Is the organization part of a coalition or an alliance?
- How is the organization perceived by regulatory bodies, government contracting agencies, professional organizations, accrediting bodies, and the general public in relation to its peers and competitors?

FOCUS B: ANALYZING THE ORGANIZATION

Task 7: Identify Corporate Authority and Mission

- What is the basis for and extent of the organization's corporate authority?
- What is its mission?

- Is the organization operating in a manner that is consistent with its authority and mission?
- To what extent is the mission supported by staff who perform different roles within the organization?
- Are policies and procedures consistent with mission and authority?

Task 8: Understand Administration, Management and Leadership Style

- How is the workplace organized and work allocated?
- Is appropriate authority and information passed on along with responsibility?
- How close is supervision and what, exactly, is supervised? Is it tasks, is it functions, or is it the employee?
- How are decisions made? Is information solicited from those affected?
- Do employees feel valued at every level? Do they believe they are making a contribution to the success of the organization?
- How is conflict handled?

Task 9: Understand Organizational and Program Structure

- What are the major departmental or program units on the organizational chart?
- What is the rationale for the existing organizational structure?
- Is this the most logical structure? Is it consistent with and supportive of the mission?
- Is supervision logical and capable of performing expected functions? Are staff capable of performing expected functions?
- Is there an informal organization (people who carry authority because they are respected by staff, and thus exert influence) that is different from those in formally designated positions of authority?

Task 10: Assess the Organization's Programs and Services

- What programs and services are offered?
- Are the services consistent with the goals and objectives of the program?
- Are staffing patterns appropriate to the services to be provided? Are workload expectations reasonable given expectations for achievement with each client and within each service and program?
- Is there a common understanding among management and line staff within each program about problems to be addressed, populations to be served, services to be provided, and client outcomes to be achieved?
- Are there established standards for quality of services?

Task 11: Assess Personnel Policies, Procedures and Practices

- Is there a written human resources plan?
- Is there a job analysis for each position?
- Is there a plan for recruitment and selection?
- Is there a plan for enhancing agency diversity?
- Is there a plan for staff development and training?
- Is there a performance evaluation system in place?
- Are there written procedures for employee termination?

Task 12: Assess Adequacy of Technical Resources and Systems

- Are program staff involved in a meaningful way in providing budgetary input? Do they get useful feedback about expenditures and unit costs during the year?
- Do program staff use budget data as a measure by which they attempt to improve efficiency?
- Do resources appear to be adequate to achieve stated program goals and objectives?

Budget Management

- What type of budgeting system is used by the agency?
- How are unit costs calculated? Do staff understand the meaning of unit costs? How are they used?

Facilities, Equipment, Computers

- Is the physical work environment attractive and conducive to high productivity? Do employees feel that they have enough space?
- Have problems been identified with current facilities and equipment? Is there a plan to address the problems and to fund solutions?
- Are there conditions related to facilities or equipment (especially computers) that appear to act as barriers to productivity or work flow?
- Does the agency have a computerized record-keeping and management information system that includes client data?
- Is the agency able to produce data that will answer important questions about clients, programs, and services?

PART IV

Changing Macro Systems

In the previous three parts of this book we have attempted to provide the basic knowledge necessary to understand the context of macro practice and to analyze two major macro systems—communities and organizations. In Part IV, the final part of the book, we will present a model for acting within and upon these systems. Specifically, we will detail means for bringing about change in communities and organizations that will lead to improvements in these systems' abilities to provide appropriate and effective services.

Building on the framework for understanding problems and target populations that was presented in Chapter 3, the two chapters in Part IV address the planned change process in sequential order. First, Chapter 9 outlines a variety of tasks such as developing an intervention hypothesis, identifying relevant groups, assessing political, interpersonal, and resource considerations, and setting goals and objectives. Then, Chapter 10 completes the process by discussing change tactics and the means by which all the preceding tasks are organized into a comprehensive plan.

CHAPTER 9

Developing an Intervention Strategy

Overview

Macro practice in social work can be viewed as having three major parts: (1) understanding the major components to be affected by the change—problem, population and arena, (2) preparing a strategy designed to get the change accepted, and (3) implementation and follow-up of the planned change. Chapters 3 through 8 dealt with part one. This chapter and the next focus on the preparation of a strategy and a plan. Implementation issues are incorporated into these chapters as well, but they are not discussed as a separate topic. Implementation and follow-up issues are highly individualized to the change effort, and sound professional practice involves constant interaction between the plan, the strategies and tactics proposed, and the realities of the actual intervention experience.

Strategy is a critical element of macro practice. Rothman, Erlich, and Tropman (1995) define strategy as "the fabric of action options that are available for the practitioner's choices in order to achieve change goals" (p. 3). Brager, Specht, and Torczyner (1987) link strategy to long-range goals and tactics to the short-range and specific behaviors of groups: "Groups having widely different long range goals (strategies) may engage in the same kinds of behaviors (tactics). And a specific group may utilize a wide range of tactics in pursuit of their goals" (p. 177).

The terms *strategy* and *tactics* as used here are intended to be consistent with the definitions of Brager et al. Strategy refers to the overall efforts designed to ensure that the proposed change is accepted. Tactics, to be discussed at length in Chapter 10, refer to the specific techniques and behaviors employed in relation to the target system designed to maximize the probability that the strategy will be successful and the proposed change adopted. The development of strategies and tactics involves some critical decisions. The approach taken can have far-reaching effects on the success of the change effort and its impact on the problem and the target population.

GUIDELINES FOR DEVELOPING AN INTERVENTION STRATEGY

As in previous chapters, we will present the process of developing a strategy in terms of a number of areas toward which the macro practitioner must focus his or her attention. These foci include: (A) developing the intervention hypothesis, (B) defining participants, (C) examining system readiness for change, (D) selecting a change approach, (E) assessing political and interpersonal considerations, (F) assessing economic considerations, (G) weighing the likelihood of success, (H) setting goals and objectives, (I) selecting appropriate tactics, and (J) preparing a written plan. This chapter is organized around the first eight foci, whereas Focus I and Focus J will be discussed in Chapter 10. Table 9.1 summarizes the major foci and relevant tasks involved in developing an intervention strategy.

Focus A: Developing the Intervention Hypothesis

During the early phases of problem identification, many people involved in change efforts, both professionals and volunteers, are eager to propose a specific intervention. Many have experienced the frustration of working in what they perceive to be flawed programs or under what they perceive to be oppressive organizational policies, and they are eager to propose immediate change.

A disciplined, scholarly approach to macro-level change requires that the foregoing tasks associated with problem identification and analysis in Chapters 3 through 8 be addressed first. However, it is the unusual change agent who is not constantly mindful of a preferred intervention and who is not continually molding and shaping it as the analysis unfolds.

Decisions about the nature, shape, and design of the intervention should wait until the problem analysis has been completed. When an acceptable degree of consensus has been achieved about the nature of the problem and its etiology, an intervention hypothesis is proposed.

Task 1: Develop a Working Hypothesis of Etiology.   Questions to be asked in relation to this task are:

- What factors gleaned from the problem analysis, the population analysis, and the arena analysis help in understanding cause-and-effect relationships?
- How should the working hypothesis of etiology be framed?

TABLE 9.1   Framework for Developing an Intervention Strategy

Focus	Tasks
A. Developing the Intervention Hypothesis	1. Develop a Working Hypothesis of Etiology
	2. Develop a Working Intervention Hypothesis
B. Defining Participants	3. Identify the Initiator System
	4. Identify the Change Agent System
	5. Identify the Client System
	6. Identify the Support System
	7. Identify the Controlling System
	8. Identify the Host and Implementing Systems
	9. Identify the Target System
	10. Identify the Action System
C. Examining System Readiness for Change	11. Assess General Openness to Change
	12. Identify Anticipated or Actual Response
	13. Determine Availability of Resources
	14. Examine Outside Opposition to Change
D. Selecting a Change Approach	15. Select a Policy, Program, Project, Personnel, or Practice Approach
E. Assessing Political and Interpersonal Considerations	16. Address Public Image and Successful Change
	17. Identify Alternative Perspectives
	18. Assess Duration and Urgency
F. Assessing Resource Considerations	19. Determine the Cost of Change
	20. Determine the Cost of Doing Nothing
G. Weighing the Likelihood of Success	21. Assess Support from Individuals, Groups, and Organizations
	22. Assess Support from Facts and Perspectives
H. Setting Goals and Objectives	23. Identify Goals
	24. Formulate Outcome and Process Objectives
	23. Plan Activities

Study and analysis of the problem, the population, and the arena invariably produces a wide variety of data and information. It is the nature of this type of study that not all findings are helpful. They must be sorted out, and only those that are useful and relevant to the change effort should be retained. For example, in a study of teen suicide, a study of the problem may reveal the demographic makeup of the target population, a profile of academic performance, extracurricular activities of the target population, socioeconomic characteristics of parents, divorce rate of parents, as well as other findings.

A study of the population may reveal that they are in a stage at which they need to develop an identity, peer relationships are critical to their social development, and parental neglect often leads to a sense of rebellion or despair.

A study of the community may reveal that there are clearly defined groups of teens, and that associations are almost exclusively along racial lines. It may be further discovered that patterns of participation in extracurricular activities tend to favor white students, and that Hispanic and African-American students are left to develop their own activities.

Not everything discovered can be used. To be useful, the data and information produced in the analysis phase must be distilled into a working hypothesis about etiology. In short, the change agent must ask: Having studied problem, population, and arena as well as their areas of overlap, what do I now believe to be the causal factors that have led to the need for change? A working hypothesis of etiology can be expressed in a statement (or series of statements like the example below.

Example of a Working Hypothesis of Etiology. The following factors (drawn from analysis of the problem, population, and/or arena):

1. High levels of stress experienced by some teens due to feelings of exclusion;
2. Failure of family to support teen during difficult times;
3. Need to develop a positive, socially acceptable identity while, at the same time, being denied opportunities

seem to result in:

1. Social isolation;
2. Depression;
3. Suicide attempts;
4. Suicide.

This example is a bit oversimplified for the sake of illustration. Completion of this task should result in a working statement that expresses a consensus of what participants currently see as the cause-and-effect relationships as applied to the need for change.

Task 2: Develop a Working Intervention Hypothesis. Relevant questions include:

• What interventions (based on an understanding of etiology) are most likely to reduce or eliminate the problem?
• What results can be expected from these interventions?

Based on a distillation of the information gathered in the problem-analysis phase as expressed in the working hypothesis of etiology, a working intervention hypothesis is developed. The hypothesis is a declarative statement (or series of statements) that proposes a relationship between a specific intervention and a result or outcome. The statement identifies the following: (1) a target population (or specific subgroup) and problem, (2) the change or intervention proposed, and (3) the results expected from the intervention. These elements combine to form a complete package that makes clear the expected relationship between problem, intervention, and result. A working intervention hypothesis to deal with prevention of teen suicide might read something like the example below.

Example of a Working Intervention Hypothesis.   If the following interventions are implemented for teens identified as being at risk of suicide:

1. Outreach by school counselors;
2. Identification of interests and concerns;
3. Pairing with another student or volunteer in areas of interest;
4. Follow-up support services in the home

then the following results can be expected:

1. Higher levels of extracurricular participation by teens at risk of suicide;
2. Reduction in symptoms of isolation and depression among the target group;
3. At least a 25 percent reduction in the rate of teen suicide by the end of the first year

This would be considered a testable hypothesis. The expectation would be that the intervention would be designed to provide the features specified in the hypothesis, and that the results would be tracked so that the relationship between intervention and results could be established.

Probably the most critical issue in relation to developing working hypotheses of etiology and intervention is that they be developed based on the problem, population, and arena analysis. It is not unusual for people involved in change to attempt to impose their own perceptions and agendas on change efforts. A principal or school board member may have had a positive experience imposing strict discipline on an individual, for example, and firmly believe that this is the answer for all teens who experience problems. Every effort must be expended to resist having these pat solutions imposed. Solutions should come from well researched analysis.

It is not necessary at this point to flesh out the intervention in detail. However, for the change effort to proceed, it is necessary to make at least a preliminary decision about the nature and form of the intervention so that planning a strategy to introduce the change may proceed.

Summary of Steps in Developing the Intervention Hypothesis.   The following is a summary checklist reviewing all the important points made so far about developing an intervention hypothesis:

1. The change agent or an appropriate representative should reexamine everything relevant that has been learned about problem, population, and arena.
2. Relevant data and information should be distilled into a clear working hypothesis of etiology (cause and effect).

3. Based on the working hypothesis of etiology, creative ideas should be generated about interventions that appear to be relevant to the need as it is currently understood.

4. Using these proposed interventions, a set of intervention hypotheses (and possibly subhypotheses) should be developed. These statements should lay out a clear set of understandings about the nature of the intervention and the expected outcomes.

5. These hypotheses and subhypotheses should be spelled out in a series of if/then statements; for example: If (population) with (problem) can be identified and recruited into this program, and if they receive (services), then we can expect that they will achieve (outcomes).

Focus B: Defining Participants

Up to this point in the change process it is not unusual for the people involved to be a small core of committed individuals, possibly even close friends or fellow employees, who recognize a condition or problem and are concerned enough to take action. It is perfectly appropriate for this small group to undertake some of the early activities of problem identification and analysis, as long as they do not become totally committed to a particular perspective on the problem.

In order for effective macro change to occur it is necessary to have allies. A good deal of strategy development involves the building of coalitions. People willing to commit themselves to change rarely accept someone else's definitions and perspectives without some revision. (If full participation of all critical actors was accomplished in the problem identification and analysis phases, then achievement of consensus on the problem and proposed solution should not be a barrier to progress at this point.)

One method of identifying, in an orderly, systematic manner, the participants critical to the success of a change effort is to identify people who are affiliated in some way with certain groups or organizations that make up the many systems and subsystems of the change effort.

We will use the term *system* to describe these critical participants. This term is used in the context of systems theory, implying that participants should be viewed as more than simply a collection of individuals who happen to have some common interests and characteristics. As a system or subsystem critical to the success of the change effort, they represent a complex set of interrelationships having system-like attributes that must be recognized and attended to by the core planning group. One of these attributes, for example, is entropy, which refers to the natural tendency of systems to expire without input and regeneration from outside the system. The concept is directly applicable to the types of systems involved in planned change. (For further discussion of systems theory, see von Bertalanffy 1950, or Katz & Kahn 1966.)

The systems to be considered include (1) an initiator system, (2) a change agent system, (3) a client system, (4) a support system, (5) a controlling system, (6) a host system, (7) an implementing system, (8) a target system, and

(9) an action system (see also Kettner, Daley, & Nichols 1985). It is worth noting here that these terms are used strictly for conceptual purposes to assist in understanding who should be involved and why. They are not terms commonly used among people involved in change efforts. It is more likely that terms like *committee* or *task force* will be used to designate groups, but the professional person who coordinates the effort should be aware, conceptually, of what systems are represented by the significant participants.

Task 3: Identify the Initiator System.   Questions for this task are:

- Who first recognized the problem and brought attention to it?
- How should/can the initiators be involved in the change effort?

The initiator system is made up of individuals who first recognize the existence of a problem and bring attention to it. This could be a group of parents raising concerns with a school board about increasing violence in their schools or a group of staff members concerned about a lengthening waiting list for service in the counseling program. Individuals who first raise the issue may or may not also become a part of the initial planning process.

It is sometimes necessary and worthwhile to work with a group of individuals who fill appropriate roles and have a thorough knowledge of the problem, but see themselves as powerless to affect the system. Empowerment strategies such as teaching, training, group counseling, or consciousness-raising efforts at this point can pay rich dividends in the long run, and can place appropriate spokespersons in leadership positions rather than substituting less-appropriate leaders.

Task 4: Identify the Change Agent System.   The key question to be asked for this task is:

- Who will be responsible for leadership and coordination in the early stages of the change effort?

From the initiator system, the issue moves to identification of the change agent system. In a professionally assisted change effort this involves an individual designated as the leader of the change effort. We will refer to this person as the change agent. The change agent, together with an initial core planning committee or task force, comprises the change agent system. If the change activity will require drawing on the resources of an organization, it is essential that the organization sanction the change and also be identified as part of the change agent system. This may involve getting formal approval from executive or board, and may require release time from other duties, secretarial support, and other allocation of resources.

The makeup of this system is critical to the change effort because much of what is accomplished will be framed in the perspectives of these individuals. Ideally, this system will include representation from the initiator system, people who have experienced the identified problem, people who have had experience in trying to solve the problem, and people who can be influential in getting the change accepted.

The function of the change agent system is to act as a central coordinating point. Many participants in the change effort will be taking on different activities at the same time. It is the job of the change agent system to ensure that the change effort is properly organized and carried out from its early conceptualization to the point at which it is turned over to others for implementation. As the major systems and perspectives are identified and the action system (discussed in a later section) is formed, the coordinating functions are shifted to the action system.

The work of the change agent system begins with carrying out the problem identification and analysis as described in Chapter 3. This planning effort continues as each of the systems and participants is defined and a strategy is developed for getting the change accepted.

Task 5: Identify the Client System.   Questions relevant to this task are:

- Who will be the primary beneficiaries of change?
- Who will be the secondary beneficiaries of change?

The client system is made up of individuals who are asking for and will become the direct beneficiaries of the change if it is implemented. In Chapter 3, we pointed out that macro change efforts begin with identification of a target population and a problem. The client system would be a subset of the target population for whom the specific change effort is being undertaken. In some cases it is possible that the target population and the client system could even be synonymous. For example, if the target population is all homeless people in the town of Liberty, and the purpose of the community change effort is to provide housing and services for all homeless people in Liberty, then the target population and client system are the same.

Different terms are used for conceptual purposes. A *target population* brings focus to the population analysis and usually represents a broader spectrum of people. A *client system* refers to the people who are intended to benefit from the change effort. In the town of Liberty, for example, for a specialized project, the client system could be homeless women and children.

In defining the client system, the change agent should resist the temptation to jump to the easy and obvious definition of the primary beneficiaries, and should patiently and carefully analyze details. For example, if the identified problem is drugs in the schools, several potential beneficiaries could be considered as the client system. A partial list of people who would benefit from eliminating drugs from the schools would include students, teachers, administrators, parents, local police, campus security, neighbors, the school board, and the community as a whole. The question, then, becomes one of establishing priorities for direct benefits and distinguishing between primary and secondary beneficiaries. The decision will have an important impact on the change effort. If "students who want a good education in a drug-free environment" are identified as primary beneficiaries, then the intervention may well be directed toward tighter security and stricter discipline. If, on the other hand, primary beneficiaries are described as "students who use drugs and are unable to maximize their educational opportunities due to impairment," then the intervention may be directed toward treatment.

The boundaries for macro-level changes tend to be defined in a way that the primary focus is on a segment of a community or organization. Total communities as defined by political boundaries (entire towns, cities, counties) or total organizations are rarely the focus of a professionally directed change effort led by a social worker, but it is certainly not out of the question that they could be.

However the primary beneficiaries are defined, the remaining groups should be identified and listed as secondary beneficiaries. Secondary beneficiaries may be important and may need to be called on when the change effort needs public support. We will refer to this group as the support system.

Task 6: Identify the Support System.   The key question to be asked for this task is:

- What other individuals and groups (in addition to the primary and secondary beneficiaries) will support the change effort?

The support system is a catch-all system that refers to everyone in the community or organization who has an interest in the success of the proposed change. Some may receive secondary benefits. This group is expected to be positively inclined toward change, and may be willing to be involved in supporting and advocating for the change if they are needed.

The support system is defined largely by who is in the target population (or client system) and by the nature of the problem. People have an interest in certain populations and problems for a variety of reasons: a loved one is afflicted with the problem, their employment brings them into close contact, their church or service organization has selected this population for assistance. They are sometimes described by the related concern or issue, such as the "mental health community," or the "foster care community." These are the people the change agent will count on to become involved if decision makers need to be persuaded that the change is necessary. Figure 9.1 illustrates the relationship between initiator, change agent, client, and support systems.

Initiator, change agent, and client systems can be seen as incorporated within the boundaries of the support system in that they all have an interest in addressing the need for change. Initiator, client, and change agent systems may overlap or may represent separate and distinct constituencies.

Task 7: Identify the Controlling System.   The key question to be asked for this task is:

- Who has the formally delegated authority and the power to approve and order implementation of the proposed change?

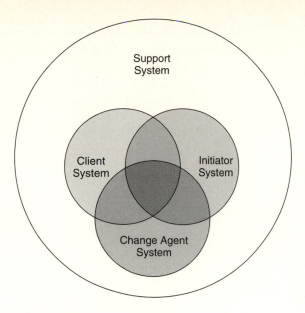

FIGURE 9.1   Relationship of Systems

The controlling system is defined as that person or group of individuals with the formally delegated authority and the power to approve and order the implementation of the proposed change. Macro-level change invariably involves approval by some formally designated authority. If the change involves a public agency or publicly funded or regulated services, control may rest with a body of elected officials. If the change involves a private agency, control may rest with a board of directors. The question that must be answered in defining the controlling system is: What is the highest level to which one must appeal in order to receive sanction and approval for the proposed change? These individuals or bodies are significant to acceptance and implementation of the change effort, and their positions on the proposed change must be known and considered.

Task 8: Identify the Host and Implementing Systems.   Among the important questions are:

- What organization will be responsible for sponsoring and delivering the activities of the change effort?
- What individuals will be involved in direct delivery of services or other activities necessary to implement the change effort?

The host system is the organization or group responsible for implementation of the change—usually an organization, a department, or a unit. Within the host system is a smaller group of employees or volunteers who will have day-to-day responsibility for carrying out the change. We refer to this as the

TABLE 9.2   **Examples of Controlling, Host, and Implementing Systems**

	Controlling	Host	Implementing
School System	School Board	A particular school and its principal	Teachers in the school involved in the change
Law Enforcement System	City Council	Police Chief and Department	Police Officers involved in the change

implementing system. Implementers are employed by or volunteer for the host system. In most instances of macro-level change the host system will be an organization that will be expected to implement a policy change, a new program, or a project. The listing of systems in Table 9.2 identifies controlling, host, and implementing systems in a school system and in a law enforcement system.

The change agent should be careful not to assume that the positions of the controlling system, host system, and implementing system about the proposed change are identical. It is not unusual for those involved in the execution of policy to disagree with the policy makers and vice versa. Each system should be assessed separately. Figure 9.2 depicts the typical relationships of the controlling, host, and implementing systems.

Task 9: Identify the Target System.   Relevant questions include:

- What is it that needs to be changed (e.g., individual, group, structure, policy, practice, etc.) in order for the effort to be successful?
- Where (within the organization or community) is the target system located?

The target system is the individual, group, structure, policy, or practice that needs to be changed for the primary beneficiaries to achieve the desired

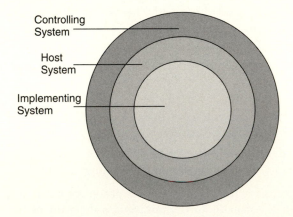

FIGURE 9.2   **Relationships Between Systems Controlling, Host and Implementing Systems**

benefits. The target system (not to be confused with our earlier use of the term *target population*) is a complex concept that cannot always be defined in clear and simple terms. Often what needs to be changed may include philosophy, values, attitudes, practices, and policies as well as the provision of services. Another complicating factor is that many change efforts must address multiple targets. For example, in addressing the high school's drug problem it may be necessary to educate the faculty and staff about what is happening before they are willing to allow the change to occur. They are targeted for change first. Next, it may be necessary to target the school board to gain their approval to intervene. Finally, having gained the approval and support of teachers and school board members, the intervention, focusing on the "real" target group—high school students using drugs—can be implemented.

Two questions need to be answered in defining the target system: (1) What change (or series of changes) needs to take place in order for the primary beneficiaries to achieve the desired benefits? and (2) What individuals or groups need to agree to the change (or series of changes)? We have defined these individuals or groups as controlling, host, and implementing systems. The target system may lie within the boundaries of any or all of these systems, or it may lie entirely outside of any of them. The target system in the school experience could include selected school board members, a principal and assistant principals, or a subgroup of teachers, or the target system could be a selected group of students. The decision will be made based on what change is proposed and who needs to be convinced to support it.

Task 10: Identify the Action System.   The key question to be asked for this task is:

- Who should be represented on a central "steering committee" or decision-making group that will see the change effort through to completion?

As all other systems are being defined and participants selected, an action system is being formed. The action system is made up of individuals from other systems who have an active role in planning the change and moving it toward implementation. Clearly there is a good deal of overlap here with the change agent system, earlier defined as the professional change agent, sanctioning organization, and sometimes a core planning group. While the change agent system forms the core of the action system, other actors also have important roles in providing input into decision making and should be added as the change effort proceeds. The action system should include, whenever possible, representatives from all other systems, including those systems in need of change, if the relationship is not excessively adversarial.

For example, if the social problem under consideration is the unmet needs of the homeless, the concern might first be raised by a person who passes by a few old men sleeping in doorways every day on her way from the bus to her place of work (initiator). She finds that several other employees at her place of

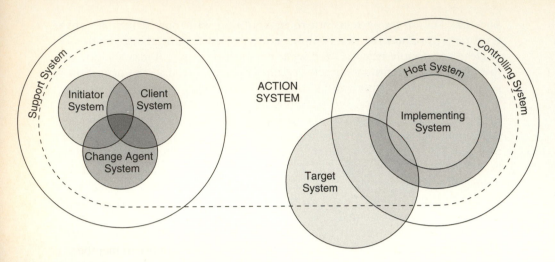

FIGURE 9.3   Systems in Interaction

work have the same concern, and she raises the issue to the city council (controlling system), where it is assigned to the City Department of Human Services (change agent system and host system). The social worker (change agent and possibly implementer) forms a task force that includes those who brought the issue to the council. As the condition is researched and analyzed, more people are added to the task force. Professionals who work with the homeless (support system) would be asked to join, as would some current or former homeless people (client system) and someone from the city's political or administrative structure who understands the potentialities and limitations of the city's participation (controlling system). When all the significant participants have been identified, this group would become the central decision-making body in the change effort and would be defined as the action system.

Systems in Interaction.   In examining these systems in interaction, it is important to remember that we distinguish among them and define them separately for conceptual purposes only. In actual practice, all systems could be within one organization, and it is highly probable that many systems will overlap. The interrelationships of all systems is depicted in Figure 9.3.

One side of the diagram includes the systems proposing and favoring change. The larger system is the support system, and includes all systems favoring change. Contained within the support system we find the initiator, client, and change agent systems, all with possibly varying degrees of overlap. On the other side of the diagram we find the systems identified as in need of change. The controlling, host, and implementing systems are represented by concentric circles in that each subsystem is typically contained within the span of control of the next larger system. The target system may lie within any of these systems or even outside all three. The action system may overlap any or all of these systems. An example illustrating all systems within one organization would be a situation in which an organizational change is proposed. For example, a human service agency may have a special program for "crack babies" (babies born addicted to drugs) and their mothers (the client system) that includes detoxification, rehabilitation, counseling, and parent training. After six months, a supervisor (initiator system and change agent system) notices that the case managers (implementing system) have been practicing "creaming," providing the bulk of services to the most highly motivated clients and ignoring the needs of the least motivated. In this example, this practice of "creaming" would be the target—that which is to be changed. The supervisor calls the problem to the attention of the executive director (representing the host system) and the executive director raises it with the board (the controlling system), and recommends that incentives (the proposed change) be developed for case managers to work with less motivated clients. A task force (action system) made up of the supervisor, a case manager, a board member, an administrator, and a former client now volunteering for the agency examines the problems and possibilities of directing more service to unmotivated clients.

All this has taken place within the boundaries of a single organization with essentially no input from extraorganizational sources. This illustrates the nature of the shifting boundaries of systems, while demonstrating the value of retaining conceptual clarity in defining the systems. Even though the terms *controlling, host,* and *implementing* may never be used, it is important that the change agent understand the domain, authority, and power of each, and keep roles, responsibilities, and expectations for each clear and distinct.

Focus C: Examining System Readiness for Change

As the change process unfolds, each of the systems defined above should be assessed for its readiness to support the proposed change. An assessment of readiness should include consideration of an openness to change in general, commitment to the proposed change, availability of resources to implement the proposed change, and the degree of outside resistance to the proposed change. These considerations should be assessed for each system. However, it is likely that there will be some similarities among those systems promoting change (initiator, change agent, client, support, and action systems) and among those with whom they are hoping to bring about change (controlling, host, implementing, and target).

Task 11: Assess General Openness to Change.   The central question for this task is:

- What has been the past experience with each of the systems with regard to organizational or community change?

General openness to change involves an informal assessment, based on experience, of how people in decision-making positions have dealt with earlier proposals. This is not likely to be a consideration for those systems promoting change, since these systems are clearly in support of (and therefore open to) change in this instance. However, when examining the systems to be changed, it can be a very different story. Much has been written about the difficulties of getting organizations (especially bureaucracies) to change (see, for example, Brager & Holloway 1978). Analyzing past experiences and general openness to change may be helpful in finding the subsystems or individuals that are most likely to be responsive to the proposed change.

Task 12: Identify Anticipated or Actual Response.   Under this task the main question to ask is:

- What level of commitment to the proposed change is anticipated from each of the systems?

Commitment to the proposed change should be examined in terms of each system's enthusiasm in endorsing the change in its existing form. It is characteristic of community and organizational change that there will be differences in perspective on what form changes should take, even when there is enthusiastic agreement that change is needed. Low levels of commitment to the change as proposed can have a negative effect on its acceptance and eventual implementation. Assessment of commitment should involve examination of degree of enthusiasm as well as degree of internal consensus about the design of the proposed change.

Task 13: Determine Availability of Resources.   Relevant questions include:

- From what sources will resources be solicited?
- What resources will be requested?

Availability of resources, for many change efforts, will be the key question. While openness to change and commitment to the proposed change are helpful, availability of resources is a *sine qua non*. Resources for the systems to be changed usually refers to budgeted dollars, but should also be understood to include reassigning staff, use of volunteers, in-kind resources such as computer time, supplies, space, and others. Resources for the systems promoting change usually refers to numbers of people, time available, and the willingness to persist if opposed.

Task 14: Examine Outside Opposition to Change.   The primary question here is:

- What individuals or groups outside the systems identified can be expected to oppose the change effort?

The final factor to be explored with each system is the degree of external resistance or opposition experienced. There may be instances in which a controlling system—elected local officials, for example—supports a proposed change

TABLE 9.3 Assessing System Readiness for Change

	Systems Promoting Change	Systems to Be Changed
	Initiator, Client Change Agent, Support, Action	Controlling, Host, Implementing, Target
General Openness to Change	Probably not an issue, since these groups are promoting change.	If these systems have shown tendencies in the past to resist changes of this type, this should serve as an early warning.
Anticipated or Actual Response to Proposed Change	How committed are those promoting change to the type change being proposed? What are the differences, if any? Are some committed only to a highly specific solution?	Is there consensus or disagreement about the type of change being proposed? How strong are feelings for and/or against it?
Availability of Resources	Do the systems promoting change have the skills and human resources to see the change effort through to completion, even if there is resistance?	Do the systems to be changed have the funding, staff, facilities, equipment, or other resources needed to implement the proposed change?
Opposition to Change	What forces outside these systems are opposing change? How strong is the opposition?	What is the source of outside opposition? How strong are the pressures to reject the proposed change? What significant actors are most vulnerable to pressures?

but the constituency it represents—grass-roots groups, for example—is opposed. Almost any proposed change that requires public funds will find external resistance from groups that are competing for the funds. If pressure tactics are to be used, the change agent should ascertain whether the pressures that can be brought about through this change effort will be able to offset pressures brought by those resisting the change. For the systems promoting change it is important to identify possible vulnerable targets within its ranks. People who can be pressured to back down may represent a liability, and those promoting change should be aware of it. A summary of considerations is illustrated in Table 9.3.

Focus D: Selecting a Change Approach

One of the first agenda items for the action system is selecting a change approach. As the change agent moves toward completion of all of the problem identification and analysis tasks covered in Chapters 3 through 8, the nature of the problem and significant supporting information should be coming into focus. This makes clear what needs to be changed. An important question yet to be answered is how the change should come about. For example, if one of the client service programs within an agency is providing a poor quality of services, improving the services may require a policy change (e.g., redefining eligibility). This same situation could also require a program change (e.g., changing the type of counseling provided), or a project change (e.g., testing a new service with a limited number of clients). Changes in personnel and practices are also options, but we recommend that their use be limited to situations in which policy, program, or project approaches are determined not to be feasible. These five change approaches will be discussed below.

Task 15: Select a Policy, Program, Project, Personnel, or Practice Approach.   For this task the critical question is:

- What approach (or combination of approaches) is most likely to achieve the desired change?

The professionally assisted change efforts discussed in these chapters are intended to fall into two very general categories: (1) those that lead to an improved quality of life for the clients served, or (2) those that lead to an improved quality of work life for employees so that their energies can be devoted toward providing the best possible services to clients. In order to address these two categories, we propose five approaches to change. The approach selected becomes the focus of the target system.

1. *Policy.* Policy is represented by a formally adopted statement that reflects goals and strategies or agreements on a settled course of action. Policies may be established by elected representatives, boards, administrators, or by a vote of the people affected. In some instances, a policy may be needed in order to change a situation. For example, a new policy that outlines a grievance process for clients may be empowering to the persons who feel they have no recourse when they disagree with agency practices. In other situations, existing policy may be unnecessarily restrictive and need to be amended. For example, administrators of congregate housing for the elderly may find that policies created to facilitate transfers and relocations actually tie their hands rather than enable them to make individualized and caring decisions.

2. *Program.* Programs are prearranged sets of activities designed to achieve a set of goals and objectives. In macro practice, programs are usually intended to provide services directly to clients. Sometimes they are of a supportive nature, such as fund-raising or public relations programs.

   Program change will vary. Some change efforts will result in the establishment of new programs to serve a special population group. Other change efforts may focus on altering existing programs so that they are designed to be more sensitive to client needs.

3. *Project.* Projects are much like programs but have a time limited existence and are more flexible so that they can be adapted to the needs of

a changing environment. Projects, if deemed successful and worth-while, are often permanently installed as programs.

Often change agents will find that creating a project that demon-strates a new or different intervention is more palatable to decision makers than making a long-term program commitment. Therefore, it is likely that change will result first in a demonstration or pilot project before a program change is possible.

4. *Personnel.* Many types of activities take place in communities and organizations. Sometimes people experience seemingly insurmount-able differences and engage in ongoing conflict. Employees occasion-ally get involved in an attempt to depose an unpopular administrator. The professional change agent should proceed very carefully before getting involved in personnel-related issues. Several factors should be considered. First, is the proposed personnel-related change effort being considered because of the reasons stated above: improvement of the quality of life of clients or improvement of work life so that clients can be better served? Second, will the proposed change be dealt with through regularly established channels? When the target of a change effort is an individual, there is often a temptation to proceed "underground."

Brager and Holloway (1978) suggest that, under certain circum-stances covert tactics may be appropriate. First, one must determine if agency officials are ignoring client needs in favor of their own interests. Second, the change agent must decide if the use of formal, overt sources may jeopardize self, clients, or colleagues. Third, if overt means have failed or are clearly not feasible, one may consider covert tactics. In any case, the professional change agent should recognize the potential risks, including loss of job, should be convinced that the change is worth the consequences, and should be prepared to accept them if necessary. Ethi-cal practice is basic to social work, and ethical dilemmas often emerge in situations in which one has conflict over where loyalties lie—with an agency employer or with clients. Ethical dilemmas were discussed in Chapter 1 and will be re-examined in the final chapter.

5. *Practice.* The fifth focus of change—practice—refers to the way organi-zations or individuals within them go about doing business. Practices tend to be less formal than policies. They may even be specific to indi-viduals or groups, and, therefore, are more elusive than policies. Well-designed policy, together with monitoring and evaluation capability, is usually a stronger and more permanent remedy for inappropriate or offensive practices. For example, if a receptionist treats clients rudely and proves to be insensitive to their concerns, several options are avail-able. He or she could be reprimanded, sent for training, or even fired. These actions may or may not change behavior, but even if they do, they are unlikely to solve the problem because they focus only on the practice of one person. A more permanent solution would be to incorporate into

the personnel-processing system for receptionists an expectation of courtesy to clients. This would include job description, recruitment literature, and criteria for hiring, performance evaluation, merit increases, and promotion. Dealt with in this way, not only is one employee encouraged to change practices or behaviors but all future employees as well.

Approaches in Interaction.   A decision about the change approach is obviously intimately connected to a decision about the nature of the problem and the target system. The important issues to be resolved in defining the change approach are: (1) What is needed to remedy the problem? and (2) How ready are the people in decision-making positions to recognize, accept, and implement the remedy? For example, many changes can be handled in a very simple and straightforward manner. More day-care slots are needed for single mothers in employment training programs; the change agent calls this to the attention of the appropriate people in the human service department and more slots are added. Parents want drug and alcohol education in the high schools; the school board agrees to provide it.

Other changes, however, may require, first, policy, then program change. The state department of human services may recognize a need to provide preventive educational and counseling services to teens who are at high risk of becoming pregnant. Conservative legislators may be opposed to allocating funds seen as violating parental prerogatives. The change may require that enabling legislation be passed first and that a project or program then be implemented. The change agent and action system should carefully analyze the proposed change and system readiness for change and should prepare a plan that allows for the appropriate sequencing of policy, program, and/or project changes.

Focus E: Assessing Political and Interpersonal Considerations

Several times throughout the book we have discussed the importance of politics in bringing about change. We address these considerations more directly in this section. *Politics* is used here in a broad sense of having to do with the different ways individuals important to a change effort may respond when asked to support the change. This includes consideration of partisan politics, but is not limited to that arena.

Task 16: Address Public Image and Successful Change.   Among the questions to be asked are:

- Who can serve as effective spokespersons for the proposed change?
- Who should keep a low profile when the proposed change is presented to decision makers?
- Has anyone key to the success of the change effort been left out?

An early question to ask is: Who is involved in promoting the proposed change, and how are they perceived by decision makers? Preparing a list of participants in each system and assessing the political and interpersonal strengths and liabilities of each participant can assist the change agent and action system in making the best use of each participant. Some people with valuable technical expertise may be seen as highly controversial and a liability when viewed from the interpersonal/political perspective. Previous negative experiences with decision makers should serve as a "red flag" but should not necessarily rule someone out from assuming a high-profile role. Much depends on whether collaborative, campaign, or contest tactics (discussed in the next chapter) are selected. Regardless of who is designated as the public spokesperson, careful consideration should be given to how well and by whom this person is perceived and respected. This principle applies to both community and organizational change efforts, but may be even more important in organizational change because of the closeness of working relationships and the greater likelihood of people knowing more about each other than they would in the community arena.

An additional question to be asked all the way through is: Has anyone critical to the success of this change been left out? Failure to involve people who can help can be as damaging as involving people who may harm the effort.

Task 17: Identify Alternative Perspectives. The key question here is:

* How will opponents of the change effort frame their opposition?

A second consideration is perspective. People involved in change in the field of human services are often amazed to learn that there is almost no concern raised that does not have an opposing view. For every advocate of a woman's right to have control over her own body, there is one who will support a fetus's right to survive. For every person concerned about child abuse, there is one who is equally concerned about perceived abuses of parental prerogatives by child welfare workers. It is tempting to dismiss opponents' views as uninformed and unenlightened, but in undertaking macro-level change it is unwise to do so. Alternative perspectives should be carefully analyzed for their merit and their potential or actual political appeal. Even plotting a spectrum of opinions, together with some educated estimates of levels of public support of each, can be an informative exercise for action system participants. Each perspective should also be weighed for the intensity of its support. The likelihood is that the closer to the extremes, the more intense the feelings. Figure 9.4 illustrates a continuum of possible perspectives on services to AIDS patients.

Task 18: Assess Duration and Urgency. Relevant questions are:

* How long has the problem existed?
* Is the problem considered an emergency?

A third area of consideration that affects perception of a problem is the length of time a problem has existed and the extent to which it is considered

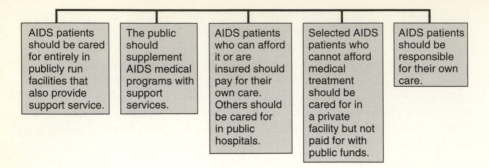

FIGURE 9.4   A Continuum of Perspective

threatening to individual or organizational survival. We refer to these as duration and urgency, and deal with them together because in many ways they are interrelated.

Longstanding problems are hard to change. People become desensitized, and community and organizational leaders are not easily persuaded that there is really a problem that needs attention. For example, it took a class action suit on behalf of the chronically mentally ill citizens of Arizona to force the state legislature to address their needs. Recently emerging problems like homelessness among young families tend to have more popular support for change. Occasionally, longstanding problems can be presented in a new way, as has been done with alcohol abuse in the campaign against drunk driving over the past decade.

For newly emerging or newly defined problems, the change agent should examine the issue of urgency. The closer the problem is to threatening survival needs such as food, clothing, shelter, safety, and medical care, the more likely those in a position to make changes will attend to it. Within organizations, problems that directly or indirectly affect the budget, and therefore the capacity of the organization to survive, tend to receive a relatively higher priority than non–budget-related problems. The proposed change should be weighed in terms of their duration and urgency, and these factors used appropriately in preparing a strategy for promoting the proposed change.

Focus F: Assessing Resource Considerations

The major concern of decision makers about proposed change in most cases comes down to how much it will cost. Whether or not social workers agree with this value perspective, we operate within a money-oriented system. Decision makers often look at the cost before they even consider the rationale for implementing the change. Improved quality of life is not, in itself, enough of a rationale for persons responsible for managing limited resources to agree to support a particular change effort.

Task 19: Determine the Cost of Change.   Among the questions to be asked under this task are:

- What anticipated costs related to the proposed change can be itemized? What must be estimated?
- What sources of financial support or in-kind donations should be approached?

For reasons stated above, the change agent must make some estimates of what the proposed change will cost. This can be difficult, because in many cases the details of the intervention design are not even worked out until there are some assurances that the change will be accepted. Take, for example, a situation in which the parents in a community want the school board to sponsor more organized and supervised after-school activities. Some may want arts and crafts, some athletic activities, some drama and music options. When the school board is approached these details have probably not been addressed. The change agent must be prepared for a response that "the proposed change will cost too much and resources are not available." To counter this, some preliminary calculations must be prepared, at least to the point of estimating the number of staff persons, approximate salaries required, estimated square feet of space needed, cost per square foot, and other rough calculations. Technical expertise may have to be consulted to arrive at realistic cost estimates. While most decision makers will want to conduct their own analysis of costs, estimates by the proposers of change can at least serve as standards for comparison.

Task 20: Determine the Cost of Doing Nothing.   Relevant questions are:

- What will this problem cost the organization or community if nothing is done?
- How can this cost be framed so that it will impress decision makers as a good investment to support the proposed change?

A very valuable statistic for comparative purposes, if it can be calculated, is the cost of nonresolution of this problem or nonimplementation of the proposed change. It is important to impress upon decision makers that there are also long-term costs associated with doing nothing. For example, costs for inpatient or residential services can run as high as $5,000 to $6,000 a month. At first blush, an intensive vocational training program for high-risk adolescents costing $10,000 per client per year may appear outrageously expensive. However, if presented side by side with data demonstrating that 90 percent of the clients who complete this program become self-sufficient and do not need residential treatment, decision makers may be persuaded that it really represents a long-term cost savings.

Focus G: Weighing the Likelihood of Success

When the major participants, the proposed change, and the political and economic issues have been identified, the time has come to weigh the relative strength of supporting and opposing forces and to decide if the change effort is to be a "go" or a "no-go." This can be done in an orderly fashion by adapting Kurt Lewin's techniques of force-field analysis (1951). The issue for consideration here is whether or not to invest additional time, energy, and resources. The experienced change agent recognizes that there is little value in moral victories. If a change effort is to be undertaken, there should be some chance of succeeding. Force-field analysis can enable the change agent to make an informed decision about the likelihood of success.

We propose a modification of Lewin's framework that examines two areas: (1) support from individuals, groups, and organizations, and (2) support from facts and perspectives.

Task 21: Assess Support from Individuals, Groups, and Organizations.
Questions to be asked relative to this task are:

- Who supports the proposed change?
- Who opposes the proposed change?
- Who is neutral about the proposed change?

Applying the force-field analysis model, support from individuals, groups, and organizations should be laid out in three columns. Column one represents the driving or supporting forces. Column two represents neutral forces, and column three represents the restraining or opposing forces. Identifying each of the systems involved, together with their key individuals or groups will provide a graphic depiction of supporting and opposing forces and will help in determining the possibility of success if the change effort goes forward. Figure 9.5 illustrates a force-field analysis.

Task 22: Assess Support from Facts and Perspectives.   The key question to be asked here is:

- What facts and perspectives gleaned from the problem, population, and arena analysis support, and what oppose, the proposed change?

Following the identification of individuals, groups, and organizations supporting and opposing the change effort, we propose that facts and perspectives be identified in the same way. It is unlikely that any new research or analysis is necessary at this point. Identifying supporting and opposing facts and perspectives involves drawing on everything now known and available in terms of statistics, history, theory, research, etiology, interpersonal and political factors, and resource considerations. Each should be examined for its potential driving or restraining effects on the change effort. Figure 9.6 illustrates examples of support from facts and perspectives.

Using this format, action system participants next initiate a discussion session focused on making the "go/no-go" decision. An option, of course, is to gather more facts or to postpone the decision to a more opportune time. Additional fact gathering, if absolutely necessary, is considered advisable only if it

SUPPORT FROM INDIVIDUALS, GROUPS AND ORGANIZATIONS		
System	Driving/ Supporting Forces ⟶	Neutral Entities ⟵	Restraining/ Opposing Forces
Initiator system	Homeless Advocates T. Johnson L. Stearns		
Change Agent System	St. Catharine's Parish and Youth worker J. Foster		
Client System	Homeless teens in Douglas County		
Support System	Homeless Advocates Parents of Runaway, Inc. Existing homeless programs		
Controlling System	City Council members supporting change	City Council members not yet taking position	City Council members opposed to teen shelter
Host System		City Department of Human Services	
Inplementing System	Potential contract agencies		
Target System		City Council member votes in favor of funding proposed teen shelter	
Action System	Youth worker J.Foster, Advocates, two homeless teens, two social workers from existing shelters		
Others		A large percentage of the general public	Taxpayers Against Increased Public Social Services (TAPS) City Newspaper Task Force on CMI Homeless (who are competing for funding)

FIGURE 9.5   Force-Field Analysis of Individuals, Groups, and Organizations Supporting and Opposing a Proposed Project to Serve Homeless Teens

Driving/Supporting Forces ----→ | ←---- Restraining/Opposing Forces	
1. Teen homelessness is increasing by 20% per year.	1. Resources are already inadequate to meet existing needs of homeless families.
2. Homeless teens have been drawn into drug trafficking, prostitution, and many property crimes.	2. No federal or state funding is available; homelessness is considered a local problem.
3. Media have increased coverage of the problem; the public increasingly favors some action. Etc. . . .	3. Suburban cities are not willing to contribute needed support; major urban city council feels it should be considered a regional problem. Etc. . . .

FIGURE 9.6   Support from Facts and Perspectives on the Problem of Homeless Teens

is highly focused and time-limited. If, however, fact gathering is proposed as a delaying tactic or intended simply to avoid making a difficult decision, it should be recognized for what it is and rejected. It should also be recognized that this may be the point in which some participants will believe the proposed change to be unattainable and will decide to drop out, while others may choose to pursue the effort. Here again, it should be emphasized that the professional person acting as change agent must make as sound a decision as possible in the interest of achieving the change objectives. Necessary changes that have a good chance of success should be supported. Causes that are likely to be defeated as currently conceptualized should be tabled until they are more fully developed or the timing is better.

Focus H: Setting Goals and Objectives

Goals are brief—one sentence or phrase—general statements of expected outcomes (e.g., to reduce the number of dropouts in the Jefferson district). Objectives spell out the details for each goal in measurable terms, including expected outcomes and the processes to achieve them. Activities are lists of tasks that must be undertaken and completed in order to achieve each objective.

If the decision is made to proceed, the final step before selecting tactics is to establish a set of goals, objectives, and activities for the change. Goals and objectives are intended to act as a beacon to aid in keeping the change effort on track. Activities specify precisely what is to be done, by whom, and within what time frame.

Setting goals and objectives is probably as much art as it is science. The purpose is to take what can be a very large and complex undertaking and to break it up into manageable subsets. Each subset has its own set of goals, objectives, and activities.

The process begins with re-examining the change effort and organizing it into categories or sections. This takes some practice and requires knowledge of the subject area, which is why problem analysis is so important in macro-level change. The problem, as analyzed and conceptualized in the problem analysis phase, becomes a theme that is repeated throughout the change episode. The following examples illustrate how one might go about this first step of breaking a large and complex change effort into subsections or categories. They are built on the assumption that the problem analysis, the population analysis, and the community or organizational analysis have been completed.

Example 1   The proposed change is a three-year project to reduce teen pregnancy and enable at-risk teens to graduate from high school.

Project Subcategories

1. Building self-esteem.
2. Providing health, hygiene, and sex education.
3. Providing academic support.
4. Providing financial support.

In the example, we have depicted a four-part project designed to achieve the purpose as stated above. In both examples, each of the four areas listed above would have its own set of goals, objectives, and activities.

Example 2   The proposed change is a policy change that provides for financial incentives for programs demonstrating measurable improvement with alcohol-abusing clients.

Project Subcategories

1. Developing valid and reliable indicators of client progress.
2. Developing a fiscal incentive package for staff.
3. Developing quality assurance measures.

By dividing the change effort into subcategories, each part of the effort can proceed toward achieving its own set of goals and objectives in a way that is more concentrated and focused than if all objectives and activities were organized under a single goal. The exception to this principle of subdividing is when the change effort is so clear and simple that it does not require subcategories. For example, a project to conduct a client satisfaction survey might be a project that requires only a single set of goals, objectives, and activities. It is often true, however, that simple, unopposed change efforts come about without complications, and do not require the type of change process described in this book. If one follows the steps recommended in this book, it is likely that one is dealing with relatively complex change.

Once the subcategories are selected, a set of goals, objectives, and activities should be developed for each. They should always be thought of as a set or package, not as items that stand alone, even though they are occasionally used alone.

Task 23: Identify Goals.   For this task the critical question is:

- What are the major areas (in terms of client outcomes) that will be affected by the proposed change?

A goal is a general statement of expected outcomes or a desired future state (Kettner et al. 1985). It need not be observable or measurable. It is simply a statement of hopes or expectations, stated in a positive and general enough way to get agreement and support. Continuing with the above examples, the following goal statements would be appropriate:

Example 1: Teen Pregnancy Project.

Goal 1: To improve client self-esteem.

Goal 2: To increase client knowledge of health, hygiene, and contraception.

Goal 3: To strengthen client academic abilities.

Goal 4: To increase client financial resources.

Example 2: Measuring Client Outcomes of Services to Alcoholic Clients.

Goal 1: To develop indicators of client change.

Goal 2: To develop fiscal incentives to promote client improvement.

Goal 3: To develop methods for ensuring service quality.

Task 24: Formulate Outcome and Process Objectives.   Relevant questions include:

- What client outcomes are expected to be achieved if the proposed change is implemented?
- What steps will be necessary for the achievement of each client outcome?

Once a goal statement is written, the next step is to specify objectives. Objectives are intended to move the change effort toward the goal. They are highly specific and measurable. There are two types: (1) outcome objectives, and (2) process objectives. One outcome objective is written for each goal, and specifies the results or outcomes to be achieved. One or more process objectives then specify the process to be followed in order to achieve the result. When the outcome objective and all its related process objectives are completed and written out, it should be evident that the process objectives, when completed, will lead to achievement of the outcome objective, and that the outcome objective, when accomplished, will move the effort toward the goal. A complete objective, whether outcome or process, has four parts: (1) a time frame, (2) a target, (3) a result, and (4) a criterion for measuring or documenting the result (Kettner et al. 1985). In the following pages, examples will be given of both outcome and process objectives.

The time frame is stated in terms of the month, day, and year by which the result will be achieved. In situations in which a project's start date is unknown, the time frame may be specified in terms of time elapsed from the beginning of the project (e.g., "within three months of the beginning of the project," or "by the end of the first year"). Once a start date is known, it is wise to go back and fill in actual dates, since objectives are often also used as monitoring tools.

The second part of an objective, the target, specifies the individuals or focal point for which the objective is written. Outcome objectives are focused on a quality-of-life change and will identify the individuals for whom the change is intended. Process objectives may have an object (such as a program or a department) as a target, instead of a population.

Statements should be as precise as current knowledge will allow. An outpatient drug treatment program, for example, might specify "24 cocaine addicts at least 18 years of age and currently employed" as its target. A process objective might specify "the counseling program" or the "performance evaluation system" as its target or focal point. For reasons stated in earlier chapters in this book, the more precise the target, the greater the likelihood of a successful intervention. As an example, the teen pregnancy program mentioned above will be used to illustrate how outcome and process objectives fit together to form a plan of action.

The third part of an objective is a phrase that specifies the expected outcome or result to be achieved when all activities are completed. This phrase differs depending on whether the objective is an outcome or a process objective. An outcome objective focuses on a quality-of-life change for the target population; that is, something must happen to make their lives better or more stable. Outcome objectives refer to such factors as improved knowledge and skill, improved relationships with spouse, reduction of alcohol abuse, and other such changes. Process objectives focus on the result expected that indicates that the process is complete. Results might include such products as a completed report, a plan, or a new data-collection form.

The final part of an objective is the criterion that will be used to determine whether or not the objective has been achieved. Objectives must be precise and measurable, yet sometimes the result to be achieved seems vague and elusive. Some programs, for example, are designed to improve self-esteem. The question is, how does one know whether or not self-esteem has been improved? The criterion specified in the objective ensures that only one standard will be used. If improving self-esteem is the result, then it must be measured by a standardized test designed to measure self-esteem. The criterion for an outcome objective usually begins with the phrase, "as measured by . . . ." Increased self-esteem might be measured by the Index of Self-Esteem (Hudson 1982). Process objectives generally produce products or achieve milestones in a process, and use a different type of criterion to measure the result. In most cases, process objectives will use the phrase, "as documented by" indicating some formal product or result that will be accepted as documentation that the process objective has been completed. Continuing examples of outcome and process objectives on the teen pregnancy project follow:

TABLE 9.4   Sample Outcome and Process Objectives

	Outcome	Process
Time Frame	By June 30, 20XX	By February 1, 20XX
Target	50 teens considered to be at risk of pregnancy	For teens considered to be at risk of pregnancy
Outcome/Result	Will increase their knowledge of health, hygiene, and contraception	A training curriculum on health, hygiene, and contraception will be developed
Criterion	As measured by a pretest/post-test developed for the course	As documented by receipt of a completed training package

Outcome objective:
[time frame]
By June 30, 20XX,

[target   ]
at least 50 teens considered to be at risk of pregnancy

[outcome   ]
will increase their knowledge of health, hygiene, and contraception

[criterion   ]
as measured by a pretest/posttest developed for the course.

Process objective:
[time frame]
By February 1, 20XX,

[result   ]
a training curriculum on health, hygiene, and contraception will be
developed

[target   ]
for teens considered to be at risk of pregnancy

[criterion   ]
as documented by receipt of a completed training package.

When all four parts—time frame, target, result, and criterion—have been
written, the objective is complete. The foregoing examples are reproduced in
Table 9.4 to reinforce the understanding of the differences between outcome
and process objectives.

Typically a set of goals and objectives will include one goal, one outcome objective, and several process objectives. For example, in the program outlined in Table 9.4, the following might be the focus of goals and
objectives:

Goal:

To increase knowledge about health and pregnancy for teens at risk.

Outcome objective:

By June 30, 20XX, to increase knowledge of health, hygiene, and contraception for 50 teens considered to be at risk of pregnancy as measured by a pretest/posttest developed for the course.

Some possible areas in which process objectives might be developed:

Develop training curriculum.

Develop and reproduce training materials.

Recruit 50 teens at risk of pregnancy.

Secure a suitable training location.

Hire trainers.

Implement the program.

Evaluate the program.

Task 25: Plan Activities.   The important question to be addressed here is:

- What tasks or activities must be undertaken for each process objective to be achieved?

The final step in Focus H is to itemize activities. Activities represent the highest level of detail incorporated into the plan. Each activity represents a step that, when accomplished, moves the project closer to achievement of a process objective. Activities should specify the work to be done, the person responsible, and a time frame. The Gantt chart, originated early in the century by management pioneer Henry L. Gantt, has proved to be a useful format for setting up activities.

A Gantt chart is made up of columns and rows. Each row represents an activity, and columns are used to identify activity number, person responsible, and the beginning and ending month. Illustrated below is an example of a Gantt chart applied to one of the process objectives for the pregnancy prevention program.

The Gantt chart in Figure 9.7 depicts a training project beginning July 1, phasing in each activity sequentially over the next seven months, and delivering the completed training package as promised on February 1. The horizontal lines across the columns indicate the approximate anticipated beginning and ending times for those activities. The *1* in the February column next to activity number 7 indicates that the completed training package is due on that specific date.

In preparing an action plan for a macro-level change, each subsection of the intervention should include a set of goals, objectives, and activities. When these are developed at an acceptable level of precision, with responsibilities and time frames clearly specified, the action plan is complete. The last steps in macro-level change involve the selection of tactics and the development of a written plan. These final steps are discussed in Chapter 10.

Process Objective: By February 1, 20xx, to develop a training curriculum on health, hygiene, and contraception for teens at risk of pregnancy, as documented by receipt of a completed training package.

Activity Number	Activity	Person Responsible	Time Frame J F M A M J J A S O N D
1.	Develop course objectives.	J. Smith	├—
2.	Prepare content outline modules on health, hygiene, and contraception.	J. Smith/ L. Black	┤
3.	Select teaching methods for each module.	L. Black	├—
4.	Prepare workbooks and handouts for each module.	C. Rich	├———┤
5.	Print up workbooks and handouts.	B. Wood	—
6.	Develop pretest/posttest.	J. Smith	—
7.	Deliver complete training package.	J. Smith	1

FIGURE 9.7   A Gantt Chart

REFERENCES

Brager, G., and S. Holloway. (1978) *Changing human service organizations: Politics and practice.* New York: Free Press.

Brager, G., H. Specht, and J. L. Torczyner. (1987) *Community organizing.* New York: Columbia University Press.

Hudson, W. W. (1982) *The clinical measurement package.* Homewood, IL: Dorsey.

Katz, D., and R. L. Kahn. (1966) *The social psychology of organizations.* New York: Wiley.

Kettner, P. M., J. M. Daley, and A. W. Nichols. (1985) *Initiating change in organizations and communities.* Monterey, CA: Brooks/Cole.

Lewin, K. (1951) *Field theory in social science.* New York: Harper & Row.

Rothman, J., J. L. Erlich, and J. E. Tropman. (1995) *Strategies of community intervention* (5th ed). Itasca, IL: F. E. Peacock.

von Bertalanffy, L. (1950) An outline of general system theory. *British Journal for the Philosophy of Science, 1*(2): 493–512.

SUGGESTED READINGS

Bargal, D., and H. Schmid, guest eds. (1992) Organizational change and development in human service organizations. *Administration in Social Work, 16* (3/4), entire issue.

Brueggemann, W. G. (1996) *The practice of macro social work*. Chicago: Nelson-Hall.

Fatout, M., and S. R. Rose. (1995) *Task groups in the social services*. Thousand Oaks, CA: Sage.

Lawlor, E. F., and K. Raube. (1995) Social interventions and outcomes in medical effectiveness research. *Social Service Review,* 383–404.

Monkman, M. M. (1991) Outcome objectives in social work practice: Person and environment. *Social Work, 36*(3), 252–8.

Salipante, P. F., and K. Golden-Biddle. (1995) Managing traditionality and strategic change in nonprofit organizations. *Nonprofit Management and Leadership, 6*(1), 3–20.

APPENDIX

Framework for Developing an Intervention Strategy

FOCUS A: DEVELOPING THE INTERVENTION HYPOTHESIS

Task 1: Develop a Working Hypothesis of Etiology

- What factors gleaned from the problem analysis, the population, analysis, and the arena analysis help in understanding cause-and-effect relationships?
- How should the working hypothesis of etiology be framed?

Task 2: Develop a Working Intervention Hypothesis

- What interventions (based on an understanding of etiology) are most likely to reduce or eliminate the problem?
- What results can be expected from these interventions?

FOCUS B: DEFINING PARTICIPANTS

Task 3: Identify the Initiator System

- Who first recognized the problem and brought attention to it?
- How should/can the initiators be involved in the change effort?

Task 4: Identify the Change Agent System

- Who will be responsible for leadership and coordination in the early stages of the change effort?

Task 5: Identify the Client System

- Who will be the primary beneficiaries of change?
- Who will be the secondary beneficiaries of change?

Task 6: Identify the Support System

- What other individuals and groups (in addition to the primary and secondary beneficiaries) will support the change effort?

Task 7: Identify the Controlling System

- Who has the formally delegated authority and the power to approve and order implementation of the proposed change?

Task 8: Identify the Host and Implementing Systems

- What organization will be responsible for sponsoring and delivering the activities of the change effort?
- What individuals will be involved in direct delivery of services or other activities necessary to implement the change effort?

Task 9: Identify the Target System

- What is it that needs to be changed (e.g., individual, group, structure, policy, practice, etc.) in order for the effort to be successful?
- Where (within the organization or community) is the target system located?

Task 10: Identify the Action System

- Who should be represented on a central "steering committee" or decision-making group that will see the change effort through to completion?

FOCUS C: EXAMINING SYSTEM READINESS FOR CHANGE

Task 11: Assess General Openness to Change

- What has been the past experience with each of the systems with regard to organizational or community change?

Task 12: Identify Anticipated or Actual Response

- What level of commitment to the proposed change is anticipated from each of the systems?

Task 13: Determine Availability of Resources

- From what sources will resources be solicited?
- What resources will be requested?

Task 14: Examine Outside Opposition to Change

- What individuals or groups outside the systems identified can be expected to oppose the change effort?

FOCUS D: SELECTING A CHANGE APPROACH

Task 15: Select a Policy, Program, Project, Personnel, or Practice Approach

- What approach (or combination of approaches) is most likely to achieve the desired change?

FOCUS E: ASSESSING POLITICAL AND INTERPERSONAL CONSIDERATIONS

Task 16: Address Public Image and Successful Change

- Who can serve as effective spokespersons for the proposed change?
- Who should keep a low profile when the proposed change is presented to decision makers?
- Has anyone key to the success of the change effort been left out?

Task 17: Identify Alternative Perspectives

- How will opponents of the change effort frame their opposition?

Task 18: Assess Duration and Urgency

- How long has the problem existed?
- Is the problem considered an emergency?

FOCUS F: ASSESSING RESOURCE CONSIDERATIONS

Task 19: Determine the Cost of Change

- What anticipated costs related to the proposed change can be itemized? What must be estimated?
- What sources of financial support or in-kind donations should be approached?

Task 20: Determine the Cost of Doing Nothing

- What will this problem cost the organization or community if nothing is done?
- How can this cost be framed so that it will impress decision makers as a good investment to support the proposed change?

FOCUS G: WEIGHING THE LIKELIHOOD OF SUCCESS

Task 21: Assess Support from Individuals, Groups, and Organizations

- Who supports the proposed change?
- Who opposes the proposed change?
- Who is neutral about the proposed change?

Task 22: Assess Support from Facts and Perspectives

- What facts and perspectives gleaned from the problem, population, and arena analysis support, and what oppose, the proposed change?

FOCUS H: SETTING GOALS AND OBJECTIVES

Task 23: Identify Goals

- What are the major areas (in terms of client outcomes) that will be affected by the proposed change?

Task 24: Formulate Outcome and Process Objectives

- What client outcomes are expected to be achieved if the proposed change is implemented?
- What steps will be necessary for the achievement of each client outcome?

Task 25: Plan Activities

- What tasks or activities must be undertaken for each process objective to be achieved?

CHAPTER **10**

Selecting Appropriate Tactics

Overview

Chapter 9 addressed strategy, which refers to the development of a written plan directed at bringing about the proposed change. Deciding on a strategy can be a time-consuming and detailed process. Although many may agree that a problem exists, getting agreement on just how the situation should be changed is seldom easy. Special efforts must be concentrated on tactics designed to get the change accepted.

Tactic selection tests the professional judgment of the change agent, particularly in how to approach the target system. Certain tactics can raise ethical dilemmas. Selecting tactics calls for mature, professional judgment in community and organizational change. Social workers should be open to the possibility that practices in many of the arenas in which they operate are well entrenched and that there will be a natural tendency to resist. The fact that agency missions are stated in inspiring words does not mean that all agencies carry out those missions. Practitioners must be aware that they are a part of legitimized systems that often contribute to the oppression experienced by the client group they are trying to serve. Selecting appropriate tactics requires one to think critically and to analyze the target system carefully.

FOCUS A: SELECTING TACTICS

The choice of tactics is a critical decision point in planned change. Tactics have been defined as "any skillful method used to gain an end" (Brager, Specht, & Torczyner 1987, p. 288). Whereas strategy is the long-range linking of activities to achieve the desired goal, tactics are reflected in day-to-day behaviors (Brager & Holloway 1978). As the change agent engages in tactical behavior, it is important not to lose sight of the goal toward which these behaviors are directed.

Brager et al. (1987) identify four essential properties of tactics used by professional change agents: "1) they are planned . . . , 2) they are used to evoke specific responses . . . , 3) they involve interaction with others . . . , and 4) they are goal-oriented" (p. 288). In addition, it is our contention that a fifth property must be in place in professional social work change efforts: 5) the tactic will do no harm to members of the client system and whenever possible members of that system will be involved in tactical decision-making.

Task 1: Consider a Range of Tactics.   Question to be asked:

- Given a knowledge of the current level of support and opposition, what tactic (or combination or tactics) is most likely to succeed?

Change almost always involves influencing the allocation of scarce resources—authority, status, power, goods, services, or money. Decisions about tactics, therefore, must take into consideration whether the resources are being allocated willingly or whether someone must be persuaded to make the allocation. If there is agreement on the part of the action and target systems that the proposed change is acceptable and that resources will be allocated, a collaborative approach can be adopted. If there is agreement that the proposed change is acceptable but there is reluctance or refusal to allocate resources, or if there is disagreement about the need for the proposed change, then a more conflictual approach may be necessary if the change effort is to proceed.

For example, a change effort may focus on the inability of persons with physical disabilities to get around the city and travel to needed service providers. A thorough study documents the problem, and a dial-a-ride transportation service is proposed. The planning commission and city council graciously accept the report, agree on the need, and thank the Transportation Task Force for Disabled Persons. Three city council members favor funding, three are opposed, and one is undecided. If the undecided council member can be persuaded to favor funding, then collaborative tactics can be adopted. If, however, she decides to oppose funding or if a compromise would undermine the change effort, then tactics designed to compel her support must be adopted. For collaborative approaches to be adopted, there must be agreement on both the proposed change and the allocation of needed resources.

In the social work literature tactics have been divided into three broad categories: collaboration, campaign, and contest (Brager & Holloway 1978; Brager et al. 1987). In this chapter, we use these terms to describe the relationship between the action and target systems. *Collaboration* implies a working relationship in which the two systems agree that change must occur, whereas *contest tactics* indicate disagreement between the two systems. *Campaign tactics* are used when the target must be convinced of the importance of the change, but when communication is still possible between the two systems. The effectiveness of the "campaign" may determine whether collaboration or contest follows. *Contest tactics* are used when neither of the other two are possible any longer. Change efforts that begin with one set of tactics may progress to other sets, depending on the evolving relationship between the action and target systems. The continuum along which these tactical categories fall is as follows:

Collaboration ◄------------► Campaign ◄------------► Contest

Although we categorize three types of relationships, success may hinge on the change agent's ability to keep the action and target systems in a state of continual interaction. It is possible that what begins as a collaborative relationship will move to conflict when new issues arise during the change process. It is equally likely that the relationship will vary across different qualities and gradations of communication, with both systems uncertain about the other, even when compromise can be reached. In short, these relationships ebb and flow, sometimes unpredictably given the political situation and sometimes all too predictably given the change agent's prior experience with the target system.

TABLE 10.1   Tactical Behaviors

Relationship of Action and Target Systems	Tactics

Collaboration
Target system agrees (or is easily convinced to agree) with action system that change is needed and supports allocation of resources
	1. Implementation
	2. Capacity Building
	   a. Participation
	   b. Empowerment

Campaign
Target system is willing to communicate with action system, but there is little consensus that change is needed; or target system supports change but not allocation of resources
	3. Education
	4. Persuasion
	   a. Cooptation
	   b. Lobbying
	5. Mass media appeal

Contest
Target system opposes change and/or allocation of resources and is not open to further communication about opposition
	6. Bargaining and negotiation
	7. Large-group or community action
	   a. Legal (e.g., demonstrations)
	   b. Illegal (e.g., civil disobedience)
	8. Class action lawsuit

Our concern is that the social worker never take the relationship between the action and target systems for granted. To assume that the target is immovable before communication has been attempted demonstrates poor professional judgment. To assume that the target will embrace the cause once the facts are known is naive. Assumptions have little place in assessing the relationship between the action and the target system. We believe that regardless of what types of tactics are used, communication should be maintained with the target system if at all possible. If communication ceases, it should be because the target system refuses to continue interaction.

Within each of the three categories are tactics that are typically used. The framework in Table 10.1 guides our discussion. Some of the following conceptualization is drawn from previous literature (Brager & Holloway 1978; Brager et al. 1987). In some areas we offer slightly different perspectives and add new tactics. Throughout the following discussion we attempt to provide an analytical framework to guide an action system in selecting the most appropriate mix of tactics.

Task 2: Consider the Pros and Cons of Collaboration.   Questions to be asked:

- Are we certain that there is no opposition?
- Can the desired change be achieved by identifying appropriate roles for participants and implementing the change?

Collaborative approaches include instances in which the target and action systems agree that change is needed. Under collaboration, we place (1) implementation and (2) capacity-building tactics.

Implementation.   Implementation tactics are used when the action and target systems cooperatively work together. When these systems agree that change is needed and allocation of resources is supported by critical decision makers, the change simply needs to be implemented. Implementation will most likely involve some problem solving, but it is not expected that adversarial relationships will be a concern in these types of collaborative efforts.

Capacity Building.   Capacity building includes the tactics of participation and empowerment. *Participation* refers to activities that involve members of the client system in the change effort. *Empowerment* is the process of "helping individuals, families, groups, and communities to increase their personal, interpersonal, socioeconomic, and political strength and to develop influence toward improving their circumstances" (Barker 1995, p. 120).

For example, a problem may be defined as exclusion of a neighborhood from decisions that affect them. The focus of the intervention is on building a capacity for greater self-direction and self-control—that is, actually teaching people how to get involved in the decision-making processes in their communities and taking greater control over the decisions that affect their lives. This approach often emerges in situations in which disenfranchised communities become targets for development, freeways, airport expansion, and other such encroachments.

Through professionally assisted change efforts, perhaps led by a neighborhood social service organization (change agent system), neighborhood residents (client system) and the city council (controlling system and perhaps target system) agree that community citizens should have a greater voice in developments that affect their community. The focus of the change or intervention, however, is not on the target system (city council/planning commission) but on educating, training, and preparing community citizens for fuller participation in decisions that affect their communities. Tactics would include education, training, and actual participation in civic organizations and activities.

Empowerment involves enabling people to become aware of their rights, and teaching them how to exercise those rights so that they become better able to take control over factors that affect their lives. Mobilizing the efforts of self-help groups and voluntary associations identified in Chapter 6 as well as involving the client system's informal support structure are methods that may be used to assist in guiding the target system toward consensus with the change effort.

Task 3: Consider the Pros and Cons of Campaign.   Questions to be asked:

- Who needs to be convinced that the proposed change is needed?
- What persuasive techniques are most likely to be effective?

Campaign implies a group effort to convince target-system members that a cause is just or a change is needed, and that resources should be allocated. Campaign tactics require a good deal of skill on the part of the change agent and action system. Lack of consensus rules out collaboration, yet it is not certain that a clear disagreement exists. Under this heading we include the use of education, persuasion, and mass media appeals designed to influence public opinion.

Education.   Educational tactics can be an integral part of campaigns. *Educational tactics* are interactions in which the action system presents perceptions, attitudes, opinions, data, and information about the proposed change with the intent of convincing the target system to think or to act differently. The objective is to inform. The assumption is that more and better information will lead to a change in behavior. It is a difficult tactic to use because opponents of the change can also be expected to inform decision-makers about different sets of data and information, and there is no absolute "truth" in dealing with complex organizational and community problems. In many cases in which education fails to produce the desired result or falls short of having the desired impact, the change agent turns to persuasion.

Persuasion.   *Persuasion* refers to the art of convincing others to accept and support one's point of view or perspective on an issue. Social workers must frequently use persuasive tactics in addition to collaboration because their causes are not always embraced by decision makers, who often must be convinced through persuasion that the change is worth pursuing. This means that the change agent must understand the motives and reasoning of the target system in order to identify what incentives or information might be considered persuasive by members of the target system.

Skillful communication requires that the action system must carefully select its leadership from persons who have the ability to persuade. Persons who are seen as nonthreatening to the target system and who can articulate the reasoning behind the planned change are particularly useful. For example, in a change effort particular actors may be perceived as unreasonable, as troublemakers, or as chronic complainers by members of the controlling system. It is not in the best interest of the client system for those persons to be the only spokespeople for the change. Clients themselves can also be powerful spokespersons, providing information and a viewpoint that persuades people of the need for change.

Framing the problem statement to make it more palatable to target-system members is a persuasive technique. This requires the ability to think as the target thinks. For example, a social worker hired as a long-term–care ombudsperson was working closely with a coalition of advocates for nursing home reform to end abuse in long-term–care facilities. Nursing home administrators were very upset over the nursing home reform coalition and perceived them as not understanding the difficulties with which they coped on a daily basis. They sincerely wanted to provide quality care but were frustrated by staff who were not properly trained to work with geriatric populations. By framing the problem as a training issue involving the need to better prepare employees and reduce turnover, the ombudsperson was able to persuade administrators to cooperate with the action system. When the ombudsperson met with the local nursing home association, she acknowledged that she was aware that the administrators wanted to operate high-quality facilities. She also noted that recent studies revealed that high staff turnover rates often contributed to lack of continuity and lower quality of patient care, sometimes leading to abuse. She explained that she and her colleagues would be willing to develop training for nurses aides because they interacted most intimately with patients, yet were most vulnerable to high turnover. Essentially, one of the contributing factors leading to abuse was being addressed, but it was framed as reducing an administrative nightmare—high staff turnover.

Cooptation is defined as minimizing anticipated opposition by absorbing or including members of the target system in the action system. Once target-system members are part of the planned change effort, it is likely that they will assume some ownership of the change process. Persuasion is used to coopt new persons into the action system. This is valuable to the success of the change effort because it is important to include persons who are viewed as powerful by the target system. These persons may be relatively neutral and may have little interest in obstructing the change effort. However, if they can be convinced to support the change effort (or even to allow their names to be used in publicity), their participation may sway others who respect their opinions. Cooptation is most effective as a tactic when opponents or neutral parties can be helped to recognize a self-interest in the proposed change.

Cooptation can be formal or informal. Coopting individuals is called "informal cooptation," whereas coopting organized groups is referred to as "formal cooptation." *Formal cooptation* means that an entire group agrees to support a cause. Because their governing structure agrees that the change effort is worthwhile, the group may issue a statement to that effect. This formalizes the commitment, even though there are always members of any group who may, as individuals, disagree with the proposed change.

Formal cooptation of a number of groups leads to *coalition building*. A coalition is a loosely woven, ad hoc association of constituent groups, each of whose primary identification is outside the coalition (Haynes & Mickelson 1986). For example, the purpose of the National Health Care Campaign was to provide health care coverage to all American citizens. This change effort brought together hundreds of organizations such as the National Association of Social Workers and the American Public Health Association. On a state-by-state basis, health care campaign chapters were forming. Interested change agents encouraged local groups to join in the efforts—forming a coalition dedicated to the stated goal. The diversity of the coalition contributed to a powerful alliance of individuals and groups that alternated between collaboration and campaign tactics as they attempted to address health care needs.

Lobbying is a form of persuasion that addresses policy change under the domain of the controlling system. Members of the action system will have to determine if it is necessary to change agency policy, to amend current legislation, or to develop new legislation in order to achieve their goal. Haynes and Mickelson (1986) delineate three essential concepts for social workers/lobbyists to consider. First, one should always be factual and honest. Trying to second guess or stretching the facts to support one's position is devastating to one's professional reputation as well as to the change effort's credibility. Second, any presentation should be straightforward and supported by the available data. The problem identification and analysis process discussed in Chapter 3 will assist the change agent in organizing the rationale for change. Third, any discussion should include the two critical concerns of decision makers—cost and social impact of what is proposed. If the cost is high, the social worker is advised to calculate the costs of allowing the identified problem to remain unresolved.

Mass Media Appeal.

Mass media appeal refers to the development and release of newsworthy stories to the print and electronic media for the purpose of influencing public opinion. This tactic is used to pressure decision makers into a favorable resolution to the identified problem. The expectation is that if the proposed change can be presented to the public in a positive way and decision makers' refusal to support the proposed change can be presented as obstructionist or somehow negative, then decision makers will feel pressured to change their position. Because decision makers are high-profile people like elected representatives who depend on a positive public perception, this can be an effective tactic. Use of mass media depends on news reporters' agreements that the proposed change is a newsworthy story, and assurance that one's cause will be presented accurately. Use of any media must always include consideration of clients' rights to privacy.

Task 4: Consider the Pros and Cons of Contest.

Questions to be asked:

- Is opposition to the proposed change so strong that it can only be successful by imposing the change on an unwilling target system?
- Can the proposed change be effective if it is forced?
- What are the anticipated consequences of conflict?

Under the heading of *contest* we include the use of bargaining and negotiating, the use of large-group or community action, or class action lawsuits. Large-group or community action can be further divided into legal and illegal tactics. Contest tactics are used in situations in which: (1) the target system cannot be persuaded by the action system, (2) the target system refuses to communicate with the action system, or (3) it is perceived that only lip service is being given to the proposed change. *Contest tactics* mean that the change effort becomes an open, public conflict as attempts are made to draw broad support and/or to pressure or even force the target system into supporting or at least accepting the change. Once this occurs, the action system must be prepared to face open confrontation and to escalate its coercive techniques.

Conflict is inevitable in social work practice. There will be times in the experience of every macro practitioner when formidable resistance is encountered in addressing the needs of oppressed population groups. Social work as a profession developed in response to a basic societal conflict—the persistent antagonism over individualism and the common good. Conflicts over the rights of various population groups have spawned violent confrontations rooted in basic value systems and beliefs. We believe that physical violence and terrorism cannot be condoned in any professionally assisted change efforts in a civilized society. Nonviolent confrontation, however, including civil disobedience, is an option when there is a communication stalemate between the target and action systems.

Contest tactics will require widespread commitment and possible participation from members of the support system. It is critical to the success of these tactics that the support system and its subsystems—initiator, client, and change agent—are comfortable with contest tactics because there are risks that are not present when using collaboration and campaign tactics. It is likely that the time and energy necessary for effective change will increase and relationships can become disrupted. When collaborative and campaign tactics are employed, tactics can move toward contest. However, once contest tactics are employed it is not likely that one can return to collaborative or campaign tactics. Without a clear understanding of what contest tactics involve and without full commitment from the support system, contest tactics are not advised.

Bargaining and Negotiation.   Bargaining and negotiation refer to situations in which the action and target system confront one another with the reasons for their opposition. Bargaining and negotiation occur when there is a recognized power differential between parties and a compromise needs to be made. These tactics are more formalized than persuasion, often involving a third-party mediator. Members of the target system will typically agree to negotiate when the following factors are in place: (1) there is some understanding of the intentions and preferred outcomes of the action system, (2) there is a degree of urgency, (3) the relative importance and scope of the proposed change is known, (4) there are resources that facilitate the exercise of power, and (5) they perceive the action system as having some legitimacy. In order to negotiate, both the action and the target systems must perceive that each has something the other wants, otherwise there is no reason to come together (Brager et al. 1987).

Bargaining and negotiation can result in a win/win situation, in which both target and action systems are pleased with and fully support the outcome. The result can be a win/lose, in which one system is clearly the victor, or a lose/lose, in which both systems give something up and are disappointed in the results.

Large-Group or Community Action.   *Large-group or community action* refers to the preparing, training, and organizing of large numbers of people who are willing to form a pressure group and advocate for change through various forms of collective action such as picketing, disruption of meetings, sit-ins, boycotting, and other such pressure tactics. Peaceful demonstrations are legal activities, often used by both groups at either extreme of an issue to express their views. Civil disobedience activities intentionally break the law. When action-system members deliberately engage in illegal activities (such as staging marches when permits have been denied or refusing to discontinue a sit-in when ordered), they must be ready to take the consequences of their actions. The change agent is responsible for making potential participants fully aware of these risks before the decision is made to proceed.

Class Action Lawsuits.   *Class action lawsuits* refer to instances in which an entity is sued for a perceived violation of the law and it is expected that the finding of the court will apply to an entire class of people. These tactics are often used with highly vulnerable populations such as the chronically mentally ill, the homeless, or children, who are unlikely to have the capacity or the resources to protect their own rights. Public interest law organizations may be resources for the action system in developing class action tactics.

Task 5: Weigh Relevant Considerations in Selecting Tactics.   Questions to be asked:

- What are the current objectives of the change effort?
- What is the perception (by those promoting change) of the controlling and host systems?
- What is the perception (by those promoting change) of the role of the client system?
- What resources are needed and available for each tactic?
- What are the ethical dilemmas inherent in the range of tactical choices?

Objectives.   Objectives often tend to evolve as the change process moves along, and a reexamination prior to selection of tactics is in order. For example, with the problem of domestic violence, the condition may have been brought to public awareness by the perceived need for additional emergency shelter space for battered women. However, as the problem is analyzed and better understood, the objectives may shift toward consciousness raising for all women in the community who are perceived to be at risk for violence. Thus, strategy and tactics would move from advocating for service provision to educating for empowerment. Since tactics can change as objectives change, it is worthwhile to make one last check to ensure that all are clear and in agreement on current objectives. The following questions can be used to guide the action system's reexamination of the change objectives.

TABLE 10.2   Relationship of Current Objectives to Tactics

Current Objective	Relationship of Target and Action System	Possible Tactics
1. Solving a substantive problem; providing a needed service	Collaborative	Implementation through joint action
2. Self-direction; self-control	Collaborative	Capacity building through participation and empowerment
3. Influencing decision makers	In disagreement but with open communication	Education, and persuasion through cooptation, lobbying, etc.
4. Changing public opinion	In disagreement but with open communication/ Adversarial	Education, persuasion, mass media appeal, Large-group or community action
5. Shifting power	Adversarial	Large-group or community action
6. Mandating action	Adversarial	Class action lawsuit

> 1. What are the stated objectives of this change effort?
> 2. Given what has been learned in the change process thus far, do the stated objectives need to be revised?
> 3. Which best describes the intent of the current objectives?
>   a. to solve a substantive problem or provide a needed service;
>   b. to increase self-direction or self-control of the client system;
>   c. to influence decision makers;
>   d. to change public opinion;
>   e. to shift power;
>   f. to mandate action.
> 4. Do members of the action system have any concerns about the intent of the current objectives that require further discussion?

The range of objectives and likely accompanying tactics are indicated in Table 10.2.

Controlling and Host Systems.   The controlling and host systems can be perceived in a variety of ways. If they are seen as employers or sponsors of the change, then collaboration is likely. If they are seen as supporters of, but not participants in the change, capacity building (through participation and empower-

TABLE 10.3   **Relationship of Controlling and Host System Roles to Tactics**

Perception of Role of Controlling and Host Systems	Relationship of Controlling, Host, and Action Systems	Possible Tactics
1. Sponsors; supporters; coparticipants; colleagues	Collaborative	Implementation through joint action
2. Neutrality or indifference	Collaborative	Capacity building through participation and empowerment
3. Uninformed barriers/ not sure about change	In disagreement but with open communication	Education and persuasion
4. Informed barriers/ opponents to successful change	Adversarial	Bargaining; large-group or community action
5. Oppressors	Adversarial	Large-group or community action
6. Violators of rights	Adversarial	Class action lawsuit

ment) may be the tactic of choice. If they are seen as neutral or indifferent, a campaign strategy may be in order. If, however, they are seen as oppressive or unresponsive to their primary clientele, then some type of contest approach will likely be selected. Discussion of the following questions may assist members of the action system in assessing their relationship with the controlling and host system.

---

1. Who are the critical actors in the host and controlling system(s)?
2. What term(s) best describe(s) the action-system members' perceptions of the host and controlling system actors?
   a. sponsors, supporters, coparticipants or colleagues;
   b. neutral or indifferent actors;
   c. uninformed barriers who are not sure about change;
   d. informed barriers or opponents;
   e. oppressors;
   f. violators of rights.
3. Are action system members' perceptions similar or dissimilar?
4. If they are dissimiliar, what are the different perceptions and what are the implications of this divergence of opinion for the change effort?

Table 10.3 illustrates the various perceptions of roles that might be assigned to the controlling and host systems, and the logical tactic for each.

Primary Client.   The role of the primary client can vary, and the way in which this role is perceived can affect selection of change tactics. Sometimes it may be difficult to determine who the primary client really is. For example, in addressing the needs of elderly persons, the change agent may discover that caregivers are suffering from stress and fatigue. In this situation, one must ask if the primary beneficiaries of a change effort will be the older persons themselves or their caregivers.

If the primary client is seen as a consumer or recipient of service, then a collaborative change approach is the most likely tactic. If the primary role is as a resident of a community or potential participant in an effort to achieve self-direction and control, then a capacity-building approach is, perhaps, more appropriate. If the primary client is seen as a person who needs a service (but this need is not acknowledged by the controlling system), as a victim, or as a voter or constituent with potential power to influence decision makers, then some type of contest approach is likely to be employed. The following questions guide the action system in assessing the role of the primary client.

---

1. Who is defined as the primary client?
2. How do members of the action system describe the primary client?
   a. consumer or recipient of service;
   b. resident of the community in need of self-direction or self-control;
   c. citizen/taxpayer not permitted full participation;
   d. victim, underserved needy person;
   e. victim, exploited person;
   f. person denied civil rights.
3. Do action-system members agree or disagree in their descriptions of the primary client? Do clients agree or disagree?
4. What role does the primary client play within the action system?
5. How much overlap is there between the client and the action systems?
6. What mechanisms does the action system use to obtain input from the client system?

Table 10.4 displays client roles, approaches, and tactics.

Resources.   A key consideration in choosing tactics is the amount of resources available to the action system, since different tactics require more or different types of resources than others. If collaboration is the tactic of choice, for example, one necessary resource will be technical expertise capable of understanding whether or not the change is being properly implemented, monitored, and evaluated. In order for a capacity-building tactic to be used, grass-roots organizing ability, together with some teaching and training expertise must be available to the action system. If there is conflict, either skilled persuaders, media support, large numbers of people willing to do what is necessary to bring about change, or legal expertise must be available. The following questions may assist the action system in assessing resources.

TABLE 10.4   Relationship of Client System Role to Tactics

Perception of Role of Client System	Relationship of Client and Target Systems	Possible Tactics
1. Consumer; recipient of service	Collaborative	Implementation through joint action
2. Resident of the community in need of greater self-direction and self-control	Collaborative	Capacity building through participation and empowerment
3. Citizen/taxpayer not permitted full participation	In disagreement but with open communication	Education and persuasion
4. Victim; underserved needy person	Adversarial	Mass media appeal
5. Victim; exploited person	Adversarial	Large-group or community action
6. Person denied civil rights	Adversarial	Class action lawsuit

---

1. What tactics are being considered at this point?
2. What resources will be needed to use these tactics adequately? (e.g., expertise, training, time, funding, equipment, etc.)
3. What members of the action system have access to the needed resources?
4. If additional resources are needed, should the boundaries of the action system be expanded to include persons/groups who have access to additional resources?

Resource considerations are illustrated in Table 10.5.

Professional Ethics.   In Chapter 1 we discussed the importance of values in social work practice. Ethics are the behaviors that bring values into action. An ethical dilemma is defined as a situation in which a choice has to be made between equally important values. Tactical choices are no exception. Decisions regarding what tactics to use are based on the values held by action-system members. It is often the clash of action- and target-system values that leads to the selection of contest tactics.

Three ethical principles were highlighted in Chapter 1: autonomy, beneficence, and social justice. These principles are deeply enmeshed in macro-practice change. A clash between autonomy and beneficence occurs when the client system is not willing to risk the little they have, yet when the action system wants to push for a quality-of-life change. Members of the client system may have limited control over their lives, but their right to decide (self-determina-

TABLE 10.5   Resources Needed by Action System
for Each Tactic

Tactic	Resources Needed
1. Collaboration—joint action or problem solving	Technical expertise; monitoring and evaluation capability
2. Capacity building	Grass-roots organizing ability; teaching/training expertise; opportunities for participation; some indigenous leadership; willing participants
3. Persuasion	Informed people; data/information; skilled persuaders/lobbyists
4. Mass media appeal	Data/information; newsworthy issue or slant; access to news reporters; technical expertise to write news releases
5. Large-group or community action	Large numbers of committed people (support system); training and organizing expertise; informed leadership; bargaining and negotiating skills
6. Class action lawsuits	Legal expertise; victims willing to bring action and provide information; at least enough money for court costs

tion) that they do not want to risk the little control they have must be respected by action-system members if it is clear that client-system opinion is being fairly represented. Alternatively, the action system may be heavily composed of professionals who are acting on the principle of beneficence. They may sincerely believe that they know what is best for the client system. Rights of clients take precedence over the wishes of the action system when such a conflict emerges.

This clash was illustrated in a social work intern's first field experience. Working for a small community center in the southwest, she discovered that many of her Hispanic clients lived in a crowded apartment complex with faulty wiring and inadequate plumbing. With the backing of her agency, she began talking with clients to see if they would be willing to engage in a change process directed toward their living conditions. As she analyzed the situation, she realized that any change process would involve housing and public health personnel in the action system. Her clients begged her not to bring these concerns to the attention of local authorities. Many members of the client system were illegal immigrants and they feared that their exposure to public authorities would ensure their deportation. The client system was willing to accept poor housing conditions rather than risk the consequences of exposure. The client system's autonomy was in conflict with the change agent system's beneficence.

The clash between social justice and autonomy is exemplified when the action system demands redistribution of resources and the target system believes that in giving up their control over valued resources they have less freedom. Macro change frequently appeals to the principle of justice, for it is usually through the redistribution of valued resources (e.g., power, money, status, etc.) that change occurs. Because social justice is a basic ethical principle that raises emotions when it is violated, change agents can become so obsessed with injustice that any means is viewed as an appropriate tactic if it leads to a successful end. It is our contention that this type of thinking can lead to professional anarchy, whereby tactics are perceived as weapons to punish the target system rather than as actions to enrich the client system. In these situations it may be too easy for the change to take on a life of its own and for the professional to assume a beneficent role. Righteous indignation may overtake sound judgment.

In the previous chapter we discussed the use of covert tactics in situations in which legitimate channels of communication have been tried and clients agree that covert means may be their only chance for success. These considerations must be carefully weighed because the use of covert tactics usually raises ethical concerns.

To guide the action system in discussing professional ethics, we pose the following questions:

---

1. What are the value conflicts between the target and action systems?
2. What ethical principle(s) appear to be guiding the activities of the action system?
3. Is there the potential for a clash of ethical principles between the client and action systems?
4. If covert tactics are being considered, what conditions have led to this decision?
   a. The mission of the target agency or the community mandate is being ignored.
   b. The mission of the target agency or the community mandate is being denied for personal gain.
   c. Change efforts have been tried through legitimate channels but the target system will not listen.
   d. Client system members are fully aware of the risks involved, but are willing to take the risks.
   e. Other.

There are very few situations in which there is clearly a "right" or "wrong" tactic. Berlin (1990) explains, "we are all vulnerable to oversimplified bipolarizations. We search for order, find meaning in contrasts, and learn by maintaining an 'essential tension' between divergent experiences, events, and possibilities. It is this allowance of contrasts that differentiates either-or, narrowing and excluding bipolarizations from those that are encompassing or transforming" (p. 54).

It is common to think dichotomously (e.g., win-lose, right-wrong, good-bad, consensus-conflict). In conflict situations dichotomous thinking may assist the radical change agent in believing that the target system represents evil, whereas the action system represents good. This fuels the fire of confrontation and is appropriate in some situations. However, we believe that the professional social worker has a responsibility to carefully analyze what is happening before making assumptions that lead directly to the use of contest tactics. This means that the majority of change efforts will utilize collaboration and campaign tactics, as the action and target systems attempt to communicate with one another. Although consensus-conflict is a dichotomy, we believe that the majority of interactions happen in the various gradations in between—where varying degrees of communication occur.

If the action system attempts to collaborate or is willing to compromise but the target system remains unmoved, then contest tactics may have to be employed. What we want to guard against, however, is action-system members making assumptions about target-system members without attempting to communicate with them. In short, decisions about what tactics to use depends on the situation, the proposed change, and the relationships among actors in the action, client, and target systems.

FOCUS B: PREPARING A WRITTEN PLAN

When all the foregoing tasks have been completed, the proposed change should be written up in the form of a short, concise plan. This will include a few pages on the purpose, the problem, and the proposed change. A page on costs, and a few pages on expected benefits should make clear what resources will be requested, how they will be spent, and what benefits will be derived from implementation of the proposed change.

A few pages should be used to lay out the strategy and tactics, outlining roles, responsibilities, and time lines in Gantt-chart form. This will be helpful in ensuring that the proposed strategy and tactics are well coordinated as they are implemented. Any documents from the data-collection and problem-analysis phases that are felt to be helpful and are clear and concise can be attached to the plan.

This brings the change effort to the point at which it is ready for action. A community or organizational problem affecting a target population has been identified and thoroughly thought out. A general approach to an intervention has been proposed and a hypothesis developed proposing a relationship between problem, intervention, and outcomes. Alternative strategies have been carefully thought through, participants selected, issues weighed, and tactics selected.

Clearly there is more to be done prior to the full implementation of change. It is not the intent of this book, however, to get into the details of project or program implementation. The macro practitioner, as conceptualized here, has a decision to make at the point when the proposed change has been accepted and funded. If the change is to be implemented by a formal organization, roles may have to be redefined. The change agent must either attempt to hold the action system intact and define new roles, or disband the action system. One appropriate role, should the action system remain intact, is that of monitoring the implementation. An example would be an action system advocating for improved transportation for disabled persons. Once funded, the program is assigned to the city's Transportation Department, but the action system may remain involved by periodically surveying client satisfaction of users of the system.

If on the other hand, the change is to be implemented by the action system, new roles and responsibilities need to be defined. Formal organizational activities such as incorporating, selecting a board and executive, and hiring staff may be necessary. An example would be an action system advocating after-school activities for children of working parents and subsequently volunteering or being paid to plan and supervise the activities.

In any case, once the change has been endorsed and funded, the change agent should make clear to the action system that an important milestone has been reached, that there is cause for celebration, and that the change effort will now move into a new phase. It is critical that the action system acknowledge that implementation does not automatically mean that the change will occur as planned. Many plans have come to implementation, only to lose sight of the original intent of those who advocated for the change to occur. Therefore, implementation will bring a new host of challenges, expectations, barriers, insights and additional changes to be addressed.

CONCLUSION

We began this book with a chapter on the history and values of the social work profession. We discussed the struggles of gaining a professional identity and the ethical dilemmas those struggles impose on macro practice. Parts II and III focused on approaches to understanding community, social service systems, and health and human service organizations.

Part IV has proposed a systematic approach designed to produce the strategy and tactics that offer the potential for successful change. The approach includes a carefully thought-out series of tasks intended to maximize participation, to think through all possible types of change, and to select the options that will most likely achieve the desired results.

Next, the planners of change consider a number of political, interpersonal, and economic factors in order to be able to assess strengths and weaknesses of the proposed change. Itemizing the supporting and opposing people and factors allows the planners of change visually and cognitively to assess the likelihood of success. If it appears that the chances for success are good, the change effort moves to the stage of selecting appropriate tactics. Finally, a proposed plan of action is sketched out, including specification of key participants, activities, and time lines.

As with all professional practice, the approach is modified by the practitioner to fit the situation. If conditions dictate immediate action, some procedures will be shortened or streamlined. If time allows and the significance of the proposed change dictates, each task will be carried out with careful attention to detail.

In any case, it is our position that some changes will always be needed in the field of human services, both in organizations and in communities. These changes, we believe, require the professional assistance and consultation of social workers knowledgeable about macro-level change. They require informed, and sometimes scholarly, participation and guidance in order to ensure that what is achieved is what is most needed to address the social problem in the best interest of the target population.

We believe that social workers are well qualified to lead or coordinate the planning stages of such change efforts, and this book is intended to assist in that process. As the change effort moves to implementation, roles and responsibilities may change. It may be that new areas of expertise—legal, media, clinical, organizing, planning, designing, managing—are needed and would be sought from additional available sources and from elsewhere in the social work literature. At this point the change agent notes the success in achieving necessary support and funding for the proposed change, and coordinates either the disbanding of the action system or the transition into new roles.

REFERENCES

Barker, R. L. (1995) *The social work dictionary.* Washington, DC: National Association of Social Workers.

Berlin, S. B. (1990) Dichotomous and complex thinking. *Social Service Review,* 64(1), 46–59.

Brager, G., and S. Holloway. (1978) *Changing human service organizations: Politics and practice.* New York: Free Press.

Brager, G., H. Specht, and J. L. Torczyner. (1987) *Community organizing.* New York: Columbia University Press.

Haynes, K. S., and J. S. Mickelson. (1986) *Effecting change: Social workers in the political arena.* New York: Longman.

SUGGESTED READINGS

Amidei, N. (1991) *So you want to make a difference: Advocacy is the key.* Washington, DC: OMB Watch.

Bailey, D., and K. M. Koney. (1996) Interorganizational community-based collaboratives: A strategic response to shape the social work agenda. *Social Work,* 41(6): 601–11.

Gutierrez, L., A. R. Alvarez, H. Nemon, and E. A. Lewis. (1996) Multicultural community organizing: A strategy for change. *Social Work,* 41(5): 501–08.

Lakey, B., G. Lakey, R. Napier, and J. Robinson. (1995) *Grassroots and nonprofit leadership: A guide for organizations in changing times.* Philadelphia: New Society.

Lee, J. A. B. (1994) *The empowerment approach to social work practice.* New York: Columbia University Press.

McInnis-Dittrich, K. (1994) *Integrating social welfare policy and social work practice.* Pacific Grove, CA: Brooks/Cole.

Mondros, J. B., and S. M. Wilson. (1994) *Organizing for power and empowerment.* New York: Columbia University Press.

Tropman, J. E., J. L. Erlich, and J. Rothman. (1995) *Tactics and techniques of community intervention,* 3rd ed. Itasca, IL: F. E. Peacock.

APPENDIX A

Framework for Selecting Appropriate Tactics

FOCUS A. SELECTING TACTICS

Task 1: Consider a Range of Tactics

- Given a knowledge of the current level of support and opposition, what tactic (or combination of tactics) is most likely to succeed?

Task 2: Consider the Pros and Cons of Collaboration

- Are we certain that there is no opposition?
- Can the desired change be achieved by identifying roles for participants and implementing the change?

Task 3: Consider the Pros and Cons of Campaign

- Who needs to be convinced that the proposed change is needed?
- What persuasive techniques are most likely to be effective?

Task 4: Consider the Pros and Cons of Contest

- Is opposition to the proposed change so strong that it can only be successful by imposing the change on an unwilling target system?
- Can the proposed change be effective if it is forced?
- What are the anticipated consequences of conflict?

Task 5: Weigh Relevant Consideration in Selecting Tactics

- What are the current objectives of the change effort?
- What is the perception (by those promoting change) of the controlling and host systems?
- What is the perception (by those promoting change) of the role of the client system?
- What resources are needed and available for each tactic?
- What are the ethical dilemmas inherent in the range of tactical choices?

FOCUS B. PREPARING A WRITTEN PLAN

APPENDIX B

Case Example: Jackson County Foster Care

The following example illustrates the major components of a written plan for a macro change effort.

BACKGROUND

Jackson county incorporates a major city, several medium-sized suburbs, and a small amount of rural area. The Child Welfare Services Division of its Department of Social Services recently undertook an analysis of foster children for which it had responsibility during the past five years. The findings revealed that there was a disproportionately low number of white children in this population and a disproportionately high number of children from other racial or ethnic groups.

In response to a newspaper article which reported these results, over 30 representatives of various minority communities attended an open hearing held by the County Board of Supervisors. They expressed serious concerns about the findings. The County Director of Child Welfare Services was instructed to appoint a task force to study the situation and to make recommendations. The 14-member task force included:

- Three parents of ethnic minority foster children;
- Four leaders from minority communities;
- Two foster parents;
- Two foster-care social workers;
- A foster-home recruitment coordinator;
- A child welfare researcher from the local university;
- The top administrator from the foster care program.

Analysis of the Problem. The group began with an initial statement of the problem that focused on the fact that ethnic minority children comprised a higher proportion of children in foster care than would be expected based on the overall proportion of these children in the county. They then began to review available literature to familiarize themselves with issues associated with foster care and return to natural families. The literature review they conducted uncovered the following facts:

341

1. Placing children in foster care may be necessary if it is the only way to ensure their safety, but all possible efforts should be made by workers to avoid the need for foster care by facilitating solutions to family problems while the child is still in the home.
2. If it still becomes necessary, foster care is supposed to be temporary. Workers should attempt to facilitate solutions to problems in the family in order to allow the child to return home as quickly as possible. If this cannot be done, the next best option is to find some other permanent placement such as an adoptive home.
3. Foster care that is intended to be temporary but that continues indefinitely is harmful to children. This is because it jeopardizes their ability to form developmentally critical attachments with a parent or permanent parent surrogate.

Analysis of the Population.   The task force members then directed their efforts toward gaining a better understanding of the population of interest, which they defined as ethnic minority children in foster care. To accomplish this, they reviewed five-year statistics from the Department's child welfare division, studied in detail the findings of the division's recent report, and examined other research on minority children and families. The most important results they found were:

1. Children of color were overrepresented in foster care not only in Jackson County but elsewhere in the country as well.
2. Racial or ethnic minority children can become overrepresented in foster care in two ways: (a) they can be placed in foster care at a higher rate than white children and/or (b) they can leave foster care at a slower rate than white children and thus account for a greater number in care at any given point in time.
3. Once child welfare services in Jackson county had commenced, white children were less likely to be placed in foster care than nonwhite children.
4. Research reports suggested that ethnic minority children, once placed in foster care, were adopted or placed in other permanent arrangements at the same rate as nonminority children. However, minority children who were returned to their parents' homes did so much more slowly than nonminority children.

Based on these findings, the task force refined its problem statement to focus on the specific concerns of children of color being too likely to be placed in foster care and too unlikely to be reunited with their biological families in a timely fashion.

Analysis of the Arena.   Initial findings of the research efforts of the task force also implied that the arena in which a change effort would need to take place was not the community as a whole but the Jackson County Social Services organization. Under this assumption, the task force collected the following information from records within the Department and from interviews with current and former clients and professionals in other agencies in the community.

1. The proportion of persons of color who held professional positions in Jackson County's foster care services division was much lower than the proportion of children of color who were placed in foster care in the county.
2. Foster parents licensed by the division were also much less racially and ethnically diverse than the population of foster children in the county.
3. Many child welfare workers and foster parents were seen as lacking an in-depth understanding of the meaning of culture and tradition to ethnic minority families. This meant that children's behavior tended to be interpreted from a white perspective, which might be inconsistent with norms established and understood in minority communities.
4. Support services offered to help families deal with problems when a child was been removed were seen as lacking the cultural sensitivity necessary to help strengthen ethnic minority families.

As per Figure 1.1 in Chapter 1, the change effort that task force members began planning therefore assumed that the situation was one involving an overlap of problem (too great a likelihood of children entering foster care and staying too long), population (children of color), and arena (Jackson County Social Services and its clients). It was felt that biological families served by the Department's foster care division needed more resources and supportive services. Also, the division's professional staff and its foster parents needed a better understanding of family norms and the variables critical to healthy family environments for minority children.

Intervention Hypothesis.   Based on the preceding analysis, the task force members proposed the following as their intervention hypothesis:

If minority families who place children in foster care can be recruited into a program of supportive services, and

If more effective supportive services can be provided to these families than in the past, and

If the number of ethnic minority foster families and child welfare workers can be increased, and

If child welfare workers and foster parents can increase their knowledge of and sensitivity to the needs of minority children and their families,

Then the number of successful post-foster-care returns to biological families will be increased.

After proceeding through each of the tasks outlined in Chapters 3, 9, and 10, they produced the following written plan.

PART I: THE PROBLEM AND THE PROPOSED CHANGE

In the Jackson County Division of Child Welfare Services it was recently discovered that the rate of return of minority children from foster care to their natural families was significantly less than the rates for white children. A task force was appointed and a study was undertaken. A number of causal factors have emerged from the study.

There is some evidence that minority families whose children go into foster care have more serious economic, social, and emotional problems and are in need of a network of supportive services that will enable them to strengthen the family and better parent the child. On the whole, such services, with a special emphasis on serving ethnic minority families, have generally not been available to these families.

Second, there is evidence that child welfare workers and foster parents lack knowledge about minority families that could be important in the decision-making process about the needs of minority children and what should be considered realistic behavioral and performance expectations for return to biological families.

The task force proposes a series of interventions aimed at improving the cultural sensitivity of child care workers and foster parents and strengthening families who place children in foster care.

The first set of interventions will be directed toward child welfare workers and foster care parents. Cultural sensitivity training for these persons will include:

- Assessing one's values and perceptions as they relate to work with minority children and their families;
- Understanding African-American families and children;
- Understanding Hispanic families and children;
- Understanding Native-American families and children;
- Understanding Asian families and children.

Foster parents who complete cultural sensitivity training courses will:

- Receive a higher level of payment, and
- Be certified to receive minority foster children.

The second set of interventions will include support services, under contract with agencies that have demonstrated an understanding of and sensitivity to ethnic minority cultures. These services will be directed toward minority families. They are:

- Case management;
- Economic incentives;
- Individual and family assessment and counseling;
- Remedial education and GED opportunities;
- Job preparation, training, and placement;
- Self-esteem building workshops; and
- Self-help groups.

PART II: KEY ACTORS AND SYSTEMS

1. *Initiator System:* Black Families United, a community organization that organized the effort to meet with the County Board of Supervisors.
2. *Change Agent System:* The task force, staffed by an experienced child welfare supervisor.
3. *Client System:* Ethnic minority children who are placed in foster care and their families.
4. *Support System:* At least eight ethnic community organizations, two child welfare advocacy groups, several minority clergy and their congregations, many child welfare professionals, and the foster parents' association.
5. *Controlling System:* The County Board of Supervisors.
6. *Host System:* The Jackson County Division of Child Welfare.
7. *Implementing System:* Three units within the Jackson County Division of Child Welfare—(1) the Foster Care unit, (2) the Staff Development and Training unit, and (3) the Purchase of Services Contracting unit.
8. *Target System:* Since this will be a multiphase process, there will be phase-specific targets. The initial target will be the funding sources needed to underwrite the proposed interventions. This includes the Board of Supervisors and several local foundations. Subsequent targets include (1) child welfare workers and foster parents who need to become more ethnic-sensitive, and (2) minority families with children in foster care.
9. *Action System:* The Task Force, together with key representatives from the Division of Child Welfare and potential service providers.

PART III: GOALS, OBJECTIVES AND ACTIVITIES

This change effort is proposed as a three-year pilot project, during which time the Division of Child Welfare will correct any problems discovered in implementing the original design. Following the three-year trial period the project, if successful, is to be implemented as a permanent part of Jackson County Child Welfare Services.

GOAL 1

To improve and strengthen the cultural sensitivity of the Jackson County Child Welfare system.

Outcome Objective 1.1

By December 31, 19xx, to increase the knowledge of four ethnic minority cultures on the part of at least 50 trainees (including child welfare workers and forster parents), as measured by a 50% increase between pretest and posttest scores on tests developed for the training course.

Process Objectives

1.1   By July 19xx to present a proposal to the County Board of Supervisors for funds to develop culturally sensitive curricula for child welfare workers and foster parents in Jackson County.
1.2   By September 19xx to develop four training courses on understanding African-American, Hispanic, Native-American, and Asian-American families designed for child welfare workers and foster parents who serve minority children.
1.3   By October 19xx to produce 50 copies of all handouts associated with the training courses and distribute them to the Child Welfare Staff Development and Training Unit.
1.4   By November 19xx to recruit at least 50 child welfare workers and foster parents to take the training courses.
1.5   By January 19xx to administer pretests and to train at least 50 child welfare workers and foster parents in cultural sensitivity.

GOAL 2

To strengthen ethnic minority families who have children who are placed in foster care.

Outcome Objective 2.1

By September 30, 19xx, at least 100 ethnic minority families with children in foster care will have additional economic, social, emotional, and/or family support resources as measured by at least 30% higher scores on the Multidimensional Family Assessment Inventory.

Process Objectives

2.1   By November 19xx to inventory economic, social, emotional, and family support resources needed to serve African-American, Hispanic, Native-American, and Asian families in Jackson County.

2.2   By April 19xx at least 100 ethnic minority families with children in foster care will have been initially assessed to determine what resources are currently used and what resources are needed but not available or accessible.

2.3   By June 19xx gaps between available and needed resources for minority families will be documented in writing.

2.4   By September 19xx formal proposals for funding services designed for minority families will be presented to the Jackson County Board of Supervisors and at least two local foundations.

Activity Chart for Process Objective 2.1

By November 19xx to inventory economic, social, emotional, and family support resources needed to serve African-American, Hispanic, Native-American, and Asian families in Jackson County.

Activity Number	Activity	Person Resposible	Time Frame											
			J	F	M	A	M	J	J	A	S	O	N	D
1	Form task force to identify resources	Change agent	–											
2	Hold meeting of task force	Change agent		–										
3	Develop subcommittee	Members of task force		–	–									
4	Conduct inventory of resources a. economic b. social c. emotional d. support	Members of task force					–	–	–	–	–	–		
5	Prepare final report	Change agent									–	–	–	
6	Report results along with identified gaps in available resources													–

PART IV: TACTICS

It is anticipated that this change effort will proceed through a series of phases, as follows:

Phase 1

The objective of phase 1 is to get the change accepted by potential funding sources. The focus of this phase is on the County Board of Supervisors, several private foundations interested in minority concerns, and people capable of influencing their decisions. Campaign tactics will include education, persuasion and lobbying. In the event that campaign tactics are not successful and funding sources are not open to change, contest tactics may be used. These tactics would include mass media appeals to mobilize the support system as well as bargaining and negotiation and large-group social action.

Phase 2

The objective of phase 2, if the project is funded, is to increase cultural awareness and knowledge. The focus of this phase is on child welfare staff and foster parents who serve minority children and their families. Collaborative tactics will include joint action, capacity building, and education.

Phase 3

The objective of phase 3 is to ensure that improved services are provided to minority families who have placed children in foster care. Services should be adapted to the unique needs, concerns, interests, and traditions of each ethnic group, and will involve the application of knowledge and skill gained in phase 2. The focus of this effort will be on child welfare workers, foster parents, and contracted service providers. Collaborative tactics will include capacity building and joint action.

Index